About Gary Null

With the American public's dramatically increasing concern with health and the food we eat, the name of Gary Null is gaining ever greater renown as one of the leading nutritional authorities and spokesmen for organic living of the modern generation. His books—written in collaboration with his brother Steve and with his dedicated staff—as well as his many magazine articles and lecture tours have helped spread the good word about good health all over the nation. In addition, Gary Null is proprietor of one of the country's most successful health food stores.

In *The Complete Handbook of Nutrition,* Gary and Steve Null have succeeded in setting down in easy-to-read form all that is known and that we need to know about the food we eat and its effect for good and for ill. No home library is complete without this invaluable guide.

D0042628

The Complete Handbook of Nutrition

GARY AND STEVE NULL

A Dell Book

Published by
DELL PUBLISHING CO., INC.
1 Dag Hammarskjold Plaza
New York, New York 10017

ISBN: 0-440-11613-9

Reprinted by arrangement with
Robert Speller & Sons, Publishers, Inc.
New York, New York 10010

Printed in the United States of America

First Dell printing—May 1973
Second Dell printing—January 1974
Third Dell printing—June 1975
Fourth Dell printing—September 1976
Fifth Dell printing—August 1977
Sixth Dell printing—February 1979
Seventh Dell printing—September 1979
Eighth Dell printing—October 1980

TO
J. I. Rodale and Staff
Adelle Davis
Carlton Fredericks
Gayelord Hauser
Linda Clark
John Lust
Lelord Kordel
Carlson Wade
Herbert Shelton
Paul C. Bragg
Bob Hoffman
H. E. Kirschner
Linus Pauling
Ralph Nader

TABLE OF CONTENTS

INTRODUCTION

To compile the information for this book required assembling facts gleaned from the examination of books (nearly 800) containing material on health and nutrition. In addition, dozens of articles, clinical reports and other research data from government and foundation sources were examined so that no reference source would go unchecked. We traveled across America interviewing doctors, food consultants, nutritionists, and noted individuals skilled or knowledgeable in the field of health and nutrition. The final result is a handbook as comprehensive and detailed as any work ever before prepared on the subject of health and nutrition.

Important information about Vitamins, Minerals, Protein, Enzymes, Food Values, Food Combining, Fruit & Nuts, Acid & Alkaline Balancing, Raw Juice Diet, Pollen, plus many other vital subjects is explained in layman's language.

This is a handbook, guide and reference encyclopedia for all who care about health and are seeking to maintain and improve it.

Before beginning this book, it is important to understand the spirit in which it is written. The information presented here is *not* intended as a cure-all. We wish to make no radical claims for cures or revolutionary types of therapy. Rather, we wish to present scientifically substantiated evidence which will give the reader insight into how his body functions and what it needs to maintain optimal health. You will be presented with an array of constructive alternative methods for achieving and maintaining a sense of personal well-being. At first the variety of possibilities we have presented may seem conflicting in some instances. In one chapter, for example, we tell you that meat is one of the best sources of protein. Yet in another chapter we discuss the common arguments for vegetarianism. This is because we do not wish to prescribe any one method of natural therapy. We wish to present as many sound options as possible for people to choose from. We strongly recommend that any diagnosis and prescriptions for specific therapeutic programs should be left to the professional nutritionist or physician, taking into consideration individual circumstances and preferences. *Under no circumstances* do we recommend that you try to diagnose and treat yourself without professional help.

HOW TO USE THIS BOOK

It is important to note that we have grouped our material into clusters of related chapters. For example, the chapters on vitamins, minerals, protein, enzymes and glands will be found side by side because in bodily functions, they are also closely related. Yet each chapter is definitive and complete unto itself. This is markedly different from most other health and nutrition books where you must skip from chapter to chapter to obtain a full picture of the concept discussed.

While this book can be read from cover to cover, it is also meant to be a concise and useful reference guide to answer specific questions on health and nutrition.

CLARIFICATION

At the beginning of each chapter where essential statistics are used (for example the food value chapter) the charts or diagrams presented are based on the United States Government's food value statistics. We have used these statistics as a barometer and assigned specific nutritional values to foods in relationship to their figures. All of the government's statistics for vitamins, food value, etc., are based upon non-organic foods since the vast majority of people reading this book are not in a position to buy natural organic foods. However, we have also listed the variations between the organic and non-organic in most instances so that you can see the difference. An example can be found in the chapter on vitamins. Whereas the government's statistics and minimum daily requirements for a particular vitamin might be very small, most health food advocates will suggest a much higher amount.

While it is true that there are often discrepancies between the food values of organic and non-organic substances, we wish to emphasize that it is the practical application of a sound nutritional program which is most essential. While we hope that eventually organic foods will become the staple rather than the exception in the American diet because we feel that their benefit is significantly higher, we do not wish to dismiss as worthless the food which is readily available to the vast majority. What we do recommend is that you eat raw and fresh foods as much as possible and that you wash them thoroughly. If carefully selected, they will also serve your nutritional purposes well.

Above all, we have emphasized in chapters such as raw juice therapy, fasting, fruits, and herbs where specific illnesses or diseases are mentioned and associated with specific therapies we are not advocating that any of these methods are cures. What we are saying is that if some of these methods are used it is possible that they can be helpful in aiding a specific illness, to some degree. Of necessity our list of specific deficiencies related to specific ailments is only partial and quite limited. This is meant only as a guide to some of the more common possibilities. For example, a diseased thyroid may be caused by an iodine deficiency and some improvement might therefore be possible with iodine therapy or juice therapy. It is also possible, however, that the diseased thyroid is caused by something entirely different than an iodine deficiency and that therefore iodine therapy would be of little help and might even further aggravate the condition. It is for this reason that we again suggest you seek professional advice before trying to implement any of these programs.

Anyone who believes that one glass of juice or two weeks of fasting or even a good diet for a short period of time will provide any lasting beneficial effects is certain to become disillusioned. Healthy habits and sound nutrition are a way of life which must be followed as long as one lives if one is to reap the fullest benefits of a healthy body and mind. There is no quick or easy crash program of lasting value. It is possible, however, that by chance one might accidentally discover something which makes him feel positively alive, if only for an hour, after years of feeling numb and half-dead. For some, even one such spark is enough to get them hooked again on pursuing life. That's what this book is all about: the active pursuit of life. We do feel that suggestions given here concerning specific ailments may possibly be of benefit and in some cases may even cause significant improvement.

What we hope to do is open the doors for the uninitiated, and give a helping hand to those already on their way towards feeling the full totality of their life force.

Gary & Steve Null, Nutrition Consultants
January 1972
New York City

*The Complete
Handbook of
Nutrition*

VITAMINS

VITAMIN A

Vitamin A is one of the easiest vitamins to obtain in a well-rounded diet, for it is not lost to any great extent in cooking or storing. Yet, borderline deficiency of this vitamin is thought by nutritionists to be common in this country. What this means is that most people get enough Vitamin A to protect them from serious consequences but not enough to keep them in the peak of health.

Both plants and animals are sources for Vitamin A, animals being the better source for us because A comes as a complete vitamin, whereas in plants we eat "carotene" which is then converted to Vitamin A in the body. But plants should not be overlooked as a Vitamin A source; they provide other important vitamins as well.

Vitamin A is stored in the body (mainly in the liver), which allows a considerable depletion before symptoms of deficiency occur. Mobilization of Vitamin A from the liver depends on adequate dietary protein. Inadequate Vitamin A and protein frequently occur together and are considered as the two most common causes of malnutrition. People with liver problems have faulty absorption and metabolism of Vitamin A. Infants and children are much more susceptible to the effects of Vitamin A deficiency because they haven't had time to build a reserve. The first obvious symptom is night blindness. This is chiefly an inability to adapt to bright lights or to darkness. If you can't see for a while when you come into a bright room from darkness, or can't make out anything at night after being exposed to a sudden glare, such as headlights, you probably have Vitamin A deficiency. If you are only comfortable when wearing sunglasses on bright days, or you squint excessively, you'd better have an examination for Vitamin A deficiency.

Part of Vitamin A's job is to protect what doctors call the "specialized epithelial surfaces" of the body—the mouth tissues, and those of the respiratory system, the salivary glands and those of the digestive tract and the organs of the reproductive system and the skin. Lack of Vitamin A can naturally cause disorders of any of these or, perhaps more important, a slight A deficiency can weaken one or all of these parts so that they are candidates for any infection that comes along.

Dr. Janet Fogle of Akron University has shown that the throat and lungs of patients deficient in Vitamin A invite cold germs, for the cells there won't have the stamina to withstand viral invasions. She reports also that dry, brittle hair with dandruff is often a symptom of lack of Vitamin A.

Other symptoms of a Vitamin A deficiency are itching and burning or slight redness of the eyelids, certain skin diseases (especially in children), a horny condition of the mucous membrane of the mouth and of the respiratory system, and an inability to store fat. Scientists have observed that Vitamin A deficiency is often accompanied by colds and respiratory problems. The complete role that Vitamin A plays is still a mystery to scientists and biochemists but from present tests most agree that Vitamin A must be involved in some fundamental function in most tissues.

A very important function of A is its contribution to growth and dental health in children. Vitamin A is essential for the child while his teeth are being formed and while he is growing to full stature, for without it he cannot properly use Vitamin D and calcium, and rickets will result.

Vitamin A occurs in several forms: as retinol (an alcohol), retinal and retinoic acid. In its pure form Vitamin A is a pale yellow crystalline compound. It is soluble in fat but not in water. Because it is easily oxidized, Vitamin E may be used to help prevent oxidation. Vitamin A is also rapidly destroyed by ultraviolet radiation. The amount of Vitamin A that can be attained from vegetable sources is determined by the carotene content of the vegetable. The darker colored vegetables have more Vitamin A. The vitamin is relatively stable to heat, acids and alkalis. It can be destroyed by prolonged heating in the presence of oxygen and the activity of the vitamin is rapidly lost in rancid fats. The pure

Vitamin A from animal sources and the carotene form is absorbed like fat and requires the facilitation of bile. When one's diet is low in fat, or when there is an obstruction of the bile duct both Vitamin A and carotene absorption is impaired.

Studies on an Indian male population showed a range of absorption of carotene to be 33 to 58 percent with an average of 50 percent. Of the 50 percent absorbed about half will eventually be converted into Vitamin A; which means about one sixth of the carotene from plants eventually is utilized. The carotene is converted into Vitamin A in the body by an enzyme called carotenase. Unless one is a vegetarian and consumes large quantities of vegetables, preferably dark green or dark yellow, it is a good idea to occasionally include animal sources of Vitamin A in the diet.

Taking Vitamin A in sufficient quantity will relieve the symptoms of deficiency rather quickly, unless there are conditions that prohibit the body from absorbing it. Liver diseases and gastro-intestinal infections limit the body's capacity to use Vitamin A.

Since the foods we eat provide carotene which has to be converted to Vitamin A, and many disorders or foreign substances (such as mineral oil) can inhibit this conversion in one way or another, Vitamin A food supplements are recommended. Drs. Albert E. Sobel and Abraham Rosenberg of New York have found that diabetics are unable to transform carotene into Vitamin A. They suggest that diabetics, or anyone having difficulties with assimilating Vitamin A substances, should take a fish liver oil supplement.

Since Vitamin A is stored in the body, its intake does not have to be excessive, such as that of Vitamin C. But since there is no way for a person to know what his reserve is at any given time, Vitamin A should be added to the diet regularly to prevent deficiency. The daily recommended dosages for Vitamin A are:

Children up to 12	1500-3500 International Units per day
Children over 12	4500-6000 I.U. per day
Adults (moderately active)	5000 I.U. per day
Pregnant women	6000 I.U. per day
Nursing mothers	8000 I.U. per day

As with recommended amounts of nearly all vitamins, these figures are considered too low by some nutritionists. Since we cannot presume that our diets give us all the Vitamin A we need, we should bolster them with A-rich foods —apricots, asparagus, carrots, cantaloupe, eggs, liver, kidneys, peaches, sweet potatoes, parsley, pumpkins and green peppers. Cod liver oil (as all fish liver oils) is very rich in Vitamin A, and halibut liver oil contains many times the amount of cod liver oil.

Modern methods of farming and processing often destroy much of the Vitamin A in vegetables (fortunately, since A is not water soluble, it does not get lost when vegetables are cooked). From natural sources and in normal doses no toxic effect will develop. Vitamin A can build up a reserve in the liver. If one consumed massive doses (50,000 I.U. daily over a long period of time) it can lead to a toxic condition.

None of the Vitamin A in milk is lost in pasteurization, or in canning. Powdered whole milk loses about 60% of its vitamins on storage for nine months. Butter loses very little of its Vitamin A if stored in air-tight containers, but frying destroys this vitamin.

VITAMIN K

Dr. Dam of Copenhagen observed in 1935 that chickens on a diet adequate in all known nutrients developed a severe hemorrhagic disease but after adding liver fat and alfalfa to the diet returned to normal. He concluded that the hemorrhage was due to a fall in prothrombin, a compound required for normal clotting, and the unknown substance in alfalfa was required for proper blood clotting. He named this substance "Koagulations Vitamin" and in 1939 it was isolated and named Vitamin K.

Vitamin K is fat soluble and requires the presence of bile to be absorbed. Vitamin K is stable in heat but is destroyed by sunlight. There are several forms of Vitamin K (all belonging to a group of chemical compounds known as quinones): K_1 is found in green plants, K_2 is formed by bacteria in the intestinal tract, and the fat soluble synthetic compound, menadione. Menadione is twice as biologically active as the natural K_1 and K_2 but when taken orally will induce vomiting. None of the three forms is stored in any significant amount. The biological activity of Vitamin K in food substances is determined by the ability to prevent hemorrhage in young chickens. (Menadione is used as a standard of comparison.)

The richest sources of Vitamin K are alfalfa, kale, spinach, cabbage and grass.

Vitamin K can be synthesized by bacteria in the lower intestinal tract. Certain medications containing sulfa drugs and antibiotics suppress the action of the bacteria flow required for proper synthesis. In newborn infants synthesis by the sterile intestinal tract does not take place for several days. This potentially dangerous period can be safeguarded against by administering Vitamin K to the expectant mother or to the infant upon delivery.

The main function of Vitamin K is to stimulate the production of the prothrombin of the blood by the liver. If there is a Vitamin K deficiency blood clotting time is prolonged. Vitamin K is recommended by most surgeons to their patients before having surgery. People who are taking dicumarol, an anticoagulant often used to treat coronary thrombosis, are advised to take Vitamin K to counteract it.

It is known that diets containing 1 to 2 mg will correct Vitamin K deficiency, but no quantitative estimate of Vitamin K has been recommended. Vitamin K occurs in abundant quantities in a good diet, also it can be synthesized by intestinal bacteria flow, so there should be little chance of a deficiency in a healthy individual. If an individual has fat absorption impaired or severe liver disease, constant use of antibiotics or sulfa drugs, or extremely poor diet then a supplement of Vitamin K may be necessary.

VITAMIN E

Vitamin E is perhaps the most maligned, ignored and neglected natural substance ever to come out of medical research. It was serendipitously discovered in 1922 by two American doctors, Herbert M. Evans and Katharine S. Bishop, who stumbled upon it while conducting experiments with rats to establish a correlation between fertility and growth. They found that some unknown substance in lettuce and wheat germ oil corrected a reproduction problem brought on by certain diet deficiencies.

One of Dr. Evans' acquaintances, a professor of Greek

at the University of California, labelled the fertility substance *tocopherol*—tocos (childbirth), phero (bring forth), and ol (a non-Greek suffix for alcohol). Greek scholars and esoteric scientists notwithstanding, tocopherol became known as Vitamin E.

There are at least four tocopherols (alpha, beta, delta, gamma) and they are widespread throughout nature. The most active is alpha-tocopherol. The test to determine the biological activity of a tocopherol is based upon the function of the tocopherol in the prevention of fetal reabsorption in rats, the measure of E storage in liver and plasma responses, and the increase in susceptibility of erythrocytes to hydrogen peroxide radicals. Other tocopherols have biological activity ranging from 0% to 50% of alpha. Alpha may be the most active because it is absorbed easily but delta-tocopherol is the most potent antioxidant.

Scientists knew for a long time that a lack of Vitamin E caused dramatic body ailments, but there was no definite disease linked with its shortage—such as night blindness (Vitamin A deficiency), beriberi (Vitamin B), scurvy (C), and rickets (D)—until 1952. In that year, using a new laboratory technique, Dr. Paul Gyorgy of the University of Pennsylvania showed that a Vitamin E deficiency in infants generally brought about hemolysis, a weakness of the red blood cells which causes them to rupture easily.

Subsequent findings that a Vitamin E deficiency led also to edema (water retention), skin lesions, and cerebellitis (a degenerative brain disease), prompted the American Academy of Pediatrics to recommend, in 1967, a minimum level of 0.3 International Units of Vitamin E per 100 kilocalories in infant formulas. The Food and Drug Administration proposed this amount, also.

This same Vitamin E deficiency anemia has been found in premature human infants. Doctors at Case Western Reserve University in Cleveland found that 80% of the premature infants they studied between 1968 and 1971 had weak blood cells . . . and low levels of Vitamin E.

Vitamin E is an antioxidant, which means that it inhibits the reactions created by oxygen in the blood. Oxygen makes body fat turn rancid, and these rancid fats then damage red cell membranes.

Vitamin E deficiency makes red blood cells, which produce oxygen in the body, more susceptible to damage from body stresses and from such medications as iron. If the iron supplement, ferric chloride, is introduced to the body, the remaining Vitamin E will be destroyed.

In 1900, heart attacks were practically unknown. People had congestive heart failure and strokes, but they didn't have coronary arteries clogged with fat. The heart attack, known as coronary thrombosis, is a modern malady, limited only to a few western countries—the United States and nations that have been "Americanized" since World War II.

One historical explanation may be the discovery of a more efficient milling process in 1911. This new process, which separated the hull on the wheat from the kernel, soon dominated the bakery industry in this country. The result was, and is, the proliferation and sole use of almost completely nutritionless white flour products. The wheat hull is an excellent source of Vitamin E for man, and it has been eliminated from our diet.

The good ole American heart attack, as native to us as hot dogs and Mom's apple pie (both of which contain white flour), is a product of atherosclerosis, more commonly known as hardening of the arteries, or more correctly described as hardening and thickening of the walls of the arteries. This thickening constricts the flow of blood. Dr. Paul Dudley White, the father of modern cardiology, has called atherosclerosis "the great 20th century epidemic." Some nutritionists blame the American diet of white flour products, and have coined atherosclerosis as "the White Plague." Whatever this scourge is called, it has reaped a vast harvest among the small percentage of the world's population that is able to afford it. The Black Plague found its most ready victims among the poor; the White Plague is an affluent man's disease. Not only has it grown to epidemic proportions in the industrial nations in the past 50 years, but it is afflicting younger and younger men.

According to a study of autopsies performed on bodies of American G.I.s in Vietnam, the average youth fighting in the U.S. Army is the victim of atherosclerosis. "In all cases," writes Wolfgang Mellors in a recent *New York Times* article, "some degree of hardening of the arteries was found in the bodies of these soldiers, who represent the cream of this nation's youth. They were all candidates for coronary thrombosis."

In 1972, the American Heart Association revealed that death rates from heart attacks among young men aged 25 to 44 years has risen 14%, from 45.7 to 52.0 per 100,000 Americans, since 1950. During this same period, the heart attack rate for men 45 to 64 years has risen from 574.9 to 597.9 (a 4% increase) per 100,000. In all, over 570,000 Americans die from heart attacks each year.

Many doctors attribute this frightening rise in atherosclerosis to richer foods, more calories, tobacco consumption, emotional stress, and sedentary lives. Others, like Drs. Wilfred and Evan Shute, heart specialist brothers who head the Shute Institute for Clinical and Laboratory Medicine in London, Canada, put the blame on Vitamin E deficiency. The answer lies somewhere in between.

Since we have already discussed tocopherol's role as an antioxidant, we may touch upon how its action upon fats affects the level of Vitamin E in our bodies. Dr. Max Horwitt of the University of Illinois has reported that the high percentage of polyunsaturated fats in our diets depletes the Vitamin E in our bodies as it is called into action to inhibit the activity of the oxygen in the blood. Therefore, the rich American diet eventually makes us deficient in Vitamin E.

In 1955, Dr. M. Aloisi found that laboratory rabbits deprived of Vitamin E soon develop muscular dystrophy, a degenerative disease (actually several diseases) of the voluntary or skeletal muscles. Rabbits are vegetarians whose diet consists mainly of leafy greens, so Vitamin E comprises a large part of their nutrition. Rabbits are therefore more susceptible to Vitamin E deficiency and are excellent subjects for experiments, for they offer exaggerated and accelerated examples of what Vitamin E deprivation can do to other animals.

Correlations between rabbits and humans have yet to be made. However, we do know that humans whose diets are deficient in Vitamin E develop maladies related to the muscle system—muscle weakness, oxidized fat deposits, and an increased excretion of creatine in the urine (which precedes muscular dystrophy).

Drs. Richard Mihan and Samuel Ayres of the University of California, while experimenting with tocopherol in treating skin diseases, accidently found that Vitamin E was effective in relieving muscle cramps. Treating 26 patients suffering from severe night cramps, they were able to achieve nearly 100% satisfactory results in all cases. These findings match those of Dr. Robert Cathcart III, a California orthopedist who has prescribed Vitamin E treatment for muscle cramps to over 100 patients and found it much more effective and safe than previously used medications.

Though the full extent of Vitamin E deficiency's influence on the human muscle system has not yet been ascertained, we can safely say that good muscle tone requires a sufficient diet of Vitamin E substances. People who should know—joggers, baseball pitchers, coaches, and race horse trainers—swear by this miracle vitamin.

The latest role of Vitamin E is its usefulness as a cosmetic and skin rejuvenator. There is very little evidence to back these claims. Vitamin E has been proven to effect scar tissue formation but it has no efficient healing properties. Vitamin A proved to speed healing. One test did show that taking E and A increases the effectiveness of the A, possibly because of E's antioxidant effect. Vitamin E not only helps A's absorption in the body (by sixfold) but preserves it while it's being stored in the liver.

According to Dr. Aloys Tappel of the University of California, the basic deterioration reaction in the human cell is the destruction of fat by oxygen. If this is true, then the chemical deterioration which we know as aging might be slowed by the increased use of dietary antioxidants. Vitamin E, as we discussed earlier, is an antioxidant.

Dr. Samuel Ayres says that the damaging effect of spontaneous peroxidation (the combining of fat with oxygen) on body cells may be retarded to a considerable degree by Vitamin E.

Dr. Denham Harmon of Nebraska reports that rats given added tocopherol live longer than rats on normal diets. He contends that Vitamin E or some other effective antioxidant added to man's diet could extend his useful lifespan perhaps five to ten years. Still, much more research will have to be done before we even think about pronouncing a Fountain of Youth. The findings give cause for optimism, however.

The best way to sell a product is by using sex. If Vitamin E can ever be determined to aid sexuality, its neglect and malignment will come to an orgasmic end. However, we do not wish to pander to the reader's sexual instincts. Reportage, not titillation, is our job.

As we have said, Vitamin E was discovered by Drs. Herbert Evans and Katharine Bishop during their experiments with fertility in rats. Since that time, Vitamin E deficiency has been found to cause reproductive failures in the female turkey, cow, and hen; and sterility in male rats, guinea pigs, dogs, hamsters and roosters.

In his work with hamsters at the University of Oregon, Dr. A. L. Soderwall showed that when wheat germ oil was added to their diets, aging female hamsters became pregnant more frequently, had more successful pregnancies, and gave birth to larger litters than "control" hamsters on a normal diet. Fertility in the Vitamin E fed hamsters was 83.9%, compared to 36.1% for the untreated hamsters.

In dealing with human subjects, doctors have found that Vitamin E affects hormones necessary for reproduction. It has been established as a factor in curing female hormone-related disturbances, and may be capable of preventing the genetic malfunctions that produce Downs Syndrome (mongolism) in children. However, no evidence has pointed to male potency increase.

Since Vitamin E is widespread in nature and in food, it would seem that a normal American diet would provide more than enough to maintain good health. Unfortunately, this is not the case. Professor Robert Harris of the Massachusetts Institute of Technology in Cambridge, tells us that the Vitamin E activity of foods is always less—perhaps 40% less—than the total tocopherol content. Add to this the "damage" of food processing. Heating and storage cause food to lose some of its Vitamin E content. Our processing of cereal grains destroys as much as 90% of their tocopherol. Freezing strips food of much of its Vitamin E. It appears that the more processed foods we eat and the longer our food is stored, the less Vitamin E we get. And what's worse, our diets of saturated fats deplete the little tocopherol we do ingest.

Unfortunately, most of the Vitamin E in this country is being fed to animals—they get the best grains. Humans are left with the stripped-down, processed bulk.

Dr. David Herting of Kodak Research Laboratories tells

us that borderline Vitamin E deficiency is fairly common throughout the world, even in this country. He warns that there is a danger "of a marginal deficiency or gradual depletion which does not show any immediate overt signs."

Food processors are notorious for removing key vitamins from foods, and then "enriching" their products with synthetic vitamins. However, Dr. Max Horwitt of the University of Illinois points out that there is no complete non-toxic, fully capable antioxidant that can substitute for tocopherol. Synthetic alpha-tocopherol has the same activity as natural alpha-tocopherol, but it differs slightly in the manner in which it transfers across the cell walls and accumulates in desirable concentrations when needed.

Vitamin E is lost in storage and processing; fresh virgin olive oil contains 15.5 mg per 100 grams, stored 4.1 mg, and refined has none. Whole wheat flour, untreated, loses 65% of alpha after being stored for 190 days. When wheat flour is treated 19% of alpha remains. Frozen foods fried in vegetable oil lowers alpha content and frying destroys some E. The amount of tocopherols found in plants differs greatly. Soybean oil contains much greater amounts of gamma than alpha tocopherol. Alpha is found in all seeds but is in the majority in only three: almond, oats, and peanuts. All tocopherols are derived from plant sources, primarily seed. Vegetable oils, in contrast to seeds, generally have simpler tocopherol patterns and contain principally the saturated forms; the amount of E found in vegetables and fruit as compared with seeds and seed oils is small.

Some authors suggest taking vegetable oil or lecithin with the E for better absorption. Laxatives, especially mineral oil, interfere with the absorption of alpha. People with fat absorption problems should take the water dispersible form of E, as should people with gastrectomy and gastric surgery. If man is deficient in E there is no compensatory mechanism to increase the efficiency of its absorption. Some E advocates recommend 800-1200 I.U. a day for people with heart trouble. Many doctors believe one needs only 25-30 I.U. a day. The Recommended Dietary Allowance is 30 I.U. per day. One should consider such factors as the polyunsaturated fat content in his diet, the amount of unprocessed flours, seeds and grains he eats, his physical activity, the air quality, his absorption ability and his present health in determining his own requirements.

There is no doubt that natural E is more biologically active than synthetic E. Test results vary in activity from 20% to as high as 36% more active. The dosage is measured in international units, 1 milligram = I.U. Vitamin E has never been shown to be harmful even at massive dosages.

We add to this, however, a word of caution. Anyone with high blood pressure should not begin taking over 100 I.U. daily until he shows a capability of handling more without raising his blood pressure even higher.

VITAMIN B-COMPLEX

The B-vitamins constitute the most important members of the water soluble group of vitamins. There are many kinds of them and they interact together in fulfilling their various roles.

Vitamin B could refer to any one of a dozen different nutrients which comprise what is known as the B-complex. The B group is instrumental in the metabolic processes of all living cells by serving as co-factors in the various enzyme systems needed to provide the cells with energy.

The B-complex vitamins are, for the most part, dependent upon one another for their interrelation and an inadequate intake of one may impair the utilization of others. This is the reason why single discrete deficiencies of the B-complex are seldom isolated although the signs and symptoms of deficiency of a particular member of the group may predominate. Furthermore, it is unwise to take the B-complex vitamins in large amounts individually because the use of a single member of the group therapeutically may create a vitamin imbalance and precipitate deficiency of other members of the complex. Therefore, better than taking one or two individual members of the complex, take them all together in one supplement or in a food where they are balanced, such as dry yeast.

White bread, white flour products, polished rice and other processed grains do not contain sufficient quantities of the B-complex. This is important to the average American because half of our national diet consists of foods made from white sugar and white flour. These two carbohydrates (from which all B-vitamins have been removed during refining) must have B vitamins in them or our bodies cannot use them properly. Thus, the more refined foods you eat, the more B-vitamins you need.

Since B-vitamins are water soluble, they are lost when the water in which meats or vegetables are cooked is thrown away. They are destroyed by intense heat, slow cooking, and by light. Baking soda and baking powder destroy Vitamin B.

It is important to remember that the B-vitamins should be taken together, which is easily possible if one takes 3 teaspoons of brewer's yeast or eats liver daily. These, of course, are not the only Vitamin B foods, but they are the richest. Synthetic Vitamin B preparations do not supply you with the same effective B-complex you get from natural sources.

The B-complex consists of B_1 (thiamin), B_2 (riboflavin), B_6 (pyridoxine), B_{12}, niacin, pantothenic acid, choline, inositol, biotin, Paba, B_{15} (pangamic acid), and folic acid. They are closely related to each other in chemical structure and activity, and most of them cannot function without their fellow vitamins of the B-complex, all being in the proper proportion provided by natural foods.

The B-complex is chiefly responsible for the health of the digestive tract, the skin, mouth, tongue, eyes, nerves, arteries, and liver.

There are official recommendations for only a few of these B-vitamins. Many of them are recent discoveries and have not been exposed to enough research. Others are yet to be isolated, though we know they exist.

B_1—*Thiamin* B_1, also called thiamin, has been known as an important factor in nutrition for almost 60 years. From time to time scientists discover new effects that it has on the human body. Thiamin primarily serves as a coenzyme essential for the proper metabolism of carbohydrates.

Severe thiamin deficiency results in the disease beriberi, which was once a scourge upon the Oriental people who ate polished rice. A Japanese naval doctor found that a diet of fish, barley, vegetables and meat eliminated the problem.

Beriberi's symptoms are numbness and tingling in the toes and feet, stiffness in ankles, pains in legs and finally paralysis of the leg muscles, and heart dysfunction. A Vitamin B_1 deficiency usually results in a mild, "sub-clinical" form of beriberi.

Thiamin, the substance which is found in the outer part of cereals and in yeast is necessary for growth. Laboratory animals that are deprived of it grow more slowly than their siblings and do not reach full development. It promotes good appetite and improves the operation of digestion.

It also plays a part in oxidation of the human cell; therefore thiamin deficiency affects every cell in the body. Especially susceptible are the nerve tissues, which, without B_1, cause depression, irritability, fatigue and thought dysfunction. During thiamin deficiency, degeneration of myelin sheaths of nerve fibers in the central nervous system and the peripheral nerves develops.

Thiamin is not stored in the body and therefore must be replenished every day, especially in those who do physical work. Sugar, tobacco and alcohol destroy thiamin, so allowances should be made by those who indulge.

Thiamin has a good survival rate in storage, but it is lost when dry heated or exposed to any high temperature.

Vitamin B_1 deficiency is quite common in America because our milling methods remove wheat germ (high in B_1) from the flour we use. This country has suffered from what James Dawson has called "the White Plague" since 1911, when white flour products took over the American diet (see Vitamin E).

In its pure form, thiamin hydrochloride, thiamin is a crystalline yellowish white powder having a yeastlike odor and salty nutlike taste. Thiamin is unstable in heat or alkali so one should use low temperatures, little water, and no baking soda while cooking.

Dr. Ruth Flinn Harrell wrote a book called *The Effect of Added Thiamin on Learning*, in which she relates a curious phenomenon that she witnessed at Johns Hopkins Hospital. A young patient had been in an accident and had lost his power of speech and writing. During his lengthy reeducation process, he suddenly began to learn at a much faster rate, and was soon cured and released.

While investigating this case, Dr. Harrell found that five or six days before the improvement began, the patient had had Vitamin B_1 added to his diet. She could find nothing else that might point to the change.

To investigate her suspicions, Dr. Harrell experimented with white rats and found that they learned to follow intricate mazes much more rapidly when thiamin was added to their diet. She then began a program working with handicapped children who had been diagnosed as mentally incapable of learning speech, and reports that they learned more rapidly after being given thiamin in their diet. Two of the children, in fact, learned to read and were able to go on and live as normal human beings.

It would appear that a certain nutritional state must exist in the nervous system for a learner to effectively utilize what he is being taught. We still do not understand the complex biological, chemical, nervous, mental or electrical processes that go on in the body when we are learning, but we can safely say that B_1's effect of oxidation to nerve tissues may very well have something to do with increased learning capability. Bruno Minz of the Sorbonne University in Paris found that a cut nerve dripped a liquid containing thiamin, and that an electrically stimulated nerve gave off a high rate of thiamin, 80 times more per unit than a resting nerve.

Any doubt of thiamin's capability in increasing the learning process was erased in a six-week experiment at a Lynchburg, Virginia, orphanage, involving 104 children. The experiment, ingeniously handled by Dr. Harrell to prevent any extra variables, proved that children given thiamin tablets improved their physical and mental skills. The thiamin group of children gained about one-fourth more in learning ability than the control group.

If your diet is deficient in Vitamin B_1 you will begin to exhibit the following symptoms. At first you'll experience easy fatigue, loss of appetite, irritability and emotional instability. Then comes confusion and loss of memory, followed by abdominal pains and constipation. Finally, heart irregularities and leg problems (numbness, prickling sensations, tenderness) crop up.

The *Journal of Pediatrics* claims that thiamin is essential to pregnant women. Not only will a deficiency affect her, but the child as well. Mothers' milk should be thiamin-rich. B_1 has also been successful in the relief of morning sickness —nausea and vomiting.

The daily minimum requirement for B$_1$ is small compared to that of other vitamins. Active men need at least 2.3 mg; teenagers 2.0 mg; pregnant women 1.8 mg; others 1.5 mg. These amounts are minimum standards set by the Committee on Foods and Nutrition of the National Research Council, however, and will protect you only from the symptoms of deficiency. For good results, you should take more in your daily diet.

The amount of thiamin one needs to promote proper health will depend mainly on one's carbohydrate consumption. The richest sources for thiamin (B$_1$) are brewer's yeast (over 3.25 mg in 3 teaspoons), soybeans (1.14 mg in ½ cup), lean pork (1.04 mg in one slice), almonds, asparagus, bacon, barley, lima beans, beef heart, wheat bran, cashew nuts, cornmeal, rye flour, soy flour, lean ham, dried lentils, calves' liver, peas, pecans, pork spareribs, and wheat germ. Quality wise the vegetables, fruit, and milk categories are not rich in thiamin, but in quantity they can be important in obtaining one's daily requirement.

B$_2$—Riboflavin   Riboflavin is an intense yellow pigment found in the outer parts of cereals and yeast. It is one of the B-complex vitamins, occurring mostly in foods in which the other B vitamins occur. It is a water soluble vitamin and is not destroyed by cooking unless an alkaline solution such as baking soda is used.

B$_2$ is sensitive to light. Daylight will destroy about half of it.

Nutritionists believe that riboflavin deficiency is this country's most common vitamin deficiency. Alcoholics suffer severe B$_2$ deficiencies because alcohol destroys this vitamin. Riboflavin is an active part in several enzymes necessary to body oxidation and metabolism, and its deficiency seriously weakens the body. The organs most affected by a riboflavin shortage are the skin, mouth (cracked lips, purple tongue), and eyes (burning and dryness, cornea disorders, sensitivity to bright light). In some cases the legs and feet are affected by B$_2$ deficiency—burning sensations, trembling. Anemia may also develop.

Other deficiency symptoms may be loss of hair, split fingernails, eczema and other scaly skin problems, spinal pain, and loss of weight. The central nervous system may suffer impairment.

B_2 is stored in the body much more efficiently than B_1 and is conserved by fibrous foods (besides alcohol, fats and minerals deplete the riboflavin supply).

Riboflavin is responsible for promoting growth and general health. It is essential for the normal functioning of the gastrointestinal tract, and helps the body to assimilate iron.

The Food and Nutrition Board of the National Research Council has set the daily standard requirements for riboflavin as follows: active men, 3.3 mg; nursing mothers, 3.0 mg; teenagers, 3.0 mg; pregnant women, 2.5 mg; others, at least 2.5 mg.

Foods richest in riboflavin are cheeses, lima and soybeans, dried milk, kidneys, liver (3.3 mg in 2 slices), brewer's yeast and whey (extremely high), wheat germ, wheat bran, hickory nuts, wheat hearts, wheat and soy flour, eggs, and peanut butter.

B_6—Pyridoxine   In 1934 Gyorgy reported that Vitamin B_2 consisted of two factors, one being riboflavin; the other he named B_6. In 1938 pyridoxine was isolated and in 1939 Kuhn and Wendt synthesized it. Later it was discovered that two derivatives of pyridoxine (pyridoxamine and pyridoxal) were also active.

Pyridoxine is an odorless white crystalline compound which is stable to heat and to acid. It is unstable in alkali medium and is destroyed by light. Of the three forms of B_6, pyridoxine represents the principal form in food products because it is more resistant to food processing and storage than the other two. Since Vitamin B_6 is water soluble, little is stored in the body. Vitamin B_6 serves as a coenzyme in a significant number of metabolic functions, most of which are involved in amino acid metabolism. It is necessary for transaminations of amino acids. During this process B_6 acts as a coenzyme that separates an amino group from an amino acid and forms a new amino acid. This reaction is important in the formation of the non-essential amino acid. B_6 is required to convert tryptophan into niacin. Most of the biological reactions concerned with changing the chemical properties of amino acids and creating new substances require B_6. Vitamin B_6 also plays a role in the conversion of the essential unsaturated fatty acids (linoleic acid). Pyridoxine helps release glycogen from the liver and muscle as glucose. In animal tests Vitamin B_6 deficiency is characterized by skin lesions, nervous symptoms, and blood disorders. Unlike the previously discussed vitamins no clearcut symptoms are observed in man. Some tests have resulted in seborrheic dermatitis around the eyes and mouth, depression, nausea, vomiting and central nervous system abnormalities appear in extreme deficiency. Infants depleted of B_6 have been shown to develop irritability and convulsions. A deficiency syndrome has been identified in mentally retarded children with uncontrollable convulsions from birth due to inborn error of B_6 metabolism.

Pyridoxine should be taken in its natural form, in combination with other B-vitamins. Several pieces of liver or three tablespoons of brewer's yeast will supply a daily quota of B_6. The daily recommended dosage is 1.5 to 20 mg, depending on your activity. For people with high protein intake (over 100 grams) more B_6 is required.

The only known side effect for large doses (100 mg) of B_6 is sleepiness.

Pyridoxine is destroyed by roasting or stewing, and it will dissolve during slow cooking. Fast cooking is recommended for B_6 foods.

Besides brewer's yeast and liver, other good sources of pyridoxine are lima beans, wheat germ, peas, peanuts, sweet potatoes, bananas, cabbage, and molasses. Milk, meat, fish and poultry are not rich in B_6 but because of the quantity consumed collectively account for most of the dietary B_6.

B_{12} *or Cobalamin* B_{12} is such a recent discovery that very little is known about it. It made a dramatic appearance in 1948, when researchers found and isolated it (from liver). B_{12} was shortly credited with being the substance in liver that combatted the fatal pernicious anemia.

B_{12} is not easily absorbed or utilized fully because it requires the presence of several other factors necessary for absorption and utilization, i.e., a micro-protein enzyme called Castle's intrinsic factor, hydrochloric acid, calcium,

B_6, iron, and folic acid. The body will excrete excessive amounts through the urine. Vitamin B_{12} is found in most tissues but is primarily stored in the liver and kidney. It is released as needed to the bone marrow and other tissues. The total body stores of B_{12} are high; with no B_{12} intake it may take as long as five years for a deficiency symptom to appear.

Vitamin B_{12} has many cellular functions but it is primarily essential for the functioning cells of the gastrointestinal tract, nervous system, and the bone marrow. It acts as a coenzyme in the synthesis of DNA. It is more potent than folic acid in stimulating blood cell formation.

Pernicious anemia results from a lack of intrinsic factor in the gastric juice, which is essential for the absorption of B_{12}. If any of the previously mentioned factors, iron, folic acid, calcium, are deficient a Vitamin B_{12} deficiency could result. Very rarely will a B_{12} deficiency be caused by low dietary intake (the exception being a vegetarian diet that lacks any B_{12}). B_{12} deficiency is normally caused by faulty absorption.

B_{12} recently acquired the name cobalamin, because it contains the trace element, cobalt. Cobalamin cannot be synthesized in the body and, like all other B-vitamins, cannot act in the body without the presence of the other B-vitamins.

Minimum requirements for Vitamin B_{12} have not yet been established. It is found in liver, kidney, milk, fish and meat, but not in grains or vegetables. However, it may be present in kelp—2 or 3 ounces of seaweed daily may provide a minimum requirement for vegetarians.

Doses of B_{12} are measured in micrograms (1/1000 of a milligram) and the daily requirement is small. Apparently, large doses of it are not harmful when taken in concentrated forms.

B_{12} is a product of fermentation by bacteria, so it may be naturally "manufactured," or controlled, by scientists.

B Vitamin—Niacin   Niacin in pure form is a whitish crystalline material. It is quite chemically stable when dry; resistent to heat, light, air, acids and alkalies. Niacin is water soluble, therefore one should not drain off the water after cooking. Niacin is absorbed from the small intestine; once in the body niacin is converted into the active form nicotin-amide. Excessive intakes are excreted in the urine. Trypto-phan is converted into niacin in the body, but requires the presence of B_6 for this conversion. Brewer's yeast is the rich-est source of niacin. It also occurs in meats, fish, poultry and peanuts. Vegetarians may need to supplement their diets with peanut butter or yeast because of the low con-centrates of niacin in vegetables and fruits. The protein foods rich in tryptophan, milk and eggs, even though low in niacin will help furnish one's need for niacin.

Niacin serves as a functioning group in the molecule of a coenzyme concerned with tissue respiration and fat syn-thesis. The enzymes serve as hydrogen acceptors capable of accepting and releasing hydrogen atoms. They also act in metabolism of carbohydrates and amino acids. A deficiency of niacin normally takes months to develop.

Niacin deficiency symptoms, besides pellagra, are ten-der gums, diarrhea, indigestion, abdominal pain, nausea, irritability, insomnia, appetite loss, anxiety, back- and head-ache, depression, fatigue, numbness, and dizziness. Lack of niacin can change a person's whole personality, for the worse. Since niacin is found in the same foods as thiamin (B_1), deficiency symptoms of both generally occur together.

Since niacin forms enzymes that are part of the chemical chain that assimilates sugars and starches, an insufficient amount of this B-vitamin causes dysfunction of carbo-hydrate digestion, resulting in disorders of the digestive tract and nervous system. A breakdown in niacin-contain-ing enzymes also causes a breakdown in the functions of thiamin and riboflavin (B_1, B_2).

Synthetic niacin is commonly used to enrich breakfast foods and bread, but is not efficient in filling natural niacin's role.

Active men need 23 mg of niacin daily; active and pregnant women, 18 mg; nursing mothers, 23 mg; teen-agers, 20 mg; and others, 18 mg. Because of its function (metabolism of fats, carbohydrates, and protein) the amount of niacin needs will depend on one's acceleration of me-tabolism; exercise, stress, surgery, and illness. The dietary requirement of niacin will also be related to the amount and quality of proteins in the diet. A person on a high protein rich diet will require less niacin (60 mg of tryptophan is needed to convert 1 mg of niacin).

Richest sources of niacin are brewer's yeast, desiccated liver, and wheat bran. Other good sources are peanut butter (excellent), chicken, pork and beef heart, mackerel, swordfish, turkey, veal, salmon, mushrooms, lamb, and whole wheat flour.

B Vitamin—Pantothenic Acid   Dr. R. J. Williams isolated pantothenic acid in 1938. In 1946 Lipman showed that coenzyme A was essential for acetylation reactions in the body. Coenzyme A is the form in which pantothenic acid functions in the body. The name for pantothenic acid is derived from the Greek word "panthos" meaning "everywhere," because pantothenic acid is widely distributed in biologic materials.

Pantothenic acid is an unstable, yellow oil, soluble in water. There is little loss from cooking except in acid or alkaline solutions. As a crystalline compound (calcium pantothenate) it is bitter tasting and quite stable. Pantothenic acid from animal sources is in the form of coenzyme A.

Pantothenic acid is essential in the intermediary metabolism of carbohydrates, fats, and protein. Pantothenic acid functions as coenzyme A in the body and is involved with many metabolic roles in the cells. It is involved in the synthesis of cholesterol, steroid hormones, porphyrin for hemoglobin, and phospholipids. Coenzyme A is synthesized within all cells and does not cross cell membranes, therefore there is no coenzyme A in the blood. It plays an important role in the release of energy from carbohydrates. The highest concentrations of pantothenic acid are found where metabolic activity is the greatest: liver, kidney, brain, adrenal, and heart tissues. It may affect the adrenal glands, for its shortage results in fatigue, fainting and disturbed pulse rate.

Being a B-vitamin, it works with the other B-vitamins. More specifically, it works in conjunction with riboflavin and inositol, and its lack disturbs the body's manufacture of other B-vitamins. Since pantothenic acid is a recent discovery, much of its action is still theoretical; scientists have not yet determined its daily requirement in humans (possibly 1/200 gram) nor its symptoms of deficiency.

However, we do know it works as an antihistamine

against undigested amino acids, and that it is related to the body's production of cortisone. Lesser symptoms of its deficiency are graying hair, burning feet, chronic fatigue, cracked fingernails, depression, and tendency to contract infection.

Pantothenic acid is needed by the body in stress conditions, increases vitality, and speeds recovery in many illnesses. It is present in highest amounts in liver, yeast, egg yolk, peanuts, peas, and wheat germ. Like other B-vitamins, it dissolves in water. Baking soda and other alkalines destroy it.

B Vitamin—Biotin The B-vitamin biotin is so potent that no human cell contains more than a trace of it. Liver is one of the richest sources of biotin, yet it contains less than one part biotin per billion.

It is required as a coenzyme in the synthesis of fatty acids, and for other metabolic processes, including the removal of carbon dioxide to or from active compounds, and the oxidation of carbohydrate. The body has the ability to synthesize biotin by intestinal bacteria.

Biotin is also an antidote for skin rashes and hair loss brought on by avidin, a substance in egg whites. Biotin deficiency results in severe rash, Leiner's disease (skin has a burned lobster appearance), and eczema (skin is scaly, itching). These conditions are corrected by daily injections of 5 mg of biotin.

Because biotin is needed in such minute amounts, its lack is a rarity. But it must be in the body. The best foods for obtaining biotin in your diet are beef and lamb liver, unpolished rice, soybeans and soy flour, sardines, cauliflower, cow peas, and brewer's yeast.

B Vitamin—Inositol Inositol's status as a B-vitamin was only recently established, and there is still much to be learned about its activity in humans. Though inositol was isolated from diabetic urine over 100 years ago it did not gain attention until 1950, when a *Newsweek* magazine article reported an experiment with rabbits that showed evidence of inositol's power in lowering cholesterol levels.

Later research has borne out that inositol is essential in the production of lecithin. Synthesis of inositol occurs within the cell. Inositol is concentrated in the brain. When 750 mg of inositol was administered, along with choline (a B-vitamin), to patients recovering from heart attacks, the size of the cholesterol particles and the amount of fat in their blood quickly decreased. and within two months the cholesterol levels were back to normal.

People wishing to lose weight should get plenty of inositol to stimulate lecithin action.

Giving inositol to patients about to be operated upon for stomach cancer is considered to be a valuable pre-operative procedure. It apparently has a mild inhibitory action on certain types of cancer. An experiment in 1943, in which mice with transplanted cancers were injected intravenously with inositol, showed that the growth of the tumors was retarded in proportion to the amount of the dosage given.

J. I. Rodale reports that Drs. Herbst and Bagley administered inositol to six patients suffering from cancer of the bladder. The original tumors lessened in size because of this treatment.

Conversely, however, Adelle Davis states that inositol does not retard cancer growth.

Adelle Davis and others recommend inositol to those whose hair is falling out. Dosages of inositol, folic acid and biotin, they report, will not only stop the falling but will stimulate new growth. Inositol deficiency leads to poor lecithin production, high cholesterol and fatty liver, nephritis (a fatal liver disease), blood sugar, coronary disease, and all dysfunctions caused by lecithin deficiency.

Diabetics throw it off; inositol appears in much greater amounts in their urine than in the urine of healthy people. This may lead to severe atherosclerosis and fatty liver if not treated.

Rich sources of inositol are dried lima beans, beef brains and hearts, cantaloupe, grapefruit, peaches, peanuts, oranges, peas, raisins, wheat germ, cabbage, brewer's yeast, and other meats, fruits and vegetables in lesser amounts.

B Vitamin—Folic Acid Folic (or pteroylglutamic) acid is a recently discovered B-complex vitamin. It was isolated from spinach leaves in 1941 and called folic because of its apparent abundance in foliage.

Its chief function is the prevention of several types of anemia. Folic acid, therefore, aids in the proper growth and reproduction of red blood cells. Vitamin C facilitates the conversion in the liver. It plays an important role in the synthesis of compounds needed to manufacture DNA and RNA, which are essential to cell division and the transmission of inherited traits. Folic acid and B_{12} are co-workers in many processes necessary to keep the blood cells in proper health. It is required in the conversion of amino acids. Three linked components make up folic acid, para-aminobenzoic acid, glutamic acid, and pteridine group. Folic acid can be synthesized in the intestinal tract by certain bacteria, such as coliform organism. Poor protein diet may impair the utilization and function of folic acid. Its deficiency results in diarrhea, inflammation of the tongue, gastrointestinal disorders, a decrease in white cells, and all the accompanying symptoms of anemia.

Of the B-vitamins, folic acid is most easily destroyed by high heat and light exposure. Nutritionists believe that the quantity of folic acid in greens can be determined by the green coloring. Deep green vegetables are therefore higher in folic acid.

The minimum daily requirement has not yet been set, but to insure proper nutrition you should eat plenty of folic acid-rich foods. They are brewer's yeast, salmon, wheat germ, spinach, watermelon, cantaloupe, broccoli, beef, asparagus, lima beans, chicken, lettuce, liver, and oysters.

B Vitamin—Para-Aminobenzoic Acid Para-aminobenzoic acid, known for convenience as Paba, is one of the latest B-vitamins to be studied, and therefore we still know little about it.

Most importantly, we know that Paba is, in chemical terms, "antagonistic" to sulfa drugs. That is to say, sulfa drugs and Paba are so chemically alike that they can fill the same position in the linking of certain molecules. Paba, then, is usurped when sulfa drugs are introduced into the body, and the subsequent chain of events is disrupted.

The bad effects of sulfa drugs are actually symptoms of

para-aminobenzoic acid deficiency. When these drugs are given to a person who is Vitamin B-deficient, they will normally take over Paba's function. The results are digestive disorders, nervousness, and extreme depression.

Paba serves as an excellent skin ointment for burns, sunburns, dry skin (eczema), aging skin (wrinkles), and possibly skin cancer. Paba is also essential for healthy hair. In animals, a Paba deficiency has been associated with graying of the hair.

It is necessary for the body's production of folic acid (a B-vitamin), which in turn helps to assimilate pantothentic acid.

Paba is found in the foods plentiful in other B-vitamins: liver, brewer's yeast, eggs, milk, rice bran, whole wheat, wheat germ, and molasses.

B Vitamin—Choline   In humans, the main function of choline is the metabolism and transportation of fat from the liver. Choline also plays an important role in the transmission of nerve impulses. Lack of choline in the body causes low production of acetylcholine, which then results in muscle weakness, damage tomuscle fibers, and excessive scarring.

In 1949, Drs. L. M. Morrison and W. F. Gonzales conducted an experiment with 230 acute heart disease patients. After their release, these patients were observed for three years. Half (115) of them served as controls, and the other half were given a choline supplement. Three years later, 29 of the control patients had succumbed to heart disease and died. In the choline group, only 9 died of heart disease.

German doctors have reported success in treating hepatitis with choline. They found that choline treatment reduced the duration of viral hepatitis to nearly half.

Researchers in Italy experimented with choline's effect in reducing hyperthyroid conditions. They found that choline hydrochloride medication gave relief to thyroid sufferers. The body can synthesize choline from the amino acid serine, providing methionine is present along with folic acid and B_{12}, which act as coenzymes.

Choline has also been shown to be useful in controlling

diabetes when used with other B-vitamins.

Foods rich in choline are snap beans, soybeans, egg yolk, lamb kidneys, pork and calves' liver, peas, spinach, brewer's yeast, and wheat germ.

Choline is best known for its rich concentration in colostrum, the extra-rich mothers' milk of the first days of nursing which nature provides for the infant in his first, weakest days. Fruit, milk, and vegetables are poor sources of choline.

Adelle Davis says that the average daily American intake of choline is about one-fifth the minimum requirement. However, if other B-vitamins and proteins are present, the body converts its supply of methionine to choline when normal levels of choline are low.

Choline's action in the body is inhibited by the presence of alcohol.

Researchers at the University of Toronto found choline to be essential to the health of the heart and circulatory system of young rats. Choline-deficient rats developed damaged arteries and aorta that were clogged with fat deposits. The fat deposits also inflamed the liver and kidneys of these rats, pinching their blood supply. Their cells became so engorged with fat that many burst and allowed the fat to seep into the blood and bile. When the condition of these rats was not allowed to go too far, their blood cholesterol could be lowered with choline. Choline forms lecithin in the liver.

Nephritis (a liver disease) has been produced in animals by choline deficiency. The coils of their capillaries are damaged, blood lecithin drops far below normal, severe hemorrhages occur, and cholesterol and fat deposits clog the body's circulatory system. The result is edema (or dropsy), a swelling caused by fluid accumulations in the body. Choline can also alleviate these symptoms.

B Vitamin—B_{15} B_{15}, or pangamic acid, is one of the newest discoveries. We know little about it so far. However, we do know that it aids in regulating fat metabolism, heightens oxygen assimilation in tissues, stimulates the glandular and nervous systems, and has been beneficial in certain types of heart diseases. It helps increase the body's tolerance to lowered oxygen supply, and protects the body from slow carbon monoxide poisoning.

It is found in the common B-vitamin foods.

VITAMIN C

Vitamin C is probably the best-known and the most underestimated nutrient of all. In truth, it is active in more functions of more organs in the body than any other.

Though the existence of vitamins was not known until 1912, Vitamin C was actually discovered by Dr. James Lind in 1750. A British naval physician aboard the *H.M.S. Salisbury*, Captain Lind took the task upon himself to find out why sailors would return to port from long months at sea with a disease called scurvy—marked by weakness, aches, bruising and internal hemorrhaging, bleeding gums, swelling joints, shortness of breath, and eventually, death.

Scurvy had become one of the accepted hazards of seafaring in Lind's time. Hippocrates wrote about it in 460 B.C. Epidemics of scurvy often spread through early Europe. In 1593, Sir Richard Hawkins discovered a correlation between reasonably good health of sailors and citrus fruits aboard ship, but this coincidence was generally dismissed. Easily, more sailors have died from scurvy than have been killed in all the naval battles of history.

Dr. Lind did not accept this disease as others had before him, and he began a scientific investigation of scurvy. He noticed that it didn't occur aboard ships that sailed the coastline, or on local fishing ships, but only on long voyages. Lind finally suspected that the lack of fruits and vegetables may have been the cause of scurvy.

Nobody accepted his findings until 1795, when his persistence convinced the British Admiralty. Limes were then issued as a dietary staple for British sailors (hence their nickname, limeys) and remained so until the First World War.

The missing ingredient that those limes and other fruits provided was ascorbic acid. We know it now as Vitamin C.

Most animals have an enzyme in their livers that allows for the manufacture of ascorbic acid from a commonly found body chemical—glucose. But for a small group of mammals—the monkey, the guinea pig, the bulbul, and man—ascorbic acid is a daily and essential dietary requirement; they cannot produce this vitamin in any sufficient amount to sustain health. An adult human, for instance, who is kept on a Vitamin C-free diet, will lose his blood level of ascorbic acid in six weeks. After ten weeks, symptoms of scurvy will begin to appear.

There are still many people, some of them affluent, who suffer from Vitamin C deficiency. There are those who are poor, those who eat the wrong foods because of a lack of any nutritional knowledge, children of working mothers, families who have their meals prepared improperly (boiling destroys Vitamin C), dieters, alcoholics, the elderly and senile, heavy smokers, and bachelors who eat as best they can.

In 1968, the U. S. Department of Agriculture announced that 20% of the American population was eating a nutritionally poor diet, and that 25% had an intake of Vitamin C below the minimum standards. Our reliance on processed foods and our poor eating habits have deprived us of some of our basic requirements. Most of us never get scurvy (Boston City Hospital, for example, reports only seven to ten cases a year), but many suffer from "subclinical" scurvy, which is difficult to detect without careful laboratory tests. So we have millions of Americans who feel they do their daily deed for their bodies by drinking orange juice at breakfast, and then forget about Vitamin C for the rest of the day, and suffer minor ailments.

Vitamin C is concentrated in the white blood cells, which fight infection; a deficiency results in lowered resistance to bacteria and viruses. It also functions in the synthesis of the cement substance that binds cells together. Deficiency results in a breakage of small capillary cells—hemorrhages under the skin. Personality disorders may also result from not getting sufficient Vitamin C.

What *is* a sufficient amount of Vitamin C? The National Research Council in 1963 gave the daily requirement as 70 milligrams for both men and women. Teenagers need about 80 mg per day, and pregnant women and elderly persons need at least 100 mg. We should add, however, that many nutritionists believe these quantities to be minimal. Vitamin C is not stored in the body and must be replenished constantly. Unlike other vitamins, too much Vitamin C cannot be taken.

Vitamin C has been credited as a cure for many ailments and diseases. Dr. Fred R. Klenner of Reidsville, N. C., states emphatically that 10 or more grams of ascorbic acid every day will preclude any danger of having kidney stones, for C lowers the pH of the blood and neutralizes the alkaline solution required for stones.

Dr. Kenner also recommends Vitamin C for preventing tooth decay.

Vitamin C is a good natural laxative. It dilutes bile and aids in elimination.

Vitamin C carries hydrogen into the body and aids in the proper burning of foodstuffs. It nurtures small blood vessels, the teeth, bones and skin. It aids in healing wounds and fighting germs, and helps in the body's absorption of iron.

One of the most dramatic claims for Vitamin C came from Nobel Prize winner Dr. Linus Pauling, who in his book, *Vitamin C and the Common Cold,* announced that massive doses of Vitamin C far above the daily minimum requirement—up to 10,000 mgs a day—can prevent and help cure the common cold.

Dr. Pauling also stated that a 10-fold increase in the daily intake of ascorbic acid would bring about a 10% increase in the well-being, both physically and mentally, of everyone, and increase the body's healing rate.

All persons need to increase their daily Vitamin C intake because prolonged hard muscular work, consumption of chemically fertilized food, severe climatic cold, infections, air pollution, mental stress, and cigarette smoking all bring about a need for added amounts of ascorbic acid. Persons living in Los Angeles, New York, and other pollution centers need 2 to 3 times more Vitamin C than those living in Arizona. Smokers need more than non-smokers. All these stresses cause the body to use more ascorbic acid, or actually destroy the vitamin.

Strengthening the body against diseases is not Vitamin C's only claim to health. British rheumatologists claim that C seals the cell walls of joint linings that let arthritis-causing enzymes loose in the joint cartilages, causing arthritis and rheumatism. Dr. Irwin Stone reports that Vitamin C given to children builds people resistant to the rheumatoid disease process.

Five million Americans have cataracts over their eyes,

and one million of these people are between the ages of 30 and 60. Scientists know that the healthy eye lens is very rich in Vitamin C. Adelle Davis claims that Vitamins C, E, and B$_2$ have improved cataract conditions in patients. Many observers, like Dr. Donald T. Atkinson, say that poor diets and high stress of aging contribute to the poor nutrition of old persons. What Vitamin C they get is quickly burned. This could explain their high rate of cataracts.

Psychiatrists Abram Hoffer and Humphry Osmond wrote in *How to Live with Schizophrenia* that schizophrenia has a physiological, biochemical basis. Most authorities in medicine and psychiatry agree with this view to some extent. Drs. Hoffer and Osmond claim some success in helping schizophrenics with injections of Vitamins B (niacin) and C. Dr. Michael H. Briggs of New Zealand reports that schizophrenics excrete more Vitamin C than other mental patients, and that they have high amounts of copper—which destroys Vitamin C—in their blood. Russian scientists report success with schizophrenics by starving them for a week to clean their systems and then putting them on a special, high-nutrition diet. Dr. Linus Pauling has also written of his success in dealing with mental illness with ascorbic acid. Further research into this matter would be valuable, for 1 in 10 Americans—over 17 million —suffer mental illness. New York City, a polluted city that creates profound stress in its inhabitants, is a city of sickness—at least 80% of New York City dwellers suffer some form of mental illness.

Dr. Iain W. Dymock of Glasgow, Scotland, wrote in the *British Medical Journal* that patients with duodenal ulcers are short on Vitamin C. They may be intaking enough of the vitamin, but their digestive tract's condition is such that they can't absorb it. Dymock reports that most ulcer patients he has treated showed evidence of Vitamin C depletion, but that this may be due to previous treatment for their ulcers; physicians try to cut off the flow of hydrochloric acid, which assimilates C. In any case, huge doses of Vitamin C aid in healing stomach perforations and may be the best treatment for ulcers.

Dr. Peter Schwartz, formerly of Camp Lejeune Naval Hospital, North Carolina, contends that surgery patients need large doses of C because their bodies lose it during surgery. Another surgeon agrees, recommending 200-300 mgs daily for surgery patients, because the usual drugs administered to these patients may cause an increase in the excretion of Vitamin C, the one substance they will need for body healing after surgery. Collagen, the body's product that actually closes over a wound and protects it, is formed with the aid of Vitamin C.

Vitamin C is effective in dealing with poisons. Experiments with rats have shown that ascorbic acid protected them from suffering extreme effects of rat poisoning (strychnine). Hungarian scientists have found C to have the capability of breaking down DDT in the body. Dr. Henry A. Schroeder of Dartmouth College writes that the element cadmium (found in high amounts in those with high blood pressure) is neutralized by Vitamin C.

Working with guinea pigs which, like us, cannot manufacture their own ascorbic acid, researchers have found that the blood of these animals, when they had scurvy, coagulated abnormally. In addition to fragile blood vessels, these guinea pigs developed fatty liver and an inability to coagulate blood properly. Apparently, the blood substance which aids in this process could not be made in the liver without Vitamin C.

On this same line, Dr. Emil Ginter, Chief of the Biochemistry Department of the Institute of Nutritional Research at Bratislava, Czechoslovakia, studied 1000 Slovakian school children and found that they suffered a Vitamin C deficiency in winter and early spring. When testing their blood during these times, he found that it contained far larger than normal amounts of cholesterol, the fatty substance that causes hardening of the arteries. To prove that a definite correlation existed, he experimented with two colonies of guinea pigs—one given 10 times the amount of Vitamin C as the other. After a year, according to Dr. Ginter's report, "cholesterol accumulation in the liver, adrenals, brain and other tissues, including the aortic wall, was 30% higher in the vitamin C-deficient animals than in the controls."

A Russian scientist is quoted by Dr. Ancel Keys of the University of Minnesota as having found that adding Vitamin C to the diet hinders the development of hardening of the arteries. Another Russian scientist, a member of the Academy of Medical Sciences in Moscow, stated that the fabled longevity of many people in the Caucasus region of South Russia (the life expectancy in some tribes is over 100) may be due partly to their high Vitamin C intake.

All of this naturally leads us to the effect of C in reducing the risk of heart attacks and strokes. Dr. J. Shafar, a Glasgow physician, has noted significant heart trouble in patients diagnosed as having scurvy. But after a week of Vitamin C treatment, these heart troubles disappeared.

To go on and on would be redundant. It is sufficient to say that Vitamin C may well be the key to good health and immunity to disease. It protects against colds and their complications, helps build resistance to fatigue and stress, and generally improves health.

The best sources of Vitamin C are the citrus fruit juices: orange, grapefruit, lemon, lime, grape, etc. An average orange contains approximately 60 milligrams of ascorbic acid. Orange and lemon peels have twice as much Vitamin C as the juice.

Foods rich in Vitamin C are alfalfa meal, almonds, asparagus, bananas, blueberries, brussels sprouts, cabbage, cantaloupe, carrots, celery, chard, collards, cranberries, currants, endives, parsley, peas, peppers, radishes, spinach, strawberries, tomatoes, tangerines, turnip greens and watercress.

Meat and other sources of Vitamin C are liver (chicken), milk, apple juice and watermelon.

VITAMIN P (BIOFLAVONOIDS)

The bioflavonoids (bio meaning active rather than inert; flavonoids meaning the crystalline substance which provides the yellow color in certain foods such as an orange and lemon) provide a source of healthful nutrition to the system. It has proved beneficial in helping in the treatment of hemorrhoids, respiratory infections, high blood pressure, varicose veins, habitual abortions, rheumatic fever, anemia and damage caused by X-rays.

The principal constituents of the chief bioflavonoids include several types of vitamins: Vitamin C, Vitamin K, Vitamin P and hesperidin, a crystalline substance largely concentrated in the peel and pulp of citrus fruits. Also contained in the bioflavonoid foods are other vitamins, amino acids, protopectin and minerals.

The main value of the bioflavonoids is their ability to increase the strength of the capillaries and regulate their permeability (P stands for permeability). Vitamin P also assists Vitamin C in keeping the collagen in a healthy condition. Vitamins P and C are synergists (the combined effect of both substances administered together is greater than the sum of the individual effects).

The orange and lemon are full of bioflavonoids.

Vitamin P is also called the flavone factor and citrin. By helping to prevent the passage of serum proteins through the capillary walls into the tissues, it has proved helpful in edema.

While the functions of the essential vitamins are definitely known, it is not advisable to use isolated vitamins for specific conditions. Vitamins are interrelated in their functions and there is a functional relationship between the vitamins and minerals. A proper balance of vitamins and minerals, as obtained with a varied and well chosen diet, is the best procedure and if necessary as a supplement to the diet the use of a reliable nutritionist is recommended, to give you the vitamins and minerals desired.

VITAMIN F

This vitamin is more commonly known as essential fatty acids.

The function of Vitamin F in human nutrition has not been definitely established. It is credited with helping to maintain the proper resilience and lubrication of all cells. It is necessary for normal glandular activity, especially of the adrenal glands. It is helpful for the prevention of cholesterol deposits in the arteries. It helps protect you to a small degree against the harmful effects of X-rays. It assists the assimilation of calcium to the cells. It also promotes a healthy skin and is useful in the prevention of such disorders as eczema, allergies, asthma, colds and sinus infections.

A deficiency of this vitamin can cause dry skin, weak, dry hair, brittle fingernails, baldness, acne, eczema, dandruff, and allergic conditions. No official unit has yet been established.

The richest natural sources of Vitamin F are cold-pressed, unrefined vegetable oils: wheat germ oil, linseed oil, sunflower oil, safflower oil and soybean oil.

SATURATED AND UNSATURATED FATTY ACIDS

Fatty substances are composed of various atoms of carbon, hydrogen and oxygen, linked together like chains. Some are long, meaning they have many atoms linked together; others are short. Many types of fats have open links, where other atoms can be attached to them. These are called the "unsaturated fatty acids." "Unsaturated" means that these open links in the chain are there, ready to be filled or "saturated" with an atom of some other substance.

Linolenic, linoleic and arachidonic acids are simply "unsaturated" fatty acids. They are essential for good health. Since they have open links in their chain of atoms, it is easy for them to combine with other substances in your body. They serve many purposes; they assist in carrying the food which they combine with through the miles of blood vessels and they are used in building cell structure. It is only possible for them to do this because the open links in their chains of atoms invite other substances to join with them in various chemical combinations.

In order to change an unsaturated fatty acid into a saturated fatty acid certain changes must occur. In most cases the open chains have already been filled with some other substance and there is no chance for this kind of fat to take the active role in the body's laboratory.

When oxygen is combined with the unsaturated fatty acids, an atom of oxygen moves into the empty link, joins itself chemically with the other atoms and the fat becomes rancid. When hydrogen is added, it moves into the empty link, joins itself to the other atoms and you have "hydrogenated fat," a thick, lard-like substance. In either situation, since the empty links have been filled, the fat can no longer fulfill its duties inside the body, due to its becoming "saturated."

Rancid fat in the diet is responsible for the destruction of fat-soluble vitamins. Natural fats in their natural state, such as those in the safflower seeds, carry along substances called antioxidants which prevent oxygen from turning the fat rancid.

Unsaturated fatty acids are most abundant in vegetable and cereal oils, and not very plentiful in animal fats, such as butter, eggs, milk and meat fats. Also, vegetable oils are more healthful to the body because they do not contribute a fatty substance called cholesterol, which is harmful to the heart.

VITAMIN D

This is a fat-soluble vitamin and is found in fish liver oils. It is also present in butter and eggs, fish and meat. Vitamin D is concerned with calcification of the bones. Vitamin D consists of a group of chemically distinct sterol compounds, but only those called D_2 and D_3 are of practical importance. D_2 is a plant sterol, ergosterol, and is closely related to cholesterol in structure. D_3 is synthesized in animal tissues (found in skin) from a substance named 7-dehydro-cholesterol. Both D_2 and D_3 are converted to active forms by irradiation with ultra-violet light. Ergocalciferol (D_2) is prepared commercially for use as a vitamin supplement, while cholecalciferol (D_3) is the form found in fish liver oils.

HOW TO READ LABELS

1. *NATURAL*:   Insofar as our literature is concerned, the term "natural" means as naturally found in nature or in natural food sources. It would further imply that in preparation there has been no molecular change, either biologically or biochemically in the combinations or in the activity of these natural foods. This, of course, does not mean that in the preparation moisture and fiber cannot be removed. We further believe that all label declarations should state the exact food source from which the vitamins or minerals are obtained, if they are represented to be natural.
2. *CRYSTALLINE*:   A crystalline vitamin is one that had as its original source a natural food. By means of solvents, heat, or distillation they have been reduced to one specific, pure crystalline vitamin or crystalline amino acid. In the preparation of crystalline vitamins it is practically impossible to reduce any natural food product

to an absolutely pure state. The "impurities" remaining are, perhaps, certain of the synergists and when combined with a crystalline vitamin are, in our opinion as well as that of certain other experts, superior to the synthetic.

3. *SYNTHETIC*: When a scientist in a laboratory has reconstructed the exact molecular structure of a crystalline vitamin by putting together or chemically combining molecules from other known sources, he then has a pure synthetic vitamin. Naturally, the synthetic vitamin has no synergists, no enzymes, no coenzymes, no minerals, no mineral activators, nor covitamin helpers. It is a pure vitamin. Legally, it is not necessary to give the source from which the synthetic chemical is derived.

Following is a list of the items most frequently found in food supplement formulas.

VITAMINS

You will note from the list of the sources below that few crystallines are used at the present time. The reason is that the synthetics are, in many cases, as much as sixty times cheaper to produce.

ITEM	SOURCE GIVEN	
Vitamin A	Fish Oils	Natural
Vitamin A	Acetate	Synthetic
Vitamin A	Palmitate	Syn. or Cryst.
Vitamin A	Lemon	Crystalline
Vitamin B-complex		
Vitamin B_1	Yeast	Natural
Vitamin B_1	Thiamin Mononitrate	Synthetic
Vitamin B_1	Thiamin Hydrochloride	Synthetic
Vitamin B_2	Yeast	Natural
Vitamin B_2	Riboflavin	Syn. or Cryst.
Vitamin B_6	Yeast	Natural
Vitamin B_6	Pyridoxine Hydrochloride	Synthetic
Vitamin B_{12}	Yeast	Natural
Vitamin B_{12}	Streptomycin Fermentation	Crystalline
Vitamin B_{12}	Cobalamin Concentrate	Crystalline
Para-aminobenzoic Acid	Yeast	Natural
Para-aminobenzoic Acid		Synthetic
Folic Acid	Yeast	Natural

Folic Acid	Pteroylglutamic Acid	Synthetic
Pantothenic Acid	Yeast	Natural
Pantothenic Acid	Calcium Pantothenate	Synthetic
Inositol	Soybeans	Natural
Inositol	Reduced from Corn	Crystalline
Choline	Soybeans	Natural
Choline	Choline Bitartrate	Synthetic
Biotin	Liver	Natural
Biotin	D-Biotin	Synthetic
Nicotinic Acid	Yeast	Natural
Nicotinic Acid	Niacin	Synthetic
Niacin	Yeast	Natural
Niacin	Niacinamide	Synthetic

Vitamin C-complex

Vitamin C	Citrus, Rose Hips, Acerola Berries	Natural
Vitamin C	Ascorbic Acid	Synthetic

Vitamin D-complex

Vitamin D	Fish Oils	Natural
Vitamin D	Irradiated Ergosterol	Synthetic
Vitamin D	Calciferol	Synthetic

Vitamin E-complex

Vitamin E	Wheat Germ Oil	Natural
Vitamin E	DL-Alpha Tocopherol Acetate	Syn. or Cryst.
Vitamin K	Alfalfa	Natural
Vitamin K	Menadione	Synthetic

MINERALS

Minerals are generally characterized as either inorganic or organic. An inorganic mineral is one found in soils, rocks or chemicals. Some may be obtained in pure powder form, while others are so unstable alone that they are available only as a mineral salt combined with something else. An organic mineral is one that has been changed by photosynthesis from the action of sun, soil, air and water, into plant life, and then indirectly into animal tissue.

Calciferol is a colorless, odorless crystalline material, insoluble in water, soluble in fats and oils. It is not affected by dilute acids, alkalis or oxygen. Calciferol is stable to light, heat and oxidation, the pure material retains its potency very well, but as existing in foodstuffs its stability is not very good.

Vitamin D is very similar to the substance cholesterol which is a normal constituent of all fats. Both these substances belong to the group known as steroids which also includes the cortico-steroids (cortisone), substances in the adrenal glands, and the male and female sex hormones. Another steroid, ergosterol, is present in yeast extracts. This substance, when exposed to ultra-violet light, becomes transposed to Vitamin D. This is the commercial method of preparing the vitamin. In the human skin is a similar substance called 7-dehydro-cholesterol. Exposure of the oiled or unwashed body to sunlight will convert this substance to Vitamin D. It is for this reason that this vitamin has been called the sunshine vitamin.

It is also thought that sunstroke is a toxic effect due to tremendous Vitamin D activity. During the fall and winter there is a lack of Vitamin D generated in the skin. However, an excessive amount must be avoided. The daily intake should not exceed 5,000 International Units. The results of an excess are general depression, diarrhea, severe toxic effects, and abnormal calcium deposits in blood vessel walls, liver, lungs and kidneys and stomach.

Vitamin D is also responsible for regulating the absorption and metabolism of calcium and phosphorus, the bone forming elements; essential for proper tooth formation and bone growth, controls the calcium content in the blood and so governs muscular action. It is necessary for pregnant women and essential for proper glandular functioning. For proper absorption and assimilation Vitamin D requires the presence of oil or fat and calcium.

A Vitamin D deficiency can be seen in deformities of bones, soft bones, lack of stamina and vigor, dental caries, constipation, muscular weakness and instability of the nervous system, muscle twitchings and cramps.

There is practically no Vitamin D in most of the vegetables, cereals and fruit. An important point to remember when discussing Vitamin D requirements is that, even in sufficient doses, Vitamin D is ineffective unless calcium and phosphorus requirements are met also.

LECITHIN

Lecithin is the natural extract of the fatty part of the soybean.

When soybeans are pressed, a golden-colored oil separates from the protein part of the bean. After the oil has been allowed to stand for a short period of time, a yellow-colored solution settles at the bottom of the container. This substance is Lecithin which after being defatted and dried comes to us in the form of granules.

A typical analysis of soybean powder, which is used for making soya milk or used in addition to other flours, contains the following:

Protein	42.0%
Fat	23.0%
Fibre	2.2%
Carbohydrates	22.7%
LECITHIN	2.1%
Moisture	4.4%

There have been many recent claims by leading scientists as to the medical values of Lecithin. One of the most significant statements on the use of Lecithin came from Dr. Lester M. Morrison, president and medical director of Crenshaw Hospital of Los Angeles and of Santa Ana Doctors' Hospital. He stated, "The most important nutritional supplement developed in the last 50 years is Lecithin. The least it can do for you is to improve your health and give you added vitality and it may even help save your life."

He was referring to the use of Lecithin and its beneficial effects with cases of atherosclerosis and the treatment of heart and blood vessel diseases.

Lecithin is known as a phospholipid. It is an important part of all living cells, both animal and vegetable. It is found in brain tissue and in egg yolk, but for mass consumption Lecithin is extracted from soybean oil.

Lecithin contains two very important vitamins, Choline and Inositol, which are known as lipotropic factors due to their regulatory effect of deposition of fat in the liver. Inositol is also good for maintaining healthy skin and hair.

Lecithin is also believed to help remove cholesterol from the artery walls and then dissolve it in the bloodstream.

Other recent claims for Lecithin include patients who used Lecithin regularly found evidence of increased immunity against virus infections. In other cases, patients claimed that Lecithin was beneficial in cases of rheumatic carditis, diseases of the liver, anemia, kidney disorders and metabolic disturbances of the skin, such as psoriasis.

Lecithin, chemically, is a phospholipid, and it is also the chief phospholipid contained in the bile.

Phospholipids are important in keeping bile cholesterol in solution. Because gallstones consist mainly of cholesterol that has precipitated out of bile solution, supplementing the diet with Lecithin could possibly help prevent stones from forming.

Lecithin is also an important part of a healthy nervous system. Nerve fibers are surrounded by a sheath of fatty substances, the myelin sheath. This protective sheath is very rich in Lecithin. It therefore becomes obvious that the nervous system relies, among other factors, on Lecithin for normal functioning. If this sheath is lacking in Lecithin, due to a deficiency of Lecithin in the diet, then the nerves are depleted and the results are often such discomforts as: fatigue, irritability, sexual decline, nervous exhaustion, etc.

In addition, soy Lecithin contains Inositol, Choline, Chephaline, and a high content of Phosphorus. Phosphorus in the form of Phosphoric Acid is found to be essential in human physiology, as it forms a part of all bones and is very high in brain and nerve tissue.

Keep in mind that Lecithin is not a medicine; rather it is one of nature's beneficial foods. It should be taken daily as a supplement.

MINERALS

Minerals, or trace elements as they are commonly called because they exist in such tiny amounts in the body, are needed for overall mental and physical functioning. They are important factors in maintaining proper physiological conditions and processes, such as the acid-base balance, osmotic action, elasticity, and soft tissues—muscles. Your skeletal structure's strength depends upon these magic minerals. The nerves must have them to be tranquil, strong and vibrant. Digestion and healthful assimilation of foods depend upon adequate "mineralization" in your system. From 4 to 6 percent of the body's weight is mineral matter. It is found in all tissues and fluids but especially in the bones, teeth and cartilage. There are close to 30 such minerals.

FUNCTIONS OF MINERALS:

1. Protein, the building blocks of your body, cannot be formed without the presence of calcium, nitrogen and sulfur.

2. The entire digestive system relies upon the vagus nerve; this nerve cannot function properly without potassium.

3. Vitamins cannot work unless minerals are present. For example, vitamin B12, needed for a strong bloodflow, requires the presence of the cobalt mineral.

4. Minerals are needed to combine with some vitamins to remove internal gaseous waste products.

5. Since the insulin molecule contains zinc, and since diabetes results from an insulin shortage, there is the possibility that a deficiency of the zinc mineral may be involved with the ailment.

6. Minerals influence muscular contraction and also dominate the making of nerve response.

7. Minerals have the power to control body liquids and to permit other nutrients to pass into the bloodstream. Without minerals, these other nutrients cannot do their proper jobs.

8. Blood coagulation is controlled by a mineral action. This means that bruises, cuts, scratches, wounds, etc., must have minerals for the healing processes.

9. Your alertness, youthful zest, energy, and thought power, all require such minerals as manganese, copper, cobalt, iodine, zinc, magnesium and phosphorus for maximum efficiency.

10. Minerals in your bloodstream act to create a germ-killing action. Therefore, minerals have the power to help create antibodies directly within your body's system, provided that other essential raw materials are present.

11. Minerals are essential for strong bones and teeth, which are about 95 percent composed of calcium and phosphorus.

Minerals have the unique power of maintaining a delicate internal water balance that is needed for all mental and physical processes. Minerals draw substances into and out of your cells. Minerals aid in keeping blood and tissue fluid from becoming either too acid or too alkaline. Minerals stimulate the hormonal secretion of glands and cause the nervous system to send commands, mentally communicated, to all parts of your body.

When minerals are ingested in combination with foods, they create what is known as an ash which then enters into the composition of every single body tissue and fluid. Your body must have minerals to serve as detoxifying (purifying) agents by combining with acid wastes from your cells. Minerals neutralize these wastes and prepare them for elimination. Otherwise, waste products decompose and make you sluggish, sleepy, ache, grouchy and generally unpleasant.

Minerals are also required for osmotic equilibrium, which refers to the most dynamic power minerals can offer the body. Your blood and lymph are liquids in which solids are kept in solution. Your cells are always being bathed in lymph fluids. Your cells, too, are semi-fluid containing dissolved matter. If the lymph outside your cells contains as much dissolved solid as found within the cells, you run the risk of having your body's cells shrink and dissolve. But minerals go to work to equalize the amount of dissolved solids both inside and outside the cells. Therefore, internal and external pressures are equalized and the body cells remain normal.

There are a few simple rules concerning the need for a complete intake of minerals. The first is that you need *all* elements, not just one or two. This means that if you have a shortage of just one mineral, the entire body machinery can become upset. Although the amounts may vary the need is constant.

While there are close to 30 "essential" minerals, all of which are vital, we shall take up the 14 most important ones because they control the use of the others.

CALCIUM

Calcium must have vitamin D, phosphorus, vitamin A and C in order to function. These other nutrients must have calcium to do their work, too. About 99 percent of your calcium is found in your bones and teeth. Only 1 percent circulates in your body fluids and tissues. Calcium is needed for blood clotting, to activate enzymes (digestive juices), and to regulate passages throughout cellular walls.

Calcium works to normalize the contraction and relaxation of the heart muscles. If your blood calcium level drops, you become nervous and irritated. An adequate calcium intake means that some is stored in the ends of the bones in long, needle-like crystals called trabeculae. This reserve storage is used when you face a stress situation. If you do not have it, your body seizes calcium from your bone structure, usually the spinal and pelvic bones.

Calcium and phosphorus must exist in a certain proportion if they are to be used properly. The ratio is two to one, or, twice as much calcium as a given amount of phosphorus. The presence of vitamin D helps to normalize this ratio and maintain a good balance.

A deficiency may cause height reduction because of fractures of the vertebrae which result from pressure. Osteoporosis, or brittle bones, is one symptom. Osteomalacia is another calcium-deficiency disease: the adult version of rickets.

Calcium is vital for your nerves; this mineral helps transport impulses of your nerves from one part of your body to another. With a calcium deficiency, cramps or convulsions may occur. Heart palpitations and slow pulse are also traced to low calcium intake. Calcium, too, helps in maintaining the delicate acid-alkaline body balance.

Prime sources of calcium are all dairy and milk products and green vegetables. The best calcium source is bone meal, a supplement made from cattle bones and dried in a vacuum process so the minerals are not depleted. Bone meal is excellent because the calcium-phosphorus balance is built in: other minerals exist in bone meal to facilitate proper calcium absorption.

Bone meal is available in tablet, powder, and flour forms at most special diet and health food stores.

PHOSPHORUS

This mineral is present in every body cell. About 66 percent of body phosphorus is in the bones in a form known as calcium phosphate; 33 percent is in soft tissue as organic and inorganic phosphate. This mineral converts oxidative energy to cell work. High energy phosphate influences protein, carbohydrate and fat synthesis, and also stimulates muscular contraction, secretion of glandular hormones, nerve impulses and kidney functioning.

Phosphorus sparks internal energy. It works to neutralize excess blood acidity; it also helps create lecithin and cerebrin, ingredients needed for mental power; it metabolizes fats and starches.

A deficiency of this mineral may cause appetite and weight loss, nervous disorder, mental sluggishness, general fatigue. In extreme difficulties, there is irregular breathing and a pale, wan appearance. Try to avoid white sugar because the delicate calcium-phosphorus balance is interfered with in the presence of white sugar in your body.

Your brain also needs phosphorus. Although 85 percent of your brain consists of water, the solid matter is made up of phosphorized fats. These fats should increase in proportion as your nervous system matures.

Veal bone meal is an excellent source of phosphorus, as is the calcium from eggs, known as chalaza. Chalaza is dense cords of albumen that hold yolk near center of egg—not eggshells! These can both be found in food supplement form at most health stores.

IRON

Every cell needs iron for giving oxygen to the system. Without iron, about 300 quarts of blood, rather than the present six or so, would be necessary to handle oxygen needs. Iron is found in the red blood cells and is needed to form the red colored substance called hemoglobin. Iron influences proteins. Iron must have calcium and the other nutrients in order to properly function.

A shortage of iron may lead to anemia, a sickish skin pallor, and a poor memory. Iron carries oxygen to your brain so it can work properly.

Since you have five million red cells in just one cubic millimeter of blood, and since iron is needed for every cell, you can see how valuable this mineral can be. Iron also works with other nutrients to influence respiratory action.

Good food sources for iron include egg yolks, green leafy vegetables, molasses and sun-dried raisins. The strongest concentration of iron is found in desiccated liver.

IODINE

You have about 25 milligrams of iodine in your system. Two thirds is in your thyroid gland; the other third is distributed in blood and tissues.

Iodine stimulates the thyroid (a two-part gland that looks like a butterfly, resting against the front of the windpipe) to secrete the thyroxine hormone which regulates metabolism and energy. An iodine deficiency may cause goiter, obesity, and sluggish metabolism.

An iodine shortage causes impairment of several body reactions, including slow mental reaction, dry hair, rapid pulse, heart palpitation, tremor, nervousness, restlessness and increased irritability.

Iodine is needed to utilize fat and influence other nutrients. Iodine is found in all seafoods and vegetables grown in iodine-rich soils. The best source of iodine is found in kelp, a dehydrated seaweed. Another good source is in onions. Dulse is also a good source of iodine.

SODIUM

This mineral works with potassium to help maintain the favorable acid-base factor in your system. It also helps maintain a normal water level balance between cells and fluids. Sodium enables your nerves to respond to stimulation and transmit it, and provides strength to your muscles so they can contract. It joins with chlorine to improve blood and lymph health. Its main purpose is to render other blood minerals more soluble and prevent them from becoming clogged or deposited in the blood distribution system.

A sodium deficiency may cause stomach and intestinal gas, weight loss, muscle shrinkage. Carbohydrate foods cannot be changed into fat for digestion. You may have ample amino acids, but sodium must process them. Sodium favors the formation and free-flow of saliva, gastric juices and enzymes and other intestinal secretions.

Sodium is found in sea foods, poultry, beets, carrots, chard and dandelion greens. Since this mineral is needed to build a resistance against cramps and heat stroke, it's wise to take one tablet of 1.5 milligrams each day during the summer.

POTASSIUM

This is another "balancing" mineral; it works with sodium to help normalize your heartbeat and feed your muscular system. It joins with phosphorus to send oxygen to your brain. Sodium and potassium have to have a balance. Sodium is found basically in the fluid circulating outside your cells and only a tiny amount is inside. Potassium is found largely inside the cells and a tiny supply is outside.

Potassium stimulates the kidney to dispose of body wastes. Your blood also needs potassium. A deficiency may cause constipation, nervous disorder, insomnia, slow and irregular heartbeat and muscle damage. Often, the kidneys enlarge and bones become brittle.

Good food sources include all citrus fruits, watercress, mint leaves, green peppers and chicory, as well as black-strap molasses and figs.

MAGNESIUM

This mineral is closely related to both calcium and phosphorus in its location and its functions in the body. About 70 percent of the magnesium in the body is in the bones. The rest is in the soft tissues and blood. Muscle tissue contains more magnesium than calcium. Magnesium acts as a starter for some of the chemical reactions within the body.

It plays an important role as a coenzyme in the building of protein. There is some relation between magnesium and the hormone cortisone as they affect the amount of phosphate in the blood.

Food sources rich in this mineral are figs, lemons, grapefruit, yellow corn, almonds, oil-rich nuts and seeds, wild rice, apples and celery.

COPPER

Although iron is used to make blood, copper must be present to convert iron into hemoglobin. This mineral makes both tyrosine, an amino-acid, and vitamin C usable. In many cases where a deficiency is present, skin sores develop and fail to heal. Also, general weakness and impaired respiration are among the symptoms of a copper deficiency.

Foods containing this mineral include almonds, dried beans, peas, whole wheat, prunes, calf and beef liver, egg yolks and shrimp.

SULPHUR

This mineral is important for a smooth and youthful complexion. It also keeps your hair glossy and smooth. It acts by invigorating your bloodstream, rendering it more powerful to resist bacterial infections.

It works to cause the liver to secrete bile, maintain overall body balance and helps in the maintenance of oxygen which the brain uses to function properly.

Sulphur works with the B-complex vitamins that are needed for metabolism and strong nerve health. Human hair contains sulphur, too. Sulphur is part of the amino acids that build body tissues and cells.

This mineral is found in fish, eggs, cabbage, lean beef, dried beans and brussels sprouts.

SILICON

A silicon deficiency may be traced to skin flabbiness, a feeling of chronic fatigue and eyes that are dull and glazed.

Silicon is found in hair, muscles, nails, cellular walls, and connective tissues. It joins with other minerals to create tooth enamel and build strong bones.

Good food sources are buckwheat products, mushrooms, carrots, tomatoes, and liver.

ZINC

This mineral is a constituent of insulin and also of the male reproductive fluid. It is made in the pancreas (a large gland located behind the lower part of the stomach) where it helps in the storage of glycogen, an energy producing substance. It combines with phosphorus to aid in respiration. It also sparks vitamin action. Zinc helps in tissue respiration (the intake of oxygen and expulsion of carbon dioxide and toxic wastes). Insulin is dependent upon zinc for functioning. Insulin shortage leads to diabetes. Zinc helps food to become absorbed through the intestinal wall. It helps manufacture male hormones. Since it is so intimately connected with carbohydrate utilization, a deficiency of this mineral may cause fatigue.

Zinc is found in abundance in liver.

MANGANESE

Manganese is a mineral which works with the B-complex vitamins in helping to energize the system. It also combines with phosphatase (an enzyme) to build strong bones. Much of the body's supply of manganese is found in the liver. Manganese is needed for good enzymatic function so foods can be digested and vital nutrients extracted for overall body utilization. Manganese helps build resistance to ailments, strong nerve health and, in the expectant mother, promotes milk formation.

Foods containing this mineral are green leaves, peas, beets, egg yolks, and unmilled grains.

CHLORINE

This mineral works by cleaning out toxic waste products from your system. Chlorine acts by stimulating your liver to act as a filter for waste substances. It stimulates production of hydrochloric acid, the enzymatic digestive juice needed for tough, fibrous foods. Chlorine helps in keeping a youthful joint and tendon condition; it also helps to distribute hormones secreted by your endocrine glands.

A chlorine deficiency may cause hair and teeth loss, poor muscular contractibility and impaired digestive power.

Good sources of chlorine include kelp, dulse, sea greens, leafy greens, rye flour, and ripe olives.

FLUORINE

This mineral helps to strengthen tooth enamel. But, too much of it may cause abnormal and unsightly tooth mottling.

Studies have shown that when an excess is taken, such as by means of fluoridated water, bones become weak and there is an adverse reaction upon internal organs.

This mineral can be found in almost any of the food sources listed for the other thirteen minerals.

GLANDS

The minerals, including calcium, phosphorus, magnesium, all aid in the vital function of digestion. Good digestion depends upon the power of minerals. You may eat the best quality food, prepared by the most natural of methods, but if this food is mineral-deficient then your digestive process cannot extract those substances needed to give you mental and physical energy.

The main influence in the digestive process is the hormone system, those powerful substances secreted by your glands. Hormones and glands, when properly mineralized by foods, have the power to turn fatigue into energy.

The gland is a body organ which manufactures a liquid substance which it then secretes. Some glands, such as the endocrine or ductless glands, do not issue any liquids but leave them to be picked up and transported via your bloodstream to other body parts.

A hormone is the name of the liquid substance issued by the glands. These hormones influence just about all of your mental and physical activities. The word "hormone" is taken from the Greek hormaein which means "to excite." Just a few drops of any secreted hormone has the power to stimulate body growth, activity, development, tissue nutrition, sexual vigor, muscular tone, resistance to fatigue as well as numerous mental activities. Hormonal production in your body is influenced by an adequate mineralization.

You have eight major glands which create the "interlocking directorate" of your body. These are called the ductless glands because they send their hormones (chemical messengers) pouring directly into your bloodstream. These eight glands must have minerals. Each of these glands has its specific function, but all eight are ruled by the master gland or the pituitary.

PITUITARY GLAND

At the base of your brain, directly behind your nose is a tiny "pea" which is your pituitary gland. This is known as the master of your entire personality because it issues 12 different hormones. These hormones normalize your blood pressure, improve your muscle tone, build a strong bone structure, and give power and strength to your nerves. You can enjoy an improved sense of smell, better vision, better hearing with a healthier pituitary gland. Also, this gland normalizes passage of urine and waste substances.

While the thyroid gland makes available the supply of crude energy by speeding up cellular processes, the pituitary is responsible for the transformation, expenditure and conversion of that energy into a healthful, youthful vitality.

A malnourished pituitary may cause premature aging and loss of energy. The front (anterior) portion of the pituitary controls the sex-regulating hormone.

In pubertal boys this gland will issue hormones that will develop the sex organs, change the voice, grow body hair and promote other signs of healthy young manhood. In pubertal girls, the pituitary hormone is responsible for the secretion of the lactogenic hormone in her mammary glands to prepare her for eventual motherhood. Other pituitary hormones regulate the storage of fat; an internal imbalance may lead to overweight.

Your pituitary requires a calcium-phosphorus balance, together with the vitamins A and C. This gland also must have potassium, the mineral that joins with phosphorus to send precious oxygen to your brain. Your pituitary will do all this if it has sufficient minerals to work with.

THYROID GLAND

Directly before your windpipe and located in your throat is your thyroid gland. It issues the hormone thyroxine which is formed by iodine, the mineral that combines with an amino acid (digested protein) and then still another protein byproduct. When these amino acids join with iodine, then the hormone is sent to all body parts via your bloodstream.

Thyroxine determines growth, regulates metabolization (burning) of foods, influences your emotions and has been said to regulate the reproductive or sexual functions. If your diet is low in minerals, you run the risk of a malfunctioning thyroid which means you gain unnecessary weight, risk a slow heartbeat which, in turn, causes poor circulation.

Thyroid malfunctioning can also lead to constipation, senility, and lowered body metabolism. Hypothyroid (low activity) may cause the ailment known as myxedema. It leads to "cretinism." These victims are mentally and physically slow, have low blood pressure, and look prematurely aged.

There are about 25 milligrams of iodine in your body which are needed by your thyroid. If you are tense or subjected to excitement your thyroid secretes more of this hormone. Thus, more iodine is needed to meet the challenge. You also need more iodine-produced thyroxin during situations of growth, ailment, infection, adolescence, menstruation, pregnancy, and increased activity.

Sources of iodine are sea salt and sea vegetables.

ADRENAL GLANDS

You have two adrenal glands: shaped like Brazil nuts, they sit astride each kidney. The adrenals issue adrenalin, known as the "emergency hormone" and related closely with a healthy automatic nervous system.

In times of personal danger or emotional stress, extra adrenalin is released into the bloodstream, where it quickens the heartbeat, increases the energy-yielding sugar in the blood, slows up or stops digestion, pours blood into the massine muscles, dilates the pupils of the eye for greater perception and in general, makes you extremely alert.

The adrenals also influence a normal mineral balance between blood and body tissues. Adrenalin has the power to open up the air passages in the lungs to relieve asthmatic convulsions.

Healthy adrenals will give you a healthy complexion. A deficiency of adrenalin may cause the skin to develop deep lines, grow sallow and dark and cause congestion and swelling of the nasal passages. A deficiency of adrenalin (called hypoadrenia) leads to chronic tiredness, poor appetite, weak pulse, and low blood pressure. It was found to neutralize toxic substances in the bloodstream and build resistance to infection. You need potassium and magnesium as well as the calcium-phosphorus balance to maintain a healthy adrenal.

PANCREAS

This is a narrow gland which lies across the back of your upper abdomen. The major part of the pancreas consists of glandular tissue that issues enzymatic juices by way of a duct into the upper intestine. The pancreas secretes insulin, the substance that aids in sugar storage in the liver for use in energy requirements.

A malfunctioning, mineral-starved pancreas secretes little or no insulin. This means that sugar, the sole source of brain and nerve power, can neither be stored nor burned. It is passed off through the organs of elimination. An insulin deficiency leads to extreme tiredness, weakness, dizziness and excess weight since sugar is not burned, and some is converted into fat before being passed off from the body as waste material.

Diabetes is traced to an insulin-weak pancreas gland. In due time the cells that make insulin will wear out because they have the heavy job of digesting more quantities of sugars than that for which they were originally created.

A possible pancreas malfunction may be seen in various conditions, such as brittle nails, poor teeth, sore and bleeding gums, lip and tongue fissures, skin ailments, excess mouth dryness, craving sweets, weight loss, headaches, giddiness, nervous irritability and a feeling of numbness or tingling in the extremities.

The pancreas needs oils derived from seeds (corn, peanut, safflower, sunflower, wheat germ), combined with vitamins B1, B2, niacin, pantothenic acid, and B6 to remain healthy.

PARATHYROIDS

These are four glands that are so very tiny they can hardly be seen. The parathyroids are found behind the thyroid gland, in the upper chest, between the tonsils and thymus. If removed or damaged, they cause bone malformation, tetany (cramps and convulsions), and severe calcium deficiency. This means that the victim is nervous, easily irritated, has a poor heartbeat, poor appetite, and abnormal hair loss. Visual disorders may include cataracts. Hearing fades.

The parathyroids measure about the size of a small pea. These glands work closely with the use of calcium and phosphorus and their hormone arranges to store calcium in your long bones. If you face an important mental or physical task, calcium is sent out of the bones by means of parathyroid action.

Your kidneys may suffer if your calcium metabolism is awry because of unhealthy parathyroids. Conversely, if the quantity of calcium-phosphorus is improper, the entire hormonal system is also upset.

To obtain an ample supply of minerals feed your parathyroids with bone meal. Made from dehydrated cattle bones, this food is rich in the aforementioned minerals as well as vitamins A and D, all of which combine to normalize hormonal powers.

FEMALE OVARIES

The ovaries are olive-sized; one is situated on each side of the female womb. These glands secrete the estrogen and progesterone hormones.

Estrogen stimulates the growth of the female genital organs, the breasts and pubic hair. It stops the growth of the long bones at puberty, sensitizes the muscles of the uterus (womb) to pitocin (hormone) from the posterior pituitary, and is a primer for the action of progesterone.

Progesterone is secreted by the corpus luteum that forms after an egg cell leaves an ovary. It is essential to pregnancy, preparing the lining of the uterus for implantation of the fertilized egg cell. It stops menstruation and causes the breasts to grow. If fertilization does not occur, the corpus luteum dies and the fall in progresterone secretion brings on the menstrual flow.

Female fertility and monthly regularity are interwoven with this gland. An estrogen deficiency may cause a flat-chested condition. A progesterone shortage may cause female sterility.

These hormones create a soothing, tranquil influence on the female organs.

It is possible that the minerals in fresh vegetables combine with vitamin E in millet to stimulate the function of the ovaries.

MALE SEX GLANDS

In addition to the reproductive organs, these consist of the testes (gonads) which issue hormones to produce fertility. The male hormone is called testosterone. This hormone makes a male virile and fertile, and creates body shape. The main substance of the testes is a mass of tiny coiled tubes. If placed end to end, they'd extend for more than 300 yards. These tubules are lined with cells that produce spermatozoa. Between these coiled tubes are tiny isolated cellular groups which pour forth the male hormone (testosterone).

A deficiency may cause prostate gland disorder, a flabby muscular condition, premature aging, and a deterioration of mental energy. The hormone has the power to give vigorous tone to all body muscles and provide strength to bladder and stomach.

A testosterone extract has been made from the sarsaparilla root. This is a tropical American climbing plant with roots so deep that they extract the precious minerals from the soil that are imparted to its seeds. It has been found that some of the minerals in foods prepared from sarsaparilla helped stimulate a healthy male hormonal system. Zinc, the mineral found in male reproductive fluid, is abundant in sarsaparilla; also, this plant has B-complex and C vitamins which unite with minerals to create a strong hormonal power.

THYMUS

This gland is found in the upper part of your chest. Actually, it is on the windpipe beneath the thyroid. The purpose of the thymus is to metabolize the minerals in your body, particularly calcium and phosphorus. When your thymus has enough minerals, it produces white blood cells which then build your resistance against disease. Minerals unite with the B-complex and vitamin C nutrients and protein to function adequately.

A deficiency of minerals may react upon the thymus

and cause frequent nosebleeds and excessive bleeding from small scratches and bruises.

The thymus gland is a storage gland affording a certain amount of protection against the deleterious effects of a lack of food.

Thus we see that hormones and glands act as catalysts by promoting internal reaction and speeding up or slowing down body processes.

The nature of the food supply may be a possible factor in the production of, or the disturbances of, the glands of internal secretion. In handling such a condition, a diet calculated to affect the glands in question becomes a necessity.

The correction of dietary defects, especially in the vitamin-mineral content, is essential. Whatever affects the glands, harmfully or favorably, affects character, personality and bodily well being.

PROTEIN

It would be hard to overestimate the importance of protein in our diets. One of the most important facts about protein is that it is the only substance which supplies us with the materials of which our bodies are made. Protein is the most abundant substance in our bodies. We are 18 to 20% protein by weight. Our muscles, skin, hair, nails, eyes, teeth, blood, heart, lungs, brain and nerves are all protein.

In our bodies we find that a third of the protein is in muscles. A fifth is in bones and cartilages, a tenth in the skin, and the remainder in the other cell tissues and body fluids. Our bile and urine do not contain any protein at all.

We also rely upon proteins for the myriad reactions involved in metabolism, the process that keeps our bodies running. This metabolic process is regulated by special proteins (hormones) and catalyzed by other proteins (enzymes).

All foods we eat contain carbon, oxygen, and hydrogen. We derive these substances from starches, sugars and fats, and proteins. But only proteins contain nitrogen, sulfur and phosphorous—all essential.

There are hundreds of different proteins, and all of the basic ones come from other animals and plants. Since we cannot store proteins in our bodies, we need a continuous supply. When we take in protein our bodies will use what they need at that moment and turn the rest into fuel to be used when energy is needed. To be used for energy, protein must first be converted into starch or sugar, and once the protein has been converted it cannot be changed back into protein, no matter how badly it is needed by our bodies.

We need a continuous supply of protein because the

cells in our body are constantly breaking down and being replaced. Every cell in our body is replaced every 160 days. Our vital organs change more quickly. The liver regenerates every two weeks. Since these organs are made up of proteins, only proteins can be used to build, repair or maintain our body. While vitamins and minerals are essential to good health, and starches and sugars are essential as fuel, we need the building blocks of proteins to keep us alive.

The amount of protein we need is dependent on many factors. Our age is important; people past forty-five need more protein than younger people. Their ability to digest and assimilate proteins has fallen off. An older person cannot utilize his protein intake as completely as a youth, and if he continues to take in the same amount of protein as he always has, even if that amount had been sufficient in his younger days, he will suffer from a deficiency. Increasing age often requires an increased intake of protein for the body to be well nourished.

Another major factor that determines our protein need is lifestyle. If we are under severe stress our protein needs increase quickly. Under stress or illness as much as 135 grams of body protein can be destroyed in one day. Therefore, adjust your protein intake to your lifestyle. Your body can not synthesize the "non-essential amino acids" rapidly enough to meet a sudden demand for protein because of stress of illness. By keeping track of our daily intake of protein we can easily adjust it to protect ourselves. During a mild illness a person should increase his protein intake to 80–120 grams a day.

There are many types of proteins in our blood. One of these is called hemoglobin. Hemoglobin transports oxygen from our lungs to the tissues of the body and brings back carbon dioxide to the lungs to be eliminated from the body. Almost ninety-five percent of the hemoglobin molecule is protein (the other five percent is iron).

There are other proteins in the blood that give our bodies the means to resist certain viruses and infections. Gamma Globulin, another blood protein, also forms antibodies which can neutralize bacteria and viruses and other harmful micro-organisms. If we are deficient in our protein intake, we are in effect lowering our resistance to infection or disease. This is important as we get older and cannot utilize proteins as well.

Proteins also assist in the exchange of nutrients between cells and intercellular fluids and between tissues and the blood and lymph. They are instrumental in maintaining the fluid balance throughout the system. When the body is too low in protein, this fluid balance becomes upset.

All proteins in our bodies are in a constant state of exchange. Molecules or parts of molecules of protein are constantly breaking down, while other molecules and parts of molecules are being built up as replacements. This exchange is characteristic to all life processes. Continuous turnover of cells and molecules explains why our diet must supply an adequate amount of daily protein even after we no longer need it for growth. The rate of protein turnover is faster within the cells of the tissue, called intracellular, than in the substance between the cells, which is called intercellular.

PROTEIN AND BLOOD SUGAR

Only recently have we begun to understand the intricate relationship between the level of sugar in our blood and the foods we eat. The sugar (glucose) transported in the blood is the basic fuel for all the organs of the body. Our brain and nervous system are critically dependent upon this blood sugar to function properly.

The source of energy expended by our nervous system comes from cellular respiration, a process where complex foods are broken down into simpler substances, which are then oxidized in the individual cells. Oxidation is often compared to "burning," but this is not an exact analogy. What actually happens is that glucose, as well as other foods, is transformed through a series of intermediate compounds by the action of enzyme proteins. This is a step-by-step process, with all of the steps interlocked. Energy is formed in differing amounts and different times during the process, and these intermediates, all ultimately derived from glucose, are what supply this energy we need and use.

We can think of this energy as being released in "packets" that are formed at different stages in the energy cycle. Biochemists call these "packets" *adenosine triphosphate*, or ATP. The energy cycles in which these packets are released are called *glycolysis* and the *citric acid cycle*, which produce pyruvate (energy) and o-acetate, respectively.

The release of these packets of ATP is dependent upon a great number of reactions, each of which depends upon the successful completion of the preceding reaction. If this step-by-step breakdown of glucose is disturbed, impaired mental functioning can possibly result.

Interference in the energy cycle is most frequently found at specific points where there are great demands for enzymes, which are proteins. A deficiency in any substance needed at these points can cause critical effects on brain metabolism. Niacin (Vitamin B_3) and other vitamins and minerals must be supplied in sufficient quantities for our nervous systems to function properly.

The ability of our nervous systems to function properly in breaking down glucose for energy is affected by the kinds and amounts of fuel being utilized in other tissues of the body.

How well we produce energy depends on the rate in which we oxidize our food. Dr. George Watson, in *Nutrition and Your Mind*, classifies patients as slow oxidizers, fast oxidizers and suboxidizers. Each of these groups needs a different diet to function properly. A slow oxidation diet would be harmful for a fast oxidizer, for instance. This is one reason why anyone changing his diet should consult a physician and watch carefully for any adverse signs.

Proteins are broken down into simpler substances called amino acids. Some of these proteins are metabolized like sugar, others like fat, and the remainder by other metabolic routes. From the proteins in our diets we can get both sugar protein, which yields pyruvate (energy), and fat protein, which yields acetate. Both are necessary for energy production.

But there is another very important characteristic of protein foods that effects the energy-producing machinery of the tissues. In addition to their amino acid content, which helps to determine the amount and kind of intermediates the energy cycle will yield, proteins contain another class of substances. These are called *nucleoprotein*. These nucleoproteins are conjugated with nucleic acids, which play an important part in the energy mechanism of cells. The most important of these nucleoproteins is a purine base called adenine.

Adenine is a constituent of ATP, which you will remember is the energy packet released at various stages of the energy cycle. ATP is one of the most critical components of the body and the principal energy carrier of the cells. Adenine is also part of the complex intermediate, acetate, from which most of the energy we use is derived.

Adenine can be synthesized in the body from CO_2, formate, aspartic acid, glycine, and glutamin. But this does not mean adenine should be neglected in our diets. We also use the nucleoproteins we obtain from our food. Their inclusion or exclusion in our diet can mean the difference between ineffective nervous system function which results in anxiety, and a well-functioning nervous system essential to a forward-looking confidence. Although fish and animal sources are the highest in purine content, our need for purine does not necessitate their inclusion in our diets. Our systems can be maintained at peak efficiency from sources that range from 50 to 150 milligrams per 100 grams of food. Vegetable sources in the category include:

asparagus	lentils
spinach	beans
yeast	peas
whole-grain grains and cereals	mushrooms
cauliflower	peanuts

No matter what your metabolic type, having an abundant supply of protein at the core of your diet is very important. The brain uses up to one fourth of the total amount of glucose carried by the blood. For our nervous system to function properly it must have a steady supply of glucose in the blood, since glucose is the only fuel it can burn.

This essential blood sugar level is maintained directly by carbohydrates (starches and sugars) and protein. Indirectly the blood sugar level is influenced by the amount of fat being burned in the tissues.

All the carbohydrates we eat are transformed into glucose, but only half of the protein in the diet can be transformed in this way. Like proteins, glucose cannot be stored for later use. A person who weighs around one hundred and fifteen pounds can only store enough sugar to last about four hours. And this sugar carried in our blood is our body's principle source of energy.

The liver is the main organ for storing sugar. Here sugar is stored as glycogen, or "liver sugar." And it is in the liver that some of the protein foods we eat contribute to maintaining our blood sugar level. The protein that is to be used for energy is first converted to glycogen and then to glucose by a process called gluconeogenesis.

Briefly, here is how the blood sugar level is maintained. When we eat a well balanced meal, the carbohydrates are quickly digested and transformed into glucose. At this point part of the glucose is carried by the blood to the tissues where it is used for fuel. Some of the glucose is stored in the liver as glycogen.

Protein is digested at a much slower rate. That portion of the protein which is capable of being changed into glycogen is gradually stored between meals in the liver. It is then released into the blood as glucose when it is needed.

In this way, when the sugar in the blood that has come from the digestion of the carbohydrates begins to be depleted, we can tap the reserve supply made available from the protein. This only happens if our food intake contains enough carbohydrates in addition to protein.

Carbohydrates and proteins interact to maintain our blood sugar level. If there is an insufficient supply of one of them, neither can do its work properly. Unless sugar is being burned, protein cannot be converted into either liver sugar or blood sugar.

If our diet does not contain enough protein along with the carbohydrate, our blood sugar will be depleted within a few hours, and there will be no glycogen from the liver to help maintain it. The slow digestion of protein over a period of several hours is responsible for keeping a constant supply of glycogen building up in the liver. This supply of glycogen can then be released as blood sugar when necessary.

USING PROTEINS IN YOUR BODY

Our protein supply must be adequate. But for us to make efficient use of this supply we also need enough fats and oils and carbohydrates. Protein plays an important part in maintaining our energy supply, but other substances supply much of our energy. If we rely too heavily on protein for energy we are undermining its other functions in our bodies.

When we digest proteins, they are broken down into amino acids, which are the chemical units that make up protein. Amino acids determine protein's nutritive and biological value. To use amino acids to their best advantage we must have the right proportion of the different kinds of them. All the proteins we eat yield, through digestion, an assortment of these amino acids. The nutritional value of the protein depends on the particular assortment of the relatively few amino acids. Of the twenty-two amino acids that exist, only eight are classified as "essential." This does not mean that we do not need the other fourteen "non-essential" amino acids. What it does mean is that, while our bodies can synthesize "non-essential amino acids," we must rely entirely on our food supply for the eight essential ones.

The nutritional value of the protein we eat depends not only on the assortment of amino acids, but also on the amounts of each amino acid the protein furnishes. When we say that a protein is "complete," we mean that all of the amino acids essential to maintain good health are present.

A complete protein includes the eight essential amino acids. The remaining fourteen amino acids are produced by the body if the food does not supply them.

Protein deficiency has diverse effects on the skin, hair, nails and non-essential organs.

In digestion, after the protein is first separated into these many small pieces of amino acids, these acids are then separated according to their content: carbon, hydrogen, oxygen and nitrogen. These simple amino acids are then carried by the blood to the liver, and from there they are absorbed into the body.

When the amino acids leave the liver to be carried by the blood to the needed areas, they are reassembled into special combinations of "manufactured" proteins that replace worn-out cells, add to growing tissues, or make enzymes, hormones and other active compounds.

Amino acids that are not fully used cannot be stored in the body. They are returned to the liver, where they undergo a process called deaminization. During deaminization the substance is stripped of its amino groups. The excess nitrogen leaves the body as urea through the urine. The hydrogen, carbon and oxygen fragments are used to provide energy, on call to help maintain the blood sugar level.

ACID-ALKALINE BALANCE

Protein also plays a vital role in the maintenance of our body's balance between acid and alkaline. When the acid-alkaline balance is upset, the digestion of proteins appears to be assisted by the parotid glands. If these glands are dehydrated, the digestion and assimilation of all classes of protein are almost at a standstill.

ALKALINITY AND ACID

Alkalinity is essential to life. For instance, a grain of wheat or any other seed will not germinate until it is softened and alkalized by water. If a mother's cells are not alkalined, conception will not occur. We are involved here with the LAW OF POLARITY—the earth and everything contained therein is a manifestation of the union of two forces, a positive and a negative, with a line of balance in the center. The body must have a balance of alkaline and acid.

If an imbalance arises in the body it is sometimes difficult to blame any gland or organ. In the case of alkaline-acid imbalance, it appears that the real balancer is the pituitary gland and that the other glandular bodies are merely subsidiaries. The pituitary gland has so many duties to perform after physical exercise, shock, chill, mental strain, or even a meal, that an immediate return to zero, or balance, is impossible. It is not unusual for several hours to elapse before anything approaching balance is attained.

The symptoms of acid-alkaline imbalance—heartburn, certain gastric conditions, arthritis, and many other complaints—are not necessarily signs of acidosis. They could possibly be symptoms of alkalosis. In any case, don't prescribe or diagnose yourself. Always contact your family doctor for professional guidance.

WHAT TYPE OF PROTEIN DO WE NEED?

We have covered many of the reasons why our bodies need protein. Perhaps the best reason is that a sufficient supply of protein every day is critical to continued good physical and emotional health.

We will now turn our attention to the kinds of proteins we need to fulfill these nutritional requirements.

Proteins come in a tremendous variety. They fall into two categories: essential and non-essential proteins. Essential proteins contain the eight essential amino acids that we must take in through our diets.

For our bodies to use the eight essential amino acids, we need to eat all of them simultaneously. Only then, when all eight are present at once, can we carry out efficient protein synthesis.

If even one of these essential amino acids is missing, or it's only temporarily missing, protein synthesis efficiency drops off. It might even stop.

But this is only part of the story. Not only must we have all eight essential amino acids present at one time, but the amounts of each and the proportion of the amounts to each other is important. This is a rather recent concept in nutrition, since most of the writing on nutrition has been geared to "just getting enough," assuming that if enough protein goes into your mouth you will be all right.

Recent research, however, takes us in a new direction. Now it seems that not only must we get the right nutrients, but we must get them in the right proportions.

Dr. Roger Williams at the University of Texas has discovered that in many cases the proportion of nutrients is more critical than the amounts, particularly in developing vitamin formulas for people under stress and people with alcohol problems. It is not too surprising, then, that the same should be true for the essential ingredients of protein.

Let us summarize the three crucial factors concerning proteins in our diet.

The first is that of the twenty-two necessary amino acids there are eight that our bodies cannot make but which must be obtained from outside sources. These are called "essential" amino acids.

Secondly, all eight of these essential amino acids must be present simultaneously.

Thirdly, all of these eight must be present in the right proportions.

It is this last factor that is the most critical if we want to pursue a vegetarian diet. Most of the food proteins we eat contain all of the eight essential amino acids. However, in some plant sources, one or more of the eight are usually present in a disproportionately small amount.

These amino acids present in a disproportionately small amount are called "limiting amino acids." Their name is appropriate because they limit the use of all the seven other protein components.

If you eat a specific protein food which contains enough tryptophan to satisfy one hundred percent of the utilizable pattern's requirement, and the food contains 100 percent of the leucine level and so forth, but only 50 percent of the needed lysine, then, as far as your body is concerned you may as well have eaten only 50 percent of all the essential amino acids. Your body simply can not use more than fifty percent of the protein because of the "limiting amino acid," which determines the utilization of all the essential amino acids.

Therefore, our bodies can only use one pattern of the essential amino acids. If all the essential amino acids are not present in the right proportion, we can use them only to the extent that the "limiting amino acid" allows us to. When the protein reaches the cell, the "assembling center" in the cell will release the amino acids left over that cannot be used above the level of the "limiting" amino acid. The left-overs are than used by the body as fuel in the same way as carbohydrates.

The "biological value" of a given protein food is determined by how closely that food matches the pattern that our body can use. Another way of expressing the "biological value" is that it is the percentage of absorbed protein that your body actually uses. The absorption of the protein is a function of digestion. How much of the protein that goes into our mouths becomes absorbed is the food's digestibility factor.

There is a third term which covers both the digestibility factor and biological value. This term is Net Protein Utilization, or NPU. In the simplest terms, the Net Protein Utilization factor tells us how much of the protein we eat is actually available to our body. NPU is a key concept in understanding the role protein plays in diet and health.

Let's take a closer look at what determines the Net Protein Utilization factor. The NPU of a food is determined by how closely the essential amino acids in its protein match the body's own utilization pattern. The protein that most nearly matches this ideal pattern is that found in eggs. Ergo, egg protein can be used as a model to measure the amino acid patterns in other foods. The closer the amino acid patterns of another food comes to the amino acid pattern of egg protein, the higher that food's utilization.

HOW MUCH PROTEIN WE NEED

Our purpose here is to understand the facts of protein nutrition. This is of the utmost importance before experimenting with a new diet.

There are three separate considerations which determine the proper protein allowance for different people.

First we must determine the minimum need.

Secondly, we must make allowances for individual differences.

Thirdly, we must make an adjustment for protein quality.

The major disagreements among nutritionists are over the first consideration of the body's minimum need for protein. But even here the differences are not so great as to make meaningless some kind of average.

Your Minimum Protein Need   Nitrogen is a characteristic and relatively constant component of protein. Because of this, scientists can measure the presence or absence of protein by measuring the nitrogen. The first step taken by experimenters to determine how much protein our bodies need, is to put their subjects on a protein-free diet. Measurements as to how much nitrogen the subjects lose in urine and feces are then taken. To these measurements is added a small factor to compensate for the loss of nitrogen through the skin sweat and internal body structures. The total figure arrived at gives us the amount one must replace by eating protein and forms the basis for the minimum protein requirement for body maintenance.

A diet that is deficient in protein intake results in stunted growth, unsatisfactory reproduction, cessation of ovulation and failure to reproduce, general ill health, inadequate regulation of blood sugar level, physical inefficiency, habitual fatigue, poor muscle development, lack of resistance to infection, loss of sexual interest, and a decrease in sperm count. Protein cannot be used for growth until after the needs for maintenance have been met. When there is not enough protein in the body to fulfill both purposes, growth will suffer.

Our protein needs are increased by exercise, stress, and illness. Adjustments upward must be made in the basic protein diet when these situations are present.

Another condition that requires additional protein is the second half of pregnancy, when the fetus is growing rapidly. During this time, the woman should add an additional 20 grams of protein to her diet daily. When the mother is nursing the baby, she should take an additional 40 grams of protein daily.

The basic allowance for protein recommended by the National Academy of Sciences is 0.227 grams per pound of body weight per day. An average minimum from several sources is 0.214 grams.

Individual Differences People vary considerably not only in their basic need for protein, but in how well they can digest and assimilate the protein they take in. But there is general agreement among nutritionists that adding an increase of 30 percent to the average minimum protein requirement will cover up to 98 percent of the population, giving a figure adjusted for individual differences. The Food and Agriculture Organization of the United Nations arrived at the same figure, but did it a little differently. They added 10 percent to the minimum daily requirement to compensate for losses due to stress, then added another 20 percent to allow for individual differences.

When we add 30 percent to the average minimum figure of 0.214 we come up with 0.278. The rounded figure then is 0.28 grams of protein per pound of body weight per day.

Adjustment for Protein Quality This 0.28 grams per pound of body weight per day figure is based on the assumption that we are taking in only the highest quality protein. That is protein used completely by our bodies. The 0.28 figure is the amount of needed protein that our bodies must use. The amount of protein we must eat to make sure our body gets 0.28 grams of usable protein can be much higher.

Therefore, in determining the amount of protein we need we must examine the kinds and quality of protein. There are basic differences in food proteins as to how completely the body can use them. Since we are not able to utilize low-quality protein as well as high-quality, we must eat more of a low-quality protein to fill our daily requirements.

Since the allowances made above are based on total protein, and the total grams of protein eaten are never fully used by the body, we must make another adjustment to set an appropriate protein allowance for population groups. This allowance is based on the average usability of protein, which takes us back to the Net Protein Utilization (NPU) factor.

There is a formula for arriving at this allowance for grams of protein. This formula is quite simple. We first take the minimum population requirement for usable protein (0.28 grams per pound of body weight) and multiply it by 100 over the NPU of the population's staple food(s). The product of this multiplication is the number of grams of total protein recommended for that population. The formula in simplest terms reads: 0.28 x 100/NPU.

Since this book is concerned with meat as well as a vegetarian diet, let us take a typical value for the quality of plant protein and insert it into our formula. For example, if our sample population lives on vegetables whose NPU average is 55 percent, how much should it eat?

The average NPU for meat is 70, which means our sample group needs more vegetables to get its needed protein than if it ate meat. Inserting 55 into our formula, we come up with: 0.28 x 100/55 = 0.51 per pound of body weight per day. With 0.51 we can divide the body weight in half and change the answer to grams. For instance, a man in this population who weighs 150 pounds will need 75 grams of protein a day from his vegetarian diet. On a meat diet he would need only 56 grams.

The lands that produce vegetable sources of protein

used for grazing could be turned into inexpensive sources of protein food if people relied less on meat and more on plant sources.

An unshaking emphasis on producing meat as the backbone of the American diet not only uses up vegetable sources of protein, but also other sources of food. In 1968, up to one-half of the world's fish catch was fed to livestock.

But Isn't Meat Necessary?   There are many people who consider plant protein inferior on two counts. First they assume that meat is the highest and richest source of protein, and that it is easier to obtain more protein from meat than from plant sources. Secondly, vegetable protein is supposed to be of inferior quality.

Is meat actually the richest source of protein? Not necessarily. There are plant sources of protein that rank higher than meat in the quantity of protein they provide, particularly in their processed form. *Soybean flour, for example, is over forty percent protein, while meat is rarely more than twenty to thirty percent protein.* Some cheeses are also very high in protein. Parmesan cheese, for instance, is 36 percent protein. Meat, as a source of protein, ranks lower than these two sources, ranging from twenty to thirty percent protein, which is not that much higher than dried beans, peas, and lentils. These three are essentially in the same range as meat, with twenty to twenty-five percent protein.

What about the quality of the protein we get from plants? This quality can be measured scientifically and computed into figures, called the Net Protein Utilization, or NPU.

The NPU lets us know what percentage of the protein we eat is actually available to our bodies, and it is a good measure of the protein quality of our diets. The scale of foods in terms of Net Protein Utilization, based on a United Nations publication, ranges from 40 to 94.

Animal protein occupies the higher ranks of this scale, but meat is not at the top. Eggs and milk have the highest NUP's—94 and 82 respectively. Meat is just above the middle of the scale; its average NPU is 67 percent. Plant sources range between 40 and 70, with soybeans and whole rice at the top.

In one aspect, animal proteins are superior to plant proteins, in that they more nearly match the requirements of the human body. This does not mean, however, that we must use meat as our main source of protein, because dairy products also contain these animal proteins. The only advantage of this protein is that we need to eat less meat than plants to fulfill our essential amino acid requirements.

But we have seen that plant sources of protein are many times more plentiful than meat sources on our planet, and that it is not necessary to rely fully on meat. We can get our supply of proteins from other sources. How this is done will be examined in the following chapters.

LEGUMES
(Dried Peas, Beans, and Lentils)

Many people overlook the important role of legumes in a vegetarian diet because they think of them as being "dull food," but in fact, some legumes have a protein content equal to or greater than that of meat.

Soups can be made from lentils, peas, black beans, and soybeans. It takes only a little imagination to turn these foods into a part of your daily diet.

All legumes are at least 20 percent protein. The highest, soybeans and mung beans, have NPU's of 61 and 57 percent, respectively.

LEGUMES

¼–½ cup dry	Total Protein	Usable Protein
Soybeans or soy grits	17 grams	10 grams
Mung beans	12	7
Broad beans	13	6
Peas	12	6
Black beans	12	5
Cowpeas (blackeye)	12	5
Kidney beans	12	5
Chickpeas	11	5
Lima beans	10	5
Tofu (Soybean curd) wet, 3½ oz.	8	5
Lentils	13	4
Other common beans	11	4

NUTS AND SEEDS

Nuts and seeds are as rich in protein as the legumes, and their Net Protein Utilization (NPU) factor is often higher. Nuts are seldom given a place of any importance in the American diet. Yet they contain important minerals. The Brazil nut, for instance, is important in a vegetarian diet because of its sulfur-containing amino acids which are rare in plant protein. Nuts are also a good source of fat essential in maintaining good health. The following is a compositional break-down of nuts.

CHEMICAL COMPOSITION OF NUTS

NUTS	Water	Protein	Carbo-hydrate	Fat	Minerals
Acorns	4.10	8.10	48.00	37.40	2.40
Almonds	4.90	21.40	16.80	54.40	2.50
Beechnuts	9.90	21.70	19.20	42.50	3.86
Brazil Nuts	4.70	17.40	5.70	65.00	3.30
Butternuts	4.50	27.90	3.40	61.20	3.00
Candlenuts	5.90	21.40	4.90	61.70	3.30
Chestnuts (dried)	5.90	10.70	74.20	7.00	2.20
Chufa	2.20	3.50	60.70	31.60	2.00
Coconut	14.10	5.70	27.90	50.60	1.70
Filberts	5.40	16.50	11.70	64.00	2.40
Hickory Nuts	3.70	15.40	11.40	67.40	2.10
Paradise Nuts	2.30	22.20	10.20	62.60	2.70
Pecans	3.40	12.10	8.50	70.70	1.60
Pignons	3.40	14.60	17.30	61.90	2.90
Pignolias	6.20	33.90	7.90	48.20	3.80
Pistachios	4.20	22.60	15.60	54.56	3.10
Black Walnuts	2.50	27.60	11.70	56.30	1.90
English Walnuts	2.50	18.40	13.00	64.40	1.70
Water Chestnuts	12.30	4.00	50.00	1.20	1.77
Peanuts	7.40	29.80	14.70	43.50	2.25
Peanut Butter	2.10	29.30	17.10	46.50	2.20
Almond Butter	2.20	21.70	11.60	61.50	3.00

NUTS AND SEEDS

Average Serving 1 oz.	Total Protein	Usable Protein
Pignolia nuts, 2½ tbsp.	9	5
Pumpkin and squash seeds (3 tbsp.)	8	5

Sunflower seeds or meal (4 tbsp.)	7	4
Peanuts	8	3
Peanut butter	8	3
Cashews	5	3
Sesame seed (3 tbsp.) or meal (4 tbsp.)	5	3
Pistachio nuts	5	3
Black walnuts	6	3
Brazil nuts	4	2

The sizes of the servings here are conservative. One ounce of peanuts will supply only 7–8 percent of your daily protein needs. A 10¢ bag of peanuts (about 1½ ounces) gives 10 to 12 percent.

Some nuts are not considered good sources of protein because of their high calory-to-protein ratio. These include pecans, chestnuts, coconuts, filbers, hazelnuts, macadamia nuts, almonds, pine nuts, and English walnuts.

Nuts and seeds tend to be high in tryptophan and sulfur, but they are generally deficient in isoleucine and lycine.

GRAIN CEREALS AND THEIR PRODUCTS

Cereals are not considered a source of protein in the United States, but they provide almost half the protein in the world's diet. Their percentage of protein is not high.

As with other sources of protein, grains and cereals must be evaluated from two different aspects—the quantity and quality of the protein they provide.

There are wide differences in the quantity of protein among various grains. Wheat, rye and oats, for example, have 30 to 35 percent more protein by weight than rice, corn, barley, and millet. Not only does the protein content vary from grain to grain, but it varies within one type of grain. Wheat can range from 9 to 14 percent protein. The wheat with the highest protein content is hard red spring wheat. Durum wheat, often used in pasta, is the second highest in protein content at 13 percent.

NPU values of cereal range from the low 50's to the low 60's. There are some exceptions, however. Whole rice has a NPU of 70 percent, the same as meat. Next is whole wheat germ, with an NPU of 67. Oatmeal and buckwheat have NPU values of 66 and 65. All of these values are higher than most other vegetable protein sources and comparable with beef.

TABLE 1. Protein Supplies (1963–65) (per capita and per day—by regions and subregions)

Regions and Subregions	Calories	Animal proteins	Vegetable proteins	Total proteins
FAR EAST (incl. China Mainland)				
South Asia	2,050	8.6	46.2	54.8
Southern Asia Mainland	2,020	6.4	43.0	49.4
Eastern Asia	2,180	13.1	36.3	49.4
South Eastern Asia Major Islands	2,350	20.5	54.6	75.1
China Mainland	2,040	7.1	33.6	40.7
	2,010	8.2	50.5	58.7
NEAR AND MIDDLE EAST	2,410	14.0	57.6	71.6
AFRICA				
North Africa	2,170	10.9	47.6	58.5
West and Central Africa	2,100	10.9	44.1	55.0
East and Southern Africa	2,120	7.8	46.9	54.7
	2,270	15.0	49.8	64.8

LATIN AMERICA	2,590	24.1	43.5	67.6
Brazil	2,780	19.4	49.4	68.8
Mexico and Central America	2,500	21.3	45.0	66.3
Northern and Western countries of South America	2,220	22.2	36.3	58.5
River Plate Countries	3,090	50.5	37.0	87.5
DEVELOPING REGIONS	2,140	10.7	46.9	57.6
EUROPE (incl. U.S.S.R.)	3,050	42.8	44.8	87.6
Eastern Europe	3,180	32.4	56.7	89.1
Western Europe	3,020	45.4	41.9	87.3
NORTH AMERICA	3,140	65.3	27.8	93.1
OCEANIA	3,230	63.9	31.5	95.4
DEVELOPED REGIONS	3,070	48.3	40.8	89.1
WORLD	2,380	21.0	45.1	66.1

TABLE 2. Percentage contribution of various commodities to percentage supplies
(Protein supplies 1963–65)

	Cereals	Starchy roots and tubers	Pulses nuts and seeds	Vegetables and fruits	Vegetable proteins	Meat	Eggs	Fish	Milk	Animal proteins
FAR EAST (incl. China Mainland)	59.3	3.3	18.0	3.3	84.3	6.6	0.7	4.6	3.8	15.7
South Asia	64.5	1.0	19.6	1.0	87.1	1.4	0.2	1.4	9.9	12.9
Southern Asia Mainland	58.8	2.0	8.3	4.0	73.5	7.1	1.4	15.4	2.6	26.5
Eastern Asia	48.2	2.1	14.0	8.4	72.7	6.1	2.9	15.6	2.7	27.3
South Eastern Asia Major Islands	64.4	6.4	7.4	3.9	82.6	7.1	1.0	8.6	0.7	17.4
China Mainland	57.8	4.6	20.3	3.2	86.1	10.0	0.5	2.7	0.5	13.9
NEAR and MIDDLE EAST	67.8	1.0	6.7	4.9	80.1	8.0	0.7	1.4	9.5	19.6
AFRICA	54.7	9.1	15.7	1.9	81.4	9.2	0.5	4.1	4.8	18.6
North Africa	69.9	1.1	5.1	4.2	80.3	7.8	0.8	1.6	9.5	19.7
West and Central Africa	51.2	14.8	18.1	1.6	85.7	6.8	0.4	5.1	2.0	14.3
East and Southern Africa	55.1	4.5	15.6	1.7	76.9	12.5	0.6	3.4	6.6	23.1

LATIN AMERICA	39.8	4.0	16.9	3.4	64.3	18.3	1.9	2.7	12.7	35.7
Brazil	37.9	3.6	26.6	3.7	71.8	13.5	2.2	2.3	10.2	28.2
Mexico and Central America	44.3	2.1	18.2	3.0	67.9	12.7	1.8	2.4	14.9	32.1
Northern and Western countries of South America	41.0	7.5	8.5	4.3	61.8	18.8	1.2	4.8	13.2	38.2
River Plate Countries	32.7	4.2	2.5	2.9	42.3	41.0	2.1	1.4	13.0	57.7
DEVELOPING REGIONS	57.2	3.8	16.8	3.3	81.4	8.3	0.9	4.0	5.4	18.6
EUROPE (incl. U.S.S.R.)	36.8	5.5	3.8	5.4	51.5	21.5	3.8	4.2	18.8	48.5
Eastern Europe	50.0	6.4	3.0	4.2	63.6	16.4	2.5	1.5	15.1	36.4
Western Europe	33.5	5.4	3.9	5.6	48.4	22.8	4.1	4.9	19.8	51.6
NORTH AMERICA	17.6	2.6	4.6	5.2	30.1	36.3	5.8	2.9	24.9	69.9
OCEANIA	24.9	2.4	2.2	3.6	33.1	36.8	4.2	3.1	22.5	66.9
DEVELOPED REGIONS	31.9	4.7	3.9	5.3	45.8	25.4	4.3	3.9	20.4	54.2
WORLD	47.9	4.1	12.1	3.9	68.2	14.7	2.1	3.9	10.9	31.8

Many of the grains and cereals are deficient in isoleucine and lysine, however, and these essential amino acids must be made up by other sources that are compartively rich.

GRAINS, CEREALS, AND THEIR PRODUCTS

Average Servings	Total Protein	Usable Protein
Wheat, whole grain hard red spring, ⅓ cup	8 grams	5 grams
Rye, whole grain ⅓ cup	7	4
Egg noodles, cooked 1 cup	7	4
Bulgar (parboiled wheat), ⅓ cup, or cracked wheat cereal ⅓ cup	6	4
Barley, pot or scotch, ⅓ cup	6	4
Millet ⅓ cup	6	3
Spaghetti or macaroni cooked 1 cup	5	3
Oatmeal ⅓ cup	4	3
Rice ⅓ cup		
brown	5	3
parboiled (converted)	5	3
milled, polished	4	2
Wheat germ, commercial 2 level tbsp.	3	2
Bread, commercial 1 slice, whole wheat or rye	2.4	1.2
Wheat bran, crude 2 rounded tbsp.	1.6	0.9

FLOUR

One Cup of Flour	Total Protein	Usable Protein
Soybean flour, defatted	65 grams	40 grams
Gluten flour	85	23
Peanut flour, defatted	48	21
Soybean flour, full fat	26	16
Whole wheat flour or cracked wheat cereal	16	10
Rye flour, dark	16	9
Buckwheat flour, dark	12	8
Oatmeal	11	7
Barley flour	11	7
Cornmeal, whole ground	10	5
Wheat bran, crude	9	5

Except for soybean flour, all of these flours are deficient in isoleucine and lysine and should be complemented by other protein sources. Legumes are the ideal match for grains since they are high in these amino acids. Brewer's yeast is also an excellent complement.

Remember, it is not only important to get "enough" protein, but to get it in the right proportions. The safest way to assure this is to eat different sources of protein.

DAIRY PRODUCTS

Average Serving	Total Protein	Usable Protein
Cottage cheese, 6 tbsp.		
creamed	14 grams	11 grams
uncreamed	17	13
Egg white, dried or powdered ½ oz.	11	9
Milk, non fat dry solids 4 tbsp, 1 oz.	10	8
Parmesan cheese, 1 oz.	10	7
Milk, skim, whole or buttermilk, 1 cup	9	7
Yogurt from skim milk, 1 cup	8	7
Swiss cheese, 1 oz.	8	6
Edam cheese, 1 oz.	8	6
Egg, 1 medium	6	5
Ricotta cheese, ¼ cup	7	5
Cheddar cheese, 1 oz.	7	5
Roquefort cheese or blue mold, 1 oz.	6 5	4 4
Camembert cheese, 1 oz.	5	4
Ice cream, about ⅓ pint	5	4

FISH

Per Serving, 3½ oz (about 100 grams)	Total Protein	Usable Protein
Tuna, canned in oil and drained	24 grams	19 grams
Mackerel, Pacific	22	18

Per Serving, 3½ oz (about 100 grams)	Total Protein	Usable Protein
Halibut	21	17
Humpback salmon	20	16
Swordfish	19	15
Striped bass	19	15
Rockfish	19	15
Shad	19	15
Shrimp	19	15
Sardines, Atlantic in oil	21	14
Carp	18	14
Catfish	18	14
Cod	18	14
Pacific herring	18	14
Haddock	18	14
Crab	17	14
Northern Lobster	17	14
Squid	16	13
Scallops, 2 or 3	15	12
Flounder or Sole	15	12
Clams, 4 large, 9 small	14	11
Oysters, 2 to 4	11	9

VEGETABLES

Vegetables are not going to make a large contribution to your protein needs, but they contain many vitamins and minerals essential for good health and vitality. Most of the vegetables listed here are low in calories, so you need not be too concerned about eating too many of them.

Vegetables high in vitamins and minerals include: snap beans, beets, burdock, cabbage, eggplant, lettuce, onions, green peppers, pumpkins, radishes, rhubarb, squash, sweet potatoes, tomatoes, and turnips.

Many of the vegetables listed as sources of protein are deficient in sulfur content and isoleucine and should be complemented by sesame seeds and Brazil nuts. Millet, parboiled, rice and mushrooms are high in sulfur content.

The average serving of vegetables here is based on a fresh, uncooked weight of 3½ ounces.

VEGETABLES

Average Serving	Total Protein	Usable Protein
Lima beans, green	8 grams	4 grams
Soybean sprouts	6	3
Peas, green, shelled	6	3
Brussels sprouts	5	3
Corn, 1 med. ear	4	3
Broccoli, 1 stalk	4	2–3
Kale, w/stems cooked	4	2
Collards, cooked	4	2
Mushrooms	3	2
Asparagus	3	1.8
Artichoke	3	1.8
Cauliflower	3	1.8
Spinach	3	1.5
Turnip greens cooked	3	1.4
Mung bean sprouts	4	1.4
Mustard greens	3	1.4
Potato white, baked	2	1.2
Okra	2	1.2
Chard	2	1

DRIED FRUITS

The most important value of dried fruits is their content of carbohydrates and mineral matter. In order to maintain optimum health, one must have fats and fluid substances, vitamins and carbohydrates.

Carbohydrates form the bulk of the food most people eat: breads, potatoes, vegetables, fruits and some nuts. There are three types of carbohydrates—sugar, starch, and cellulose (gums and pectins).

The sugar content of dried fruit is far greater than of fresh fruit, but you should eat both. Fruits contain vitamins, juices and acids. Dried fruits are rich in minerals, and only sea foods such as clams, lobsters, and oysters can compare with them. The minerals found in dried fruits are potassium, sodium, calcium, magnesium, iron, sulphur, silicone, and chlorine.

CHEMICAL COMPOSITION OF DRIED FRUIT

	Water	Protein	Carbohydrate	Fat	Minerals
Apples	26.10	1.60	62.00	2.20	2.00
Apricots	29.40	4.70	62.50	1.00	2.40
Pears	16.50	2.80	66.00	5.40	2.40
Peaches	20.00	3.15	50.00	.45	2.15
Prunes	22.30	2.10	71.20	—	2.30
Raisins	14.60	2.60	73.60	3.30	3.40
Currants	17.20	2.40	74.20	1.70	4.50

ENZYMES

The enzyme reaction within our system represents one of the fascinations of the human organism. Few food and nutrition experts have given these essential elements the attention they rightly deserve. However, by the end of this chapter, you should have a pretty good understanding of the role these natural agents play in your life.

Enzyme: means or refers to a catalyst (i.e., a substance which in minute quantities promotes chemical change without itself being used up in the reaction), produced by living things, of complex structure. There are a variety of enzymes, each acting only on a very limited range of chemical reactions.

The word "Enzyme" is derived from the Greek and means "in ferment" or "to leaven" and if you can think of an enzyme in these terms you will have a much better grasp of its role in your own system.

I don't often use dictionary terms but the one stated for "enzyme" is fairly complete: "Any of a class of complex organic substances which cause chemical transformation of material in plants, man and animals."

The fact is that "enzyme" and "life processes" are synonymous. Every living thing contains and is regulated in some manner by enzymes. To reduce the term to its most fundamental operation within your system would be to say that it controls the chemical reactions by which your food is digested, absorbed, and metabolized. Enzymes also control the type and amount of physical and mental energy used by your body.

Within all living things a large number of chemical reactions are continuing the life processes. The majority of these reactions are controlled by enzymes. An enzyme, like a catalyst, significantly increases the rate of chemical change of a substance (called the substrate) to another or others. Most of the reactions of metabolism would not occur perceptibly in the absence of enzymes, at the temperature and in the other conditions in which living things exist; and so metabolism is entirely dependent on enzymes. All enzymes produce their effect on the substrate by combining with it and activating it, so that the substrate undergoes further chemical change, at the same time losing its combination with the enzyme. Because of this process the enzyme is not consumed, but at the end of the process is free to deal with more substrate. Since the activation of the substrate is rapid, a very small amount of enzyme can produce a substantial effect. One molecule of catalase can decompose 40,000 molecules of hydrogen peroxide per second at freezing point. Most enzymes are present in rather small quantities.

Most enzymes activate only one type of substrate each. Other enzymes are less highly specific but even so each reacts only with chemically related substrates. There is correspondingly a large number of different enzymes, for every type of reaction which occurs in your system.

Each enzyme needs a specific activator or co-enzyme in order to perform properly. If the co-enzyme is not present, this will cause an inhibiting effect on the main enzyme and the food will not be decomposed completely.

Enzymes are unstable elements and are easily destroyed or inactivated, e.g. by high temperature, or by a wide range of chemical substances. Although they are not consumed by the reaction, enzymes slowly break down and have to be synthesized. The micro-nutrients required by organisms probably go to regenerating enzymes and co-enzymes.

Endogenous enzymes are manufactured by the body within the cell structure and that is where most of them do their work, although they can, when needed, be extracted and sent to other parts of the system. Some enzymes (e.g. digestive enzymes of vertebrates) are normally secreted to the outside of cells. In the metabolic processes of cells, and also in digestion, enzymes work very much as systems, the products of one reaction passing on to be substrate of another.

Closely similar enzymes, and enzyme systems, have been

found in a wide variety of organisms, including plants, animals, and bacteria, and they account for the fundamental similarities of many aspects of their metabolism.

The vitamins which we have discussed at length in this book, all act as co-enzymes and are important if not essential to the effectiveness of the enzymes. If your diet is properly balanced with the necessary nutrients, then your system can produce an adequate amount of its own enzymes, but if you are in some way starving the system of the essential elements, then you lose the capacity to produce these enzymes and must take them as you would take a vitamin or mineral tablet.

Excess heat will destroy enzymes. Even at 105 degree body temperatures, enzymes will be inactivated, mainly due to enzyme proteins which are damaged. Therefore, it is only from uncooked, fresh raw foods that an ample supply of exogenous enzymes can be ingested.

Since the noted American biochemist, Sumner of Cornell University, first isolated the enzyme in 1926, more than 70 enzymes have been isolated in a pure form. The first co-enzymes were isolated in 1933 and later their structure was determined.

Many chemists think of an enzyme as a catalyst and protein. But this is not the case. And to support this is the statement by Euler, the renowned Nobel Prize biochemist who worked on enzymes and fermentation. "They are not protein, but are in colloidal combination with the cell proteins."

Enzymes should not be compared with mold or bacteria. They are rather, unorganized, colloidal, nitrogenous substances present in all tissue. They only exist in living cells.

It is enzymatic action that changes fruit juices into a frothing, turbid concoction and then into an enjoyable, wholesome drink. It causes both wine and beer to ferment, seeds to sprout, fruit to ripen and your food to digest. The enzyme also causes the leaves to change colors from one season to the next. Enzymes are prime movers and motivators of nearly every living organism on earth. The presence of live enzymes in raw milk (not pasteurized milk), in uncooked honey, raw apple juice, raw carrot juice, etc. is, from the nutritional viewpoint, completely different from the enzymes the body itself creates from protein sources.

It is the action of an enzyme which converts starch into sugar. That is the first step in the enzymatic action in your system. It begins in your mouth. Once in your stomach and intestine, a molecule of the enzyme invertase can break down a million times its own weight of sucrose into invert sugar and this in no way decreases its future working capacity. To illustrate the tremendous strength of enzymes . . . crude ptyalin (in the mouth) can digest 200,000 times its weight in starch, one tiny gram of pure rennin (in the stomach) can coagulate ten million grams of milk.

From this example you can see the advantage of eating live, raw foods, which can digest much quicker and more completely than ones which contain no enzymes. The differences in the speed of digestion are significant. A few ounces of raw grapes will digest within an hour; a can of cooked grapes will take two or more hours to digest. Why? Because they contain no enzymes. All foods which are packaged in cans must be sterilized and this heating process kills the enzymes. If you expect a normal healthy system, eat raw live foods.

Of the three basic types of food: proteins, carbohydrates and fats, the enzyme ptyalin in the saliva digests only the carbohydrates, changing them into glucose. The pepsin of the stomach works on the proteins, changing them into amino acids with the aid of hydrochloric acid. The enzyme lipase affects only the fats, hydrolyzing or emulsifying them. The completion of digestion on proteins and carbohydrates is done in the small intestine with still another enzyme, trypsin. This is not to imply that digestion is so simple that only three or four enzymes are required. In fact, it takes many enzymes to digest all proteins, fats and carbohydrates. With each type of protein, i.e. eggs, cheese, meat, nuts, fish, a different set of co-enzymes go to work. Each food has and needs a specific enzyme to properly digest and assimilate its nutrients. Cherries must have their cherry enzyme, bananas need their own banana enzyme and so on. Nature has provided every living element with its own enzyme and provided that it has not been chemically treated, heated or otherwise unbalanced from its natural state, it will provide whatever enzymatic action is necessary for proper body metabolism. Enzymes must also have normal heat, moisture and oxygen to function properly. Your mouth, stomach and intestines provide such conditions.

While each type of enzyme works on a specific chemical action, as a rule enzymes act in groups or a system.

A great deal of needless heart disease and other coronary ailments could possibly be avoided by understanding the role the enzyme plays in conjunction with fats.

Many modern day researchers are of the belief that cholesterol build-up in the arteries is caused or is directly affected to some degree by consuming fats without enzymes which the body enzymes cannot break up and they are thus stored or build up in the liver and blood vessels.

The same can be said for hydrogenated fats, which the body enzymes are unable to cope with. Thus, they also are stored or accumulate in the blood vessels where eventually they pile up to such an extent they clog up the artery; a rupture may result followed by clotting and a heart attack.

If fats containing enzymes were consumed such as unpasteurized and unhomogenized milk, butter, and cheese, the enzymes which these foods contain would properly disseminate the natural fat and make it available for distribution throughout the system. The regular use of grains, and nuts containing high quantities of unsaturated and natural oils in the diet would benefit you greatly. As an added precaution, take one or two capsules of both lecithin and safflower oil. These natural oils help burn up cholesterol in the arteries and heart and thus lessen the chance for arteriosclerosis.

Nearly 90 percent of the average American diet is devoid of essential nutrients, especially enzymes. Most people think they are getting the proper balance of nutrients in cereals such as corn flakes, shredded wheat, post-toasties, rice krispies, oatmeal, plus V-8 juice or frozen orange juice. However, these common breakfast items contain no enzymes and only a few vitamins and minerals. It is also doubtful whether frozen foods or juices have their enzymes impaired. Boiled, fried or scrambled eggs, although high in complete protein, contain no enzymes. They have been destroyed in cooking. Cheese which has been processed from pasteurized milk or cream, too, is devoid of useful enzymes. The same is true of jam, jelly, or honey, unless the honey is unpasteurized; stewed prunes, canned pineapple, peaches, apricots or other cooked fruits and vegetables contain no enzymes. In short, anything which is cooked, canned or heated is devoid of enzymes.

Dried fruits, provided they are sun dried only, are just about as beneficial as fresh fruits. Drying by natural methods only suspends the enzyme action, which is started again when warmth and moisture are added. However, there is a marked difference between natural dried fruits and fruits treated with sulphur and heat and steam to cause drying. The commercially prepared dried fruits have no enzymes due to the sulphur or the heat, both of which will kill the enzyme. A good way to see if a dried fruit has been sulphured is to check the color. It should be dark brown and rather dry.

Enzymes can live indefinitely when dried to a powder at blood heat and the cold seems to do no harm to them. It is the enzymes that start the seeds growing and then tell the seeds when to be dormant and when to come to life.

I do not want to leave the impression that all cooked foods are harmful; on the contrary, several types of food must be cooked in order to break down the cell walls, especially those containing much cellulose, thus allowing easy penetration of the digestive fluids and the digestion of the contents. But this process must be accomplished by the synthesized body enzymes, for there are no natural food enzymes, if they have all been destroyed in the cooking.

The body enzymes are not capable of completely processing or assimilating the cooked or smoked or chemically treated foods, unless however, an enzyme tablet is also taken with the meal, or a fresh or dried piece of pineapple, papaya, or apple is eaten after the meal. These three fruits contain the most enzymes of any fruit and they will assist your system in breaking down protein and fats.

Without enzymes, any food which you might eat would remain a solid mass and lie there, unassimilated in your stomach. All food must be processed by enzymes which divide it up into fine particles to form a liquid or colloid and then it can pass through the permeable membranes and be taken up by the blood.

Enzymes slow their processes or become dormant in the cold and only spring into action when the temperature rises above 40 degrees. This is the reason refrigeration tends to slow down the decaying process. Optimum temperature for enzymatic action is about 90 degrees.

However, most organic elements and their enzymes can stand freezing and thawing.

The common belief is that your system can manufacture all of the enzymes which it needs, but this is not so.

The digestive secretions, fluids and tissues of your body are not endowed with sufficient enzymes to carry out the functions without aid. You need a constant supply of natural enzymes found only in wholesome, untreated, fresh foods. These natural enzymes are not superfluous.

Enzymes stand out from vitamins and minerals mainly due to their extremely sensitive nature. Neither vitamins nor minerals will lose their potency as easily as enzymes.

Metabolism is entirely dependent upon enzymes and one could presume that persons suffering from an unbalanced metabolism could also be lacking sufficient enzymes.

As all food is pre-digested, digested and assimilated by means of enzymes, without sufficient enzymes contained within the food itself or in the body, then the normal process of absorbing the nutrients in the food is only partially accomplished.

If you have chronic gastrointestinal difficulties, then see your doctor and ask him if your symptoms could originate from a decrease in the enzymatic power of the digestive secretions. Theoretically the answer could be found in laboratory examination of the digestive secretions, but in actual practice this is not always feasible. The intestinal digestive fluids do not easily lend themselves to accurate evaluation of the enzyme constituents. If you accept the possibility that the enzymatic efficiency of the gastrointestinal tract is not up to par, then enzyme therapy could offer a more scientific approach to the problem than is possible with alkali medication and other less effective palliatives.

Through the action of the enzymes the natural elements in food are made available and assimilable to and by the system.

These gastric ferments or enzymes break through the complex biochemical bonds around natural foods in which they occur and perform the operation of releasing the elements in combination to freer combination and assimilation through the intestinal walls and bloodstream. It is then easy for your system to pick up the enzyme action through the membranes, capillaries, lymph glands and other body organs and equally and properly distribute it throughout the body.

To conclude this chapter on enzymes, keep in mind that any food which states that it is "enriched, strengthened, fortified or improved" actually contains no enzymes and very few useful nutrients. The process by which they enrich or fortify foods also destroys most of the vital elements. This is also the case of the flour which is used by millions of American housewives each day for baking purposes. The various treatments and additives result in a pure white substance which contains virtually no nutritional value. Aside from the complete lack of value, the flour is treated with any number of harmful toxic chemicals: chlorine dioxide, ammonium chloride, nitrogen peroxide, propionic acid, benzoyl peroxide, potassium bromate, oxides of nitrogen, nitrosyl chloride and sodium aluminum sulphate.

There are three classes of elements your system needs daily in order to build and maintain good health: they are vitamins, minerals and enzymes. Your system is unable to produce vitamins and minerals and it can only produce a few enzymes. Therefore, it is only common sense that you should eat foods which contain an ample supply of all three. These foods must be raw, fresh and untreated by chemicals.

FOOD VALUES

SPECIAL NOTE
The information presented in this chapter will aid the reader in gathering knowledge of the particular nutrients found in foods common to the American diet. No reference is intended to mislead the reader into thinking that any one food or any combination of foods, will *cure* or reduce any ailment. We do not believe in the *cure* or *prescriptions* which other authors in the Health and Nutrition field have tried to force upon the reader. When we state, then, that Papaya will aid digestion it does not mean that it will also cure indigestion. Please accept the following information as a guide only. It is not a prescription.

To compile the information for this chapter required the examination of more than fifty books. The primary reference books on this subject are "The Complete Book of Food and Nutrition," J. J. Rodale & Staff, *Rodale Books Inc.* "Dictionary of Foods" Hauser & Berg, *Beneficial Books.* "About Nuts and Dried Fruit," P. E. Norris, *Thorsons Publishers Ltd.* "Vitamins: what they are and how they can benefit you," H. Borsook, Ph.D., M.D., *Pyramid Books.*

The average person takes it for granted that whatever he eats has sufficient nutritional value to get him through the day. This is rather evident due to the enormous quantity of "Quick Service" foods consumed every day by millions of people. Unfortunately these consumers are unaware that hot dogs, pizza, french fries, and colas have little or no nutritional value and are, in addition, unhealthy.

Lack of basic knowledge concerning food values is quite common throughout America. Few housewives know what vitamins, minerals, fats, acids or protein are in any given food. Much less how various foods should be combined. The catchall phrase, "a balanced diet," means little when people do not know what they are balancing, or have been deceived about what they believe they are consuming.

If people were made aware of the complete lack of food values in various popular foods, it might be assumed that they would make efforts to correct their eating habits. Virtually all foods obtainable through normal supermarkets and groceries are adulterated to one degree or another through the use of preservatives, coloration, pesticide residue, and a variety of other poisons (see chapter on POISONS). We have used organic sources in arriving at the following food definitions except where specifically stated otherwise.

The following chapter deals with food values and will be a useful reference and guide to understanding nutritional values of all foods common, and sometimes not common, to the American diet.

NOTE

To avoid confusion in the use of the terms *fats* and *oils*, we might begin by saying that the fat content of nuts is very high—in some instances well over 50 percent.

There is no food over which human digestive capacity varies so much as fat, but fat in one form or another is necessary.

All fats consist of three elements; carbon, hydrogen, and oxygen. They are the most concentrated forms of fuel and give twice as much heat as either proteins or carbohydrates. When digested they are absorbed partly into the small intestine and partly into lymph, and ultimately into the bloodstream. Fat is stored in depositories under the skin; in the tissues of most organs; in the mesentery and around the kidneys; and when these fat storage deposits are replete, fat eventually passes into the liver.

You can cut down your intake of fats but there is a definite need for some fat to be consumed in your diet. Fats in the form of phospholipids play an important role in nourishing the brain, and a class of compounds derived from fats known as sterols are essential to life.

As far as we can ascertain fats and oils from nuts do

not contain vitamin D, though margarines made from nut oils can be fortified to contain this very important vitamin and are in this respect just as beneficial as butter.

It was once thought that nut butters and oils were devoid of vitamin A, but through modern research scientists have found that some nut oils contain substantial quantities. Nuts also contain a considerable quantity of basic amino-acids; butter made from nuts has a high biological value. They not only help to maintain life and growth, but if fed to nursing and pregnant mothers improve the quality of their milk.

Unless nuts are ground by the teeth and broken down, the digestive juices can work only imperfectly on them and they pass undigested into the alimentary canal. The digestibility of nuts increases by as much as 10 percent when turned into butter. Unfortunately, most commercial nut butters are made from roasted nuts which have been heavily salted, and the excessive heat under which they are treated develops free fatty acids. Nuts should be dehydrated at moderate temperatures or gently dried to make them crisp. If roasted at high temperatures, the B complex vitamins are destroyed. In addition, salting nuts, far from improving their digestive qualities, interferes with the process of digestion.

Nuts are one of the most concentrated foods and have as high a nutritional value as any animal product with the exception of cheese. The fat in all nut butters is more easily digested than butter. Animal fats are free fats and will not mix with water whereas nut fats do so and form an easily digestible emulsion.

If you have had any difficulty digesting nut butters, eat them in combination with vegetables. In order to digest fats, there must also be present organic sodium in your food. Sodium is the principal alkaline element in the process of saponification which takes place when the pancreatic juice, bile and intestinal juices come into contact with fats. The organic sodium found in fresh vegetables and fruits will accomplish this.

When eating nuts, leave the skins on, because the vitamins are usually found in this covering. These vitamins are destroyed when the nuts are salted and roasted when the fats are split into glycerine and free fatty acids.

NOTE

Since dried fruits are not mentioned in the list of food values, special notice to their nutritional qualities will be given below.

Dried fruits are important in their own right and not merely as a substitute for fresh fruits. The vitamin C in dried fruits is not as high as that of fresh fruits, but drying concentrates the sugar, and makes it an infinitely greater source of energy.

In the U.S.A. the law stipulates that there shall not be more than 350 parts of sulphur dioxide per million, but this law is often broken and much dried fruit from this country has as much as 1,000 parts per million.

Peaches, pears, nectarines and apples are prepared for dehydration by having the stones or cores removed and are then placed in a "sulphur box." This is done so that 1. Fruit may appear as transparent as possible; 2. to reveal decayed portions overlooked in trimming; 3. to prevent fermentation and decay while drying; 4. to kill flies and other insects which leave behind larvae, which may develop after storing; 5. to make the texture of the fruit porous and so facilitate drying.

Sulphured fruit generally looks more yellow and attractive which adds to its sales potential.

Sulphured fruit contains more water than sun dried fruit and weight for weight is of less value. In many packing houses the fruit is reprocessed; that is, washed and re-sulphured, increasing the sulphur content to 3,000 parts per million or more, which makes the fruit unhealthy.

Sulphur adds nothing to the flavor of fruit or its quality. Sulphurous acid interferes with the functions of the kidneys, which have to work harder to remove it from the system; and in many instances, sulphur has caused the retardation of the red blood corpuscles.

There is no need for sulphur dioxide to be used in dehydration and many manufacturers have stopped using it.

The most important value of dried fruits lies in their carbohydrate content and mineral matter. In order to maintain optimum health one must have fats for fuel and energy; minerals to supply bone, blood and fluid substances; vitamins which have many beneficial functions and carbohydrates which also supply heat and energy.

Carbohydrates form the bulk of the food most people eat: bread, potatoes, all vegetables, fruits and some nuts.

There are three types of carbohydrates: 1. sugars, 2. starch, 3. cellulose, gums and pectins. Carbohydrates are composed of hydrogen, oxygen and carbon. Hydrogen and oxygen are present in the same proportion as water: two to one. The fuel value of carbohydrates is only half that of fats because the hydrogen in carbohydrates is already combined with oxygen in the form of water and so it cannot be burned as it is in fats.

Starch ends up as sugar in the body. Some forms of sugar are assimilated straight into the bloodstream while others, in a more complex chemical form, have to be broken down before this can be accomplished.

After passing into the bloodstream they emerge from the intestines and pass to the liver to be stored in the form of glycogen. As much glucose as is needed for immediate use passes on and is transformed into glycogen in the muscles, which use up glycogen as they work, which causes a rather constant need for it.

The liver is the main storehouse of glycogen. The amount of carbohydrate needed for immediate use goes into the muscles and the remainder is stored in the liver. Even though the sugar content of dried fruit is far greater than fresh fruits, you should eat both because fruits contain vitamins, juices and acids. Dried fruits are the richest of all in minerals and only sea foods, such as clams, lobsters and oysters can compare with them in this respect. Minerals found in dried fruits are potassium, sodium, calcium, magnesium, iron, sulphur, silicon, and chlorine.

CHEMICAL COMPOSITION OF NUTS AND DRIED FRUITS

NUTS	Water	Pro-tein	Carbo-hydrate	Fat	Min-erals
Acorns	4.10	8.10	48.00	37.40	2.40
Almonds	4.90	21.40	16.80	54.40	2.50
Beechnuts	9.90	21.70	19.20	42.50	3.86
Brazil Nuts	4.70	17.40	5.70	65.00	3.30
Butternuts	4.50	27.90	3.40	61.20	3.00
Candlenuts	5.90	21.40	4.90	61.70	3.30

NUTS	Water	Pro-tein	Carbo-hydrate	Fat	Min-erals
Chestnuts (dried)	5.90	10.70	74.20	7.00	2.20
Chufa	2.20	3.50	60.70	31.60	2.00
Coconut	14.10	5.70	27.90	50.60	1.70
Filberts	5.40	16.50	11.70	64.00	2.40
Hickory Nuts	3.70	15.40	11.40	67.40	2.10
Paradise Nuts	2.30	22.20	10.20	62.60	2.70
Pecans	3.40	12.10	8.50	70.70	1.60
Pignons	3.40	14.60	17.30	61.90	2.90
Pignolias	6.20	33.90	7.90	48.20	3.90
Pistachios	4.20	22.60	15.60	54.56	3.10
Black Walnuts	2.50	27.60	11.70	56.30	1.90
English Walnuts	2.50	18.40	13.00	64.40	1.70
Water Chestnuts	12.30	4.00	50.00	1.20	1.77
Peanuts	7.40	29.80	14.70	43.50	2.25
Peanut Butter	2.10	29.30	17.10	46.50	2.20
Almond Butter	2.20	21.70	11.60	61.50	3.00
DRIED FRUITS					
Apples	26.10	1.60	62.00	2.20	2.00
Apricots	29.40	4.70	62.50	1.00	2.40
Pears	16.50	2.80	66.00	5.40	2.40
Peaches	20.00	3.15	50.00	.45	2.15
Prunes	22.30	2.10	71.20	—	2.30
Raisins	17.20	2.60	73.60	3.30	3.40
Currants	17.20	2.40	74.20	1.70	4.50

In order to clarify some of the values mentioned in this book we have prepared the following chart on the vitamin contents of common foods. This chart was originally printed in the best seller "Vitamins: What they are and how they can benefit you," by the nationally acclaimed nutritionist Henry Borsook, Ph.D., M.D., published by Pyramid Books. We reviewed dozens of food value charts for this chapter and found the following one by Dr. Borsook to be the most accurate and comprehensive of any in its field. In addition, whenever we mention that a particular food is high, medium or low in a certain nutrient, you can compare it with this chart to get a more specific and detailed analysis of the food in question.

THE VITAMIN CONTENTS OF COMMON FOODS

Unless otherwise indicated, the quantities given below are those in the dry or fresh state before cooking.

No values for vitamin D are given because except in milk, butter, and eggs, the amounts in all foods are too small to be significant.

The data is as yet too limited in research findings, or the daily human requirement is inadequately determined, to make it useful to include in this table values of vitamins B6, nicotinic acid, pantothenic acid, E and K. However, for a detailed analysis of each of these vitamins, read the chapter on VITAMINS.

Where no vitamin values are given in this table it is because they have not yet been determined. In any case, the amount present probably is insignificant for ordinary purposes, except in the case of vitamin B2.

UNIT EQUIVALENTS:

Vitamin A

    1 International unit = 2 Sherman Units

                    = 0.6 microgram (gamma, y) of B carotene

Vitamin B1 (Thiamine Chloride)

    1 International unit = 3 micrograms (gamma, y)

                    = 0.003 milligram

                    = 2 Sherman units

Vitamin C (Ascorbic Acid, Cevitamin Acid)

    1 milligram   = 20 International units

                    = 2 Sherman units

Vitamin B2 (Riboflavin)

    1 milligram   = 333 Sherman-Bourquin units

                    = 1000 micrograms (gamma, y)

	MEASURE		Vitamin A I.U.	Vitamin B1 I.U.	Vitamin C Mill.	Vitamin B2 Mill.
	Ordinary	Ounces				
BREADS & CEREALS						
Barley, whole grain	1 tblsp.	½	0	3.3	—	0.001
" , pearled	1 tblsp.	½	0	0	—	
Biscuits, baking powder	1 biscuit		19	3	—	
Bread, Boston brown	1 slice 3" diam. ⅜" thick	¾	55	13	—	
" , white, made with milk	1 slice 3"x3½"x½"	¾	10	3.8	—	0.0121
" , white, made with water	1 slice 3"x3½"x½"	¾	10	3.7	—	0.006
" , 100% wheat	1 slice 3"x3"x⅜"	1	70	27	—	
" , rye	1 slice 3"x3"x⅜"	1		14	—	
Corn, whole grain yellow	1 cup	5	1,200	72	11	0.05
" , flakes, cereal	1 cup	1½	0	trace	0	
" , meal, white	1 cup	5	0	143		
" , meal, yellow	1 cup	5	1,200	110		
Crackers, Graham	1 cracker		26	8	0	
Custard, baked	¾ cup	3	650	21	1	

Flour, rye	1 cup	5		30–70	0	
" , 100% whole, unbleached	1 cup	4	500	180	0	
" , white, bleached	1 cup	4	150	33	0	
" , white, pastry	1 cup	4	130	19	0	
" , white, plus germ	1 cup	4		49	0	
Griddlecakes	1 medium	2	200	11	0.5	
Muffins, plain w. egg	1 muffin		135	9	0	
" , plain, without egg	1 muffin		48	8	0	
" , bran, with egg	1 muffin		260	50	0	
" , bran, without egg	1 muffin		170	52	0	
Oatmeal, whole grain	½ cup	1¾	0	165	0	
" , quick cooking	½ cup	1¾	0	130	0	
Oats, rolled, packaged	½ cup	1¾	0	121	0	
" , rolled, cooked	½ cup	1¾	0	121	0	
Rice, brown	2 tblsp.	1	17	15	0	0.02
" , polished	2 tblsp.	1	0	0	0	0.022
Rolls	1 roll	1½	74	9	0	
Rye, whole grain	1 cup	5		210	0	
Wheat, whole grain	1 tblsp.	½	50	23	4	0.02
" , whole grain, cooked	1 tblsp.	½	50	23	0	
" , bran	1 tblsp.	½	85	28	0	
" , farina, light	1 tblsp.	½	0	0.2	0	0
" , germ	1 tblsp.	½	90	80	0	0.10
" , puffed	½ cup	½	0	0	0	

	MEASURE		Vitamin A I.U.	Vitamin B1 I.U.	Vitamin C Mill.	Vitamin B2 Mill.
	Ordinary	Ounces				
BREADS & CEREALS						
" , semolina	1 tblsp.	½	30	7		
" , shredded	1 biscuit	1	4	20	0	0.10
Wheat, stone-ground	1 tblsp.	½	40	22	3	0.015
DAIRY PRODUCTS						
Butter	1 square	½	315	0	trace	0.001
Buttermilk	1 large glass	8	0	35	2	0.310
Cheese, Am. Cheddar	1" cube	¾	420	3	0	0.12
" , Camembert	1" cube	¾	750		0	
" , cottage, skim	1 tblsp.	¾	70		0	0.068
" , creamed, soft	1 tblsp.	½	310	0.6	0	0.017
" , creamed, full	piece 2"x1"	1	500		0	0.02
" , Edam	1" cube	¾	300		0	
" , pimento (Kraft)	1" cube	¾	500		0	
" , Roquefort	1" cube	¾	850		0	
" , Swiss (Kraft)	piece 4"x4"	¾	440		0	
Cream, 20% fat	1 tblsp.	3/5	64	2	trace	
Cream, 40% fat	1 tblsp.	3/5	132	1.6	trace	
Eggs, whole	1 egg	1½	900	19	0	0.25
" , white	1 white	9/10	0	trace	0	0.14

	Measure					
" , yolk	1 yolk	6/10	900	19	0	0.11
" , soft-boiled	1 egg	6/10	900	19	0	0.23
" , hard-boiled	1 egg	6/10	900	19	0	1.20
Milk, whole, fresh, raw	1 quart	32	1,400	28	3.5	0.23
Milk, whole, fresh, raw	1 glass	6	260	150	19	0.20
" , whole, fresh, pasteur	1 glass	6	260	22	3.0	0.35
" , dried, reconstituted	1 tumbler	6	260	20	2.0	0.17
" , evaporated	½ cup	4	190	15	3.5	0.09
" , condensed, sweetened	1 tblsp.	¾	45	10	4.0	
" , skim, fresh	1 glass	6	trace	25	0.7	
" , skim, dried powder	1 tblsp.	¼	0	8	4	
" , shake, ice cream		12	0	37		
MEAT & FISH						
Bacon, fried	5 slices	½		5	0	0.06
Beef, lean, top round	¼ lb.	4	40	45	2.2	0.029
Chicken, light meat	¼ lb.	4		30	0	0.078
Chicken, dark meat	¼ lb.	4		42	0	2.0
Chicken liver	⅛ lb.	2	17,000	50	11	0.11
Cod, steak, fresh	¼ lb.	4	2	34	0	0.40
Crab	¼ lb.	4	2,200	45	5	0.21
Halibut, muscle	¼ lb.	4		32		
Ham, smoked, lean	¼ lb.	4		540		
Herring, whole	¼ lb.	4	1,700	20		0.12

	MEASURE		Vitamin A I.U.	Vitamin B1 I.U.	Vitamin C Mill.	Vitamin B2 Mill.
	Ordinary	Ounces				
MEAT & FISH						
Kidney, beef or calf	¼ lb.	4	450	105	12	1.6
Lamb, chop, lean	¼ lb.	4	trace	90	2	
Liver, beef, fresh	¼ lb.	4	46,000	100	34	3.4
Mackerel	¼ lb.	4		34		
Mutton, lean	¼ lb.	4		68		
Oysters, raw	⅓ cup	3½	420	75	3	0.46
Pork chop, lean	¼ lb.	4	0	515	2	0.28
Pork, loin, lean	¼ lb.	4	0	515	2	0.11
Prawns, boiled	¼ lb.	4	1,100	20	0	0.27
Salmon, fresh, canned	¼ lb.	4	340	trace		
Sardines, canned in oil	⅛ lb.	2	200	17		
Sweetbreads, fresh	¼ lb.	4		120		
Tongue, beef or sheep	¼ lb.	4		35		
Trout, fresh-water	¼ lb.	4		33		
Veal, muscle, cooked	¼ lb.	4	40	45	2	0.17
Whiting, Atlantic	¼ lb.	4	400			
FRUITS						
Apples, raw, average	1 medium	6	50	8	10	0.06
" , applesauce	½ cup	4½			9	

" , Juice	1 tumbler	6			5	
Apricots, fresh	1 medium	1⅓	1,000	3.5	2	0.04
" , dried	4 halves	⅗	540	8	0	0.009
" , dried, sulphured	4 halves	⅗	540	3	2	0.005
Avocado, California	½ avocado	4	64	40	25	0.19
Bananas	1 medium	5½	230	28	7	0.07
Blackberries	1 cup	5¾	230	10	15	
Blueberries	1 cup	5¼	150	21	8	0.021
Cantaloupe	½ mellon	13½	770	73	60	0.25
Cherries, fresh, bing	10 cherries	2⅓	75	12	13	
Cranberries, fresh	1 cup	3¾	20	0	20	0
Cranberries, Juice	½ cup	2			7	0
Currant, black fresh	1 cup	3¾		11	220	
Currant, red, fresh	1 cup	3¾		16	55	
Dates, fresh	4 dates	1½	35	12	0	0.012
Dates, dried	4 dates	1½	15	8.5	0	0
Figs, fresh	3 small	4	90	30	2.3	0.06
Figs, dried	3 small	2⅕	32	30	0	
Gooseberries, canned	1 cup	4	330	56	34	
Grape, white, seedless	½ bunch	4	22	11	2.2	0
Guava	1 guava	¾	22	2	30	0.006
Lemon	1 large	3⅗	0		55	
Lemon, Juice	2 tblsp.	1	0		15	0.001
Lime juice, fresh	2 tblsp.	1	8		10	

	MEASURE Ordinary	MEASURE Ounces	Vitamin A I.U.	Vitamin B1 I.U.	Vitamin C Mill.	Vitamin B2 Mill.
FRUITS						
Mangoes	1 mango	3	850	17	25	0.05
Olives, green	6 olives	2	85	trace	0	
Olives, mission	6 olives	2	28	trace	0	
Orange, pulp	1 large	9½	80–270	95	80	0.24
Orange, Juice Fresh	1 tumbler	6	540	59	98	0.012
Orange, Juice Canned	1 tumbler	6	540	59	72	
Papayas	1 papaya	3	1,800	7	46	0.015
Peaches, fresh	1 medium	4	900	28	3.4	0.008
Peaches, canned	2 halves	3	900	22	1.7	
Pears, fresh, Bartlett	1 pear	3⅕	6	5	3	0.015
Pineapple, fresh	1 slice ⅜"	1⅜	90	13	2.6	0.006
Pineapple, Canned	1 slice ⅜"	1⅜	90	7	2.3	
Pineapple, Juice, canned	1 tumbler	6	90	35	12	
Plums, fresh	2 plums	3⅘	210	17	5.5	0.027
Plums, canned	2 plums	3⅘	200	15	5	
Pomegranate	1 pomegranate	6	0		20	
Prunes	4 prunes	1⅖	350	24	trace	0.3
Quince	1 quince	4		11		
Raisins	¼ cup	1	28	21	0	0.04

Raspberries	1 cup	4⅗	270	trace	33	0.022
Strawberries	½ box	6	340	trace	93	0.18
Tangerines	1 tangerine	2	280	22	28	
Watermelon	1 slice 6¾"	11	0	25	15	

VEGETABLES

Artichokes	1 artichoke	8½	250	70	15	0.025
Asparagus, green	2 stalks	1⅓	130	22	19	
Beans, baked	1 cup	4	15	150	0	0.025
" , kidney, fresh	½ cup	3	27	60	0	
" , navy, dried	½ cup	3½	27	128	0	
" , lima, fresh	½ cup	3	0	100	13	0.25
" , string or snap	½ cup	3½	600	25	8	0.08
" , string, canned	½ cup	3½	600	11	2	
" , runner, green	½ cup	3½	700	40	5	
" , soy black	½ cup	3½	900	100	46	
" , soy, white	½ cup	3½	140	250		
" , wax, butter, yellow	½ cup	3½	410	30	16	
Beets, Root	½ cup diced	5	70	24	5	
Broccoli, fresh	1 cup	4	4,000	38	80	
Brussels sprouts	6 sprouts	4	1,100	65	100	
Cabbage, white, raw	1 cup	3⅓	800	25	25	0.04
Cabbage, white, cooked	1 cup	3½	50	20	12	
Carrots, raw	1 cup diced	4¾	2,700	32	8	0.03

	MEASURE		Vitamin A	Vitamin B1	Vitamin C	Vitamin B2
	Ordinary	Ounces	I.U.	I.U.	Mill.	Mill.
VEGETABLES						
Carrots, cooked	1 cup diced	4¾	2,700	32	5	
Carrots, canned, strained	1 cup diced	4¾	2,700	13	3	
Cauliflower, raw	¼ head	3	49	46	33	0.065
Cauliflower, cooked	¼ head	3		35	33	
Celery, green stems	2 stalks 7″	1½	320		2	
Celery, blanched stems	2 stalks 7″	1½	2	5	2	
Chard (beet tops) raw	½ cup	5⅕	12,000	20	43	
Chard beet cooked	½ cup	5⅕	12,000	15	28	
Chicory (escarole) raw	4 leaves	3½	9,500		5	0.022
Chives	1 teasp.	⅕			2	
Collards, fresh raw	½ cup	3⅗	2,200	68	50	0.3
Collards, cooked	½ cup	3⅗	2,200	50	22	
Corn, yellow, whole	¼ cup	1⅘	250	25	5	0.018
Corn, sweet, canned	½ cup	3½	120	30	11	
Cucumbers, raw	½ of 10″	6½	0–20	55	18	0.003
Dandelion greens	1 cup	3½	12,500			
Eggplant	3 slices 4″	6⅓	70	43	8	0.10
Endive	3 stalks 6″	7⅓	4,200	70	20	
Garlic	1 clove	¼	0		2	

Food	Measure					
Kale, raw	1 cup	3⅔	9,000	59	140	0.50
Kale, cooked	1 cup	3⅔	9,000	45	28	
Kohlrabi	1 cup ½"	5		8	39	
Leek	1 leek 7"	1	17	8	7	0.022
Lentils	2 tblsp.	1	25	14		0.03
Lettuce, Romaine	2 leaves 9"	¾	1,300	4	1	0.05
Lettuce, Iceberg, head	¼ L. Head	2½	150	20	4.5	
Mustard greens	½ cup	2⅓	100	30		
Okra	5 pods	2	85	23	6	0.26
Onions, fresh	1 medium	2	6,200			
Onions, fresh, stewed	1 medium	2	0	10		
Parsley	4 stems	½	1,000		11	
Parsnips	1 7"x2"	6¾	380	66	38	
Peas, fresh	½ cup	2½	530	85	20	0.026
Peppers, green	1 pepper	2½	600	69		0.12
Peppers, Red	1 pepper	2½	2,200		135	
Potatoes, yellow, sweet	½ medium	3⅔	8,000	31	20	0.02
Potatoes, yellow, sweet, cooked	½ medium	3⅔	4,000	25	10	
Potatoes, white	1 medium	5⅓	60	93	30	
Potatoes, white cooked	1 medium	5⅓	40	74	30	
Rutabagas	1 cup	5	10	28	22	0.13
Sauerkraut, fresh	1 cup	5		trace	16	
Sauerkraut, cooked	1 cup	5			3	

	MEASURE Ordinary	Ounces	Vitamin A I.U.	Vitamin B1 I.U.	Vitamin C Mill.	Vitamin B2 Mill.
VEGETABLES						
Sauerkraut, juice	2 tblsp.	1			4	0.065
Spinach, raw	½ cup chop	3⅗	14,000	37	53	
Spinach, cooked	½ cup chop	3⅗	14,000	30	26	
Squash, winter, Hubbard	½ cup	4	2,900	21	3.5	
Squash, summer winter	½ cup	4	170	16	3.5	
Tapioca	2 tblsp.	1	0	0	0	0
Tomatoes	1 medium	7	6,000	52	50	0.10
Tomatoes, canned	½ cup	4¼	3,600	25	24	
Tomatoes, juice, canned	1 tumbler	6	5,300	25	25	0.25
Turnip greens	½ cup	3	6,000	38	42	
Turnip, cooked	½ cup	3	6,000	25	10	
Watercress	½ bunch	1½	2,000	28	22	
NUTS						
Almonds	10 nuts	⅗	0	7	0.5	
Cashews	5 nuts	½	19	12	5	0.028
Chestnuts	2 nuts	½	0	1	0.5	
Cocoanut, shredded	1 tblsp.	⅓	0	0	0.5	0.014
Cocoanut, milk, fresh	1 cup	8			4	

Hazel	10 nuts	½		28	2	0.3
Peanuts, whole, spanish	⅓ cup	1½	17	146	4	0.3
Peanuts, shelled	⅓ cup	1½	17	146	4	
Peanuts, roasted	⅓ cup	1½		33	0	
Peanut butter	2 tblsp.	1½	17	125		
Pecans	12 nuts	½	14			
Pistachio	15 nuts	½	14			
Walnuts	12 nuts	½	190	16	3.5	
MISCELLANEOUS						
Corn oil			0	0	0	0
Cottonseed oil			0	0	0	0
Ice cream, made with skim milk		8	0	15	3	
Lard			0	0	0	0
Mayonnaise	1 tblsp.		30	0.5	0	
Pie, apple	1 serving		90	14	0	
Pie, blueberry	1 serving		62	9	3	
Pie, chocolate	1 serving		440	10	0.5	
Soup, black bean	1 cup		70	11	0	
Soup, split pea	1 cup		145	18	0	
Soup, tomato	1 cup		1,480	10	9	
Soup, vegetable	1 cup		276	9	4	
Sugar			0	0	0	0

	MEASURE		Vitamin A I.U.	Vitamin B1 I.U.	Vitamin C Mill.	Vitamin B2 Mill.
	Ordinary	Ounces				
MISCELLANEOUS						
Tea			0	0	0	0
Coffee			0	0	0	0
Cocoa	2 tblsp.	½	0	4	0	0
Beer	1 glass	6	0	4	1	1.4
Yeast, baker's compress	1 cake	2	0	100		0.5
Yeast, baker's dried	1 cake	½	0	70		0.85
Yeast, brewer's, fresh	1 cake	2	100	220		0.4
Yeast, brewer's, dried	1 cake	½		8–500		

VITAL ELEMENTS IN COMMON FOODS

Calcium
cheese (Am.)
milk (whole)
cheese (Cot.)
milk (Butt.)
cauliflower
broccoli
endive
celery
beans
rutabagas
spinach
turnips
carrots
molasses
oysters
string beans
cabbage
lettuce
eggs
nuts
fish
almonds
citrus fruit
maple syrup
fruits dried
beans dried

Sulphur
watercress
asparagus
cabbage
garlic
grape
onion
beans
bran
bread
brussels s.
cauliflower
cheese
clams
eggs
fish
meat lean
nuts
oats
oysters
peas
chard
turnips
wheat

Potassium
cabbage
cocoanut
figs
tomatoes
apricots
peaches
onions
lima beans
pineapple
milk
prunes
pears
string beans
egg plant
watercress
celery
cauliflower
raisins
potato
citrus fruit
parsley
dates
rhubarb
carrots
spinach

Sodium
wheat bread
rye bread
buttermilk
cream cheese
codfish
halibut
mackerel
salmon
bananas
celery
dandelions

Magnesium
cocoa
chocolate
almonds
cashews
peanuts
lima beans
whole wheat
brown rice
oatmeal
dates
raisins

Carbon
potatoes
brown sugar
whole wheat
shred wheat
honey

Sodium
lettuce
spinach
sweet potato
milk
am. cheese
beet
watercress

Magnesium
chard
spinach

Phosphorus
lima beans
cheese Am.
oatmeal
veal
beef liver
beef lean
fish
eggs
spinach
buttermilk
milk (Skim)
milk (whole)
almonds
grapes
lentils
pecans
rice brown
walnuts
whole wheat
brussels S.
corn
dandelion
lobster
peas
soybeans

Iron
beans
beef liver
egg yolk
peas
wheat
oatmeal
beef lean
prunes
spinach
parsley
kale
cheese
potato
chard
watercress
oysters
dates
raisins
beets
figs
oranges
mushrooms
turnips
tomatoes
banana
carrots

Iodine
lobster
clams
oysters
shrimp
blue fish
mackerel
haddock
cod
halibut
scallops
salmon
squash
radishes
asparagus
lettuce
milk
cabbage
cucumber
string beans
spinach
beets
potato
kelp
sea lettuce

Hydrogen
vegetables
fruits
milk
water

Manganese
pineapple
wheat
beans navy
blueberries

gooseberries
spinach
peaches, dry
blackberries

Nitrogen
cheese
fish
lima beans
peas
lentils
mushrooms
cheese
meats
nuts

Oxygen
in all food
and water

Manganese
tangerines
walnuts
kidney beans
beets
liver, calves
lima beans
beets
wheat bran
banana

green olives
apple
apricot
beet greens
cabbage
carrot
celery
lettuce
watercress

Fluorine
cauliflower
cod liver oil
goat's milk
egg yolk
cheese
brussel sprout
milk
garlic
sauerkraut
sea food
rye bread
cabbage
whole grains
spinach
watercress
meat broth
beets

Silicon
asparagus
spinach
lettuce
tomatoes
barley
figs
berries
oatmeal
bran
grapes
strawberries
cherries
apples
celery
beets
parsnips
black figs
radishes
chard

Chlorine
oysters
cheese
lettuce
spinach
whey
cabbage
parsnips
beets
turnips
milk
watercress
fish
celery
cottage cheese
dates
dandelion
cocoanut
carrot
tomatoes
bananas
onions
pineapple
eggs
grapes
oranges
lemons
wholewheat

VEGETABLE AND FRUIT JUICE FOOD VALUES

Juices	Vitamins	Mineral	Good For
Apple	A, B2, C	Magn., Potas., Sodi., Calci., Chlo., Iron	Bleeding gums, digestion cleansing the intestines.
Beet	A, B1, C	Sodi., Calci., Potas.	Liver, gall bladder, building red corpuscles.
Cabbage	A, B, K, E, U	Chlo., Calci., Sodi., Iron	Muscle pains, bleeding, gall bladder.
Carrot	A, B, C, E	Potas., Iron, Magn., Sodi., Silicon, Sulph., Phosphorus	Anemia, stomach and digestive ailments.
Cucumber	B, B1, C	Potas., Iron, Magn., Chlo.	Constipation, Kidney trouble, cleans blood.
Celery	A, B, C, D1	Sodi., Magni, Iron, Calci.	Rheumatism, nervousness, skin problems.
Grape	A, C	Iron, Potas.	Anemia, body energy.
Lemon	C, P	Sulph., Potas.	Common cold.
Orange	A, B, C	Calci., Phos.	Anemia, loss of energy.
Potato	A, B2, C	Potas., Sulph.	Stomach acid, skin problems.
Radish	A, C, D	Chlo., Phos.	Intestinal troubles.
Strawberries	C, D	Iron, Fruit Sugar	Anemia, constipation, skin eruption, glands, nerves.
Tomato	B, C, D, K	Magn., Iron, Chlo., Sulph., Sodi., Iodine	Liver, gall bladder, nerves.

NOTE: Magn.-magnesium. Sulph.-sulphur. Chlo.-chlorine. Potas.-Potassium. Phos.-phosphorus. Calci.-calcium. Sodi.-sodium.

A FOOD GLOSSARY

Agar-Agar A species of sea grass, commonly known as vegetable gelatin. It consists of carbohydrates and traces of iodine.

Ale Fermented extracts obtained from germinated, starchy seeds; an infusion of malt with the addition of hops, which results in a mildly stimulating alcoholic beverage. It contains excessive amounts of phosphorus acid and only a small amount of vitamin C.

Almond A nut. The kernel contains a large percentage of protein, a good deal of fat and only small amounts of vitamin A and B; having an acid excess. Almonds are very difficult to digest if not properly chewed.

Apple A tree fruit. The wild or crab apple is more preferable from the nutrition standpoint than the over-cultivated variety. Apples aid the digestion and when eaten before a meal will help overcome constipation due to their fruit-acid salts which stimulate the digestive processes and their semi-cellulose content which softens the partly digested food in the large intestine. They contain a slight alkali excess and only slight traces of the water-soluble vitamins B and C. Fresh, uncooked apple juice also aids digestion.

Apples contain 84 percent water, 0.4 percent protein, 0.5 percent fat, 13 percent carbohydrates and 0.5 percent mineral matter. An apple may be eaten raw or cooked; grated in salad or as apple sauce. While they do not combine well with potatoes, bread and pastry, they can be eaten with yogurt and several other foods (see chapter on Food Combining). Apple pectin is a natural germicide. It not only acts as a killer of organisms but also stimulates the growth of healthy tissue. Pectin is also useful as a gelatin in preserves and jellies.

Apricot The ripe fruit of the apricot tree is rich in potassium and iron and contains a high alkali excess. Apricots are extremely rich in vitamin A. One medium apricot (1¼ oz) contains 1,000 I.U. of A. Four dried halves (3/5 oz) contain 540 I.U. of vitamin A. In cases of liver or digestive disturbances apricots should be cooked or soaked well before eating.

Artichoke This bud of the flowering head of a large thistle is very rich in potassium, sodium and calcium; being a bud vegetable, over-rich in phosphorus and sulphur acids and thus causing an acid excess; containing small quantities of water-soluble vitamins, and a good amount of the fat-soluble vitamin A; possessing an oxidizing ferment (tyrosine) and an insulin having the same properties. This bud is rich in tannic acid and, therefore, is slightly constipating. Diabetics should avoid the use of artichokes due to the high percentage of purine which tends to produce uric acid.

Artichoke, Jerusalem A root vegetable containing a fairly large amount of inferior (incomplete with only a few amino-acids) protein and sizable amounts of carbohydrates, principally in the form of inulin; also containing high percentage of minerals and an alkali excess; the vitamin content is negligible.

Some doctors will recommend Jerusalem artichokes in place of potatoes due to the inulin not increasing the sugar content in the blood.

Asparagus Underground sprouts or tips of the plant; very watery, poor in nutritive values; being a bud vegetable, over-rich in acids but containing an alkali excess; rich in amino-acid known as asparagine; very little vitamins (see chart).

Avocado A tree fruit. This pulpy fruit is rich in potassium with lesser amounts of sodium and fluorine and iodine; rich in oil and containing large alkali excess. Avocado is rich in vitamin A and has fair amounts of B1, B2, niacin and vitamin C.

Avocados will assist in overcoming constipation and will also help stimulate the appetite.

Bacon Consisting principally of fat from the sides of the belly of the pig; most of which is cooked out in the process of frying, leaving a residue with a fair amount of acid excess; almost no water-soluble vitamins and only a small quantity of the fat-soluble vitamin A; very little protein which is of the non-assimilable type, thus making bacon possibly the least injurious of all animal food products.

Banana A plant fruit which is rich in potassium and calcium with a small amount of sodium. The banana has an alkali excess with a trace of vitamin B and a fair amount of vitamin C; very low on fat soluble vitamins. Bananas contain a heavy saturation of starches which, as the fruits ripen, are transformed into sugar and also protein which is incomplete.

Barley The ripe seeds of the barley grass are rich in potassium, silicic and phosphorus acids and sulphur; showing traces of iodine and fluorine; having high acid excess and almost none of the water-soluble vitamin B which is all concentrated in the seed skins. Barley is very acid forming and thus should only be eaten in small quantities.

Bean, Fresh String A pod vegetable, very rich in potassium and magnesium; having a rather small alkali excess; containing fair proportions of all vitamins.

Bean, Kidney A pod vegetable, very rich in protein which is, however, of an inferior incomplete quality; also contains much fat and carbohydrates; rich in potassium, magnesium and phosphorus and sulphur acids; has small amounts of iodine while having an acid excess, only fair amounts of vitamin B and even less of vitamins A and C. Because of their highly concentrated nature, kidney beans should be eaten sparingly.

Bean, Lima A legume very rich in incomplete protein and carbohydrates; containing per half cup: 63 mg. calcium, 158 mg. phosphorus and 2.20 mg. of iron; very high in vitamin A with good amounts of thiamin, riboflavin and pantothenic acid.

Bean, Soya A legume containing one of the few non-animal proteins which are complete and have an average of 90.5 percent digestibility. They contain a fairly equal amount of carbohydrates and protein; a very valuable vegetable fat and a high amount of potassium; fair amounts of the vitamins A and B with a trace of vitamin C.

Beef   Steer or heifer meat; rich in calcium and sodium; with high amounts of phosphorus and sulphur acids; having high acid excess; containing small percentage of vitamin B complex, and only a very small amount of vitamin A.

Meat contains a so-called meat alkali, but is composed principally of protein and fat. Beef is considered by many nutritionists as a very good source of protein. Even so, eating beef too often in large quantities is not a healthy habit, as beef contains too much acid-forming protein and so may destroy the necessary alkali excess in the body. For additional information on possible arguments for limited meat eating see (chapter on Vegetarianism).

Beet Greens (Chard)   Leaves of the sugar beet which are very rich in vitamin A and high in potassium and sodium. Like spinach, beet greens contain a considerable amount of oxalic acid which connects rapidly with calcium, forming oxalates which are then excreted.

Beet, Sugar   A root vegetable containing incomplete protein, a plentiful amount of cellulose and natural sugars. High in potassium and sodium; having alkali excess and small amounts of vitamins A, B and C. The sugar beet also contains a large amount of an oxidizing ferment which when it comes into contact with the air changes the tyrosine (amino-acid) found in the juice into a dark insoluble ✔ powder.

Blackberry   A bush fruit very rich in sugar and cellulose; high in minerals except sodium; containing high alkali excess; low on vitamin A, traces of vitamin B and only a small amount of C.

Blueberry   A bush fruit containing a small quantity of incomplete protein and a small amount of tannin and pectin; rich in potassium; with a very high alkali excess; no vitamin B and a small amount of vitamin C.

Brazil Nut   Rich in incomplete protein (a high percentage of amino-acids, but not all of the essential ones), oil and fat and starches; also rich in potassium, calcium and phosphorus; high acid excess; with a fair amount of vitamin B and smaller amounts of vitamins A and C.

Brazil nuts should be thoroughly chewed otherwise they tend to irritate the sensitive lining of the intestinal tract.

Bread, Rye   Made from the flour of the complete seeds of rye-grass and Secale cereal (cultivated rye); rich in incomplete protein, oil, starches, potassium, phosphorus and sulphur acids; having a high acid excess and a small amount of vitamin B per slice.

Bread, Wheat   Made from the ground whole grains of the wheat grass; rich in incomplete protein, oil and starches; rich in phosphorus, potassium and sulphur acids; large acid excess and having only a small amount of vitamin B per slice.

The protein content of whole wheat bread is inferior to that of rye bread.

Bread, White   Made from bleached refined flour and grains of the wheat grass with a small amount of incomplete protein and oil; very rich in starches with a little potassium, phosphorus and sulphur acids; possessing acid excess and virtually no natural occurring vitamins. In fact, white bread has very little food value.

Broccoli   A variety of the common cauliflower with the edible parts being the fleshy stalks and pollen; rich in potassium; containing small amounts of phosphorus, sulphur acids and traces of iodine; having an alkali excess; rich in vitamin B and vitamin C.

Brussels Sprouts   The bud of the common cabbage plant contains a rich supply of cellulose, potassium, phosphorus acid, and sulphur acid; also rich in incomplete protein; fairly high alkali excess with a fair amount of vitamin A and traces of vitamins B1, B2, B6 and niacin. Brussels sprouts contain sulphur acid and therefore are less valuable as a food than the other varieties of cabbage.

Buckwheat   A grain containing a small quantity of incomplete protein and fat; rich in carbohydrates, potassium, phosphorus and sulphur acids; only traces of the B complex vitamins.

Butter   Unmelted fat extracted from milk; composed of fat, small amounts of calcium, phosphorus and iron; high concentration of vitamins A and D with smaller amounts of thiamin, riboflavin and niacin.
Of all fats, butter is the easiest to digest. Care should be taken to avoid rancid butter which destroys all fat soluble vitamins upon contact. The loss of vitamin A in melted butter is negligible whereas it is completely lost when butter is used in frying.

Cabbage, Red   Has the same composition as white cabbage. The nutritional value of red cabbage is the same as white cabbage.

Cabbage, White   Unopened heads of the white cabbage plant, having a small amount of incomplete protein and little sugar; rich in potassium and calcium; containing large alkali excess and traces of iodine and iron; rich in water soluble vitamins A and D.

Cabbage, White (Sauerkraut)   White cabbage cut fine and fermented in lactic acid bacilli (brine made from its own juice with salt added); having the same composition as white cabbage with a rich amount of vitamin C. Due to its acid content it has a strong, stimulating effect upon the digestive organs.

Cakes   Made from refined flour with large amounts of sugar and condiments added; having only a small amount of incomplete protein and containing mostly starches; completely deficient in mineral value and having acid excess and virtually no vitamins and therefore no nutritional value.

Carrot   A root vegetable containing a small amount of incomplete protein; rich in carbohydrates, potassium, sodium with a fair amount of calcium and phosphorus, and traces of iodine. Very high vitamin A, only traces of the B-complex and low in vitamin C.

The vitamin A content in every 10-ounce cup of carrots is between 10,000 and 12,000 units. Although young carrots are more tender, larger, more fully mature carrots are not only sweeter but contain a larger amount of carotene; the substance which is converted into vitamin A by enzymes.

Carob Ripe pod of the Saint-John's bread or carob bean; having a fair amount of incomplete protein and some sugar; rich in potassium, calcium and phosphorus acid with traces of iodine.

There is growing evidence that chocolate (pure cocoa) is actively poisonous; many people are allergic to it while others, exposed from childhood to small increasing quantities build up a resistance. Carob is an excellent replacement for chocolate. The taste buds must be very sophisticated to tell the difference.

Cauliflower The stalk and flower bud of the brassica family which contains a small amount of incomplete protein; rich in sugar, cellulose, potassium, mustard oil, and calcium; a fair amount of vitamins A, B and C.

Because cauliflower causes mild flatulence it should be steamed or boiled. Also since mustard oil in cauliflower tends to irritate the kidneys, anyone suffering from any form of kidney disease should avoid this vegetable.

Caviar Eggs of any number of fish, but more commonly from the sturgeon, salmon and haddock; rich in incomplete protein; containing some oil; rich in potassium, calcium, phosphorus and sulphur; high acid excess and moderate amounts of vitamins A and B.

Celery, Bleached Stalks of the celery plant grown under the surface of the ground; having a slight amount of incomplete protein and a small quantity of natural sugar; good in potassium, fair amounts of sodium and calcium; high alkali excess with only traces of the B-complex, low in niacin and vitamin C.

Celery Leaves Green leaves of the celery plant growing above the ground; containing a small amount of incomplete protein and a little more sugar than the bleached celery stalk; rich in potassium, sodium and sulphur acid; having a high alkali excess; rich in vitamins A, B and C; also containing an ingredient of insulin and a ferment known as tokokinin.

Chard (See Beet Greens)   Leaves and stalk of the beet plant; containing a fair amount of incomplete protein and carbohydrates; rich in potassium and calcium; having a high alkali excess and rich in the vitamin B-complex.

Cherry   Fruit of a tree, containing a very small amount of incomplete protein; high in natural sugars and fruit acids; very rich in potassium; having an alkali excess; rich in vitamins C and B-complex.

Cherries, eaten daily, tend to regulate the eliminative process and promote a more healthy system. They also stimulate the secretion of urine without injury to the kidneys.

Chestnut   Containing a good source of incomplete protein and fat; very high in carbohydrates, potassium, sodium and magnesium; having an acid excess and only a small amount of the vitamin B-complex.

Cottage Cheese   Curdled and compressed casein (white, crumbling substances with a high acid nature) in milk; very rich in protein, rich in fat, calcium, phosphorus and sulphur acids; having a high acid excess and a small quantity of vitamins A and B-complex.

Cheese, Goat   Made from goat's milk; rich in potassium, protein, fat, phosphorus and sulphur acids; large acid excess and small quantity of vitamin A.

Cheeses   Made from cow's milk; rich in protein, fat, calcium, potassium, phosphorus and sulphur acids; high acid excess and a small amount of vitamin A. Most varieties of cheese are very nutritional.

Chick Peas (Garbanzos)   A legume rich in cellulose, fat and incomplete protein; also having a high concentration of potassium, phosphorus and sulphur acids; an acid excess and small quantity of vitamins A and B-complex.

Chicory Containing a small amount of incomplete protein; rich in potassium; having an alkali excess and a high content of vitamin A.

Chives The small, green, spear-like shoots of the chives bulb, containing a rich supply of incomplete protein, oil, potassium and calcium; rich alkali excess and fair quantity of vitamins B-complex and C.

Chives aid in dissolving the phlegm in catarrh and help to stimulate the appetite. It is primarily used as a delicate onion flavoring in salads and soups.

Chocolate Containing a mixture of sugar and cocoa; rich in incomplete protein, starches and fat; also a fair quantity of potassium, calcium, phosphorus and sulphur acids; having an acid excess with very little vitamins. Chocolate is such a heavily concentrated food that it should only be eaten in small quantities. It also contains an alkaloid, similar to the one found in caffeine, known as theobrama, from which it derives its stimulating properties. Chocolate is a common cause of constipation.

Cider Fermented apple juice; having only alcohol and fruit sugar; rich in fruit acids and very deficient in minerals; having a slight alkali excess and very little vitamin content.

Apple cider is very beneficial to digestion.

Cocoa Fermented seeds of the cocoa tree; rich in incomplete protein, starches and fat; very rich in potassium, calcium, phosphorus and sulphur acids; having a high acid excess and a very small quantity of vitamin B.

Cocoa is similar to chocolate in that it too has a stimulating effect and is also fattening. It, also, will cause constipation.

Coffee Rich in the alkaloid, caffeine, which will cause a stimulating effect; containing virtually no other nutrients.

Strong, black coffee can cause palpitation of the heart and insomnia. It can also cause a minor irritation to the nervous system, when taken in large quantities of three or more cups per day.

Cola   Dried kernels of the cola tree; rich in incomplete protein, carbohydrates, potassium, calcium and phosphorus and sulphur acids; having an acid excess and containing a very small amount of vitamins A and B-complex.

Cola nuts are rich in caffeine and thus have the same stimulating effect upon the system as coffee.

Corn-on-the-Cob   The seeds of this yellow vegetable contain a good supply of incomplete protein, carbohydrates and oil; also rich in potassium and phosphorus and sulphur acids; having an acid excess with almost no vitamins and only slight trace minerals. Foods derived from corn include corn-oil and corn flour.

White corn is inferior to yellow corn and is also not easily digestible. Corn is the least nutritious of all grains.

Crab Meat   The meat of a shellfish, containing a good source of complete protein, with very little fat; rich in potassium, sodium and phosphorus and sulphur acids; also having a high amount of iodine and a trace of vitamins B1 and B2; having a high acid excess.

Crackers   Made with wheat flour and salt. The composition and food value of crackers are the same as those of wheat bread.

Cranberry   A berry containing very little incomplete protein but fairly rich in fruit acids, especially in tannic acid; also a fair amount of potassium, and a small amount of calcium, phosphorus and sodium; traces of vitamins C and B-complex; having an acid excess.

Cream   Fat, yellowish part of milk, which rises and collects on the surface of milk; containing a small amount of complete protein; a good amount of milk-sugar; rich in fat, potassium, calcium and phosphorus and sulphur acids, having a small acid excess; rich in vitamin A with lesser quantity of vitamins B-complex and D. Cream is a very nutritious food.

Cucumber   A vegetable of the squash family, having a small incomplete protein content and a fair quantity of sugar and cellulose; rich in sodium, calcium and magnesium; very rich in phosphorus and sulphur acids; having an alkali excess; small amount of vitamin C, with a lesser amount of vitamin B-complex.

Cucumbers are an excellent food except when they have been salted or pickled, in which case they lose most of their food value.

Currant A berry, containing small amount of incomplete protein; rich in sugar and potassium; having an alkali excess and a fair amount of vitamin B-complex with a lesser amount of vitamin C. Currant juice is especially beneficial in cases of stomach or intestinal catarrh.

Dandelion Green Young leaves from the common weed, containing a small quantity of incomplete protein and also having a small amount of tannic acid and bitter ingredients (natural mineral salts and juices, which cause a bitter taste); very rich in potassium, calcium, sodium, and phosphorus acid; having a high alkali excess and fairly rich in vitamins B-complex, C and D and an extremely high amount of vitamin A. Dandelion greens stimulate the glands and cause a copious flow of bile and act as a strong urine dissolvent.

Date Fruit of the date palm, containing a fair amount of incomplete protein; very rich in sugar and cellulose; also rich in sodium, magnesium, potassium and calcium; rich in sulphur and chlorine; having an alkali excess and a small amount of vitamin B-complex.

Dill An herb containing a fairly rich supply of incomplete protein, carbohydrates and cellulose; very rich in ethereal oils, potassium, sodium, calcium and phosphorus and sulphur acids and chlorine; having a strong alkali excess; rich in vitamins A, B, and C. Owing to the heavy saturation of ethereal oil, dill should not be eaten by those who have kidney disorders.

Eggplant A bulbous, purple-skinned vegetable of the squash family containing a small quantity of incomplete protein and carbohydrates; having a fair amount of minerals and an alkali excess; rich in vitamins A, B-complex and C.

Eggs Very rich in complete protein and fat; rich in potassium, sodium, chlorine, and phosphorus acid; having an acid excess and a small amount of vitamins A, B-complex and D.

Eggs are overestimated as a food, probably due to their high protein content by weight. There has also been a misconception about the ease of digestion of the soft-boiled egg. In reality, hard-boiled eggs are much less difficult to digest. Eggs contain approximately 6 usable protein grams per 2 ounce (or 1 egg).

Egg White Rich in complete protein; also rich in potassium, sodium and sulphur acid and chlorine; having an acid excess and very little vitamin B-complex.

Egg Yolk Containing a rich amount of complete protein, fat and lecithin; rich in potassium, sodium, calcium and sulphur; containing a very large amount of phosphorus; having an acid excess and a small amount of vitamins A, B-complex and D.

Endive A vegetable plant used in salads which contains a small quantity of incomplete protein and carbohydrates; rich in potassium and calcium; having an alkali excess and a rich supply of vitamin B-complex.

Fennel A plant with aromatic seeds used as flavoring, containing a small quantity of incomplete protein and a small amount of carbohydrates; having an alkali excess with a rich supply of minerals. Fennel is principally used as a condiment, or as a flavoring for foods. It is only used in very small quantities.

Fig A tree fruit, containing a poor supply of incomplete protein but very rich in natural fruit sugar, calcium, potassium, magnesium and phosphorus acid; having an alkali excess and a rich supply of vitamin B-complex. Figs contain a beneficial protein-decomposing ferment called Papain.

Figs also stimulate the digestive organs and are one of the best natural purgatives.

Fish   Flesh of fish is far easier to digest than any animal meat; it is also very rich in complete protein; little oil (although there are some oil-heavy fish) and hardly any carbohydrates; rich in potassium, sodium, iodine, and phosphorus and sulphur acids; having an acid excess.

Fowl   Poultry meat has basically the same make-up as animal meat; rich in potassium and sulphur and phosphorus acids; having an acid excess.

Garlic   A bulb, the root of the garlic plant, containing a small amount of incomplete protein; rich in sugar and raw fiber; fair amount of mustard oil; very rich in potassium, calcium and phosphorus acid; having an alkali excess and traces of iodine; fairly rich in vitamins A, B-complex and C.

Garlic stimulates the appetite and acid secretion of the gastric juices and thus helps prevent gas formation or flatulence. Garlic also promotes peristaltic action or the movement of the bowels and so tends to heal inflammatory conditions of the intestines, created by constipation.

Ginger   Roots of the ginger plant, containing a small amount of incomplete protein, carbohydrates and ethereal oil; rich in mineral elements; having an alkali excess; it is used as an aromatic flavoring.

Ginger increases the appetite and aids digestion, helps to regulate delayed menstruation and has a fairly strong diuretic action.

Grapefruit   A hybrid citrus fruit, containing a poor supply of incomplete protein and carbohydrates; very rich in fruit acids and their salts; especially high in citric acids; rich in potassium, vitamin B-complex and C and having an alkali excess. Grapefruit serves as a natural stomach bitter which increases the flow of digestive juices.

Grape   A vine fruit, containing a poor amount of incomplete protein; rich in fruit acid salts and vinous acid;

very rich in sugar and potassium; having an alkali excess and a rich supply of vitamins B-complex and C.

Grapes increase and normalize urine and lessen the formation of uric acid while increasing the excretion of uric acid from the body and decreasing the amount of acid in the body. Grapes eaten regularly also assure better intestinal elimination.

Ham   Smoked or otherwise cured pork, containing a rich source of complete protein and fat; also rich in sodium, potassium and phosphorus and sulphur acids; having an acid excess and a fair amount of B1, B2 and niacin.

Due to its method of curing with kitchen salt and by smoking, ham is more injurious than any other kind of meat. It should be eaten no more than one meal per week and only in small quantity.

Hazelnut (Also known as Filbert)   A nut, containing a rich supply of complete protein; small quantity of carbohydrates; rich in potassium, calcium, phosphorus and sulphur acids; having an acid excess and a fair amount of vitamins A, B-complex and C.

Honey   Nectar of flowers transformed into honey through digestion in the ante-stomachs of honey bees; containing a rich supply of grape and fruit sugar with a trace of formic acid; poor in minerals; having a slight acid excess and traces of vitamins B-complex, C, D, and E; containing various animal ferments, especially oxidase (oxidizing ferment).

Honey causes a slight purgative action. It also possesses a diuretic effect which does not harm the kidneys.

Juniper Berry   A bush berry, containing a rich supply of incomplete protein, sugar, tannin, ethereal oils, potassium, magnesium and phosphorus acid; having an alkali excess and rich in vitamins B-complex and C. It is also popular as a condiment and has a slight diuretic action.

Kale   Leaves of the open cabbage which contain a small amount of incomplete protein and some carbohydrates; a good supply of potassium and calcium, some iron, phosphorus and sodium; having an alkali excess, a very high amount of vitamin A, and a rich but lesser amount of vitamins B-complex and C.

Kale, Sea Sprouts and young leaf of the sea kale; containing a fair amount of complete protein and a lesser amount of sugar; rich in potassium, sodium and iodine; having an alkali excess with a very good supply of vitamin A and a fair amount of vitamins B-complex and C.

Lamb Meat of young sheep; rich in complete protein, fat and gluten; also a good supply of potassium, phosphorus, less of sodium, calcium and iron; and a fair amount of sulphur acids; having an acid excess with some vitamin B-complex.

Lard Melted fat extracted from the waste parts of the pig; having few minerals and an acid excess and virtually no vitamins. Vegetable oils are far superior and much more nutritious than lard.

Leek A bulb and green shoot having onion-like flavor and containing a small amount of incomplete protein, some carbohydrates and a slight trace of mustard oil; rich in potassium, sodium and phosphorus acid; having an alkali excess and rich in vitamins B-complex, C and only a small amount of A.
Leeks are beneficial in that they promote urine secretion and help prevent flatulence. They also help inflammation of the air passages due to colds because they loosen phlegm. They also increase the appetite and stimulate the digestive glands.

Lemons A citrus fruit, containing small amounts of incomplete protein; very rich in citric acid and acid salts; rich in sugar, potassium and calcium; having an alkali excess and fairly rich in vitamin C with only a trace of B2. Lemons have a diuretic action without injury to the kidneys. They are recommended for mouth sores and swollen gums.

Lentil A legume, containing a rich supply of incomplete protein and carbohydrates; also rich in cellulose, purine, potassium, sodium and calcium; over-rich in phosphorus and sulphur acids; having an acid excess and traces of vitamins A and B-complex.

Lettuce, Head A salad vegetable containing some caoutchouc (rubber), chyle and bitter tasting ingredients; rich in potassium, calcium, sodium, iron with traces of iodine; having an alkali excess and fair amount of vitamin B-complex, traces of vitamin C and a good amount of vitamin A. The darker green, outer leaves contain the most vital food elements. Many types of lettuce are available including iceberg, Boston, Bib and Romaine. Only one is outstanding in its high content of vitamin A and that is Romaine.

Lime A citrus fruit, containing a small quantity of incomplete protein and sugar; very rich in citric acid and citric acid salts; fair amount of potassium and calcium; having an alkali excess and a sizable quantity of vitamin C and a fair to low amount of vitamin A.

Liver Containing a very rich source of complete protein, potassium, sodium and magnesium, also rich in phosphorus and sulphur acids; having an acid excess and a high amount of the B-complex and a very rich source of vitamin A; also a moderate amount of vitamin D. Beef liver has about a third more vitamin A than either calf or chicken liver. (¼ lb. Beef 46,000 I.U. of A; ¼ lb. Calf 32,000 I.U. of A; ¼ lb. Chicken, 32,200 I.U. of vitamin A.)

Lobster A shellfish rich in complete protein; with a small amount of fat; low in sodium, fair in potassium and phosphorus and sulphur acids; also contains a slight trace of iodine; having an acid excess and a small quantity of vitamin incomplete B-complex.

Macaroni Pasta, a form of noodles made from the meal or grits of wheat flour mixed with water and eggs to make a dough; containing a fair quantity of incomplete protein, small proportion of fat and a rich source of starches; also rich in potassium and phosphorus and sulphur acids; having an acid excess and a small amount of vitamin B-complex.

Malt   Germinated seeds of different grains, but usually barley; containing an incomplete protein and small quantity of fat and starches; rich in malt-sugar, potassium and phosphorus and sulphur acids; having an acid excess and fair amount of vitamin B-complex.

Mango   A pulpy, tropical fruit, containing a very small amount of incomplete protein and a high sugar and cellulose content; having an alkali excess and fair amounts of vitamin A and small amounts of vitamins B1, B2 and C.

Maple Syrup   Syrup boiled down from sap of the maple sugar tree; rich in potassium, sugar and calcium; having an alkali excess and rich in vitamin B-complex.

Margarine   Fat of the same consistency as butter, obtained by pressing melted vegetable fats, which have been hydrogenated and made to look like butter. Containing some mineral elements; having an acid excess and a fair amount of vitamin A, due to fortification with a synthetic. Hydrogenating the oils to make them solid destroys most of the essential fatty acids.

Melon   A pulpy fruit, of which there are several varieties, related to squash and pumpkin, containing a small amount of incomplete protein; rich in sugar, cellulose, potassium and having an alkali excess; low in vitamins B-complex and C. Melons also have a mild diuretic action which does not harm the kidneys.

Milk (from Cows)   Containing a small amount of alkali excess; very rich in complete protein, fat and sugar; low in potassium and sodium, very rich in phosphorus and sulphur acids; also rich in vitamins A, B-complex, fair C and D. Milk possesses oxidizing ferments which are not always easy to digest. For babies and small children raw cow's milk sometimes contains too much protein and should be diluted with water. Also in the boiling or sterilizing of milk, various changes, occur which affect the qualities of the milk. The vitamin content is changed, the valuable protein is partially decomposed and the bone-building salts in colloidal-loose form are changed to a combined form which is difficult to assimilate.

Milk, Butter Slightly curdled milk from which the fat has been removed. Its composition is almost the same as sour milk with the exception that it is deficient in fat.

Milk, Skimmed Milk from which the fat has been skimmed or separated. Composition is much of the same as regular milk except that it contains only traces of fat.

Milk, Sour Milk curdled due to the formation of lactic acid; the casein being transformed into gelatinous masses. The composition of sour milk is the same as ordinary, sweet milk, except that it has less sugar.
Sour milk has been used in cases of stomach or intestinal ailments.

Millet A grain, containing large quantities of incomplete protein; some fat and rich in starches, potassium, magnesium and phosphorus and sulphur acids; having an acid excess and small amount of vitamin B-complex.

Molasses Uncrystallizable, evaporated syrup obtained from the raw cane sugar residue when reduced to a fluid by boiling; rich in raffinose, sucrose, grape and fruit sugars; having no protein and very rich supply of minerals; having an alkali excess and only a trace of vitamin B1.

Mushroom (Any of a Variety of Fleshy Fungi) Containing a rich supply of incomplete protein; some carbohydrates; rich in sodium, potassium, and sulphur; having an alkali excess and a little Vitamin A and D with traces of the B-complex.

Muskmelon A fruit, containing a small quantity of incomplete protein and a fair amount of sugar; rich in potassium; having an alkali excess and a fair supply of vitamin B-complex; also possessing a strong diuretic action without injuring the kidneys.

Mustard Greens Leaves of the mustard plant, containing an incomplete protein and small amount of carbohydrates and a rich supply of minerals; having an alkali excess; high in vitamin A, small amount of B-complex, and a fair C content.

Mutton Flesh of the fully grown sheep; rich in complete protein and fat; very rich in potassium, and phosphorus and high in sulphur acids; having an acid excess with a small amount of vitamins A and B-complex. Mutton fat is very difficult to digest.

Nectarine A tree fruit, containing a rich amount of carbohydrates and sugar; a small quantity of minerals; having an alkali excess and a small amount of vitamin C.

Nuts Virtually every nut is rich in protein, fat and carbohydrates; also in potassium, sodium, calcium and phosphorus and sulphur acids; having an acid excess. (See chapter on Nuts & Dried Fruit.)

Oats A grain, containing a rich supply of incomplete protein, starches, potassium, phosphorus and sulphur and silicious acids; having an acid excess and small quantity of vitamins A and B-complex.

Okra A vegetable, a tall plant with mucilaginous green pods, containing a rich supply of incomplete protein and carbohydrates; also rich in sodium and calcium; having an alkali excess and small amount of vitamin B-complex. Okra has been used for aiding digestion and helping to overcome inflammation of the stomach and intestines.

Olive A tree fruit, having a large quantity of incomplete protein and carbohydrates; very rich in potassium, fat, sodium, and calcium; having an alkali excess and small amount of vitamins A and B1. The cold pressed oil of olives is very healthful and contains more nutritional properties than any other vegetable oil. Olives also contain more protein than any other fruit.

Onion A root-bulb vegetable, containing a small quantity of incomplete protein and a fair amount of sugar; very rich in ethereal mustard oil, potassium and calcium; having a very rich supply of sulphur and an alkali excess; possessing a fair amount of vitamins B-complex and C. Onions are strongly diuretic in their action.

Orange   A citrus fruit, containing a small amount of incomplete protein and a fair supply of sugar; very rich in citric acids and fruit acid salts; rich in calcium and potassium; having an alkali excess and a rich source of vitamins C, B-complex and A.

Oyster   A shellfish, containing a rich source of complete protein and having little fat; rich in sodium, chlorine and potassium; also rich in phosphorus and sulphur acids; strong traces of iodine; having an acid excess and a good supply of vitamins A and B-complex.

Papaya   A pulpy fruit, fairly rich in incomplete protein, sugar and fat; very rich in sodium and magnesium; fairly rich in phosphorus and sulphur; having an alkali excess; a good source of papain, which aids digestion. High in vitamin A, with traces of niacin and good C.

Paprika   A mild, powdered seasoning made from sweet red peppers; contains virtually no nutritional properties and can cause an irritation to the mucous membranes and the intestinal tract.

Parsley   An herb and a vegetable, containing a trace of incomplete protein and ethereal oil; rich in calcium, potassium and magnesium; having an alkali excess and a large quantity of vitamins B-complex and C and a very high amount of vitamin A. Parsley is diuretic in its action. It has also been used in cases of menstrual irregularities. Stimulates digestion.

Parsnip   A root vegetable containing a small quantity of incomplete protein; fairly rich in sugar and very rich in ethereal oil, cellulose, potassium and calcium; having an alkali excess and small amounts of vitamins A and B-complex.

Peach   A tree fruit, having a fair amount of incomplete protein and sugar; very rich in calcium and potassium;

having an alkali excess and fair quantities of vitamins B-complex and C.

Peaches aid digestion; they are also diuretic and laxative.

Peanut A ground-nut, containing a very rich supply of incomplete protein and fat; fair amounts of carbohydrates and purine; very rich in potassium, calcium, magnesium and phosphorus and sulphur acids; having an acid excess and a fair amount of vitamins A and B-complex.

Pear A tree fruit, having a small quantity of incomplete protein; rich in sugar, and potassium; having an alkali excess and a small amount of vitamins B-complex and C.

Pea, Fresh A legume vegetable, containing a fairly rich supply of incomplete protein, sugar and starches; very rich in magnesium, potassium, phosphorus and sulphur acids; having an alkali excess and a small amount of vitamins A, B-complex and C.

Pecan A tree nut, containing the highest oil content of all nuts. They have about 71 percent oil. They also contain all of the elements mentioned under the *Nut* listing. They have a mild laxative effect and should be chewed well before swallowing.

Pepper, Black Spice, ground from seed, used for flavoring and containing a rich supply of acrid ingredients which cause an irritation to the mucous membranes, the kidneys and urethra.

Pepper, White Spice, ground from seed, used for flavoring and containing about twice as much acrid-tasting ingredients as the black pepper, but white pepper is milder because it contains less acrid resins.

Persimmon A fruit, having a small quantity of incomplete protein and a good supply of carbohydrates; rich in potassium and fair in phosphorus acid; having an alkali excess, high vitamin A and some C. Persimmons have a strong purgative action.

Pickles Small cucumbers or other vegetables or fruits, preserved in vinegar or mustard. They have no beneficial food value and thus should not be eaten regularly.

Pineapple A bush fruit, rich in potassium, malic, citric and tartaric acids; having a high percentage of cellulose and a ferment known as papain, which neutralizes protein acids; having an alkali excess.

Fresh pineapples have been used for poor digestion and constipation. They supply the weak stomach with the lacking acid salts and act as a disinfectant for the digestion of food. They have a diuretic action.

Pine Nut (Pignolia) Containing the highest percentage of protein of any nut (33.9 percent) (see chapter on *Nuts*); also rich in mineral elements, fat, and tannic acid; having an acid excess and small amount of vitamin B-complex.

Plum A tree fruit, containing a fair amount of incomplete protein; very rich in sugar and some fruit acid salts; high content of postassium; having an alkali excess and a small amount of vitamin B-complex. Plums are beneficial for relief of constipation and hemorrhoids. Due to their stimulating effect upon the intestines they have also been used in liver ailments.

Pork Flesh of the domestic pig; rich in complete protein and fat; very rich in sulphur acids and phosphorus; having an acid excess and only traces of vitamins A and B-complex.

Potato A root vegetable, containing a small amount of valuable protein and rich in starches; very rich in potassium and traces of iodine; having an alkali excess and small amounts of vitamins A, B-complex and C.

Potato, Sweet A root vegetable, containing a small quantity of incomplete protein with larger amounts of sugar and starches; very rich in calcium and potassium with traces of iodine; having an alkali excess and containing a very good supply of vitamin A, with a small amount of vitamins B-complex and C.

Pumpkin A vegetable of the squash family, containing a poor amount of incomplete protein; fairly large quantity of sugar and cellulose; very low in sodium and a fair amount of potassium; having an alkali excess, excellent vitamin A and an adequate supply of B-complex and C.

Quince A fruit, having a low supply of incomplete protein, high sugar and fruit acid salts, also some tannic ingredients; fair in cellulose, potassium and pectin; having an alkali excess; low vitamin A, B-complex and C.

Radish A root vegetable, having a poor supply of incomplete protein; fairly rich in sugar and mustard oil; having a large quantity of cellulose and potassium; having an alkali excess and small quantities of vitamins B1, B6 and C.
Radishes are strongly diuretic. They also stimulate the appetite and digestion.

Radish, Horse A root vegetable, containing a small amount of incomplete protein and only traces of fat; having a large quantity of carbohydrates and raw fiber and ethereal mustard oil; very rich in calcium, potassium and phosphorus acid; also rich in sulphur acid; having an alkali excess and no known vitamins.
Mustard oil tends to irritate the kidneys, the bladder and mucous membranes of the digestive tract. Horse radish does stimulate the appetite and digestion and aids in loosening phlegm.

Raisin The dried fruit of the grape, containing a rich supply of incomplete protein, sugar and cellulose; also rich in calcium, potassium, magnesium and phosphorus and sulphur acids and chlorine with traces of iodine; having an alkali excess and very small amounts of vitamin B-complex.

Raspberry A bush berry, having a small amount of incomplete protein and a large supply of sugar; rich in vitamins C and B-complex with an alkali excess.

Rhubarb A vegetable (but eaten cooked as fruit), containing a small amount of incomplete protein, sugar and fruit acid salts, particularly oxalic acid; good in potassium; having an alkali excess, low in vitamin A, and only a trace of vitamins C and B-complex.

Romaine   Has the same composition as that of common lettuce with the exception of almost double the amount of vitamin A.

Spinach   A leafy vegetable, containing a good supply of incomplete protein; rich in mineral salts and having an alkali excess. Raw spinach juice has a fair amount of iron, excellent vitamin A, low B-complex and C.

Squash   A pulpy vegetable, containing a small amount of incomplete protein; rich in minerals, particularly potassium; having an alkali excess and a rich source of vitamin B-complex, a good supply of A and a small amount of C.

Strawberries   A berry, containing a rich fruit sugar and potent bactericidal elements; having an alkali excess with some minerals, incomplete protein and a fair supply of vitamin C.

Sugar   Containing virtually no food value and the most overrated mass-consumed food item in America. All sugars belong to the carbohydrate group. The unprocessed, unrefined, raw sugar is better than the white sugar which is too concentrated and acid-forming. Sugar should not be used. Raw honey makes an excellent substitute for sugar and has none of the harmful elements of refined sugar.

Tomatoes   A berry (but eaten as a vegetable), containing a rich supply of potassium, low in other minerals; also rich in vitamin A, good in B-complex and C; and having an alkali excess.

Turnips   A root vegetable, having much the same composition as potatoes and can be eaten in place of them.

Vinegar   Wine vinegar made from apple cider; having an acid excess and no beneficial food elements; lemon juice should be used in place of vinegar.

Walnut Containing a rich and incomplete protein, fat and starches; small amount of calcium, fair amount of potassium and magnesium and phosphorus and sulphur acids; having an acid excess and small amounts of vitamins A and B-complex.

Yogurt A custard-like food prepared from milk curdled by bacteria and often sweetened or flavored with fruit; containing a good supply of complete protein; rich in phosphorus and sulphur; low in potassium and sodium; very low in fat (about 96 percent fat free); because of its oxidizing ferments and natural beneficial bacteria, yogurt is easy to digest; rich in vitamin B1, traces of D and C.

FOOD COMBINING

There are two basic rules that one must follow to maintain a healthy eating program. The first is to understand exactly which foods contain what food values and secondly, how should one combine foods in order to fully utilize, digest and assimilate them.

The following chapter explains the proper combination in which foods should be eaten.

The following menus constitute properly combined meals. The amount of each food eaten depends upon the individual. It is rather obvious that most Americans are not yet ready to discipline themselves to eating all of the right combinations and foods, all of the time. This chapter on food combining should serve as an illustration and guide to what the proper combinations are and why you should try to understand them. We realize that changing the American diet and methods of eating will take years, but if they at least are shown what constitutes the ultimate method, it may help those few who wish to gradually make the change in diet. This same principle applies to every chapter in this book.

Use the information in this chapter, as well as the rest of this book, merely as guides and learn to prepare your own menus.

The following menus were compiled from the years of extensive work and research by one of the world's most renowned nutritionists, Dr. Herbert M. Shelton, at his Health School in San Antonio, Texas.

HOW TO EAT FRUITS
Fruits undergo little or no digestion in the mouth and stomach and are, as a rule, quickly sent into the intestine, where they undergo the little digestion they require. To eat

them with other foods that do require considerable time in the stomach is to have them held up there pending the completion of the digestion of the other foods. Bacterial decomposition follows.

Fruits should not be eaten between meals. To eat them between meals is to put them into the stomach while the stomach is still busily engaged in digesting the previous meal.

It is suggested that the fruit meal be eaten for breakfast. Do not add sugar to the fruits.

Oranges	Fresh Figs	Mangoes
Grapefruit	Peaches	Cherries
	Apricots	Apricots
Oranges	Cherries	Cherries
Apples	Apricots	Peaches
	Plums	Nectarines
Grapefruit	Bananas	Berries with Cream
Apples	Pears	(no sugar)
	Grapes	
Mangoes	Bananas	Apples
Cherries	Persimmons	Grapes
Apricots	Dates	Dates
		Glass of Sour Milk
Apples	Dates	Bananas
Grapes	Apples	Pear
Papaya	Pears	Figs
Figs		Glass of Sour Milk

As a variation, a very healthy and tasty meal may be made of a fruit salad and a protein as follows:

A large fruit salad composed of:
Grapefruit, orange, apple, pineapple, lettuce, celery, four ounces of cottage cheese or four ounces of nuts, or a greater amount of avocado.

HOW TO EAT STARCH

It is suggested that the starch meal should be eaten at noontime. Starches should be eaten dry and should be thoroughly chewed and insalivated before swallowing. Acids should not be eaten on the salad with the starch meal. We suggest a very large salad with the protein meal and a smaller one for the starch meal. Again, we stress, only eat until you are comfortably full, try not to stuff yourself by overeating.

Vegetable Salad	Vegetable Salad	Vegetable Salad
Turnip Greens	Spinach	String Beans
Yellow Squash	String Beans	Mashed Rutabaga
Chestnuts	Coconut	Irish Potatoes

Vegetable Salad	Vegetable Salad	Vegetable Salad
Spinach	Spinach	Asparagus
Beets	Turnips	Okra
Irish Potatoes	Jerusalem Artichoke	Peanuts

Vegetable Salad	Vegetable Salad	Vegetable Salad
Chard	Spinach	Okra
Carrots	Baked Egg Plant	Beet Greens
Potatoes	Jerusalem Artichoke	Whole Grain Bread

Vegetable Salad	Vegetable Salad	Vegetable Salad
String Beans	Okra	Yellow Wax Beans
Turnips	String Beans	Kale
Sweet Potatoes	Jerusalem Artichoke	Irish Potatoes

Vegetable Salad	Vegetable Salad	Vegetable Salad
Asparagus	Beet Greens	String Beans
White Squash	Okra	Yellow Squash
Yams	Brown Rice	Irish Potatoes

Vegetable Salad	Vegetable Salad	Vegetable Salad
Beet Greens	Turnip Greens	Okra
Cauliflower	Asparagus	Brussel Sprouts
Sweet Potatoes	Brown Rice	Irish Potatoes

Vegetable Salad	Vegetable Salad	Vegetable Salad
Spinach	Collards	String Beans
Red Cabbage	Cauliflower	Cabbage
Baked Caladium Roots	Baked Hubbard Squash	Sweet Potatoes

Vegetable Salad
String Beans
Baked Egg Plant
Steamed Cala-
    dium Roots

Vegetable Salad
Collards
Fresh Corn
Brown Rice

Vegetable Salad
Chard
Broccoli
Yams

Vegetable Salad
Turnip Greens
Okra
Jerusalem
    Artichoke

Vegetable Salad
Kale
String Beans
Baked Hubbard
    Squash

Vegetable Salad
Swiss Chard
Peas
Hubbard Squash

Vegetable Salad
Kale
Okra
Jerusalem
    Artichoke

Vegetable Salad
Green Squash
Fresh Corn
Brown Rice

Vegetable Salad
String Beans
Broccoli
Hubbard Squash

Vegetable Salad
Chard
Yellow Squash
Jerusalem
    Artichoke

Vegetable Salad
Turnip Greens
Broccoli
Peanuts

Vegetable Salad
Spinach
Cabbage
Baked Hubbard
    Squash

Vegetable Salad
Beet Greens
Yellow Squash
Irish Potatoes

Vegetable Salad
Chard
String Beans
Peanuts

Vegetable Salad
Swiss Chard
Yellow Squash
Baked Caladium
    Roots

Vegetable Salad
Kale
Okra
Brown Rice

Vegetable Salad
Spinach
Green String
    Beans
Brown Rice

Vegetable Salad
Okra
Beet Greens
Steamed Caladium
    Roots

Vegetable Salad
Spinach
String Beans
Peanuts

Vegetable Salad
Chard
Okra
Brown Rice

Vegetable Salad
Yellow Squash
Chard
Potatoes

Vegetable Salad
Okra
Cauliflower
Carrots

Vegetable Salad
Chard
Asparagus
Baked Beans

HOW TO EAT PROTEINS

The foods which combine best with proteins of all types are the non-starchy and succulent vegetables. It is suggested that the protein meal should be eaten in the evening. Acids and oils and oily dressings should be reduced to the minimum with protein meals.

Vegetable Salad	Vegetable Salad	Vegetable Salad
Green Squash	Okra	Green Squash
Spinach	Spinach	Kale
Nuts	Nuts	Cheese
Vegetable Salad	Vegetable Salad	Vegetable Salad
Chard	Chard	Collards
Asparagus	Yellow Squash	Yellow Squash
Nuts	Fowl	Lean Meat
Vegetable Salad	Vegetable Salad	Vegetable Salad
Asparagus	Beet Greens	Mustard Greens
Yellow Squash	String Beans	String Beans
Nuts	Fish	Fish
Vegetable Salad	Vegetable Salad	Vegetable Salad
Broccoli	Chard	Turnip Greens
Fresh Corn	Yellow Squash	Green Peas
Nuts	Lamb Chops	Fowl
Vegetable Salad	Vegetable Salad	Vegetable Salad
Yellow Squash	Baked Eggplant	Broccoli
Cabbage	Chard	Green Beans
Sunflower Seeds	Eggs	Nuts
Vegetable Salad	Vegetable Salad	Vegetable Salad
Spinach	Spinach	Steamed Onions
Broccoli	Yellow Squash	Swiss Chard
Lean Meat	Eggs	Cheese
Vegetable Salad	Vegetable Salad	Vegetable Salad
Chard	Turnip Greens	Green Squash
Okra	String Beans	Turnip Greens
Cottage Cheese	Eggs	Roast Beef
Vegetable Salad	Vegetable Salad	Vegetable Salad
Okra	Okra	Red Cabbage
Yellow Squash	Red Cabbage	Spinach
Cottage Cheese	Lean Meat	Cottage Cheese

Vegetable Salad	Vegetable Salad	Vegetable Salad
Chard	Asparagus	Asparagus
Yellow Squash	Cone Artichokes	Broccoli
Fish	Fowl	Eggs
Vegetable Salad	Vegetable Salad	Vegetable Salad
White Cabbage	Beet Greens	Yellow Squash
Spinach	Okra	Chard
Nuts	Sunflower Seeds	Lean Meat
Vegetable Salad	Vegetable Salad	Vegetable Salad
Spinach	Kale	Baked Eggplant
Green Squash	String Beans	Kale
Cottage Cheese	Sunflower Seeds	Fish
Vegetable Salad	Vegetable Salad	Vegetable Salad
Beet Greens	Baked Eggplant	Yellow Squash
Green Peas	Chard	Mustard Greens
Cottage Cheese	Soy Sprouts	Pecans
Vegetable Salad	Vegetable Salad	Vegetable Salad
Yellow Squash	Asparagus	String Beans
Broccoli	Green Beans	Avocado
Cottage Cheese	Walnuts	Lean Meat
Vegetable Salad	Vegetable Salad	Vegetable Salad
Spinach	Okra	Brussels Sprouts
Cabbage	Beet Greens	Kale
Fish	Sunflower Seeds	Eggs

EATING SCHEDULE FOR A WEEK

Again I wish to stress that all the menus given in this book are intended merely as guides to the reader to assist him in understanding the principles of food combining and enable him to work out his own menus.

The same foods are not always available in all parts of the country. A food that is available in one section of the country at one time of the year may be available in another part of the country at a different time of the year. Food availability varies with season, climate, altitude, soil and market facilities. The man who knows how to combine his meals may make use of the foods which are at hand and work out a meal. The man who depends on a cut-and-dried book of menus and does not know how to combine his foods may find that the particular foods listed in the menu for today are not available; he is left out on a limb. What he usually does is take the easy way out and eat indiscriminately. If you are at the home of a friend or relative, your book of menus can be of no service to you; but if you know how to combine your foods, you may usually pick out compatible combinations from the foods spread before you and eat a well-combined meal.

Learn the principles of food combining so that you may properly apply them in any and all circumstances in which you may find yourself. A child may be able to follow a chart; an intelligent adult should learn principles and learn to apply these. Once you have done this and have practiced properly combining your foods for a time, the practice becomes automatic and you do not have to spend a lot of time on it. Above all things, do not become a crank or fanatic on the matter. Eat your meal and forget it. Let your friends eat their foods and don't give them a lecture on dietetics at the dining table.

The following two weekly schedules are designed to demonstrate the proper ways to combine foods at different seasons of the year. The first week's schedule covers foods available in Spring and Summer. The second week's schedule covers foods available in Fall and Winter. Use these merely as guides and learn to prepare your own menus. The proteins are only suggestions and may be changed to suit taste.

SPRING AND SUMMER MENUS

Sunday

BREAKFAST	LUNCH	DINNER
Watermelon	Vegetable Salad	Vegetable Salad
	Chard	String Beans
	Yellow Squash	Okra
	Potatoes	Lean Meat

Monday

Peaches	Vegetable Salad	Vegetable Salad
Cherries	Beet Greens	Spinach
Apricots	Carrots	Cabbage
	Baked Beans	Fowl

Tuesday

BREAKFAST	LUNCH	DINNER
Cantaloupes	Vegetable Salad	Vegetable Salad
	Okra	Broccoli
	Green Squash	Fresh Corn
	Jerusalem	Eggs
	Artichoke	

Wednesday

Berries with	Vegetable Salad	Vegetable Salad
Cream	Cauliflower	Green Squash
(no sugar)	Okra	Turnip Greens
	Brown Rice	Lean meat

Thursday

Nectarines	Vegetable Salad	Vegetable Salad
Apricots	Green Cabbage	Beet Greens
Plums	Carrots	String Beans
	Sweet Potatoes	Fowl

Friday

Watermelon	Vegetable Salad	Vegetable Salad
	Baked Eggplant	Yellow Squash
	Chard	Spinach
	Whole Wheat	Fish
	Bread	

Saturday

Bananas	Vegetable Salad	Vegetable Salad
Cherries	Green Beans	Lean Meat
Glass of Sour	Okra	Broccoli
Milk	Irish Potatoes	Soy Sprouts

FALL AND WINTER MENUS

Sunday

Grapes	Vegetable Salad	Vegetable Salad
Bananas	Chinese Cabbage	Spinach
Dates	Asparagus	Yellow Squash
	Baked Caladium	Fish
	Roots	

Monday

Persimmons	Vegetable Salad	Vegetable Salad
Pear	Kale	Brussels Sprouts

BREAKFAST	LUNCH	DINNER
Grapes	Cauliflower	String Beans
	Yams	Fowl

Tuesday

Apples	Vegetable Salad	Vegetable Salad
Grapes	Turnip Greens	Kale
Dried Figs	Okra	Yellow Squash
	Brown Rice	Lean Meat

Wednesday

Pears	Vegetable Salad	Vegetable Salad
Persimmons	Broccoli	Okra
Banana	String Beans	Spinach
Glass of Sour Milk	Irish Potatoes	Fish

Thursday

Papaya	Vegetable Salad	Vegetable Salad
Orange	Green Squash	Red Cabbage
	Parsnips	String Beans
	Whole Grain Bread	Fowl

Friday

Persimmons	Vegetable Salad	Vegetable Salad
Grapes	Carrots	Chard
Dates	Spinach	Yellow Squash
	Steamed Caladium Roots	Cheese (Swiss, American, Cheddar etc.)

Saturday

Grapefruit	Vegetable Salad	Vegetable Salad
	Fresh Peas	Spinach
	Kale	Steamed Onions
	Coconut	Lamb Chops

Sunday

Honey Dew Melon	Vegetable Salad	Vegetable Salad
	String Beans	Baked Eggplant
	Vegetable Soup	Kale
	Yams	Eggs

It is impossible to overestimate the importance of good digestion. Upon the efficiency of the digestive process depends the preparation of the raw materials of nutrition; hence, upon good digestion depends, to a very large extent, the well-being of the body. There can be no such thing as good assimilation and nutrition without good digestion. The best of diets fails to yield up its greatest good when the digestive process fails in the work of preparing it for use by the body.

Good digestion means more normal tissue change throughout the body. Improved digestion results in general improvement in all of the functions of life. Take the time to make sure your digestion is proper.

FOODSTUFFS CLASSIFIED

Foodstuffs are composed of water and a few organic compounds known as proteins, carbohydrates, sugars, starches, pentosans, fats, mineral salts, and vitamins. These types of foodstuffs constitute the raw materials of nutrition. As proteins, carbohydrates and fats, they are not usable by the body. They must first undergo a disintegrating, refining and standardizing process more commonly known as digestion. Although this process of digestion is partly mechanical, as in the chewing, swallowing and emulsifying of food, the physiology of digestion is very largely a study of the chemical changes foods undergo in their passage through the alimentary canal. For our present purposes, we will concentrate on the mouth and stomach digestion.

Before a study of the enzymatic digestion process is examined, you should first be able to distinguish different foodstuffs. The following classifications of foods will guide you in your combinations. Some complex foods appear in more than one section.

PROTEINS

Nuts	All Cereals	Dry Beans
Dry Peas	Soy Beans	Peanuts
Avocados	Cheese	Olives
Fowl	Milk	Cocoanut
Lean Meat	Fish	

CARBOHYDRATES
The carbohydrates are the starches and sugars.

STARCHES:

All Cereals	Potatoes	Banana Squash
Dry Peas	Hubbard Squash	Jerusalem
Peanuts	Caladium Root	Artichokes
Pumpkin	Cakes	Flour
Bread	Pies	Pastas
Dry Beans	Chestnuts	

MILDLY STARCHY:

Cauliflower	Beets	Carrots
Rutabaga	Salsify	

SYRUPS AND SUGARS:

Brown Sugar	Cane Syrup	Molasses
Maple Syrup	Milk Sugar	
White Sugar	Honey	

SWEET FRUITS:

Banana	Date	Fig
Raisin	Grape	Prune
Sun-dried Pear	Persimmon	

FATS

Olive Oil	Soy Oil	Butter
Sesame Oil	Corn Oil	Butter Substitutes
Cream	Nut Oils	Most Nuts
Pecans	Avocados	Cotton Seed Oil
Fat Meats	Lard	
Tallow	Sunflower Seed Oil	

ACID FRUITS

Orange	Grapefruit	Pineapple
Pomegranate	Sour Apple	Lime
Sour Peach	Tomato	Sour Grape
Lemon	Sour Plum	Sour Cherry

SUB-ACID FRUITS:

Fresh Fig	Pineapple	Sweet Cherry
Papaya	Pear	Sweet Apple
Apricot	Sweet Peach	Huckleberry
Mango	Sweet Plum	

NON-STARCHY AND GREEN VEGETABLES

Lettuce	Cabbage	Green Peas
Chicory	Brussels Sprouts	Endive
Broccoli	Dandelion	Cauliflower
Spinach	Chard	Collards
Turnip Tops	Chinese Cabbage	Beet Tops
Cow-Slip	Mustard	Okra
Turnip	Kale	Chive
Green Beans	Green Corn	Dock
Sorrel	Cucumber	Egg-plant
Water Cress	Parsley	Kohlrabi
Leeks	Onions	Rhubarb
Escarole	Garlic	Scallions
Summer Squash	Cardoon	Zuccini
Sweet Pepper	Asparagus	Bamboo Shoots
Celery	Broccoli	Radish

MELONS

Water Melon	Musk Melon	Honey Dew
Honey Balls	Banana Melon	Pie Melon
Cantaloupe	Casaba	Crenshaw Melon
Christmas Melon	Persian Melon	Nutmeg Melon

DIGESTION

The changes through which foods go in the processes of digestion are effected by a group of agencies known as enzymes or unorganized ferments.

It is important to know how an enzyme works. An enzyme may be appropriately defined as a physiological catalyst. Many substances do not normally combine when brought into contact with each other, yet they may be made to do so by a third substance when it is brought into contact with them. This third substance does not in any way enter into the combination, or share in the reaction; its mere presence seems to bring about the combination and reaction. Such a substance or agent is called a catalyst, the process is called catalysis.

Plants and animals manufacture soluble catalytic substances, colloidal in nature but resistant to heat, which they employ in the many processes of splitting up of compounds and the making of new ones within themselves. To these substances the term enzyme has been applied. Enzymes are known for their protein character. These enzymes are involved in the reduction of complex food substances to simpler compounds that are acceptable to the bloodstream and usable by the cells of the body in the production of new cells.

As the action of enzymes in the digestion of foodstuffs closely resembles fermentation, these substances were formerly referred to as ferments. Fermentation, however, is accomplished by organized ferments—bacteria. The products of fermentation are not identical with the products of enzymatic disintegration of foodstuffs and are not suitable as nutritive materials. Rather, they are poisonous. Putrefaction, also the result of bacterial action, also gives rise to poisons, some of them very virulent, rather than to nutritive materials.

Each enzyme is specific in its action. It acts only upon one class of food substances. The enzymes which act upon carbohydrates do not and cannot act upon proteins nor upon salts or fats. Even in the digestion of closely related substances, such as the disaccharides (complex sugars), the enzyme that acts upon maltose is not capable of acting upon lactose. Each sugar seems to require its own specific enzyme.

This specific action of enzymes is of importance, as there are various stages in the digestion of foodstuffs, each stage requiring the action of a different enzyme, and the various enzymes being capable of performing their work only if the preceding work has been properly performed by the enzymes that also precede. If *pepsin*, for example, has not converted proteins into peptones, the enzymes that convert peptones into amino acids will not be able to act upon the proteins.

The substance upon which an enzyme acts is called a substrate. Thus starch is the substrate of ptyalin. Each enzyme is apparently adapted to or fitted to a certain definite structure.

Digestion commences in the mouth. All foods are broken up into smaller particles by the process of chewing, and they are thoroughly saturated with saliva. Of the chemical part of digestion, only starch digestion begins in the mouth. The saliva of the mouth, which is normally an alkaline fluid,

FOOD COMBINING   167

contains an enzyme called ptyalin, which acts upon starch, breaking this down into maltose, a complex sugar, which is further acted upon in the intestine by maltase and converted into a simple sugar dextrose. The action of ptyalin upon starch is preparatory, as maltase cannot act upon starch. Amylase, the starch-splitting enzyme of the pancreatic secretion, is said to act upon starch much as does ptyalin, so that starch that escapes digestion in the mouth and stomach may be split into maltose and achroodextrin.

Ptyalin is destroyed by a mild acid and also by a strong alkaline reaction. It can act only in an alkaline medium and this must not be strongly alkaline. It is this limitation of the enzyme that renders important the manner in which we mix our starches, for if they are mixed with foods which are acid or that provide for acid secretion in the stomach, the action of the ptyalin is brought to an end.

Stomach, or gastric juice ranges all the way from nearly neutral in reaction to strongly acid, depending upon the character of the food eaten. It contains three enzymes: pepsin, which acts upon proteins; lipase, which has slight action upon fats; and rennin, which coagulates milk. Pepsin acts only in an acid medium and is destroyed by an alkali. Low temperature, as when iced drinks are taken, retards and even suspends the action of pepsin. Alcohol precipitates this enzyme.

The body adapts its secretions to the different kinds of foodstuffs which are consumed. The varying amounts and proportions of the various elements which enter into the composition of the gastric juice give a juice of varying character and adapted to the digestion of different kinds of foodstuffs.

Weak acids occasion a copious flow of saliva, while weak alkalis occasion no salivary secretion. Disagreeable and noxious substances also occasion salivary secretion in an effort to flush away the offending material.

An excellent example of this ability of the body to modify and adapt its secretions to the varying needs of various kinds of foods is supplied us by the dog. Feed him flesh and there is a secretion of thick, viscous saliva, chiefly from the submaxillary gland. Feed him dried and pulverized flesh and a very copious and watery secretion will be poured out upon it, coming from the parotid gland. The

mucous secretion poured out upon flesh serves to lubricate
the bolus of food and thus facilitate swallowing. The thin,
watery secretion, on the other hand, poured out upon the
dry powder, washes the powder from the mouth. Thus, the
kind of juice poured out is determined by the purpose it
must serve.

RIGHT AND WRONG COMBINATIONS

To fully understand what combinations of foodstuffs you
can digest, it will be necessary to consider, one by one,
the possible combinations and analyze these in their relation to the facts of digestion.

ACID-STARCH COMBINATIONS

A weak acid will destroy the ptyalin of the saliva. With
the destruction of the ptyalin, starch digestion must come
to a halt. Yet we constantly eat acid fruits before our
breakfast cereal and notice no ill effects. Starch which
escapes digestion at this stage is destined to be acted upon
by the pancreatic juice, and the final result may be entirely
satisfactory. Still it is reasonable to assume that the greater
the work done by the saliva, the lighter will be the task
remaining for the other secretions and the greater the
probability of its complete accomplishment.

There is sufficient acetic acid in one or two teaspoonsful
of vinegar to entirely suspend salivary digestion. The acid
of tomatoes, berries, oranges, grapefruits, lemons, limes,
pineapples, sour apples, sour grapes, and other sour fruits
is sufficient to destroy the ptyalin of the saliva and suspend
starch digestion.

Therefore, until it can be shown that saliva is capable
of digesting starch without the presence of ptyalin, we shall
have to insist that acid-starch combinations are indigestible.

Our advice then, should be: Eat acids and starches at
separate meals.

PROTEIN-STARCH COMBINATIONS

The acid which is highly favorable to gastric digestion
is quite prohibitive to salivary digestion. The power to digest protein is manifested only with an acid reaction, and
is permanently lost when the mixture is made distinctly
alkaline. The conditions which permit peptic digestion to

take place are, therefore, precisely those which exclude the action of saliva.

When we eat carbohydrates the stomach secretes an appropriate juice, a gastric juice of different composition from that which it secretes if it finds proteins coming down. This is a response to the particular demand that is being made on the stomach.

When bread is eaten, little hydrochloric acid is poured into the stomach. The juice secreted upon bread is almost neutral in reaction. When the starch of the bread is digested, much hydrochloric acid is then poured into the stomach to digest the protein of the bread. The two processes, the digestion of starch and the digestion of protein, do not go on simultaneously with great efficiency. On the contrary, the secretions are nicely and minutely adjusted, both as to character and to timing, to the varying needs of the complex food substance.

Herein lies the answer to those who object to food combining because "nature combines various food substances in the same food." There is a great difference between the digestion of a single food, however complex its composition, and the digestion of a mixture of different foods. The body can easily adjust its juices to a single article of food that is a starch-protein combination, both as to strength and timing. But when two foods are eaten with different, even opposite digestive needs, this precise adjustment of juices to requirements becomes impossible. If bread and flesh are eaten together, instead of an almost neutral gastric juice being poured into the stomach during the first two hours of digestion, a highly acid juice will be poured out immediately and starch digestion will come to an almost abrupt end.

The first steps in the digestion of starches and proteins take place in opposite media—starch requiring an alkaline medium, protein requiring an acid medium in which to digest. Since gastric juice digests protein and saliva digests starch, it is obvious that for efficient digestion the meat (protein) part of a meal should come first and the starch part second. If you eat your protein first and your starch last, the protein will digest in the lower end of the stomach while the starch will digest in the upper end.

When the average man or woman eats flesh, eggs, cheese,

he or she takes bread with the protein. Hot dogs, ham sandwiches, hamburgers, toast and eggs, ham on rye and similar combinations of protein and starch represent the common practice of eating such foods. The stomach has no mechanism for separating these thoroughly intermixed substances and partitioning them off in separate areas.

Mixing foods in this manner is not seen in nature.

On the basis of these facts we offer our second rule for food combining. It is: Eat protein foods and carbohydrate foods at separate meals.

By this is meant that cereals, bread, potatoes and other starch foods should be eaten separately from flesh, eggs, cheese, fish, and other protein foods.

PROTEIN-PROTEIN COMBINATIONS

Two proteins of different character and different composition, and associated with other and different food factors call for different modifications of the digestive secretions and different timing of the secretions in order to digest them efficiently. For example, the strongest juice is poured out upon milk in the last hour of digestion, upon flesh in the first hour. Eggs receive the strongest secretion at a different time to that received by either flesh or milk. Therefore, eggs should not be taken with flesh or milk.

The digestive process is modified to meet the digestive requirements of each protein food and it is impossible for this to be modified in such a manner as to meet the requirements of two different proteins at the same meal. This may not mean that two different kinds of flesh may not be taken together or that two kinds of nuts may not be eaten together at the same time; but it does mean that such protein combinations as flesh and eggs, flesh and nuts, flesh and cheese, eggs and milk, eggs and nuts, cheese and nuts, milk and nuts, etc., should not be taken. One protein food at a meal will assure greater efficiency in digestion.

Our rule, then, should be: Eat but one concentrated protein food at a meal.

An objection has been offered to this rule that is as follows: the various proteins vary so greatly in their amino-acid content and the body requires adequate quantities of certain of these so that it is necessary to consume more than one protein in order to assure an adequate supply of amino-acids. But inasmuch as most people eat more than one meal a day and there is protein in almost everything we eat, this objection is invalid. One does not have to consume all of his protein at any one meal.

ACID-PROTEIN COMBINATIONS

The active work of splitting up (digesting) complex protein substances is accomplished by the enzyme, pepsin. Pepsin acts only in an acid medium; its action is stopped by alkali. When proteins are eaten the gastric juice is acid, for it must furnish a favorable medium for the action of pepsin.

Because pepsin is active only in an acid medium, the mistake has been made of assuming that the taking of acids with the meal will assist in the digestion of proteins. Actually, on the contrary, these acids inhibit the outpouring of gastric juice and thus interfere with the digestion of proteins. Fruit acids demoralize gastric digestion, either by destroying the pepsin, or by inhibiting its secretion. Gastric juice is not poured out in the presence of acid in the mouth and stomach.

The normal stomach secretes all the acid required by pepsin in digesting a reasonable quantity of protein. An abnormal stomach may secrete too much acid (hyperacidity) or an insufficient amount (hypoacidity). In either case, taking acids with proteins does not aid digestion.

Based on these simple facts, our suggestion is: Eat proteins and acids at separate meals.

When we consider the actual process of protein digestion in the stomach and the positive inhibiting effects of acids upon gastric secretion, we realize the fallacy of consuming pineapple juice or grapefruit juice or tomato juice with meat, and the fallacy of beating up eggs in orange juice to make the so-called "pep-cocktail."

Lemon juice, vinegar or other acid used on salads, or added to the salad dressing, and eaten with a protein meal, serve as a severe check to hydrochloric acid secretion and thus interfere with protein digestion.

Although nuts or cheese with acid fruits do not constitute ideal combinations, we may make exceptions to the foregoing rule in the case of these two articles of food. Nuts and cheese containing, as they do, considerable oil and fat (cream), are about the only exceptions to the rule that when acids are taken with protein, putrefaction occurs. These foods do not decompose as quickly as other protein when they are not immediately digested. Furthermore, acids do not delay the digestion of nuts and cheese; because these foods contain enough fat to inhibit gastric secretion for a longer time than do acids.

FAT-PROTEIN COMBINATIONS

Fat exerts inhibiting influence on the secretion of gastric juice. The presence of fat in the food lessens the amount of appetite secretion that is poured into the stomach, lessens the amount of "chemical secretion" poured out, lessens the activity of the gastric glands, lowers the amount of pepsin and hydrochloric acid in the gastric juice and may lower gastric tone by as much as half. This inhibiting effect may last two or more hours.

This means that when protein food is eaten, fat should not be taken at the same meal. In other words, such foods as cream, butter, oils of various kinds, gravies, fat meats, etc., should not be consumed at the same meal with nuts, cheese, eggs, flesh. It will be noted, in this connection, that those foods that normally contain fat within themselves, as nuts or cheese or milk, require longer time to digest than those protein foods that are lacking in fat.

Our fourth suggestion, then, is: Eat fats and proteins at separate meals.

It is well to know that an abundance of green vegetables, especially uncooked ones, counteract the inhibiting effect of fat, so that if one must have fat with one's protein, one may offset its inhibiting effect upon the digestion of protein by consuming much green substances with the meal.

SUGAR-PROTEIN COMBINATIONS

All sugars—commercial sugars, syrups, sweet fruits, honey, etc., have an inhibiting effect upon the secretion of gastric juice and upon the motility of the stomach. Sugars taken with proteins hinder protein digestion. Sugars are digested in the intestine. If taken alone they are not held in the stomach long, but are quickly sent into the intestine. When eaten with other foods, either proteins or starches, they are held up in the stomach for a prolonged period, awaiting the digestion of the other food. While thus awaiting the completion of protein or starch digestion they undergo fermentation.

Based on these simple facts our suggestion is: Eat sugars and proteins at separate meals.

SUGAR-STARCH COMBINATIONS

Starch digestion normally begins in the mouth and continues, for some time in the stomach. Sugars do not undergo any digestion in either the mouth or stomach, but in the small intestine only. When consumed alone sugars are quickly sent out of the stomach into the intestine. As they tend to ferment very quickly under the conditions of warmth and moisture existing in the stomach, this type of eating almost guarantees acid fermentation.

Jellies, jams, fruit butters, commercial sugar (white or brown, beet, cane, or lactic), honey, molasses, syrups, etc., added to cakes, breads, pastries, cereals, potatoes, etc., produce fermentation. The regularity with which millions of people eat cereals and sugar for breakfast and suffer with sour stomach, sour eructations, and other evidences of indigestion as a consequence, would seem to verify the need for a better understanding of proper food combining.

Sweet fruits with starch also result in fermentation. Breads containing dates, raisins, figs, etc., are improper combinations. In many quarters it is thought that if honey is used instead of sugar this may be avoided, but such is not the case. Honey with hot cakes, syrup with hot cakes, etc., are sure to ferment.

There is every reason to believe that the presence of the sugar with starch definitely interferes with the digestion of starch. When sugar is taken into the mouth there is a copious outpouring of saliva, but it contains no ptyalin for ptyalin does not act upon sugar.

Foods that are wholesome by themselves or in certain combinations often disagree when eaten with others. For example, bread and butter taken together cause no unpleasantness, but if sugar or jam or marmalade is added, trouble will follow. Mixtures of starch and sugar invite fermentation.

Upon these facts we base this suggestion: Eat starches and sugars at separate meals.

EATING MELONS

Many people complain that melons do not agree with them. Yet melons are such wholesome foods and are so easy to digest that even the most feeble digestions can handle them.

Melons undergo no digestion in the stomach. The little digestion they require takes place in the intestine. If taken properly, they are retained in the stomach but a few minutes and are then passed into the intestine. But if taken with other foods that require a lengthy stay in the stomach for salivary or gastric digestion, they are held up in the stomach. As they decompose very quickly when cut open and kept in a warm place, they are prone to give rise to much gas and discomfort when eaten with other foods.

Therefore, we suggest that you eat melons alone.

TAKE MILK ALONE

It is the rule of nature that the young of each species takes its milk alone. Milk is the food of the young. There is no need for it after the end of the normal suckling period. The dairy industry and the medical profession have taught us that we need a quart of milk a day as long as we live. In fact, this is simply a commercial program and expresses no human need.

Due to its protein and fat content, milk combines poorly with all foods. It will combine fairly well with acid fruits. The first thing that occurs when it enters the stomach is that it coagulates—forms curds. These curds tend to form around the particles of other food in the stomach thus insulating them against the gastric juice. This prevents their digestion until after the milk curd is digested.

Our suggestion is: Take milk alone.

ACID-ALKALINE BALANCE

In no condition of imbalance that arises in the body functions can we place the blame on one gland or organ and say it is entirely to blame; every disease or illness is pluri-glandular or pluri-organic in effect.

When attacking the problem of the acid-alkaline balance and the effects of imbalance, it is difficult to decide where to begin. Because of the collapse of the parotid gland, it would seem that a knowledge of the functions of the salivary glands was of primary importance, but later, we realize that the real balancer is the pituitary gland, and that the other glandular bodies are merely subsidiaries.

Among the eleven or more distinct activities of the pituitary gland is the stimulation of the thyroid gland, the stimulation of growth, of sexual development, of metabolism, that is, of digestion and assimilation, the regulation of the fluid intake and output, and the stimulation of lactation. It also initiates the flow of blood of menstruation and has a steadying influence on gaseous metabolism.

The question now arises—with such a versatile gland in control of practically all bodily functions, how could anyone ever suffer an imbalance?

There is only one answer. When the food intake is of such a quality, or lack of quality, that one by one the subsidiary glands become overworked and congested, the whole of the body mechanism is thrown out of action. It is a well-established fact that, apart from accidents, a well-nourished person does not lose balance because of shock, disappointment, emotional upset or such.

Take, for instance, the functions of the chief subsidiary, the thyroid gland, and trace the reason for the breakdown of this greatly misunderstood organ. Its very name, taken from the Greek, Thureos, meaning shield, gives us an indication of its tremendous implication. Its special duty, from the nutritional point of view, is to shield the body from absorbing and neutralizing the toxic waste from proteins. For this purpose it uses iodine, which, because of its alkaline basis, has the power to neutralize acid. From this brief analysis, we affirm that the chief cause of thyroid imbalance is probably the over-consumption of animal protein.

Aside from the amount of protein that the average person requires to replace tissue and supply heat it is also important to know what the capacity is of the individual to handle it. The same applies to all classes of food. It is what we are able to digest and assimilate that makes the difference between health and illness.

The largest gland in the body is the liver, whose chief function is the secretion of bile which passes into the intestines, where it assists digestion by emulsifying fats. This gland also stimulates peristalsis, which is the term used to describe the wave-like contractions which travel along the alimentary tract, thus forcing the contents onward. Another important duty of the liver, carried out with the assistance of the spleen, is that of breaking up worn-out blood cells, and in this way, is constantly detoxicating the circulation.

The pancreas gland measures about six inches in length and secretes a digestive fluid containing ferments which act upon all classes of foods. Its most important function is the secretion of insulin which regulates sugar metabolism as well as that of fats. Although it is seldom given any credit for it, the pancreas is also a detoxicator. In this, it appears to work with the suprarenal glands. The latter attend to the healing of cuts and wounds and, while the pancreas is working normally, provide immunity against infection. This explains why the advanced diabetic has little or no defense against infection and why a simple cut or wound will remain unhealed for a long time.

To appreciate the importance of the suprarenal glands and their relation to the subject under discussion, it is necessary to recount some of the functions of the kidneys, with which they are closely associated. In common with the lungs, the alimentary tract and the skin, the kidneys belong to the excretory system and the suprarenals play a large part in the stimulation of all the excretory processes. In fact, they are the energizers of the entire body activities, whether mental, emotional, physical or spiritual.

The urine of a healthy person consist of about 95 percent water and contains inorganic salts and organic waste material which includes urea, creatinin and uric acids. In its role of defender, the kidney has the ability to separate harmful substances and iron tablets, pep drugs, animal hormones and undigested proteins from the fluids and eliminate them in the urine. Permanent injury could result from an overaccumulation of these substances, if the system cannot eliminate them completely.

Since nothing depletes the suprarenals as quickly as toxemia, symptoms of imbalance of these glands are easy to detect. They include dryness of the mouth; hot flushes and sudden chills, due to circulatory troubles; muscular weakness; a sense of overall weakness; a fall in blood sugar; and nervous tension.

Attention is now directed toward the almost unheard of parotid glands: two important glands situated in front of each ear. These are the largest of the mucous and salivary glands whose function is to produce the fluids necessary for digestion. Saliva, which is the colorless fluid produced by the combined secretions of these glands, contains digestive enzymes and ferments. One of these ferments, which does not appear in human saliva until the child is a year old, is called ptyalin, which converts starch into dextrin and sugar.

It is not fully known what ferments and hormones are secreted by the parotids but when these secretions fail, and, if at the same time, the oxyntic cells in the digestive glands in the stomach are unable to produce hydrochloric acid in sufficient amounts to convert proteins into aminoacids, the body rapidly loses its acid-alkaline balance, and the condition known as alkalosis results. Of the two conditions, alkalosis and acidosis, the former is the more difficult to overcome, chiefly because persons have been drugging themselves for what they thought was an excess of acid, and thus worsened the condition.

Although the pituitary gland is the acknowledged director of endocrine activities, it is interesting to note that the functions of the parotids run parallel with those of the pituitary, especially in relation to the development and well-being of the sex organs. Indeed, it is difficult to determine which of these glandular bodies has the greatest influence over these organs.

The oustanding features of parotid gland and common symptoms of a loss of acid-alkaline balance in relation to it will now be analyzed.

Radiesthetically speaking, since it takes a negative and a positive force to form a chemical compound, it is easy to see why parotid secretions, which are alkaline and therefore negative, would be unable to function without gastric acids, which, being acids, are positive. Consequently, if the parotids are secreting, say, 15 percent of their normal quota, the body would derive only 15 percent of nourishment. Except for the deterioration of muscle and other tissues, this lack of nourishment would not necessarily produce undue distress. Meanwhile, the deficiency of liver fluids means a serious slowing down of peristaltic action and a condition amounting almost to a paralysis of the bowel, which the strongest aperients fail to relieve, results. Except in young children, where prolonged malnutrition over the years reaches alarming proportions as puberty approaches, the real menace of parotid dysfunction lies not as much with slow starvation as with the remaining 85 percent of undigested food substances that are stagnating and decaying in the intestines.

Now, just as nature produces moss to sweeten a stagnant pool of water, the body produces a fungus, a similar form of vegetable life, to devour the decaying waste matter accumulating in the organs. Consequently, as it is the nature of fungus to devour decaying waste, it spreads to other parts of the body such as the sinuses, the ear passages, the eyes, tonsils, mastoids, liver, heart, an open wound, or the glands themselves. Actually, fungus is a protective measure and will attach itself to any organ where accumulations of toxic waste threaten to destroy the cells. This is proved by the fact that as soon as the cleansing process is complete the fungus (or germ) disappears.

If, as in the case of mumps, where the person cannot masticate for several days and no food is taken, the fungus devours the accumulation in the parotid and throat glands, the swelling disappears and the individual makes a speedy recovery.

Of even greater importance to the body economy are the services rendered by the parathyroid glands. Usually four in number, they are situated at the back of the thyroid gland and are chiefly occupied with keeping the calcium in solution in the bloodstream. These tiny glands are also concerned with the destruction of waste products, especially protein matter which seems to affect the nervous system.

The reason why the parathyroid glands have been put last on the list of subsidiaries is because of the part they play during parotid dysfunction. With the suprarenals, the parathyroids are essential to life, in that when the parotids and other glands become depleted, they automatically take control until the balance is restored.

ALKALINITY

Alkalinity is essential to life in that a grain of wheat or any other seed will not germinate until softened and alkalized by water, neither will conception occur in either the human or the animal body if the mother's cells are acid. This follows the Law of Polarity already mentioned, which explains that the earth and everything contained therein is a manifestation of the union of the two forces, that of a positive and a negative, with a line of balance in the center.

Consequently, as alkalinity is an important tenet of naturopathetic procedure, people want to know what alkalosis is. Alkalosis is a worn-out condition of the acid-producing glands of the stomach.

When the acid-alkaline balance is lost, the digestion and assimilation of protein appears to be governed by the vitality of the parotid glands. Therefore, if these glands are dehydrated the digestion and assimilation of all classes of protein are almost at a standstill. But whereas the undigested proteins from vegetables, legumes and fruit will stagnate in the organs, they will not cause the putrefaction that arises from decaying animal protein. Therein lies the difference. The fungus from decaying vegetable matter will be easier to eradicate from the sinuses, the liver, the eyes, the kidneys, etc., than the germ-laden fungus from putrefying animal proteins.

ACID: THE KEYNOTE OF ENERGY

When we accept that creation, and re-creation, of the cells of the body depend upon both acids and alkalines, we begin to understand something of the significance of both together. Alkalis are negative and we would cease to exist (that is, to re-create ourselves) if a purely alkaline state were maintained for too long a period. The same principle applies to acids. The stomach would "digest" itself and we would literally burn ourselves up if acids, which constitute the positive driving-force of life, were allowed to dominate.

Summed up, this means that the body, to re-create itself, has to be in a state of constant change, with the pituitary gland to direct activities. Unlike the indicator of a weighing machine which registers the weight of the article placed thereon, and instantly springs back to zero, or balance, when the article is removed, the pituitary gland, working through the nerves per medium of its subsidiaries, has so many duties to perform after physical exercise, shock, chill, mental strain, or even a meal, that an immediate return to zero, or balance, is impossible. Quite often, several hours will elapse before anything approaching balance is attained.

Concerning the conditions or symptoms of acid-alkaline imbalance, it must be noted that heartburn, certain gastric conditions, arthritis, and many other complaints are not necessarily signs of acidosis. Quite often the reverse is the case. In any situation, don't try prescribing or diagnosing yourself, *always* contact your family doctor for professional guidance.

RAW FOOD JUICES

Absorption of sunlight, the essence of life, takes place within plants. The organs of plants are therefore a type of biological accumulation of energy. They are the basis of all foods. Animals eat the plants and man in turn eats animals and plants. It would probably be of value to modern man to eat more plants, raw and fresh, in order to benefit from the biological accumulation of nutrients. The raw juices are the lifeblood of vegetables and contain the vital enzymes and digestive factors so essential to maintaining a healthy body.

The raw juices that are locked in the cells of plants are pure liquid which we know contain vital therapeutic properties. They are subtle in their action, but, without the toxic effect of drugs, can sometimes eliminate and often help prevent many chronic and degenerative diseases.

Raw juices require no digestion in the stomach compared with cooked foods. They remain in the stomach a very short period and are more thoroughly assimilated than any other foodstuffs. Raw vegetables, moreover, pass through the system largely as bulk, and are not fermentative, as are cooked foodstuffs, including vegetables. From such raw materials we receive live food minerals and vitamins unchanged by heating. These raw juices are absorbed right into the blood and are utilized by even the weakest stomach.

Many people ask, why use juices? Why not just eat the raw vegetables? The answer is that for optimal health you need far more than you could eat. The stomach simply could not digest that much bulk or roughage. Also, the cellular structure of vegetables must be broken down for the nutrients to become available to the body. Chewing does a relatively poor job of breaking down. Juicing, or pulverization, is much more effective.

Fresh fruit juices are the cleansers of the human system. Vegetable juices are the regenerators and builders of our system. The essential elements found in fresh juices can be grouped into seven simple types of materials. These are: carbohydrates, fats, proteins, minerals, vitamins, bioflavonoids and cellulose. These seven substances contain everything needed for nourishing the human body. The difficulty in getting them in proper proportion with regular eating habits is rather well known, whereas the raw juices of vegetables and fruits could satisfy the nutritional needs for each of the nearly twenty-six thousand billion cells which make up the body provided they could be ingested in sufficient quantity. Even in limited quantity, however, they help to revitalize the bloodstream, revivify the nerves, rejuvenate the glands and organs and soothe the acid-irritated tissues of the stomach and intestines.

Only raw honey is more easily assimilated than raw juices. Taken on an empty stomach raw juice will be absorbed into the bloodstream and glands within 15 minutes after ingestion. The most vital element of the vegetable is locked within the cellulose fibers known as roughage. Although we do need a certain amount of roughage, it is quite possible to take in too much of it. Therefore, and because we are seeking the effect of the pure raw juices without taxing our digestive tracts with excess roughage, raw plant juices provide us with the answer.

A diet which is properly balanced and uses a large amount of juices can only help prolong life and prevent illness. Most of the vitamins and minerals available to us in the form of raw juice are destroyed by cooking. A pint or more of fresh raw juice each day will aid our overall condition. However, a therapeutic effect cannot be achieved overnight or even within a very short period of time. Give yourself time. It often takes a minimum of six weeks and up to six months or longer for your system to rebuild diseased or worn out tissues. Raw juices will certainly speed up the rebuilding of the colloidal cell chemical composition which has become unbalanced through unnatural daily living and dieting habits.

Eliminative processes begin to detoxify your system

within a few hours of drinking raw juices. This process of elimination is often very powerful, having the force to dissolve and expel hardened and caked masses which have lodged in various locations throughout the body and its glandular system. As the blood becomes more alkaline, the toxins which have saturated the cells are dissolved and enter the bloodstream to be carried off via the regular excretory channels.

You should not become distressed over the discomforts which usually occur during the first few weeks of juice therapy. Such disagreeable reactions do not mean that raw juices do not agree with your system. Rather, they signify they do not harmonize with an unhealthy condition in the stomach, intestines and bowels or an acid condition of the blood. The discomforting symptoms are actually signs that your system is cleaning itself and, therefore, improving.

The list of toxic and harmful chemicals which are so common to the American diet would take a full volume to list, but many, at least, can be found in the chapter on POISONS.

Raw fresh juices, preferably from organic sources, though this isn't mandatory, can help overcome their harmful effects.

New blood cells are born every fourteen days. If you have plenty of vegetable juice your new cells will be healthier than the old ones. They can help build a disease-resisting body. Raw juices also have a normalizing effect on the intestinal flora and its absorbing effect on the mucous membranes of the intestinal tract.

You should not think that simply taking a glass of raw juice will cause ailments to disappear. True, juices are very beneficial to an ailing or diseased system, but it takes time. It also takes a knowledge of the healing and cleansing properties of each type of raw juice. For instance, carrot juice is one of the richest sources of vitamin A and contains valuable amounts of vitamins C, G and K. It assists a sluggish appetite and aids your digestion, can improve and help maintain the bony structure of the teeth. Nursing mothers should have it to assure the quality of milk. Carrot juice also helps energize the system and combat fatigue. It also acts as a resistant to infections and a protector for the nervous system. Nutrients from other vegetables and fruits help perform other services.

In order to show you which vitamins and minerals might be lacking in your diet, we have prepared some tables showing the symptoms which could arise from a deficiency of a particular vitamin. However, you must bear in mind that symptoms are rarely due to a single cause or a single deficiency, the elements that make good nutrition work inter-relatedly often being assimilable only in the presence of one another. For instance vitamin A needs the presence of vitamin E to be utilized fully. A lack in one element therefore can cause a lack of use in another.

Along with the lists of symptoms that can generally indicate a particular deficiency is a list of vegetables and fruits having particularly high quantities of that vitamin.

Please, do not assume these lists are a cure-all. If you have persistent symptoms, take them to a doctor or a qualified nutritionist. *Remember this is a guideline only.* Symptoms are most often attributable to several causes; they are part of overall health, or overall ill-health.

VITAMIN DEFICIENCY SYMPTOMS AND REMEDIES

VITAMIN A

DEFICIENCY SYMPTOMS	PLANT JUICE	
	Good	Fair
Dry skin	Carrots	Okra
Decreased resistance to infection	Escarole	Asparagus
	Kale	String Beans
Kidney and gall stones	Parsley	Beet Tops
Retarded growth	Pimento	Broccoli
Poor-weak teeth	Sweet Potato	Collards
Lack of strength and stamina	Turnip Greens	Cantaloupe
	Watermelon	Cherries
Sinus problems	Chard	Peaches
Catarrh	Corn	Raspberries
Ear problems	Endive	Bananas
Sexual gland problems	Lettuce	Pineapple
Night blindness	Apricots	
Poor appetite	Sauerkraut	
Diarrhea	Squash	
Digestive troubles	Winter Squash	
	Watercress	

VITAMIN B COMPLEX
DEFICIENCY SYMPTOMS   PLANT JUICE

	Good	Fair
General lassitude	Asparagus	String Beans
Chronic tiredness	Avocado	Beet Greens
Loss of vitality	Broccoli	Tomato
Slow heart beat	Cabbage	Turnip
Poor lactation in nursing mothers	Carrots	Watermelon
Gastric disorders	Celery	Apples
Reduced peristaltic action	Chard	Bananas
Nerve degeneration	Dandelion	Cantaloupe
Nervousness and muscle spasms	Lettuce	Lemons
Poor appetite	Okra	Oranges

VITAMIN C
DEFICIENCY SYMPTOMS

Shortness of breath	Cabbage	Asparagus
Overall weakness	Parsley	String Beans
Secondary anemia	Pea	Carrots
Rapid pulse	G. Pepper	Celery
Headache	Pimento	Cucumber
Weak teeth	Rutabaga	Kale
Tender joints	Tomato	Cranberries
Low resistance to infection	Turnip	Orange Peel
Lowered hemoglobin	Watercress	Pineapple
Poor lactation	Cantaloupe	Peaches
Restlessness	Lemons	S. Potatoes
Digestion difficulties	Lime	Strawberries

VITAMIN D DEFIENCY SYMPTOMS

Poor bone formation
Poor teeth formation
Constipation
Pot belly
Lack of vigor
Restlessness
Rickets
Convulsions
Enlarged joints
Curvature of the spine
Retarded growth

Vitamin D is almost non-existent in plants. The best source is sunlight. In the winter it is recommended you add cod liver oil to your juices. Excessive amounts are toxic.

Marked depletion of
  calcium and phosphorus

VITAMIN E

DEFICIENCY SYMPTOMS	PLANT JUICE	
	Good	Fair
Sterility in both sexes	Spinach	Parsley
Loss of hair	Watercress	Turnip
Miscarriage	Lettuce	Wheat Germ Oil
Deficient lactation	Celery	Carrot

VITAMIN K DEFICIENCY SYMPTOMS

Retardation of normal coagulation of the blood	Cabbage	Kale

MINERAL DEFICIENCY SYMPTOMS AND REMEDIES

IRON-POOR SYMPTOMS	RAW FOOD JUICES
Palpitation of heart upon arising	Wild blackberries
Perspiration and flushes on one side	Lettuce
Tendency to colds in head	Asparagus
Face alternately flushed and pale	Currants
Murky yellowish gray face	Pears
Peevish	Plums
Easily fatigued while reading	Spinach
Alternating pain in kidneys and spleen	Raisins
Dull hearing during menstruation	Black mission figs
Anemia	Strawberries
Asthma	Cherries
Neuralgia	Okra
Tense genital organs	Dandelion leaves
Small of back weak and tender	Beets
Suffocation spells	Concord grapes
Soles of feet burn	Kale
Swollen ankles	Artichokes
Oppressive respiration	Collards
Bed wetting	Leek
Partially involuntary discharges	Mustard greens
Film before eyes	Black radishes
Sore, inflamed eyes	Brussels sprouts
Pains in shoulder joints	Cabbage
Tired nerves	Pea
Partial deafness	Cantaloupe

IRON-POOR SYMPTOMS

Food only partially digested	Lemons
Blood in stool	Cucumber
Weak rectal muscles	Strawberries
Discharges burn	Carrots
Stinging headaches	Tomatoes
Dryness of throat	Lime
Tenderness in liver and abdomen	Carrots
Menstrual pains	Peaches
Cold hands and feet	Spinach
Pulsation in finger tips	Lettuce
Gas in stomach and bowels	Carrots
Weak bladder	Celery
Poor equilibrium	Parsley

CALCIUM-POOR SYMPTOMS

Slow blood clotting	Turnip leaves
Stinging pains in genitals	Cabbage
Sluggish blood circulation	Green peppers
Sensitive to moisture	Lemons
Afternoon headache	Limes
Dizzy in open air	Onions
Staggering upon arising	Oranges
Palpitation upon ascending stairs	Rhubarb
Varicose veins	Spinach
Icy sensation in spine	Cranberries
Hemorrhages	Cucumbers
Soft bones	Peaches
Cysts	Radishes
Slimy salivation	Celery
Sores do not heal	Swiss chard
Lame ligaments	Carrots
Catarrh	Sauerkraut
Discharges	Lima beans
Pus formation	Cauliflower
Suppuration	Currants

PHOSPHORUS-POOR SYMPTOMS

Neuralgia	Red cabbage
Impotence	Corn
Hardening of wax in ears	Peas
Numbness in some part of the body	Savoy cabbage
Bronchitis	Concord grapes
Jaundice	Carrots

PHOSPHORUS-POOR SYMPTOMS

RAW FOOD JUICES

Variable body temperature — Squash
Neurasthenia — Raisins
Paralysis — Mustard greens
Beanlike knots form in glands in neck — Mushrooms
Loss of control of hand or arm — Pumpkin

IODINE-POOR SYMPTOMS

Swelling in throat, goiter — Artichokes
Pale, dry, hot scaly skin — Carrots
Arms numb — Garlic
Heart, chest and head pressure — Green grapes
Urine turbid, violet-yellowish-green — Sea lettuce
Sweet and putrid saliva, alternately — Dulse
Ailments usually on left side — Mushrooms
Hurried, short respiration — Bartlett pears
Dullness under shoulder blade — Pineapple
Numbness in fingers and hands — Avocado
Swelling of feet or toes — Potato skin
Enlarged glands — Chives
Stinging migratory pain sensations — White onions
Squinting of eyes — Broccoli
Tenderness of lower ribs — Chard
Watery discharge from nose — Celery
Greasy taste in mouth — Tomatoes
Strawberries
Watercress
Asparagus
Brussels sprouts
Chervil

SODIUM-POOR SYMPTOMS

Gout — Carrots
Indigestion — Celery
Vomiting — Okra
Rheumation — Spinach
Dry tongue — Strawberries
Dry skin — Apples
Cold feet — Asparagus
Acid stomach — Beets
Asthma — Cucumbers
Constipation — Gooseberries

SODIUM-POOR SYMPTOMS

Chlorosis

Catarrh of lungs

Poor digestion of fat, starches and
    sweets

Throat ailments

Bloating

Catarrh of nose

Cramps

Stomach ulcers

Hardening of arteries

Neuritis

Dry salivary glands

Low specific gravity of urine

Plums

Radishes

Swiss chard

Turnips

POTASSIUM-POOR SYMPTOMS

Weak heart

Periodic headache

Distress in pit of stomach

Bitter taste in mouth

Nausea from excitement

Profuse perspiration

Atrophied muscles

Itchy dry skin

Eczema on legs

Painful pustules

Pain in side

Throbbing feet

Nosebleed

Pyorrhea

Tendency to blister

Defective bowel movements

Feeling of sand in eyes

Stinging pains in left ear

Greenish ropy sputum

Pain in lower back of head

Cramp pains in heart

Constriction in urethra

Tingling in rectum

Throbbing over eyes

Tickling in nose

Enlarged ovaries

Kidney trouble

Dandelion leaves

Blueberries

Beet tops

Cocoanut

Cabbage

Endive

Lettuce

Mint leaves

Parsley

Pineapple

Spinach

Swiss chard

Carrots

Artichokes

Brussels sprouts

Grapes

Green peppers

Leek

Wild black cherries

Yellow tomatoes

Turnip leaves

Celery

Rhubarb

MAGNESIUM-POOR
SYMPTOMS

RAW FOOD JUICES

Inflated intestines	Oranges
Catarrhal discharges	Lemons
Acid blood, body gas	Grapefruit
Constipation	Tangerines
Fainting spells	Limes
Peritonitis	Plums
Yellow expectorations	Dandelion leaves
Yellowish whites of eyes	Mustard greens
Hardening of the liver	Lettuce
Weakness of abdominal muscles	Apples
Jaundice	Grapes
Pale urine	Savoy cabbage
Oily perspiration	Pomegranates
Burning sensation in stomach	Sugar beets
Falling sensations	Cherries
Frequent burning urination	Corn
Diarrhea	Peaches
Neuralgia	Pears

SILICON-POOR SYMPTOMS

Tumors	Calimyrna figs
Tuberculosis	Lettuce
Boils	Strawberries
Neurasthenia	Mustard greens
Lame sensation in small of back	White onions
Frequent urination	Parsnips
Weak lower limbs	Olives
Painful scant menstruation	Asparagus
Fingertips burn	Dandelion greens
Pain in genitals	Cabbage
Nervous exhaustion	Cucumbers
Rheumatism	Radishes
Excessive perspiration	Alfalfa
Soles of feet itch	
Headaches	
Painful piles	
Parched lips	
Brittle, dull hair	
Ovary troubles	
Enlarged liver	
Dizziness	

SILICON-POOR SYMPTOMS
Cold on left side of body
Small, rapid pulse
Prostatic pains
Premature emissions
Loose gums
Twitching of left eyelid
Fainting spells
Sore thighs
Large warts

CHLORINE-POOR SYMPTOMS

Purple extremities	Asparagus
Blue lips	Carrots
Grayish nail roots	Celery
Tension in stomach	Red and white
Facial muscles twitch	cabbage
Bones ache	Cucumbers
Constipation	Lettuce
Sore, burning mouth	Radishes
Rheumatic pains in muscles	Spinach
Burning in kidneys	Collards
Bloody saliva and urine	Ripe olives
Hot flashes	Tomatoes
Pyorrhea	Sauerkraut
Nervous prostration	Kale
Bladder troubles	
Bloating in abdomen	
Mucus forms in throat	

FLUORINE-POOR SYMPTOMS

Decay of bones and teeth	Cabbage
Tumors in liver and spleen	Cauliflower
Stones in kidneys	Garlic
Hard crusts form in nose	Sauerkraut
Urethral catarrh	Spinach
Hard shrunken prostate	Sprouts
Sclerosis	Watercress
Enlarged uterus	Endive
Pus formation	Chervil
Dilated blood vessels	Blackeyed beans
Mucus and ammonia in urine	Avocado

FLOURINE-POOR SYMPTOMS RAW FOOD JUICES

Ulcerative processes
Rheumatism in bones, numbness
Loose, tender spongy gums
Ailments with nails, bunions,
    eyelashes
Puffy lips, neck and eyes
Decay taste sensation in mouth
Bleeding gums
Red, swollen nose
Dark tongue
Clammy, decayed sweat
Hypertrophy of the spleen
Tendency to diphtheria
Ulceration
Glandular catarrh
Bone tumors
Tumors in cerebellar structures
Degenerative processes in the
    intestines

Juniper berries
Quince
Sea cabbage

SULPHUR-POOR SYMPTOMS

Granulated eyelids
Thick mucus concentrations in
    throat
Chronic problems with stomach
    and colon
Acid stomach
Gas generation
Red, shiny nosetip
Pulsations in liver, spleen, uterus
Swelling in abdomen
Saliva fetid, throat burning
Urine fetid and green
Milk causes nausea
Feet burn
Tingling, chiming in ears
Heart palpitates upon climbing
Night sweats on chest
Burning sensation in abdomen
Dryness of skin, gums
Swelling of liver, spleen, uterus

Red cabbage
Carrots
Chestnuts
Cocoanut
Figs
Nuts
Oranges
Spinach
Brussels sprouts
Chervil
Cranberries
Dill
Endive
Mustard greens
Leeks
Marjoram
Nasturtium
Red raspberries
Loganberries
Sorrel

SULPHUR-POOR SYMPTOMS

Rhubarb
Turnips
Watercress
Cauliflower
Onions
Parsnips
Peaches
Radishes
Rutabagas
Apples
Asparagus
Cherries
Cucumbers
Gooseberries
Grapes
Horseradish
Potatoes
Roebuck berries
Blackberries
Dewberries

MANGANESE-POOR SYMPTOMS

Gout

Dry catarrh

Profuse sweating

Nerve pain from shoulder to toes

Very tender nipples

Heart palpitation

Excreta yellowish, drawing in anus

Clay-like sediment in urine

Stomach contracts, trouble holding food down

Enlargement of ovaries

Stiffness in arms

Greasy taste in mouth

Spasmodic equilibrium

Hot face

Red and swollen eyes

Erratic taste functions

Fainting spells

Glands swell

Weakness in rectum muscles

Chives
Endive
Watercress
Nasturtium
Almonds
Chestnuts
Walnuts
Parsley
Peppermint Leaves
Wintergreen
Acorns
Blackeyed beans
Butternuts
French beans

SPECIAL JUICE PREPARATIONS
FOR SPECIFIC AILMENTS

The nutritional value of various specific juice combinations and their role in the maintenance of health is of prime concern. The following list of juice combinations will suggest to you various formulas that could benefit ailments and diseases.

A few juices are too potent to be taken alone and should always be combined with other juices: beet, spinach, parsley, garlic, dandelion, asparagus, lemon, turnip and watercress.

Regardless of the juice being combined, always take a minimum of 16 ounces of juice per day. With certain terminal or extremely hazardous diseases, the daily need should be four to six times the normal amount.

Acne, Pimples, etc.: Often and commonly resulting from impurities which the body is trying to eliminate through the skin.
Juice combinations:
Carrot juice alone
Carrot 10 oz., spinach 6 oz.
Carrot 8 oz., lettuce 5 oz., spinach 3 oz.

Adenoids: Inflammation and/or enlargement of pharyngeal tonsil or adenoid tissue.
Juice combinations:
Carrot juice alone
Carrot 10 oz., spinach 6 oz.

Albuminuria: Albumin present in the urine.
Juice combinations:
Carrot 10 oz., spinach 6 oz.
Carrot 10 oz., beet 3 oz., cucumber 3 oz.
Carrot 11 oz., beet 3 oz., coconut 2 oz.
Carrot 9 oz., celery 5 oz., parsley 2 oz.
Carrot 12 oz., parsley 4 oz.

Allergies: Extreme sensitiveness to certain foods, animals, pollens, dust and other substances which cause running eyes, hay fever, nettle-rash, asthma, dyspepsia, eczema and headache. The mucous membrane in the throat and sinus areas is agitated.

Juice combinations:
Carrot 6 oz., beet 5 oz., cucumber 5 oz.
Carrot 8 oz., celery 8 oz.

Anemia: A chronic lack of the necessary red corpuscles in the blood.
Juice combinations:
Carrot 12 oz., spinach 4 oz.
Carrot 8 oz., celery 6 oz., beet 2 oz.
Carrot 6 oz., beet 5 oz., cucumber 5 oz.
Carrot 8 oz., celery 4 oz., spinach 2 oz., parsley 2 oz.

Angina Pectoris: Excessive impurities in the bloodstream which cause muscular and or valvular heart problems.
Juice combinations:
Carrot 12 oz., spinach 4 oz.
Carrot 6 oz., beet 5 oz., cucumber 5 oz.
Carrot 8 oz., celery 4 oz., spinach 2 oz., parsley 2 oz.

Arteries (Hardening of): Thickening of the walls of the artery, which causes a partial blocking of the bloodstream to one or more of the organs due to the presence of inorganic calcium.
Juice combinations:
Carrot 10 oz., spinach 6 oz.
Carrot 8 oz., celery 4 oz., beet 4 oz.
Carrot 8 oz., celery 4 oz., spinach 2 oz., parsley 2 oz.
Carrot 8 oz., garlic 2 oz., pineapple 6 oz.

Arthritis: Deposits of inorganic calcium in the cartilage of the joints, often traced to an excess of carbohydrates and other concentrated starches in the diet.
Juice combinations:
Carrot 8 oz., celery 8 oz.
Carrot 6 oz., beet 5 oz., cucumber 5 oz.
Celery 10 oz., grapefruit 6 oz.

Asthma: An excess of mucous accumulation in the bronchial tubes which causes difficulty in breathing.
Juice combinations:
Carrot 10 oz., spinach 6 oz.
Grapefruit 10 oz., celery 6 oz.
Carrot 8 oz., celery 8 oz.

Astigmatism: An error of refraction in the eye due to the cornea being unequally curved in various directions,

thus causing rays of light in different meridians not to
be able to focus together in the retina.
Juice combinations:
Carrot 8 oz., celery 8 oz.
Carrot 6 oz., beet 5 oz., cucumber 5 oz.
Carrot 8 oz., celery 6 oz., parsley 2 oz.
Carrot 12 oz., spinach 4 oz.

Bad Breath: Often stemming from such common disorders
as constipation, indigestion, chronic tonsillitis, diseases
of the nose, decayed or ulcerated teeth and or gums.
Juice combinations:
Juice of ½ to one lemon in glass of warm water upon
arising, then:
Carrot 8 oz., celery 8 oz.
Carrot 8 oz., spinach 4 oz., cucumber 4 oz.

Biliousness: An improper flow of bile from the liver due
to the incomplete or partial digestion of fats.
Juice combinations:
Carrot 10 oz., spinach 6 oz.
Carrot 10 oz., cucumber 3 oz., beet 3 oz.
Carrot 9 oz., celery 5 oz., parsley 2 oz.

Bladder Disease: Several varying ailments which affect the
proper function of the bladder; gallstones, sand in the
gallbladder, inflammation of the urinary bladder, etc.
Juice combinations:
Carrot 6 oz., beet 5 oz., cucumber 5 oz.
Carrot 8 oz., celery 4 oz., spinach 2 oz., parsley 2 oz.

Blood Pressure: High blood pressure is excessive tension
of blood in the arteries caused by improper diet, lack
of exercise and in some cases, neurasthenia, worry,
anxiety. Low blood pressure is caused by excessive use
of devitalized foods in the diet, which results in deficiency of vital elements in the bloodstream. It frequently
is the result of exhaustion, weakening disease, fevers
and, in general, degeneration of the heart muscle.
Juice combinations:
Carrot 12 oz., spinach 4 oz.
Carrot 6 oz., beet 5 oz., cucumber 5 oz.
Carrot 8 oz., celery 4 oz., spinach 2 oz., parsley 2 oz.

Boils, Carbuncles: Purulent tumors caused by impurities in the bloodstream resulting in bacterial infection through the sweat glands or the follicles of the hair.
Juice combinations:
Carrot 12 oz., spinach 4 oz.
Carrot 6 oz., beet 5 oz., cucumber 5 oz.
Carrot 10 oz., beet 3 oz., cucumber 3 oz.
Carrot 8 oz., lettuce 5 oz., spinach 3 oz.

Bright's Disease: Disease of the kidneys characterized by albumin in the urine. Excessive uric acid.
Juice combinations:
Carrot 6 oz., beet 5 oz., cucumber 5 oz.
Carrot 12 oz., spinach 4 oz.
Carrot 8 oz., celery 6 oz., parsley 2 oz.

Bronchitis: Severe inflammation of the bronchial tubes due to an excess of mucus in the system.
Juice combinations:
Carrot 12 oz., spinach 4 oz.
Carrot 8 oz., celery 8 oz.
Carrot 6 oz., beet 5 oz., cucumber 5 oz.

Cancer: Any malignant form of tumor; groups of epithelial cells, half-starved from lack of proper organic matter, thriving on concentrated starches and protein.
Juice combinations:
Carrot 16 oz.
Carrot 8 oz., celery 8 oz.
Carrot 12 oz., spinach 4 oz.
Carrot 12 oz., cabbage 4 oz.

Cataracts: Opaque films over crystalline lens of the eye due to a lack of proper nourishment of the optic nerves and muscles.
Juice combinations:
Carrot 16 oz.
Carrot 8 oz., celery 6 oz., parsley 2 oz.
Carrot 6 oz., beet 5 oz., cucumber 5 oz.
Carrot 12 oz., spinach 4 oz.
Carrot 12 oz., spinach 2 oz., parsley 2 oz.

Catarrh: Copious secretions from the mucous membranes due to the inability of the body to assimilate properly milk and concentrated starches.

Juice combinations:
Carrot 6 oz., celery 6 oz., parsley 2 oz., lemon 2 oz.
Carrot 6 oz., beet 5 oz., cucumber 5 oz.
Carrot 14 oz., spinach 2 oz.
Carrot 10 oz., spinach 4 oz., parsley 2 oz.

Colds: The body is not strong enough to resist infection. Deficiency in vitamins and minerals is usually the major cause. Overexerting oneself mentally or physically and not supplying the body with the important nutritional elements to rebuild the dead or fatigued cells. This common type of condition opens the way for any number of viruses to infect the system.
Juice combinations:
Carrot 12 oz., lemon 2 oz., garlic 1 oz., onion 1 oz.
Carrot 16 oz.
Carrot 6 oz., spinach 2 oz., garlic 1 oz., watercress 1 oz., celery 4 oz., cucumber 2 oz.

Colitis: Inflammation of the large intestine or colon, with the most prominent symptom being the passage of mucus with the stools, with alternate periods of constipation and diarrhea. One known cause is an unbalanced diet and a lack of the essential vitamins and minerals.
Juice combinations:
Carrot 8 oz., apple 6 oz., lemon 2 oz.
Carrot 8 oz., apple 8 oz.
Carrot 6 oz., beet 4 oz., watercess 1 oz., cucumber 5 oz.
Carrot 10 oz., celery 6 oz.

Constipation: Lack of coordination in the nerve and muscle functions of the colon and bowel due to excessive use of concentrated starchy foods, and poor food combining, which results in sluggishness of bowel action.
Juice combinations:
Carrot 8 oz., apple 8 oz.
Carrot 8 oz., celery 4 oz., apple 4 oz.
Carrot 12 oz., spinach 4 oz.

Coronary Thrombosis: Often, when the coronary arteries become diseased they narrow to the point where blood, slowing down its flow, clots or forms thrombosis. This cuts off the supply of blood to part of the heart and the result is often fatal.

Juice combinations:
Carrot 8 oz., parsley 2 oz., garlic 2 oz.
Carrot 8 oz., parsley 2 oz.
Carrot 6 oz., beet 5 oz., cucumber 5 oz.

Dermatitis: A rather severe inflammation of the skin, usually found around the cuticle where the skin peels off in large flakes, leaving red surface beneath. Deficiency in vitamins A and E and pantothenic acid and the multiple minerals.
Juice combinations:
Carrot 8 oz., celery 8 oz.
Carrot 6 oz., celery 5 oz., apple 5 oz.
Carrot 6 oz., celery 5 oz., beet 5 oz.
Carrot 6 oz., beet 5 oz., cucumber 5 oz.

Diabetes: Inability of the pancreas to metabolize carbohydrates due to excessive use of concentrated starches and sugars in the diet.
Juice combinations:
Carrot 10 oz., spinach 6 oz.
Carrot 7 oz., celery 4 oz., parsley 2 oz., spinach 3 oz.
Carrot 6 oz., lettuce 4 oz., string beans 3 oz., Brussels sprouts 3 oz.
Carrots 7 oz., celery 5 oz., endive 2 oz., parsley 2 oz.

Diarrhea: A looseness of the bowels, usually caused by an infection in the intestines.
Juice combinations:
Carrot 8 oz., apple 8 oz.
Carrot 16 oz.
Carrot 6 oz., celery 5 oz., apple 5 oz.
Carrot 6 oz., celery 6 oz., spinach 2 oz., parsley 2 oz.

Eye Ailments: The most common ailment being eyestrain, usually caused by improper lighting conditions, such as glare, or a deficiency of vitamin A and minerals in the diet.
Juice combinations:
Carrot 12 oz., spinach 4 oz.
Carrot 8 oz., celery 8 oz.
Carrot 8 oz., celery 6 oz., spinach 2 oz.

Fever: Abnormal rise in temperature. Very common with almost every serious virus infection.
Juice combinations:

Carrot 8 oz., orange 8 oz.
Orange 14 oz., lemon 2 oz.
Grapefruit 8 oz., orange 8 oz.
Grape 8 oz., orange 8 oz.
Lemon 4 oz., grape 4 oz., orange 4 oz., grapefruit 4 oz.

Gallstones: Pigments deposited from the bile in the finer vessels produce bile-sand. This bile sand may collect into small masses in the larger duct or gall bladder, and chemical changes in the mucus take place, so that a large gallstone may be produced. One of the prime causes of gallstones is an unbalanced diet and diets heavy in spicy, fatty foods.
Juice combinations:
Carrot 6 oz., celery 6 oz., lemon 2 oz.
Carrot 8 oz., celery 4 oz., apple 2 oz.
Carrot 6 oz., beet 5 oz., cucumber 5 oz.

Goiter: An enlarged thyroid gland usually due to a deficiency of iodine in the diet.
Juice combinations:
Carrot 12 oz., spinach 4 oz., (plus add ¼ teaspoon of kelp or dulse to each formula)
Carrot 8 oz., celery 8 oz.
Carrot 8 oz., celery 6 oz., spinach 2 oz., parsley 2 oz.

Gout: A severe inflammation of the ligaments of a joint or bone, or bone lining, due to an excess of concentrated starches and fats in the diet, can also be traced to an excess of alcohol and drugs, which cause an excess of uric acid in the blood.
Juice combinations:
Carrot 8 oz., spinach 8 oz.
Carrot 6 oz., beet 5 oz., cucumber 5 oz.
Carrot 8 oz., beet 4 oz., cocoanut 4 oz.

Hay Fever: Abnormal mucous secretions in the eyes and air passages due to an excess of concentrated starches and fats in the diet.
Juice combinations:
Carrot 8 oz., celery 8 oz.
Carrot 6 oz., beet 4 oz., cucumber 6 oz.
Carrot 8 oz., celery 4 oz., spinach 2 oz., parsley 2 oz.

Headaches: The body's warning through the nervous system that something needs cleansing. It is best to try and clean the blood of impurities and help relieve excess nerve pressure in the head.
Juice combinations:
Carrot 10 oz., spinach 6 oz.
Carrot 7 oz., celery 2 oz., lemon 2 oz., apple 4 oz.
Carrot 10 oz., beet 3 oz., cucumber 3 oz.
Carrot 8 oz., lettuce 2 oz., watermelon 3 oz.

Heart trouble (Functional): Caused by the impure condition of the blood resulting in improper activity on the part of the heart organism.
Juice combinations:
Carrot 10 oz., spinach 2 oz., parsley 2 oz., lemon 2 oz.
Carrot 7 oz., celery 4 oz., parsley 2 oz., spinach 2 oz.
Carrot 10 oz., beet 3 oz., cucumber 3 oz.

Hemorrhoids: The lower section of the bowel is inflamed and contains a mass of dilated veins in swollen anal tissue.
Juice combinations:
Carrot 12 oz., spinach 4 oz.
Carrot 7 oz., beet 3 oz., apple 6 oz.
Carrot 10 oz., beet 3 oz., cucumber 3 oz.
Carrot 8 oz., apple 8 oz.

Hernia: Protrusion of any internal organ wholly or in part from its normal position, due to a lack of strength and tone in the surrounding membranes.
Juice combinations:
Carrot 12 oz., spinach 4 oz.
Carrot 6 oz., celery 6 oz., spinach 2 oz., cucumber 2 oz.
Carrot 8 oz., celery 8 oz.

Influenza: Caused by excessive retention in the body of morbid matter resulting in a feeding and breeding ground for pathogenic bacteria, affecting the air passages and usually accompanied by fever, nervous prostration, mental depression and debility.
Juice combinations:
Carrot 8 oz., celery 4 oz., watermelon 4 oz.

Carrot 12 oz., spinach 4 oz.
Carrot 6 oz., beet 5 oz., cucumber 3 oz., lemon 2 oz.

Insomnia: Cannot sleep due to nervous tension or excessive acidity in the system.
Juice combinations:
Carrot 10 oz., celery 6 oz.
Carrot 10 oz., spinach 6 oz.
Carrot 8 oz., apple 4 oz., watermelon 4 oz.
Carrot 8 oz., pear 4 oz., grape 4 oz.

Jaundice: Chronic fatigue of the liver which causes the liver to eliminate the excretion of bile by way of the lymph stream through the pores of the skin.
Juice combinations:
Carrot 6 oz., lemon 3 oz., watermelon 3 oz., apple 4 oz.
Carrot 8 oz., celery 6 oz., parsley 2 oz.
Carrot 6 oz., beet 5 oz., cucumber 5 oz.

Kidney Diseases: These usually include ailments deriving from an excess of uric acid and faulty and insufficient elimination of excessive meat products in the diet.
Juice combinations:
Carrot 12 oz., spinach 2 oz., lemon 2 oz.
Carrot 8 oz., celery 8 oz.
Carrot 6 oz., beet 5 oz., cucumber 5 oz.

Liver Ailments: An overindulgence in concentrated starches, fats, sugars and in general, devitalized foods.
Juice combinations:
Carrot 10 oz., beet 3 oz., cucumber 3 oz.
Carrot 10 oz., spinach 6 oz.
Carrot 8 oz., coconut 4 oz., papaya 4 oz.
Carrot 8 oz., beet 3 oz., apple 4 oz., watercress 1 oz.

Malaise: Vague feeling of feverishness, listlessness and chronic tiredness, which usually precedes the onset of serious acute disease, or accompanies disorders such as fever, virus, colds, etc. General run-down feeling. Traced to a lack of essential vitamins and minerals.
Juice combinations:
Carrot 8 oz., celery 8 oz.
Carrot 8 oz., apple 8 oz.

Carrot 8 oz., watermelon 8 oz.
Carrot 8 oz., grape 8 oz.
Carrot 8 oz., orange 8 oz.

Migraine: Too many impurities in the bloodstream and improperly nourished nerve centers which cause intense ache usually occurring on one side of the head.
Juice combinations:
Carrot 10 oz., spinach 6 oz.
Carrot 8 oz., celery 2 oz., cucumber 2 oz., spinach 5 oz.
Carrot 10 oz., beet 3 oz., cucumber 3 oz.

Mucous Membrane: These particular membranes line every cavity in the body and are lubricated by mucus derived from the glands or often from isolated cells on the surface of the membrane. Adequate intake of vitamins and minerals is essential to maintain the mucous membranes in the proper working and functioning order.
Juice combinations:
Carrot 8 oz., apple 8 oz.
Carrot 8 oz., pineapple 8 oz.
Carrot 8 oz., watermelon 8 oz.
Carrot 14 oz., lemon 2 oz.
Carrot 6 oz., beet 5 oz., cucumber 5 oz.

Nephrosis: This term is applied to any form of disorder or disease affecting the kidneys, but especially to a form of degeneration characterized by anemia, dropsy and albuminuria.
Juice combinations:
Carrot 12 oz., spinach 4 oz.
Carrot 8 oz., celery 6 oz., parsley 2 oz.
Carrot 8 oz., beet 4 oz., cucumber 4 oz.

Nervous System (Disorders of): Including such diseases and ailments as nerve injuries, neuralgia, neuritis, neurasthenia, diseases of the spinal cord, etc.
Juice combinations:
Carrot 8 oz., celery 8 oz.
Celery 14 oz., beet 2 oz.
Carrot 6 oz., beet 4 oz., cucumber 6 oz.
Carrot 12 oz., spinach 4 oz.

Ophthalmia: Also known as conjunctivitis, inflammation of the eye.
Juice combinations:
Carrot 8 oz., apple 8 oz.
Carrot 8 oz., celery 4 oz., cucumber 4 oz.
Carrot 10 oz., spinach 4 oz., parsley 2 oz.
Carrot 8 oz., orange 8 oz.

Overweight: A condition of the body where an excess of fatty tissue accumulates in different parts of the body. This condition is generally caused by poor food combining and an overall unbalanced diet.
Juice combinations:
Carrot 8 oz., celery 6 oz., lemon 2 oz.
Carrot 12 oz., spinach 4 oz.
Carrot 8 oz., pineapple 4 oz., papaya 4 oz.

Peptic Ulcer: Refers to the common stomach condition where ulcers develop in the stomach and the duodenum.
Juice combinations:
Cabbage 16 oz., celery 16 oz.
Carrot 16 oz., cabbage 16 oz.

Pernicious Anemia: A very serious form of anemia characterized by a poor quantity and quality of red corpuscles or fluid in the blood.
Juice combinations:
Carrot 12 oz., spinach 2 oz., beet 2 oz.
Carrot 8 oz., celery 6 oz., spinach 2 oz.
Carrot 8 oz., celery 4 oz., spinach 2 oz., parsley 2 oz.

Pregnancy: A balanced diet properly combined to benefit from the rich supply of vitamins and minerals needed during pregnancy and the period of lactation.
Juice combinations:
Carrot 8 oz., celery 4 oz., orange 4 oz.
Carrot 6 oz., coconut 4 oz., beet 2 oz., cucumber 2 oz., apple 2 oz.
Carrot 8 oz., apple 4 oz., orange 4 oz.
Carrot 8 oz., coconut 8 oz.
Carrot 6 oz., beet 5 oz., spinach 5 oz.

Pyelitis: A serious condition where pus forms in the kidneys, which in turn produces pus in the urine. It is due

to inflammation of that part of the kidney known as the pelvis, which is connected with the ureter (a tube carrying urine from kidney to the bladder). Pyelitis is closely associated with infection of the bladder, with symptoms of feverishness, listlessness, loss of weight, discomfort and frequent passing of water.
Juice combinations:
Carrot 8 oz., celery 8 oz.
Carrot 6 oz., spinach 4 oz., cucumber 3 oz., celery 3 oz.
Carrot 8 oz., apple 4 oz., coconut 4 oz.

Pyrosis: More commonly known as heartburn, which is a symptom of dyspepsia consisting of an irritable, burning sensation in the throat, accompanied by constant secretion of saliva. Poor food combining which causes an acid imbalance and an acid excess to form in the stomach is one of the major causes.
Juice combinations:
Carrot 8 oz., apple 8 oz.
Carrot 8 oz., celery 8 oz.
Carrot 6 oz., beet 5 oz., cucumber 3 oz., celery 2 oz.
Carrot 12 oz., spinach 2 oz., parsley 2 oz.

Rheumatism: This term is somewhat of a catch-all for several types of ailments including neuritis, sciatica, lumbago, arthritis, gout, etc. A common cause for all of these disorders is an excess of morbid matter in the system, often with as much as two or three pounds of putrefied food in the intestines alone.
Juice combinations:
Carrot 8 oz., celery 8 oz.
Carrot 8 oz., lemon 2 oz., garlic 1 oz., spinach 5 oz.
Carrot 8 oz., cucumber 6 oz., parsley 2 oz.
Carrot 8 oz., grapefruit 8 oz.
Carrot 8 oz., orange 8 oz.

Rhinitis: A severe inflammation in the nasal membrane due to the presence of excessive quantities of mucus in the sinus cavities.
Juice combinations:
Carrot 8 oz., celery 8 oz.
Carrot 12 oz., cucumber 4 oz.

Carrot 8 oz., cucumber 4 oz., spinach 4 oz.
Carrot 10 oz., lemon 2 oz., garlic 1 oz., spinach 3 oz.

Rickets: Due to a lack of calcium, and other essential vitamins and minerals, the bones become dangerously soft.
Juice combinations:
Carrot 8 oz., apple 8 oz.
Carrot 8 oz., grapefruit 8 oz.
Carrot 8 oz., orange 8 oz.
Carrot 8 oz., apple 4 oz., spinach 4 oz.

Sinus Ailments: Due mainly from an excess of mucus resulting from too much milk and other dairy products in the diet, also a heavy intake of concentrated starches and fats in the diet.
Juice combinations:
Carrot 10 oz., garlic 1 oz., onion 1 oz., lemon 1 oz.
Carrot 10 oz., beet 3 oz., cucumber 3 oz.
Carrot 12 oz., apple 4 oz.

Teeth: Tooth decay and other ailments with the teeth are caused in part by a lack of organic calcium in the diet.
Juice combinations:
Carrot 8 oz., celery 8 oz
Carrot 8 oz., apple 8 oz.
Carrot 8 oz., orange 8 oz.
Carrot 8 oz., beet 8 oz.
Carrot 8 oz., spinach 4 oz., cucumber 2 oz., parsley 2 oz.

Tonsils: Two almond-shaped glands, one on each side of the throat covered with mucous membrane. Tonsillitis is inflammation of the tonsils and may be either acute or chronic. One of the major causes of tonsilitis is an acid excess and an overall lack of the essential vitamins and minerals in the diet.
Juice combinations:
Carrot 8 oz., pineapple 4 oz., orange 4 oz.
Carrot 8 oz., apple 8 oz.
Carrot 8 oz., celery 8 oz.
Carrot 8 oz., coconut 4 oz., pineapple 4 oz.

Varicose Veins: Deposits formed in the wall structure of the veins. Essential organic nutrients in the diet and also due to poor food combining and an excess of concentrated starches.

Juice combinations:

Carrot 8 oz., beet 8 oz.

Carrot 8 oz., celery 4 oz., garlic 1 oz., lemon 2 oz., apple 1 oz.

Carrot 8 oz., celery 4 oz., parsley 2 oz., spinach 2 oz.

Varicose Veins: Deposits formed in the wall structure of the veins.

Juice combinations:

Carrot 8 oz., beet 6 oz., parsley 2 oz.

Carrot 12 oz., celery 4 oz.

Carrot 8 oz., apple 8 oz.

For general health have an 8-ounce glass of apple or orange juice in the morning, an 8-ounce glass of carrot juice in the afternoon and an 8-ounce glass of grapefruit juice before going to bed at night.

Apple juice a half hour after rising in the morning assists the overall functioning of the body, and promotes peristaltic activity and tones up the system. Carrot juice helps to keep the mucous membranes, cells, glands, bones and walls of the arteries in a healthy condition. Celery or grapefruit juice before bed soothes, relaxes and allows for a more sound sleep.

Along with an understanding of the various raw juice combinations should also be an analysis of the nutritional properties of the different fruit and vegetable juices. The following detailed descriptions will give you a more comprehensive look into the value of single and combined juices.

Raw Carrot Juice is the richest single juice for vitamin A. It helps to normalize your system and is a natural solvent for ulcerous conditions. It is also one of the strongest blood building agents, particularly when combined with beet, lettuce and turnip juices. Carrot juice also contains an ample supply of vitamins B,C,D,E,G, and K. It is beneficial to the appetite and aids digestion. Carrot juice is the single most important juice you can take because it combines well with any other juice and contains the most nutrients of any juice. Children should be given at least one 6 oz. glass of carrot juice each day for the improvement and maintenance of the bone structure of the teeth. Carrot juice is also good for nursing mothers as it enriches the quality of the milk.

Apple Juice purges the system of impurities and tones the cells. It has a good supply of potassium, sodium and phosphorus. It helps metabolize fatty foods to aid digestion, is excellent stimulation for the kidneys and promotes intestinal activity. Apple juice is good for blood purifying, cases of constipation, sluggish liver, skin eruptions, poor complexion and anemia.

Celery Juice is the most potent nerve tonic of any juice. It is beneficial for its ample potassium, calcium, sodium and phosphorus. It provides food for blood cells and is a builder and blood cleanser. Celery juice keeps calcium in distribution, which is an aid in arthritic conditions.

Carrot and Celery Juice makes a perfect combination for cleansing the system of excessive acid or acidosis. This combination is helpful in the regeneration of the tissues, especially those connected with the ligaments of the joints and the nervous system.

Due to the very high content of organic sodium in celery juice, it helps prevent inorganic calcium deposits which cause arthritis.

Carrot, Celery and Parsely Juice gives you the same beneficial nutrients as carrot and celery, but parsley is very strong and does a thorough job of cleansing the kidneys. It energizes the adrenal glands and has a very powerful therapeutic effect on the optic nerves, on the brain nerves and on the complete nerve system.

As mentioned previously, raw parsley juice is too concentrated to be taken alone. Never drink more than an ounce unless combined with carrot, apple, celery or orange juices. An overdose of parsley juice will overstimulate the nervous system.

Carrot and Beet Juice. Although the quantity of iron in beets is not exceptionally high it is enough to furnish the red corpuscles of the blood with adequate food. The sodium content is high while the calcium content is low, which is a valuable proportion for maintaining the solubility of calcium. This has proven a valuable aid to persons suffering from varicose veins and hardening of the arteries caused by inorganic calcium accumulations in the system and within the blood vessels. A similar, though more serious ailment, also caused by inorganic calcium deposits, is high blood pressure and other forms of heart trouble in which the blood vessels have thickened.

The combination of carrot and beet juice offers a high percentage of phosphorus and sulphur plus potassium and other alkaline nutrients. These elements combined with the high vitamin A from the carrot juice complete the strongest natural builder of blood cells.

If you add cucumber juice to carrot, beet and parsley juice you will have a fine cleansing and healing mixture for the gall bladder, the liver, kidneys, the prostate and other sex glands. This combination, taken a pint at a time, twice a day, has been successful in dissolving kidney stones over a few months' period.

Carrot and Cabbage Juice is high in sulphur and chlorine and very high in iodine. By combining sulphur and chlorine you have a powerful cleanser for the mucous membrane of the stomach and intestinal tract.

Many persons have found that gas pains occur shortly after drinking raw cabbage juice. If this be the case, it is almost always caused by an abnormal condition in the intestinal tract. To alleviate an excess of putrefied matter in the intestines, drink at least two 16-ounce glasses of carrot and spinach juice daily, for two or three weeks.

A fine cleansing action as well as an excellent source of vitamin C is found when combining carrot and cabbage juice. It is also beneficial where infection of the gums with resultant pyorrhea is present.

It is well known to both professionals and laymen alike that foods (vegetables and fruits) are most potent in their raw, natural state and that boiling or dehydrating juices destroys the effectiveness of the vitamins, minerals and salts. One-half pint of raw cabbage juice contains more organic food value than does two hundred pounds of cooked or canned cabbage.

Carrot and Radish Juice and Horseradish Sauce is a potent cleanser of abnormal mucus in the system. One-half teaspoonful of fresh horseradish sauce should be taken twice a day between meals. Do not add vinegar! Commercial vinegar destroys the tissues of the membranes lining the stomach and intestines. The old folk remedy of honey and vinegar is actually quite harmful to the stomach and intestines. If anything, take lemon juice and honey.

If you must mix something with the horseradish, add a teaspoon of lemon juice, but do not dilute it further, nor should you drink anything for at least a half hour before or after taking it. You may experience a slight sensation in the head which will create copious tears, depending upon the volume of mucus in the sinus cavities and other parts of the system. This is by far the most natural and safe method for cleansing the head of sinus mucus.

Never take radish juice undiluted, as it is too strong for your system. It should be combined with carrot juice, in connection with which it will have the effect of soothing and healing the membranes and cleansing the system of the mucus which the horseradish sauce has dissolved. It will then rebuild and regenerate the mucous membranes to their natural state.

The high quantities of potassium, sodium and iron and magnesium in the radishes help heal and soothe the mucous membranes.

A primary cause of excess mucus is the drinking of too much milk and eating concentrated starches, bread, sugar, cereals and dairy products.

Lettuce Juice is loaded with iron and magnesium. Iron is the most active mineral element in the system and must be renewed more frequently than any other. Iron is stored in the liver and spleen where it is ready for any sudden demand of the system, such as the rapid formation of red blood corpuscles where there is a heavy loss of blood. The iron is also stored in the liver for the purpose of furnishing essential mineral elements to any part of the body from which they may suddenly and rapidly diminish, such as in the case of a hemorrhage.

The holding of iron in the spleen serves an entirely different purpose. It acts as an electric storage generator where the blood is recharged with the necessary electricity for its necessary work.

The revitalizing powers of lettuce are due to the high content of its magnesium, which causes an energizing effect on the muscular tissues, the brain and the nerves. Organic salts of magnesium are excellent tissue and cell builders, especially of the nerve systems and of the tissues of the lungs. They also serve an important task in maintaining the normal fluidity of the blood and other functions without which the system could not operate properly.

The properties of lettuce juice are intensified greatly by combining carrot juice with its high content of vitamin A and sodium. Sodium helps to maintain the calcium in the lettuce in constant solution until utilized by the body.

Lettuce has a good proportion of several useful minerals. It contains more than 38 percent potassium, nearly 15 percent calcium, 5 percent iron, 6 percent magnesium, 9 percent phosphorus, 8 percent silicon and an ample supply of sulphur and other trace elements.

Carrot and lettuce juice combined will furnish the essential nutrients for the nerves and roots of the hair. By adding alfalfa juice to the combination it provides further therapeutic value to the growth of hair and restoration of its natural texture and color.

Spinach Juice provides food for the entire digestive tract: the stomach, duodenum and small intestines and the large intestine or colon.

All too often strong chemical purgatives used for cleansing the intestinal tract act as an irritant, and cause a chronic condition to develop, rather than providing a cure for constipation. The irritant stimulates the muscles of the intestines to expel the irritant and remove other morbid matter lodged therein. If one continues to use the purgatives over an extended period of time, the intestines will eventually fail to respond to even the strongest laxatives. This will cause the local tissues, muscles and nerves to become inactive. However, the use of saline purges has a different effect. A saline formula flowing through the intestines draws from the lymph stream large amounts of fluid which will usually be found to be excessively acid or saturated with toxic body waste. Unless this acid, or poisoned lymph so expelled is replaced by an organic alkaline solution such as natural raw juices, a serious deficiency will result. Also, if this replacement or re-alkalinization is not acted upon immediately, shortly thereafter, poisons remaining in the intestinal tract will, by being reabsorbed, find their way into the lymph stream and aggravate the original condition.

There is no better or healthier method of cleansing the

intestinal tract than by drinking raw spinach juice daily. By combining an equal amount of apple juice with the spinach juice you can correct the most aggravated case of constipation within a few days or weeks.

Many persons have been under the misconception that "roughage" is the primary stimulus of the bowel. On the contrary, it is the stimulation which results from the fermentation of hemicellulose and cellulose (undigestible food residues) by intestinal bacteria. Hemicellulose is the factor which controls the bulk of the stool. Foods which have a high hemicellulose content are very laxative. This is why a combination of the two is so effective in cases of severe constipation.

Raw spinach juice has also proven to be effective in cases of pyorrhea, where the teeth and gums become infected. Bleeding gums and a fibroid degeneration of the pulp of the teeth has become a common ailment due to the poor quality of the typical American diet, with its emphasis on concentrated starches, fats and poor food combining.

For those of you who suffer from any form of kidney disease a word of caution is necessary. Raw spinach juice contains a high quantity of oxalic acid which combines with its calcium content, making most of the latter unavailable to your system and forming calcium oxalate. Normally, calcium oxalate, an unassimilable salt, is passed in solution (dissolved) in the urine. However, in certain cases, because of an unknown disturbance of kidney metabolism, the kidneys are unable to dissolve these salts and calcium oxalate crystals are precipitated in the urine, a condition known as oxaluria. These crystals form a large part of most kidney stones. Those who suffer from oxaluria or have a history of kidney stones, therefore, should avoid spinach as well as potatoes, beans, endives, tomatoes, dried figs, plums, strawberries, cocoa, chocolate and tea, all of which have a very high oxalate factor.

Parsley Juice is a fine maintainer and rebuilder of the blood vessels, particularly the capillaries and arterioles. The natural trace minerals and vitamins found in raw parsley juice are essential to oxygen metabolism in maintaining the normal action of the adrenal and thyroid glands. It is also beneficial for the health of the genitourinary tract, and helps conditions such as calculi in the kidneys and bladder, albuminuria, nephritis and other kidney ailments.

By combining carrot and celery juice with parsley juice, you will have a potent tonic for any ailment connected with the eyes or optic nerve system such as weak eyes, ulceration of the cornea, cataracts, conjunctivitis, ophthalmia or laziness of the pupil.

Turnip Leaves have the highest quantity of calcium of any vegetable. It should be taken by anyone who has a calcium deficiency. The combination of carrot and dandelion juice with turnip juice provides for a tonic, unmatched for its effect on strengthening the teeth and overall bone structure.

Turnip leaves are also very high in potassium which makes it a good alkalinizer, particularly when combined with carrot and celery juices, and is excellent in reducing hyperacidity.

Watercress Juice is primarily composed of sulphur, phosphorus and chlorine, which is why it is so acid forming. For this reason it should never be taken alone but rather combined with carrot or celery juice. It is one of the strongest intestinal cleansers and also assists the system in maintaining a normal blood pressure.

By combining carrot, spinach and turnips with watercress you will have a powerful tonic for helping hemorrhoids or piles and a few types of tumors.

Cucumber Juice is best known for its diuretic action, secreting and promoting the flow of urine. It also stimulates hair growth, due to its high quantity of silicon and sulphur minerals.

By combining carrot juice with cucumber juice you will have a strong tonic for helping rheumatic ailments resulting from an excessive retention of uric acid in the system.

Dandelion Juice is beneficial in counteracting hyperacidity and in normalizing the alkalinity of the system. It is the richest food in magnesium and also contains good amounts of calcium and sodium. A good tonic for spinal and other bone ailments is a combination of carrot and turnip juices added to raw dandelion juice.

Fennel Juice has qualities similar to celery juice. It is very beneficial for the entire optic system and contains nearly all of the essential vitamins and minerals.

Tomato Juice is also rich in all of the important vitamins and minerals and helps neutralize an excessively acid condition. You should never drink tomato juice during the same meal where any starch or sugar is included, as these will neutralize its alkaline reaction. When taken alone, however, it is then used as a natural alkalizer.

String Beans and Brussels Sprouts provide the system with a natural insulin for the pancreatic functions of the digestive organism. Diabetics who eliminate sugars and starches from their diet and drink a combination of carrot, lettuce, string beans and Brussels sprouts juices, will find their condition much improved.

Onion and Garlic, aside from the distressing smell, provide your system with a potent tonic which helps nervousness, insomnia, rheumatism and is a good blood purifier and helps kill harmful bacteria and infections in the nose and throat. It also acts as an absorber of uric acid and is beneficial in instances of high blood pressure. Anyone suffering from diseases of the lungs and bronchi should take this combination daily.

Carrot and Coconut provide the system with ample amounts of calcium, magnesium and iron. They also help build a strong body and are good for peptic ulcers.

Cabbage, Cucumber and Grapefruit have a good proportion of chlorine and sulphur elements, a combination which is especially beneficial for cleansing of the mucous membranes of the stomach and intestinal tract. This combination is also the best natural diuretic known. It is a natural antiseptic. It should not be taken in cases of colitis.

Carrot, Beet and Coconut act as a tonic in cleansing the kidneys and gall bladder. They also contain the alkaline elements potassium, sodium, calcium, magnesium and iron.

Carrot, Celery, Endive and Parsley is a very rich combination containing nearly all of the essential minerals. It should be taken in cases of asthma, skin disease, biliousness, tired blood, gall stones, and gall bladder irritation, diseases of the urinary tract, stomach ulcers, inflammation of the middle ear and for general body building.

Carrot, Apple and Beet provide you with a very good tonic, rich in all of the minerals, and valuable in cases of anemia, constipation, arthritis, tired blood, obesity and general fatigue.

Carrot, Dandelion and Lettuce help build a healthy appetite, act as a nerve tonic and a mild diuretic. It is good for colds, rheumatism, arthritis, kidney, bladder and liver ailments and is a good blood cleanser and body purifier.

Carrot, Spinach and Orange are good for the entire digestive tract, both the alimentary section of the body (the stomach, duodenum and small intestines) and for the large intestine or colon.

Celery, Tomato and Radish are strong natural antiseptics. They protect your system against infection, sinus congestion and aid in obesity, catarrh, constipation, gall stones, kidney disorders, and nerve disorders.

Pineapple and Cucumber provide you with a mild digestive stimulant and a good general gland regulator. They are slightly diuretic and beneficial for ulcers of the stomach, kidney stones and bladder ailments.

Pineapple contains a very useful digestive enzyme known as papain. It is rich in chlorine which helps digest proteins and soothes sore throat and bronchitis.

Orange is a good cleanser of the intestinal tract and a blood purifier. It also has a rapid alkaline effect on an over-acid condition of the system. It is extremely rich in vitamin C.

Grapefruit provides the system with a natural alkaline reaction and is rich in fruit acids and sugars. It is beneficial as an aid in the removal or dissolving of inorganic calcium deposits formed in the cartilage or the joints as in arthritis.

Blueberry and Huckleberry act as a natural astringent, a good blood purifier and an antiseptic. Persons suffering from dysentery, acidosis, high blood pressure, menstruation disorders and diabetes should take an 8-ounce glass twice daily.

Strawberry, Cherry, Prune and Date provide an instant booster for the sluggish system. They are also good for sluggish skin, poor complexion, pimples, acne, ringworms, sore eyes, sore throat and quinsy.

Papaya and Lemon Juice are very good for digestive ailments. They contain a large amount of papain. They are helpful for sensitive stomachs and a good tonic in their rebuilding effect on the stomach and digestive tract.

Strawberry and Coconut are good for sore throat, stomach ulcers and gastritis. They also act as a general body builder. You should now have at least some idea of the exciting possibilities in store for you through the use of these natural healing and health maintaining juices. Even though it is but a brief glimpse into the challenging phase of dietetics, in the near future a great deal more research will be conducted with raw juice therapy to see the extent of its influence in the field of curative and preventive medicine.

THE IMPORTANCE OF FRUIT

In today's society, chronic fatigue and illness have become a routine part of our everyday existence. We seem to think that sore throat, sinus, bloodshot eyes, gas, heartburn, ulcers, indigestion, headache, overweight, thinning and receding hair, premature graying, dry or oily skin, wrinkles, poor eyesight and hypertension are all commonly accepted aspects of daily living. To treat these various ailments we consume millions of different medicines and drugs which are changed, improved or modified every few months. Unfortunately, these medicines have no real relation to the life force in the body.

Instead of attacking the cause or reason why we become ill, we pamper ourselves with drugs which, at best, treat and suppress symptoms. This is a direct contradiction to the natural laws of nature and the healthy state which mankind should have obtained. By subscribing to the drug theory we are implying that the habits of man are not responsible for his many illnesses, and that man can do as he pleases provided he takes the prescribed form of treatment. Much of this type of distorted thinking could be eliminated with a reeducation to the life process and study of just how the body works.

There is no device to compare with man's amazing structure. Your system is vastly complicated yet it is able to function more perfectly than any machine, pump, pulley, lever, electronic system, water system or chemical laboratory which man has yet devised. Regardless of how complicated your system may seem, its primary functions are quite simple: to distill everything which goes into the body: air, food, water, etc. The system's assimilating and eliminating faculties extract the finer essences from fruits and vegetables into the bloodstream.

The membranous tract is the lining which is like an inner covering throughout the internal portion of the system. It runs the length of the stomach, small intestines, colon, liver, glands, digestive tract, mouth, ears, nose, respiratory tract, lungs, heart, bladder, kidneys, vagina, veins, capillaries and arteries. Food by-products are able to travel along this membranous tract to the different areas of the system, and gives us the answer why phlegm can be regurgitated through the mouth from the small intestines. Your system absorbs much of the toxic matter from improper foods which your system cannot always eliminate. The body's internal arrangement shows that if you continually consume unsuitable food such as refined commercially produced foods, and animal products, they will leave large deposits of cholesterol and acids which will saturate the entire membranous tract. You can very easily saturate your entire system with harmful accumulations of morbid matter. Most people think that everything which is eaten is either used as energy or for cells and the remainder is eliminated through the bowel. However, through the effects of colds or fever or suppurating sores with their heavy catarrhal discharge, we can see what quantity of unusable and toxic matter can be stored in the body. Refined foods are so processed that they form thick sticky matter which will begin to glue and coat up the membranes and such special lymphatic organs as the tonsils which have a very important filtering role.

We should realize that the body is basically an assimilating organism which comprises the mouth, gullet, stomach, small intestines and the various organs which secrete digestive liquids such as the bile duct, pancreas and liver. The twenty-four feet of small intestines are used as the principal absorbing chamber but the fruits and vegetables begin to release their elements into the bloodstream within minutes of entering the stomach.

The excretory or eliminating organs are the kidneys which filter impurities from your blood; the lungs where an interchange of gases takes place between carbon dioxide being released by the bloodstream and the oxygen which is inhaled to replace it, and the skin which eliminates water and small amounts of urea and uric acid.

An important part of maintaining your health is to see that your assimilating and eliminating organs are functioning harmoniously. The cleaner your system the better your overall health will be.

Whenever you eat food your assimilating organs are in ascendancy, but when you rest, sleep or fast your body is given the opportunity of eliminating all toxic matter from the tissues. This is part of the reason why that if you are not eating judiciously you may awake the following morning with a stuffy nose, catarrh in the throat and acid, bitter and salty tastes in the mouth, etc.

You should try to eat only those foods which have an affinity with your digestive structure. The proper food in the right combinations will supply the body with the necessary nutrients and also keep the membranous tract moist and healthy.

When eating fruit for a meal, try to have a variety of fruits: oranges with apples or pears or peaches and plums. It is best to eat the more acid and juicy fruits first because of their cleansing and easy digestible qualities. Ten minutes or so later you can eat the more concentrated fruits such as bananas or avocado or papaya.

Sweet root vegetables such as beetroots, carrots, and turnip can be eaten in place of fruit.

One of the advantages of fresh fruit is that it has acids with which to stir up and eliminate waste and morbid matter. Leaves and vegetables as a rule are not so well endowed. Also, the sugar content of fruits makes them easier to digest, as well as more sustaining than vegetables. The sugars in fruits supply the blood and tissues with the finest energy-giving food; and also the sugars, minerals and vitamins in these recommended foods help to maintain the blood in solution at the normal internal pressure. Lastly, the protein foods; nuts, cheese, fish, meats, eggs, legumes, if consumed in too large a quantity can be a deterrent to good health as they are rendered acid in the system. Your system does not need more than 45-60 grams of protein a day and if you are eating properly—you should never need a protein supplement.

Large quantities of fruit can be consumed without preparation of any kind and contain essential oxygen and sun energy in addition to its sugars, minerals, organic water and vitamins and enzymes. In short, fruit, by supplying nourishment which is eliminative, at the same time becomes in complete harmony with the physiological law that among other elements to sound health, you must also have a balance between assimilation and elimination. In fact, the entire purpose of the fruit diet is to add essential nutriments and minerals in a cleansing medium, the acid fruit juices. Acids from fruits have an alkalinizing effect in your system; but it is the acids from the end products of concentrated foods such as nuts, meat, fish, cereals, etc., which really acidify your system; and it is the outpouring of these acids which is stirred up by the fruits which gives the erroneous impression that it is the fruit which is causing you the discomfort.

To better understand the purpose of fruit in your diet you should know the three stages through which fruit passes. It can be either underripe, ripe, or overripe. As far as possible only tree-ripened fruit should be eaten, or its nearest equivalent. If you eat anything that is underripe, your alkaline reserves are drawn upon in order to neutralize acids. Overripe fruit on the other hand, as it is in the process of changing into alcohol, enters the bloodstream so rapidly that the entire organism becomes stimulated. Sweet fruit then, is the best. It enters the circulation at a sedate pace and assists in moving any non-organic residue through the digestive tract.

Once you begin to include a good portion of fruit in your diet, your body begins to rest from the previous overindulgence of improper foods and the entire vascular and organicular system begins to contract, similar to an internal massage, so that excess fluids and wastes (hydrotherapy) are released for elimination. Through your body being rested, and the peristaltic motions becoming much more vigorous, a more thorough removal of wastes takes place, which causes your entire system to become cleaner, assimilation is improved and you shouldn't feel sluggish or full all of the time.

Fruits carry their own digestive juices and are much easier to digest than concentrated foods. Concentrated foods are very complex substances which the body must break down in order to release their vital elements, or for their elimination from your system. Your body is a self-healing organism and will attempt to digest anything which you eat. It removes the less concentrated foods first, and must, as the concentrated foods do not carry enough digestive juices with them, manufacture and secrete strong acids and enzymes for their dissolution. As fruits readily liberate their vital nutrients soon after mastication, these do not overtax the digestion to the same extent, and therefore permit the organism to commence the rebuilding and cleansing processes much sooner.

Acid fruits, mainly the lemon, by their cleansing effect throughout your system, assist the body in assimilating and dissolving fats.

The liver has a variety of functions which it must perform, without hindrance, if you are to maintain your health: storage of glycogen, the neutralizing of toxins, the breakdown of excess proteins into uric acid, and the manufacture of digestive juices. With all this to contend with, it is easy to see why many persons develop enlarged livers, due to the extra strain and work it must do if you continually pollute your system with toxic matter. With a good intake of fruit, however, the liver is not overburdened since it need never deal with concentrated foods.

Fruits also serve an important purpose to individuals who suffer from constipation. You should not have to resort to herbal or chemical laxatives when eating an ample quantity of fresh fruit. Fresh fruits and vegetables help cleanse the entire alimentary canal of phlegmy and acidic adhesions. Also, food must pass through the system at its own speed if your body has to extract the maximum quantity of nutrients from it; therefore, if you are a chronic laxative user, food will be forced through the system at a more rapid rate so that ultimately the organism will be deprived of nutriment.

For best results with a fruit diet, eat a sufficient amount so that adequate liquid and natural sugars are obtained. If you have not been eating an ample supply of fruit daily, then make one or two meals a day for a few weeks fruit meals. This will cause your bloodstream to be surcharged with fruit juices. This saturation helps to dilute and neutralize all toxins being released by the tissues, arteries, membranes, and glands, as well as cleansing the kidneys and bladder. The saturation of the bloodstream is one way to help purify your system and help prevent many serious ailments which might otherwise have developed in your system.

POLLEN

Pollen is the Manna given to us by nature and the intervention of insects, mainly the bee, to revitalize our bodies and aid in the cure of different illnesses. Its contents or ingredients are so complete with necessary proteins, vitamins, minerals, enzymes, natural antibiotics and hormones that it could be called nature's most complete food.

In the accounts of ancient civilizations and Biblical days we read that a combination of honey and bee bread (pollen) was the ambrosia of the gods. Much more recently royal jelly has been introduced as the complete sustaining youth food. In reviewing the pollen case we are prone to classify honey and royal jelly as a byproduct or emulsionization of nature's original Manna.

Pollen consists of single grains of the tiniest spores which are by themselves invisible to the naked eye. It is the male germ seed which fathers the world of plant life which nature or the insect carries from flowers, plants or tree blossoms. Transferred from the anther or a stamen to the stigma of a pistil it fertilizes the ovary and growth of a seed. The insects that pollinate most of our beautiful garden plants are bugs, beetles, flies, moths, butterflies and, of prime importance to man, the bee. The natural elements also carry this tiny spore (which is extremely prolific and has been seen to cover entire surfaces of lakes and ponds) to its destination. Each microscopic grain contains the power of the atom within it and is able to fruit a gigantic tree. When pollen by itself is not able to set this life process in motion it is aided by the insects, especially the bee. The completion of this cycle of life and its natural process is still a mystery to man.

Until recent times the miracle of this tiny spore was left entirely to the plant world, but intense research has proven it to be pure food from natural organic sources.

Although there are many variations of pollen, generally speaking pollen contains 35 percent protein, of which approximately half is in the form of free amino acids; that is, materials essential to life, which can be assimilated immediately by the body. Further, 40 percent of the content is made up of various forms of sugar, 5 percent fat, 3 percent minerals and oligo-elements (carriers of calcium, magnesium, iron, phosphorus, copper and manganese, etc.), 3-4 percent moisture totaling about 86 percent. The remaining 14 percent is composed of trace elements, only a few of which have been identified (amines, pantothenic acid, folic acid, biotin, nicotinic acid, cyanocobalamin); not only are the B-complex vitamins found but also vitamins A, C, D and E.

Recently doctors and nutrition advisors have been using pollen for the treatment of people of all ages. They found that your system only needs a small balanced quantity of these essential elements to maintain a proper growth and repair factor.

The amino acids in whole dry pollen fluctuate between 10 and 13 percent and this equals from 5 to 7 times the amino acids in equal weights of beef, eggs and cheese. Amino acids are vital to our good health and play an extremely important role in our lives. There are twenty-one known amino acids and the human body is able to produce all but eight which are referred to as the essential amino acids. Pollen contains all of these eight essential amino acids. Other complete protein foods which contain all these essential amino acids are soya beans, wheat germ, liver, skimmed milk, eggs, and certain nuts. All pollens contain exactly the same number of amino acids but different species of pollen have varying amounts of each.

A number of enzymes have been found in pollen which include: amylase, catalase, dehydrogenase, diaphorase, sucrase, diastase, cozymase, cytochrome, pectase, phosphatase, and lactic acids. Pollen compares favorably to yeast as a pure food. The alcoholic fermentation of both are identical. It is also revealed that a mixture of fresh pollen contains up to 1000 micrograms of coxamase per gram.

Pollens vary in colors and shades to the same extent as honey. It contains a variety of sugars and carbohydrates in the whole pollen in the form of cane sugar (sucrose), fruit sugar (fructose), and grape sugar (glucose).

Pollen to plants is as the fingerprints of man. It is an identification and has established for many years the botanical origin of honey from its contents. It is a highly concentrated substance which never contains over 18 percent water. Ten percent of the total gathered by bees in any particular hive may be removed with no ill effect on the colony. Pollen may contain up to 35 percent protein, with 15 to 25 percent amino acids and 40 percent carbohydrates or glucides. A recent discovery by two French doctors states that it contains a growth factor and an antibiotic.

Beekeepers are aware that it is a health food and it is now being marketed in many countries for this purpose. In this natural substance is to be found a fine and whole food and a medicine if it is obtained and stored without loss of vitality.

Intensive research has been taking place in Sweden, Russia, America, Canada, France and Switzerland. In the laboratories, under microscopic investigation, pollen placed on a slide with a mixture of boric acid and agar agar to accelerate germination, the grains will have grown tails. This does not occur when taken as a food, or assimilated. Its natural antibiotic can be used to cure many common ailments and may eventually be classified as a pure substance of life which may give us a clue to an innate force which will prolong human life and vitality, as it accomplishes for the bee.

FASTING

Fasting is accepted as being one of the oldest forms of therapy. Fasting means a total or partial abstinence from food or water for any length of time and for any of a variety of reasons. There are fruit fasts, water fasts, vegetable fasts, milk fasts, and so on.

A fruit fast is the elimination of fruit; a vegetable fast is abstinence from vegetables, etc. These are the recognized forms of fasting, yet the most common and often practiced form is total abstinence from all foods, but not water.

Unfortunately, most persons who undertake a fast know little if anything about fasting and often cause themselves unnecessary side effects. This chapter is written with the intention of giving all the essential facts about fasting.

Fasting is not a cure for any disease or ailment. Rather, it allows the body full range and scope to fulfill its self-healing, self-repairing, self-rejuvenating functions to the best advantage. Healing is an internal biological function. Fasting allows your system a physiological rest and permits the organism to become 100 percent efficient in healing itself. You will quickly see that with the proper workable knowledge, fasting can be a fast and safe way of regaining health.

Fasting gives the overworked, overburdened internal organs and tissues rest and time for rehabilitation. It exhilarates the internal power and vitality of your system to flush out toxic matter and poisons which have accumulated over the years. Thus it promotes the elimination of inorganic chemical accumulations and other toxic matter which cannot be flushed from the body by any normal means.

You find that all of your organs have improved after a fast. Digestion, assimilation and elimination processes will be improved. You will probably also find that your sensory powers, except eyesight, are exhilarated and raised to a much higher efficiency level than normal during and after a fast.

Fasting improves circulation and promotes vital vigor, endurance, stamina and strength. In short, fasting renovates, revivifies and purifies each one of the millions of cells which make up your body.

Fasting is not a new therapeutic discovery but has been practiced by intelligent persons since the development of civilization, and in the animal world since the development of the present forms of animal life. Among undomesticated animals it is a common practice to fast when ill, though this is obviously an instinctive procedure rather than a planned therapeutic measure. The first recorded instances of persons who fasted for therapeutic reasons go back to the Greek and Roman civilizations. Both Plato and Socrates fasted many times throughout their lives. Pythagoras fasted for 40 days before taking his examination at the University of Alexandria. Many of the early Egyptian writings refer to fasting as a remedy for syphilis and other diseases. Even the famous Greek physician, Hippocrates, prescribed fasting for any serious illness. Asclepiades and Thessalus practiced fasting; Celsus fasted to treat his jaundice and epilepsy, and the Arab physician, Avicenna, prescribed fasting for all ailments. Later Tertullian and Plutarch wrote much on fasting; Plutarch said: "Instead of using medicine better fast a day." In every century since the beginning, great men of science and medicine have practiced, spoken for and written about the benefits of fasting.

History thus affords evidence of the considerable amount of scientific and clinical work done to determine the effect of fasting, as regards its curative influence in the case of many specific diseases.

If you were to abstain from food for any length of time, certain changes in the function, chemical reactions and life processes of the cells and tissues would take place. It is these changes which give fasting its therapeutic properties.

Among the physiological effects of fasting is rejuvenescence, which is simply the reenergization of the cells and tissues of the body. Fasting also produces an increase in the metabolic rate. The effects of this can be attested to by Dr. Carlson and Dr. Kunde, of the Department of Physiology at the University of Chicago, who placed a 40-year-old man on a 14-day fast. At the end of the fast his tissues were in the same physiological condition as those of a 17-year-old youth.

You should also notice outward improvements when fasting. The rejuvenating effect upon the skin in particular is important. Lines and wrinkles become less apparent, and blotches, discoloration and pimples tend to disappear. Your skin will become more youthful and acquire a better color and texture. In short, you should look younger.

Your system is affected in many ways when fasting. One of these is through autolysis, which means self-loosing. Autolysis is the process of digestion of foods by ferments and enzymes which are generated by the body cells. Thus it is a process of self-digestion or intra-cellular digestion.

This action is quite normal for your system. The action of enzymes upon such elements as glycogen, fatty tissue and bone marrow, in preparing these substances for entry into the bloodstream, is normal autolysis. Likewise when an abscess points to the surface of the body to empty its contents, autolysis was involved when the flesh between the abscess and the surface was digested by enzymes.

Most medical men and scientists believed that the process of autolysis could not be made subject to human control. Though it is common knowledge that abnormal growths in the body might be absorbed through self-disintegration, the profound change in metabolism necessary to bring about such autolysis has been thought to result only in very rare cases following such conditions as extreme cachexia, the puerperium, or menopause. Such conditions, not always being within the area of self control, and only rarely producing the changes in question, offer no method whereby autolysis can be instituted at will and put under control.

During the fast, the system has the opportunity to redistribute its vital elements, the surpluses and non-vital nutrients being consumed and utilized first.

During the fast your assimilative powers are increased significantly. This can be seen both in the improvement of your blood during the fast and the rapid assimilation of food after the fast. Individuals who are afflicted with conditions such as anemia, with either an insufficiency of red blood cells or an excess of white cells, are usually back to normal after a fast. In many cases fasting has brought about an increase in the amount of erythrocytes from only one million to the normal five million count. The reason being that the fast improves the assimilation. The iron and other nutrients which are stored in the body are taken up by the blood and used. This could also account for a reduction of tooth decay after a fast. While fasting, swollen, inflamed and bleeding gums were restored to normal. The improvement in assimilation during the fast can help bring about recovery of certain deficiency ailments. This can be observed in people who are chronically underweight in spite of eating very heavily, who often gain weight to the normal level after a fast, even though large amounts of food are not eaten. The improved assimilation enables the system to utilize more of its food intake.

It is actually a normalization of assimilation which occurs on a fast. Persons who fast to lose excessive weight may gain weight to normal after the fast, but that is usually where the gain ends if nutrition is proper and balanced. Fasting, then, helps both those who assimilate too little, and those who assimilate too much of their food intake.

Your internal organs obtain nearly a complete physiological rest from overwork and overstimulation, while fasting. Your tissues have a chance to repair the damage caused by a constant diet of defective foods and excessive quantities of foods, which cause all organs to weaken. As there is no further intake of food while fasting, all of your organs' work is reduced to the lowest possible minimum. Assimilation in your system only involves the redistribution of the elements already stored there, while fasting. Most sores, wounds and fractures tend to heal more rapidly. In short, your system undergoes a healing process.

Associated with physiological rest of an organ is increased elimination. This is one of the most important advantages of fasting. A good portion of the body energy normally needed to help assimilation may be used to expel the accumulations of waste and toxins. Decomposing food in the digestive tract is quickly eliminated. Your entire alimentary canal becomes as germ free and clean of harmful bacteria as is possible to obtain. The surplus elements are utilized first. The effusions, dropsical swellings, fat, infiltrations, etc., are absorbed with great rapidity on a fast.

You may encounter a case of very foul breath and offensive skin odor, for the first few days of your fast, due to a greater elimination via the lungs and skin. Catarrhal climinations usually increase the first few days, as does the toxicity of the urine. In a few cases, considerable waste material is lost through vomiting. However, these symptoms do not occur in all cases.

You should also notice a marked improvement in nervous and mental functions while fasting. All enervating influences are discontinued and the entire nervous system and brain undergo the same physiological rest that the rest of the system experiences.

Fasting thus will help you in many ways:

1. It produces rejuvenation of tissues
2. It induces autolysis of abnormal growths
3. Speeds up assimilation and elimination
4. Allows all of the organs a physiological rest
5. Increases elimination
6. Promotes nerve energy recuperation
7. Speeds up the healing process for any body ailments

In many instances, individuals who have tried fasting have been ill. They usually only turned to fasting after having undergone all other forms of healing: drugs, surgery, manipulation, massage, electrical treatment, autosuggestion, etc., with varying degrees of success. Yet, even with such infections as affliction of the heart, and other vital organs, the percentage of recoveries has been surprisingly high; exceeding that resulting from the use of any other therapeutic measure.

There are no less than 100 books, foundation reports and fasting institutes' and sanatoriums' reports on the efficiency of the fasting treatment. One of the world's acknowledged experts on fasting is Dr. Shelton, who reported that 95 percent of the patients at his institute have recovered their health or claimed significant benefit, while fasting.

One of the most complete statistical reports of fasting comes from Dr. James McEachen, who used fasting in the treatment of 715 cases of disease during the period from

August, 1952 to March, 1958. The tests were recorded at Dr. McEachen's sanatorium near Escondido, California. The only negative factor was that many of the persons being treated did not stay on the fast for the recommended time. Even so, in 294 cases, there was a marked improvement or complete recovery; in 360 cases there was a moderate improvement, and for the remaining 61 cases, no improvement at all could be noticed. Thus the average percentage of improved or remedied cases was 88.4 percent. The following chart lists the ailments treated and the number of those responding, or not responding, to the fast.

AILMENT	NUMBER OF CASES	CASES WHICH IMPROVED	CASES NOT HELPED
High Blood Pressure	141	141	0
Colitis	88	77	11
Sinusitis	67	64	3
Anemia	60	52	8
Hemorrhoids	51	48	3
Arthritis	47	39	8
Bronchitis	42	39	3
Kidney Disease	41	36	5
Benign Tumor	38	32	6
Heart Disease	33	29	4
Asthma	29	29	0
Ulcers	23	20	3
Hay Fever	19	17	2
Goiter	11	11	0
Pyorrhea	8	6	2
Gallstones	7	6	1
Cancer	5	5	0
Multiple Sclerosis	4	3	1
Cataract	4	3	1

The statistics are even more important when you realize that of those individuals who were not helped, about half had fasted only a few days and some of the remainder gave stopping of the fast as the reason for the failure. To understand the benefits of fasting, one must consider the therapeutic values gained in the treatment of a number of specific diseases.

Any number of visual defects have been treated success-fully with fasting, though some mechanical defects cannot be corrected by fasting, and certain eye ailments require aid which fasting cannot give. If your eye muscles suffer from a lack of tone, strength, flexibility, suppleness and coordination, special eye exercises will do far more for you than fasting, though fasting may be used to supplement this therapy.

Among the eye ailments which are known, in many cases, to respond well to fasting are cataract, congestion of the conjunctiva, catarrhal and granular conjunctivitis, glau-coma, iritis, keratitis and stye. If you act early in cases of cataract, recovery can be rapid; however, advanced cases may disappear, but full recovery is much less likely.

Respiratory problems respond well to fasting. A climate change is not necessary to improve hay fever ailments. Catarrh improves, although eliminations may increase tem-porarily on the first few days of the fast. Polyps are ab-sorbed; the thickened membranes return to their normal thickness, though the atrophied structures of advanced catarrh cannot be rebuilt. Sinusitis responds quickly to the fast. Chronic laryngitis improves quickly, except in severe cases which usually take much longer. Chronic asthma suf-ferers who were unable to sleep lying in bed and conse-quently slept in a sitting position were usually relieved enough within 2 days to sleep full prone.

The most destructive and serious respiratory disease, tuberculosis of the lungs has been treated effectively with fasting. The tubercular cough usually becomes very mild or disappears. In many cases, marked improvement is seen after an extended fast, or several fasts, followed by com-plete recovery during a period of balanced eating with adequate fresh air and careful exposure to sunlight. Most tuberculosis cases respond best to one or two short fasts due to the difficulty some have in gaining weight after longer fasts.

Goiter has responded well to fasting. When simple goiter exists, the enlargement tends to subside to normal during the course of the fast. If the disease has reached the stage where the soft goiter becomes a form of tumor, called an adenoma, improvement or recovery though still possible, will take much longer. Even when the goiter displays rapidly developing evidences of toxicity, as in exophthalmic goiter, there is still hope for recovery. Unlike many other forms of therapy, there are no aftereffects with fasting.

Individuals who suffer from pernicious anemia will double their blood count in a week of fasting.

Another blood disease, leukemia, which does not respond well to any form of medication, has shown improvement when treated with fasting. Leukemia is generally associated with an excess of white cells in the blood, an impairment of the cells of bone marrow, and in some cases, impairment of the lymphatic glands, with enlargement of the spleen. In several cases the number of white cells in the blood decreased on the fast, while spleen diminution also occurred.

Many cases of poliomyelitis and chronic anterior poliomyelitis have been treated successfully with fasting. Even in cases where improvement was not possible, fasting caused further degeneration to be checked and the life prolonged. Bulbar paralysis, a less common form of poliomyelitis, may end fatally no matter what form of treatment is given.

Multiple sclerosis, which annually cripples thousands, has been treated successfully with fasting, even though, in most cases, recovery is not fully complete.

In several cases, lumps in female breasts have disappeared when fasting. The noted health and nutrition expert, Bernard MacFadden, remarked that his experience had shown "beyond all possible doubt that a foreign growth of any kind can be absorbed into the circulation by simply compelling the body to use every unnecessary element contained within it for food."

Whereas most abnormal growths which have been treated successfully have been benign tumors, there are many cases of the same good results with malignant ones. As a rule the chances of recovery from cancer depends largely upon the stage of the disease and the history of previous therapeutic treatment. If you catch the cancer early enough, before any surgery or radiation is needed, the prognosis is often favorable. The slow absorption of the neoplasm of cancer can then be expected in many cases. In many other cases there is not complete absorption, though further growth of the cancer can be stopped. If the neoplasm of cancer has been broken with exploratory or therapeutic surgery, with release of cancer cells to other parts of the body, and if tissues have been weakened with extensive X-ray therapy, the chances of recovery are markedly lower. If, in addition to these adverse factors, the individual has been treated for any length of time using pain-killing drugs, the prognosis becomes even less favorable. However, even when cancer is in its terminal stages, fasting may be considered some small assistance in reducing the pain, if nothing else.

Fasting has helped the treatment of appendicitis. The advantage of fasting over surgery in such cases as seen in the reduced mortality rate in cases of acute, gangrenous, ruptured appendicitis with peritonitis, is only 1.43 percent when the operation is deferred. Immediate operations for the same condition have provided a mortality rate of 10.64 percent as stated in the Journal of the American Medical Association, December 5, 1936.

Fasting has also helped treat a variety of disorders associated with the female reproductive system. It helps to relieve congestion, removes infection, relaxes tissues and restores tone to the affected area. Abnormal growths of the womb have been partially or completely absorbed during the fast. Fasting is also recommended for painful and excessive menstruation.

Several cases of diabetes have been treated successfully by fasting, as have disorders such as epilepsy, and varicose veins. In the case of varicose veins, fasting does not destroy or coagulate the veins, which occur by other methods at the cost of overworking the deeper blood vessels, but it does help heal varicose ulcers, assists in restoring tonicity to the walls of the veins, reduces their size and provides freedom from pain. Most younger people have a full recovery but for the person past forty, with severe varicosities, definite improvement with comfort can be accomplished, but complete recovery does not usually happen. In all cases, though, proper, balanced nutrition and adequate exercise after the fast are needed to prevent excess fluid in the tissues and assure continued improvement of the maintenance of normal tone of the walls of the veins.

In most cases, arthritis, rheumatism and gout respond favorably and quickly to the fast. In many cases, the severe pain and discomfort of arthritis disappears within several days of fasting. There is gradual disappearance of the swelling and complete or partial absorption of the deformity by autolysis providing complete ossification of the joint is not present. However, for those who have been long sufferers of the disease, longer fasts or more than one fast may be needed.

Simple gall bladder and bile duct infection is helped during fasts of two or three weeks or less. The pus is drained the inflammation subsides and the tissues are healed. If stones have formed in the gall bladder, then a longer fast is necessary. During the fast, the stones soften, later disintegrate and then pass through the bile duct into the small intestines.

Many sufferers from high blood pressure have found a safe and effective remedy in fasting. Even in cases where all other medical treatment has failed, fasting has caused definite improvement. In some cases the blood pressure may fall below the normal mark during the fast, but it will rise to normal later, but actual hypertension does not re-develop so long as proper balanced eating is maintained.

Heart disease responds well to fasting. Fasting can cause such heart disorders as narrowing of the coronary artery and formation of thrombus in this artery, to be improved. In most cases, excess fatty matter lining the walls of the artery is absorbed by autolysis. Other forms of heart disease also respond well to the fast; acute myocarditis, fatty overgrowth of the heart, endocarditis and ordinary peri-carditis. However, hemopericardium and calcified pericar-dium cannot be cured by fasting.

Of the dozens of common and acute skin disorders most can be improved by fasting. In most cases, especially where simple acne is involved, recovery usually takes no more than a few weeks or less. Eczema and severe skin ailments, however, will require longer fasts. In all cases, improve-ment is limited to the removal of swelling, inflammation, excess scaly tissue and ulcerations. However, once scar tissue has formed, no amount of fasting can remove it.

People of all ages can enjoy the benefits of a fast. Only in cases where the child is under six years of age is fasting not recommended. Most children have rapid recuperative power and should not have long fasts, no more than a week at most, unless and only under strict doctor's care.

The only periods of life during which no fast should be undertaken are lactation and pregnancy. Fasting will cause the secretion of milk to stop and hence prevent the mother from nursing the child.

Please understand me, fasting can and often does help the body to rebuild itself, but it is *not* a cure-all, nor is it the only method whereby health can be restored. As mentioned in the chapter on Raw Juice Therapy, there are several different approaches to rebuilding health and overcoming disease. Proper nutrition and the constant guidance of your family doctor are the first steps. The fast is important in the speed and completeness by which a person may regain health.

UNDERSTANDING WHAT A FAST IS AND IS NOT

Many laymen have argued that if you fast you also starve the body; this is probably where the common term "starvation diet" originated. However, this is not the case. It is true that in both instances, starvation and fasting, a complete abstinence from food is accomplished, but the physiological effects are completely different.

Your system can store a considerable amount of food to be used as nutritive matter over an extended period of time. From the beginning of every fast, the system begins to nourish and feed itself upon such stored reserves. The cells accordingly diminish in size and there are changes in the colloidal condition of the protoplasm. Cell proliferation itself continues. The body loses weight in the form of fat, muscle, tissue, blood and water. Such vital organs as the heart, brain, spinal cord, nerves, teeth and bones are well nourished while fasting with little if any loss of effectiveness. In children the skeletal structure continues to grow, the marrow being drawn upon for nourishment.

In short, while fasting, the system continues to work normally. There is, however, a limit to this reserve of food. When all normal food reserves have been used then the body must be given a fresh new supply of food or else true starvation commences and the system feeds upon the vital tissues and other unchanged body organs. This, of course, causes the healthy tissues to be used, the vitality is depleted, and the body is emaciated. The blood atrophies; the cells of the vital organs begin to degenerate and as the process continues, death is inevitable.

Fasting begins with the omission of food and ends with the depletion of the food reserves. There are certain very definite signs which occur when the body's food reserve is depleted and the end of the fast is at hand. There is invariably a return of hunger and a removal of coating from the tongue. The edges and tip of the tongue clear first, then the remainder follows quickly thereafter. The putrid taste and foul breath likewise disappear at the completion of the fast. The pulse and temperature, which often are abnormal, become normal. The eyes brighten, salivary secretion is normalized, and the urine, which may have been discolored, becomes clear. Of all these symptoms, the return of hunger and clearing of the tongue are the most significant.

Regardless of your condition, the fast should be broken at the first appearance of either symptom. Even if your tongue is not clear yet you feel hungry, stop the fast. In those very rare occasions where a person does not lose his sense of hunger, the clearing of the tongue will suffice as a guide in determining the end of the fasting period.

Abstinence from food can be very dangerous if one fails to recognize the great difference between fasting and starvation, and the symptoms which denote the end of one and the start of the other. You should never set the length of time for a fast before you start without regard to the differences between the two phases of inanition. The time required for the fast to reach completion varies with each individual. Some will exhaust their food reserve in two weeks, others may take six to eight weeks. Most overweight persons can fast longer than thin people. The excessive fat on the obese individual will allow much additional nourishment. Some of the old-time doctors and nutritional experts claim that no fast should be broken until the body reserves are diminished. They give as an example those persons who broke a fast prematurely and were unable to digest the foods, vomiting everything which they ate. Complete fasts may be the ideal but they are not always practical or even necessary. If the correct liquid foods are taken, a fast for chronic ailments can be broken at any time without trouble. In fact, for most diseases in their early stages, a short fast of a week or two often gives the desired results. When a person is too weak, a longer fast than a week or two would only cause additional harm.

I have only mentioned fasts of a week or more, yet everyone should fast at least one day each week, preferably Sunday. This would give your system a chance to rest and in a modified way would help clean and rebuild the system. Sunday is the best day because one should not work strenuously and fast at the same time. Refrain from all exercise while fasting. And above all, only fast under the supervision of your doctor.

Antagonists of fasting claim that a fast can do a great deal of harm and could possibly kill a person. They claim fasting is unsafe. I agree with the point that any therapeutic measure should both provide beneficial results in treating disease and at the same time be associated with a minimum of danger.

Opponents of fasting state that it weakens the vital organs, especially the heart, causes the stomach to atrophy or makes the digestive juices eat away at the walls of the stomach, produces deficiency disease, causes teeth to decay, lowers the resistance of the body to infection, causes cells to degenerate, promotes edema and acidosis and in many cases causes death.

However, instead of weakening the heart, fasting allows the heart a chance to rest and gain new strength, this also applies to all other vital organs including the stomach and the entire digestive tract. There is no atrophy or impairment whatsoever. Regarding deficiency ailments, these do not occur while fasting. It is a matter of common sense that if a person's normal diet lacks the necessary vitamins and minerals that have caused a deficiency disease, a fast, which supplies no additional minerals and vitamins, will do no worse. On the contrary, during a fast, when the system's energy is not used in the functioning of digestion and assimilation, the need for minerals is lowered. The reserves of these elements in the system are sufficient to meet all needs. It is for this reason that no deficiency diseases occur during a fast.

Contrary to lowering resistance to disease, fasting can increase the resistance to disease. The thousands of cases of complete or partial recoveries from disease which occur while fasting are in themselves evidence that the power to overcome infection is raised on the fast.

Granted, the blood alkalinity is slightly lowered while fasting, however, this never reaches the point that true acidosis exists. There are always sufficient alkaline reserves in the system to defend against this condition. In short, fasting is generally accepted as one of the safest and most practical therapeutic forms of regaining health. There are no contradictions in fasting, in the sense that one part of the body is helped while another is harmed. In this respect it differs from other forms of therapy, which suppress one symptom, only to create others. Fasting helps the diseased organ in the same sense that it helps all other organs and tissues.

You will probably notice a few discomforts during the initial stages of the fast. The first day, a strong desire for food is usually present by afternoon or early evening. The second day the desire increases but by the third day the hunger usually abates with the complete disappearance of hunger coming on the fourth or fifth day. Some individuals have developed nausea and vomiting at the sight of food, while on a fast. There does seem to be a marked repugnance for food during the first week of fasting. As I mentioned previously, the tongue usually becomes heavily coated and the breath very offensive, usually beginning a few days after the fast has begun.

The body reactions vary significantly with each person. When there is acute disease, with fever, the temperature gradually drops to normal during the fast. When the temperature is below normal at the outset of the fast, it gradually rises to normal and remains there. In a few exceptions, the temperature rises above normal for short periods, but this usually only occurs when no acute ailments exist. If one fasts for an extended period of time, say six to eight weeks, a marked drop in body temperature occurs. Such conditions should be a warning to you and cause you to break the fast immediately. Whenever the body temperature drops rapidly it is a sign that the system is entering the starvation period and the fast must be stopped. On occasion a slight chilliness may occur. This is caused by the decreased cutaneous circulation, but can be countered by wearing warmer clothing. Too, the feet may become cold, again for the same reason, and additional socks should be worn. In most cases a slight variation in the pulse rate can be observed. In instances of chronic illness, the pulse rises slightly during the first few days, then drops to about 40 or slightly more, after which it rises again to about 60. An erratic pulse is not uncommon during a fast. However, if it becomes persistent and remains very high or very low for more than a few days the fast should be broken off.

An increase in the strength may be noticed, especially for those who are very weak at the outset of the fast. Though most individuals lose strength from the beginning of the fast to the end of it. As the fast lengthens, weakness intensifies. Extreme emaciation, with weakness to the point of fainting or inability to walk properly is, of course, an indication that the fast must be stopped.

You will probably lose about one pound of weight per day, while fasting, at least for the first week or two and then it slows down to one pound every two or three days. In cases of extreme overweight or obesity, more weight is lost per day, often up to three pounds. One should not worry about the loss of weight as there is no danger in losing weight while fasting, in fact, the body will regain any weight it needs to reach a normal strength level, after the fast. However, obese persons are far more apt to experience nausea as the body uses up stored fat, thereby releasing toxic agents such as DDT, which accumulate in fatty tissues, into the bloodstream.

Once you have eaten your final meal before beginning the fast the digestive tract will become inactive and there is usually very little bowel movement. The intestines become empty. Bowel movement will be restored to normal right after the end of the fast. When it does occur on the fast, the action may be easy or difficult, depending on the type of food which was consumed immediately prior to the fast.

There is no set pattern for determining the sexual motivation and activity while fasting. In most instances the desire is either reduced or abolished, with temporary impotency developing during the fasts. After the fast the sexual abilities return, often with renewed vigor. Men who had been impotent prior to fasting have often regained virility.

In women previously affected by congestion in the ovaries and uterus, the menses may appear at irregular intervals while fasting and appear almost viscid in consistency with an offensive odor. This should not alarm you as it is a purely natural cleansing of the reproductive system.

Among a variety of other irritations which may or may not occur are: vomiting, skin eruptions, backaches, headaches, dizziness, hiccoughs, sore throat, slight colds and cramps. Though these symptoms are discomforting they do not pose any danger and should go away in a day or two, if you get any one of them at all. Most persons do not experience any of these.

Anyone who has had extensive drug therapy will find that fasting is the exact opposite of drug therapy. Whereas drugs often suppress the symptoms of illness, fasting will bring the disease out and attempt to eliminate all toxins and provide for a permanent recovery. Often, a disease which has been inactive, due to being suppressed by drugs, may become active through fasting, as tissues are healed and elimination increased. A fast helps the weakest tissues and organs of the body first, and thus allows for renovative activity. Often, a subdued ailment may flare up and become quite intense during the first few days of fasting, and as renovation continues to completion, all symptoms gradually subside until recovery is completed.

Once you have made it through the hunger pains and minor discomforts of the first few days of the fast, the remainder should be very easy with no further annoyance.

To prepare oneself for a fast requires little preparatory treatment. The only thing you should do is to eliminate all concentrated starches from your diet, the week before your fast. Eat only raw, fresh fruits, vegetables, and juices. This will allow your bowels a chance to loosen themselves and promote copious elimination. If your alimentary canal is clean and free from excessive residues, the fast will be much more comfortable and effective.

During the fast you will require more than the usual amount of rest. The active person consumes his nutritive reserves and energy more rapidly than the individual who takes it easy and doesn't overexert himself. Proper rest will also allow you to fast longer and emerge in better condition.

In the advanced stages of fasting you should wear warm clothing. A lack of warmth will cause the process of elimination to be adversely affected. If you should become extremely cold, break the fast.

The emotions and mental character also play an important role in the fast. Try to avoid fear and negative thoughts or influences while fasting. Anger, grief and shock tend to drain the reserve energy from the system and can cause ill effects. Therefore, if you are under these influences, don't fast.

Try not to bathe in water which is either too cold or too hot. Drink about a quart of water each day during the fast. You may encounter individuals who advocate water-free fasting, or others who recommend several quarts of water per day. Experience shows us that either of these two extremes could prove harmful if not fatal while fasting. We recommend thirst as a reliable guide. You may not feel a great need for water while fasting, but still try to drink a four- to six-ounce glass every few hours anyway.

Many old-timers will tell you that you need an enema while fasting. However, again experience and modern techniques and knowledge show us that you should refrain from using it altogether. Persons who have used it will argue that toxins and waste matter are being deposited in the colon during the fast, and that the same materials are in turn re-absorbed by the blood. They say cleansing the lower bowel with an enema each day will prevent such re-absorption.

In fact, this is *not* the case. The colon is not fundamentally an organ in which much absorption occurs, and the entire alimentary canal, including the colon, becomes free of all morbid waste during the fast. There is no substantial evidence to prove otherwise. The use of the enema would also cause additional drain on the individual's vitality. It washes away the mucus which normally protects the lining of the colon, and it breaks some of the tiny muscles of the intestinal wall, which causes the muscle tone to be impaired.

Do not take drugs while fasting. Drugs are quickly absorbed into the system of a person who is fasting. They will usually cause adverse effects. This also applies for serums and injections of any kind.

If the fast is not ended properly the results will often be unfavorable. When the intake of food is stopped, the system adjusts itself to the new conditions. The digestive organs cease to exercise their natural function; the digestive glands do not produce the usual juices, and the stomach shrinks to less than its normal size. This is all a part of the physiological rest.

It only takes a few days for your system to lose its natural ability to digest and assimilate food in the regular manner. The system is slow to regain this digestive power once the fast has ended. If the first intake of food is of the heavy concentrated type, difficulty occurs; the food will very likely be vomited up or, if retained, no digestive activity will take place, with the food decaying and fermenting, causing distress and discomfort. If this occurs in the lower section of the digestive tract, in the small intestine, the reactions are quite serious.

The first food to enter the system after the fast should be of a liquid nature, due to its rapid absorption and ease in digestion. It is soothing and less abrasive to the delicate mucous membrane lining.

Fruit and vegetable juices and broths are recommended. Discomfort is practically unknown when these foods are consumed. Unstrained orange juice is given preference by most practitioners.

End your fast with one-half glass of juice, followed by the same amount every hour, or one glass every two hours. On the second day the same schedule should be followed; a three-meal-a-day program can be followed provided that one pint of juice is taken with each meal. On the following days the amount of juice can be increased. Do not take more than one pint of juice at a sitting after the fast.

Cold and iced juices should *not* be taken. Sip the first juices very slowly, allowing the juice to be "chewed" in the mouth before being swallowed, the acid and sugar of the fruit mixes with saliva and work of the stomach is thereby reduced.

If you drink your juice too fast and too cold, stomach cramps could ensue.

The juice diet should last about six days. The ratio of the fast to the juice diet may be only two or three to one in the case of very short fasts, about four to five to one for moderate fasts, and seven to one for longer fasts. The following list will represent a suggested time schedule for correlating the juice diet with the length of the fast.

Length of Fast	Length of Juice Diet
1–3 days	1 day
4–8 days	2 days
9–15 days	3 days
16–24 days	4 days
25–35 days	5 days
over 35 days	6 days

Following the juice diet, you may eat any form of uncooked food. On successive days the quantity of food may be gradually increased. Do not try to eat large meals to compensate for previous restriction. Moderate eating habits are the safest and healthiest.

Do not feel that because you have had a successful fast that you are now immune to illness or disease. The only insurance you have to keep ailments out of your life is to live properly. Try to control your eating habits in order to preserve your good health. So understand fasting for what it is: a means of promoting the remedy of illness and the creation of health. It is not a method of maintaining health.

A RATIONAL ALTERNATIVE
TO MEAT EATING

This chapter on the benefits of a vegetarian diet is not meant as a contradiction to any other reference in this book, which deals with the nutritional elements found in different meats, fowl, and fish; rather it will serve as a guide and answer the most important questions concerning vegetarianism.

It is rather obvious that the vast majority of Americans, and this includes health food advocates, are meat eaters. Nothing that anyone says in any book, article or consumer report will cause them to suddenly change their own eating habits and become vegetarians. However, during the past three years literally thousands of individuals, mainly younger ones, have tried, and accepted the vegetarian method of diet. It is the belief of the authors that, while the percentage of vegetarians to meat eaters is only 1 or 2 percent, the trend in the next few years will be toward a diet with less meat consumed; therefore, to allow those persons who want a better understanding of the vegetarian diet, we have assembled the best arguments for vegetarianism. These facts were gleaned from more than thirty books on vegetarianism and meatless diets. The opinions stated in this chapter are not necessarily those held by the authors. It is not our intention to promote vegetarianism, but rather give it an equal forum to present its arguments for the cause of a more healthy system.

AN ARGUMENT FOR VEGETARIANISM

Perhaps no word has met with as many false interpretations as "Vegetarianism." This is mainly due to the similarity of the words "vegetarian" and "vegetables." The average person thinks that a vegetarian is a vegetable eater. Vegetarian is derived from the Latin word "vegetare," which means "to enliven." The old Romans used the term "homo vegetus" for a lively, vigorous person, sound in body and mind. All too often, false arguments against vegetarians are based on this misunderstanding.

The notion that meat is in some manner predigested plantfood, ready to be swallowed and assimilated, is entirely erroneous from a chemical as well as a physiological standpoint. This chapter will investigate and hopefully enlighten everyone whose interpretations of meat eating and vegetarianism are similar to the above statements.

Whatever other function food may or may not have, its primary purpose is to replace wornout tissue. The tissue-wastes are eliminated; the tissues themselves replenished by the food eaten; so, in the average case, the body remains about the same in weight no matter how much exercise is participated in, or how much tissue is broken down. These tissues are very complex in their nature, and a variety of food is consequently needed to restore and renourish the tissues destroyed—food containing a number of elements being necessary to offset the waste. Protein, fats, carbohydrates, mineral salts and vitamins are therefore necessary in the food; and no foods that do not contain these constituents, in larger or smaller quantities, can be classed as an all-round, sufficient food. Other things being equal, therefore, it may be said that a food must be nutritious and capable of sustaining life in proportion to its complexity. If an article of food in the diet contains only one of the essential elements necessary for supporting life, the body, if fed upon it, will waste away, no matter how much of that food is eaten. In certain experiments conducted upon dogs, it was found that, when they were fed upon fat, they became round, plump, and yet died of inanition! The same would be true of any other single article of food.

Proteins supply most of the muscle-forming elements, and a part of the energy expended by the body; fats and carbohydrates are used chiefly in supplying heat and energy to the system. Minerals and vitamins are absolutely essential. It is apparent, therefore, that foods rapidly and forcibly affect the state of the health and life force of the individual. Food, it should be remembered, makes blood; and the blood is dependent upon it for its character and composition. If the food is poisonous in character, the blood soon becomes tainted and shows the effects of this poisoning process. On any theory we may hold as to the nature of mind and its connection with the body, that theory is certainly dependent upon the body for its manifestation, in this life, and is colored and influenced by the state of the body, and the condition of the blood.

Although an adequate supply of food is necessary to all organisms, including man, there is little danger that anyone in a civilized community would run the risk of actually starving because of lack of food. (Malnutrition is something else again.) Indeed, the tendency is almost the opposite, with persons eating not too little, but too much food. The average person eats at least three times as much food as his system really requires, and it is for this reason that much of the poor health of most Americans is due. This excess is especially true of the protein foods.

The average diet is far too rich in proteins. True, people eat too many fats and carbohydrates too; but this excess is not so immediately dangerous, since such material can be stored as fatty tissue, whereas proteins at once create uric acid and a variety of toxic substances, which poison and devitalize the system. An excess of carbohydrates will produce fermentation; an excess of proteins, putrefaction. Both are harmful, but the second is more so than the first.

Meat contains a high percentage of protein; but unfortunately it also contains other substances—decaying cell-nuclei, which form a part of its own structure. Meat is by no means a clean article of diet, but on the contrary a very unclean one; and many foods supplying an equal amount of protein are to be preferred, for the reason that they supply less of the toxic material which invariably accompanies meat eating. It must be remembered that the tissues of all animals contain a certain amount of poisonous material, simply by reason of the fact that the animals are constantly creating poisons within their bodies, by the very process of living. These poisons are constantly being thrown off by the body, and it is only because of this fact that the animal is enabled to remain alive. Were this process of elimination checked for a few days, death by poisoning would inevitably result in consequence of the poisons formed by the body itself. All animals, then, create these poisons; and it would be impossible to find an animal body without them. So that, when we eat the flesh of any animal, we must eat, together with the nutritious portions, these poisons, which are practically inseparable from all animal tissue.

To contend, as so many persons do, that meat is an essential article of diet, and that man cannot live without it, is of course erroneous, in view of that fact that a goodly proportion of the human race never touch meat. There are various religious sects which never touch it at all. Meat may be preferred to other forms of protein, but it is not necessarily better than cheese, nuts, soy beans, wheat germ and other non-flesh protein.

If meat is not necessary, is there any evidence to show that man is better off without it, mentally or physically? What is the scientific basis of vegetarianism? Upon what principles does it rest? Once these are understood, you shall be in a far better position to appreciate the advantages for a vegetarian diet.

These reasons must be both logical and scientific. From a scientific standpoint, the study of this subject is founded upon the fact that the diet of any animal, in its natural state, is always found to agree both with its anatomical structure and its physiological processes and general bodily functions. So clearly is this fact recognized, indeed, by comparative anatomists and scientists generally, that animals have been divided, according to their dietetic habits, into four great classes; herbivorous, frugivorous, carnivorous and omnivorous. There are various sub and minor divisions that can be and in fact are made, such as the gramnivors, or grain-eaters; the rodentia, or gnawers; the ruminants, or cud-chewers; and the edentata, or creatures without teeth. These sub-divisions need not concern us here, however. For practical purposes, the gramnivora may be included in the class of frugivora, since most frugivorous animals eat grains to some extent.

In order to classify an animal, and place it in its proper division, it is necessary first of all to make a careful examination of its physical structure, and examine its organs in turn. By comparing these with those of other animals, you can at once place the animal in the right category. Make such comparisons in the case of man, and see where they lead. In what class should he be placed?

Consider, first of all, *the teeth*.

The Herbivora The horse, the ox and the sheep are typical of this class of animals, living as they do almost entirely upon grass and herbs. The character of their food is peculiar. It is bulky, coarse, and covered with sharp, cutting edges, ill-suited for tender mouths and gums. It must be mashed and ground thoroughly between the teeth and in the mouth before it is fit to be swallowed; and teeth of peculiar construction and mutual relation are necessary in order to perform this function. Just such teeth they possess. There are twenty-four molars, six on each side of each jaw; and in the lower jaw, in front, eight incisors, or cutting teeth, with none on the upper jaw. In place of any of these teeth on the upper jaw, there is simply a horny plate, upon which the long incisors of the lower jaw impinge when the jaws are closed. This renders possible the tearing, grinding motions necessary for biting off and masticating the food upon which these animals live. Not only that. The actual structure of their teeth is peculiarly suited to their food and its mastication. Unlike our teeth, they are not covered with enamel, but are composed of alternate layers of enamel and dentine; a soft bony substance lying between the layers of enamel, and wearing away more rapidly than it does. The result is that there is soon formed a series of jagged edges, which form cutting, grinding surfaces, and are especially adapted for the food which these animals feed upon. No such formation is present in any other class of animals, since their food is different from that of the herbivora. It is a wise provision of nature, precisely adapted to the desired ends.

The Insectivora The insect-eaters are more nearly related to the Carnivora. The form of teeth varies with the species. The incisors and canines are not especially prominent, but the molars are always serrated with numerous small-pointed eminences, or cusps, adapted to crushing insects. The three leading families of the Insectivora are the moles, the shrew-mice and the hedgehogs. They are of

small size, and are found in all countries, except in South
America and Australia.

The Rodentia The Rodentia is a peculiar order of animals, characterized by two very long and strong teeth in
each jaw, which occupy the place of the incisors and
canines in other animals. Back of these there is a toothless
space, and then four or five molars, which, when they have
a roughened crown, indicate a vegetable, but when pointed,
an insectivorous diet. Their principal foods are grains and
seeds of all kinds, and with these, often, fruits, nuts and
acorns. To this order belong the families of the squirrel,
marmot, all species of mice, the beaver, porcupine, hare,
etc.

The Edentata Occasionally, though rarely, animals of
this class have rudimentary back teeth. Their food consists
of leaves, blossoms, buds, and juicy stalks. Some also devour insects, especially ants. To this order belong the sloth,
armadillo, the anteater, etc.

The Omnivora Omnivorous animals have very distinctive teeth. The canines are markedly developed, forming
regular tusks on the side of the mouth. These are used for
attack and defense, and also to dig up roots, upon which
these animals largely feed. The hog is typical of omnivorous animals of this character. Animals of this class can
live upon both animal and vegetable food.

The Carnivora Here the teeth are very distinctive, and
their shape and arrangement are entirely different from
those of any of the other animals. These are the incisor
teeth in front, and molars behind; but the most distinctive
teeth are the canine, which especially distinguish this class
of feeders. There are four of these, two in each jaw, placed
upon the sides, and they are long, sharp and pointed. The
more nearly the animal is purely carnivorous, the more
these teeth developed, and the less meat the animal eats,
the less they are developed.

Man has two eye teeth and two lower, which are more
or less pointed, and these have been pointed to by some
as evidence of man's naturally carnivorous nature. But

these teeth bear no real resemblance to the true canines found in the mouths of the carnivora.

The Frugivora The orangutan and the gorilla are the best examples of this class of animals. Such animals have thirty-two teeth—sixteen in each jaw: four incisors or cutting teeth; two pointed teeth, known as cuspids, four small molars, known as bicuspids, and six molars.

The Teeth of Man When we consider the teeth of man, we are at once struck by the fact that they correspond, in almost every particular, with the teeth of the gorilla and other frugivorous animals. The number, the arrangement, the structure, are all alike. There are no spaces, no canines, no tusks. In carnivorous animals, the movements of the jaws are in one direction only; they open and shut, like a pair of scissors. Herbivorous animals, on the other hand, have three distinct motions: a vertical, or up-and-down motion; lateral or sidewise, and forward and backward. Man has all these, but to a limited degree. Whatever else man may be, he is, to this extent, certainly not carnivorous.

As for other parts of his anatomy, it is essential that a condensed, brief summary be given.

The length and character of the alimentary canal show such similarities, and differences. In the carnivora, the length of the canal is only three times the length of the body; in the herbivora, thirty times; in the monkey, twelve times; in man, twelve times. These differences are admirably suited to the differing character of the food eaten by these animals.

The stomach, the liver, the placenta, and other parts of the anatomy show similar identifications. So that, from the point-of-view of comparative anatomy—from which the nature of an animal's diet is largely judged, man is entirely different from flesh-eating animals, while bearing close resemblances to the vegetarian animals, and particularly the frugivora. This conclusion is highly significant.

From the standpoint of physiology, also, these various classes of animals differ radically. In vegetarian animals, and in man, the saliva is *akaline*, while in the carnivora it is *acid*. In the latter, the gastric juice is far more acid and powerful, dissolving the food quickly; the liver is also larger and more active. Since meat rapidly putrefies in a moist, warm place, the long, corrugated bowel possessed by vegetarian animals would be highly unsuitable; while the short, smooth bowel of the carnivora is well adapted to rid the body of this material as rapidly as possible. Meat retained in the human bowel becomes exceedingly dangerous, because of its toxic quality.

The structure and functions of the skin are entirely different. In general, vegetarian animals perspire, while carnivorous ones do not. We have all seen how a horse sweats, after a hard run. It is interesting to note, in this connection, that, whereas lions and tigers have sweat-glands in the skin, these are inactive; but the very fact that they still exist, in rudimentary form, seems to indicate that they were, at one time, possibly vegetarian animals. This is a wise provision on the part of nature. For, in sweating, a goodly percentage of the bodily fluids are suddenly lost. In the case of vegetarian animals, this does not particularly matter; but with the carnivora this would prove disastrous, since an excess of uric acid would at once be precipitated, and the animal would be crippled by rheumatism.

The argument from chemistry has been much stressed in the past, by vegetarians and meat-eaters alike. Everyone should know by now that the only important element meat supplies is its protein; it is notoriously lacking in other essential food factors. But modern researchers have conclusively shown that many other foods contain as high a percentage of protein as does meat: beans, peas, lentils, eggs, cheese, whole grains, and especially nuts, being rich in protein and other important mineral elements. Therefore, if a person could obtain these protein requirements from non-meat sources it would make meat eating nonessential.

It must be remembered that protein is only one element of the food required; carbohydrates, fats, minerals and vitamins must also be supplied; and these are to be found in high percentage only in vegetables, cereals, salads and fruits. These, therefore, could constitute the backbone of a diet.

When man eats meat, he really only eats vegetables, but at second hand; for the bodies of animals are built from vegetables, directly or indirectly; but while these are in pure form, when eaten in their natural state, they are admixed with the poisons of the animal's body, when meat is eaten. Common sense should tell you which is preferable.

All of this brings us to an argument from the hygienic point-of-view, the argument, that is, that meat is an unhealthful food.

When an animal is killed, it does not instantly die. It loses consciousness, and the body as a whole dies, but the tissues continue to live for several hours. During the time which elapses between somatic (bodily) death, and the actual death of the cells and tissues of the body, the activity of the animal tissues consumes the soluble food-material which is in contact with these cells and tissues, at the same time continuing to produce those waste substances which, during life, are rapidly removed from the body through the kidneys, lungs and other excretory organs.

It is by the accumulation of these poisons after death that the tissues are killed. When the heart ceases to beat, this cleansing process ceases, and the poisons which are ever-forming accumulate at a rapid rate until the vital fluids are so saturated that every living structure is killed. The arteries continue to contract after death until all the blood which they contain is forced on into the tissues, and still further on into the veins, so that the flesh of a dead animal contains a good percentage of venous blood and poisonous juices. In addition to the useful and necessary nitrogenous matter which is contained within the flesh of the animal, there are also contained within the tissues, these poisons created during life, and retained within the body of the animal after death. It is almost impossible to extract these poisons by any process which will leave the tissues of the animal free from them. Such being the case, why not eat only those foods which supply the nutriment, without the poisons?

Furthermore, meat is often a dangerous food. It is true that meat-inspection is far stricter now than it used to be; but this is after all purely perfunctory, and is not based upon detailed chemical and microscopical tests. Tapeworm, trichinosis, tuberculosis and many other diseases have been known to be transmitted by meat eating.

Pythagoras, Zeno the Stoic, Diogenes, Plato, Plautus, Empedocles, Socrates, Herodotus, Hippocrates, Pliny, Galen,

Zoroaster, Seneca, Ovid, Aristotle, Hesiod, Gautama Buddha, Theophrastus, and a host of others in antiquity were all vegetarians, and wrote strongly on its behalf.

It could be contended that many vegetarians are themselves poor specimens of health, and this is doubtless true. But there are several answers to this objection. Many only take up the reformed diet when they have been driven to it by prolonged ill-health, and only maintain life at all because of their greater care. Then again, many vegetarians do not balance their diet carefully, partaking of wrong combinations of foods, and eating far too much, under the delusion that they must do so because of their vegetarian fare. Many of them unduly neglect fruits and other essentials. It is always possible to find individuals, here and there, who are poor representatives of the system they advocate. But there are many who do not suffer by comparison with any chosen representatives of a mixed diet, and there are an increasing number who will be found to excel. After all the percentage of vegetarians, in our modern civilization, is comparatively small; and in that limited number the proportion of outstanding examples is relatively high.

Other sound arguments could be advanced in favor of vegetarianism, aside from the above, but I must content myself here with merely mentioning them.

From the humanitarian point-of-view, there are many who are opposed to the needless destruction of life, which is necessitated by our modern dietetic standards. Millions of cattle, sheep, etc., are raised for the express purpose of slaughtering them. Butchering is in itself a degrading business, as Upton Sinclair showed most conclusively in his book, "The Jungle." From the aesthetic point-of-view, it can hardly be compared with gardening or tending a fruit orchard.

Furthermore, and from the purely practical side, any area of land will supply far more food per acre in the one case than in the other. When the soil is given up to the feeding of cattle, the given area of land would supply far less nutriment than would the same soil, if grains and fruits were raised upon it, perhaps twenty times less.

But, it may be objected, if flesh-eating might be as harmful as I have been endeavoring to show, then why is it still practiced so universally? The answer is not a complex one. Mankind as a whole follows custom and habit, often without questioning the basis for doing so. So long as the food tastes good, that is all that matters. People will take the greatest care of their dogs and cats, and of their cars, homes and guns, their lawns and clothes, giving them the utmost attention, but of their own dietetic habits they are often extremely careless and usually uninterested. Only when sickness strikes do they concern themselves with their health. It is unfortunate that due to a lack of proper nutritional guidance mankind continues to suffer, largely by reason of its dietetic indiscretions.

The value and importance of fresh fruit cannot be too freely emphasized. The organic salts in fruit arouse the appetite, and aid digestion, by increasing the flow of saliva, and, indirectly, of the gastric juice as the fruit reaches the intestines, the acids increase the activity of the chyme, and stimulate the secretions of the liver and the pancreas, the intestinal glands and muscles; their influence upon the blood is marked: they render it less alkaline, but never acid. By combining with a portion of the alkaline salts of the serum, the phosphoric acid increases the phosphates in the red blood cells; they are antiscorbutic and of value in anemia, general debility, and convalescence from acute illness. Fruits containing oxalates, as tomatoes, gooseberries and strawberries, are useful in amenorrhea and for persons subject to bronchitis and asthma. The final stage in the digestion of fruit is the conversion of fruit acids and salts into alkaline salts, chiefly carbonates; they are therefore useful in scurvy, rheumatism, gout, and other diseases of the uric acid diathesis; they increase the secretion of the urine and its alkalinity and thereby increase the total excretion of salts and other materials. Fresh fruit also tends to correct constipation. However fruit alone *does not* contain the amount of nutriment that the average person needs. The person who is very active, physically, needs additional complete protein. This additional protein can be supplied through the proper combinations of nuts, grains and seeds.

Should you decide to experiment with this type of diet, make the transition gradually. Your stomach and system generally have grown accustomed to cooked foods and to their greater variety; also, the chemistry of your body needs a certain alteration before this diet can be undertaken with maximum benefit. If this is not done, fermentation and the formation of gas may result. Taper off, and make a more or less gradual transition, introducing more fruit into the diet.

Another important point of vegetarianism is that animals cannot appropriate mineral or inorganic elements directly; they must obtain all these substances by means of the vegetable world. Vegetables have the power of utilizing these inorganic materials, and building them into their bodies; but animals have to obtain all such substances in organized form, and cannot utilize inorganic elements. Mineral iron, e.g., cannot be used directly, but must be supplied by the fruits and vegetables rich in iron. Vegetables feed upon minerals and animals upon vegetables. It should be somewhat obvious by now that the vegetable world is that designed for man's food, and from it he could derive all his nourishment.

Vegetables should be dropped into boiling, not cold water, and should be cooked rapidly. The purpose of this is to coagulate and condense the outer rind or layer of the vegetable, and thus prevent the juices and valuable food-properties from boiling out, into the water.

A diet low in concentrated starches and rich in alkaline elements means smaller quantities of food, fewer waste products, quick elimination and a general over-all physical and mental vitality.

There is nothing in the protein of flesh that the animal did not derive from the plant. Not being able to synthesize amino-acids, the animal merely appropriates these, ready-made, from the plant, in the form of plant proteins. We consume several vegetable protein foods, and the deficiencies of one are made up by the richness of another. The excess of amino-acids in vegetable proteins is never great, but contains a sufficient amount to meet the needs of man. Most vegetables contain a very high grade of protein.

Today, our general sanitary and hygienic conditions are better than at any time in our history. Our food, air, water and other natural resources can not claim the same healthy conditions. This, in part, could be the principal reason for the number and complexity of our "diseases" which have been on a steady increase.

256 THE COMPLETE HANDBOOK OF NUTRITION

Consider the logic and reasoning of all the illness and fatal diseases which are currently afflicting millions of persons. One explanation for these illnesses could be constantly over-eating, and eating the wrong foods. Nothing enters the body except by way of the mouth. When the body develops a state of toxemia, therefore, this could be because of the materials introduced into it, which are themselves toxic. And of these, meat is the most poisonous. Judge then if you think that meat eating is really a healthy part of our lives. Vegetarianism, by reducing the toxemia, could help reduce illness and lengthen life.

When following a vegetarian diet, however, one or two points should be kept in mind. The first is the necessity for thorough mastication. This is especially true for nuts. One should never eat when excessively tired, excited or worried. It would be far better to take a few minutes' rest before the meal, to allow the nervous energy to be replenished and reach a state of equilibrium. Do not indulge in heavy exercise soon after eating. Take some deep breathing exercises two or three times a day. Do not think that more food is required under a vegetarian diet than the ordinary diet, for such is not the case. Too many carbohydrates are to be avoided. Finally, the mental condition and confidence in the efficiency of the diet are essential.

BEAUTY HINTS

This chapter will serve to give some insight into the most commonly asked questions on beauty through natural techniques. It is not intended to be an all-inclusive, comprehensive analysis of health and beauty. For that type of in-depth information, please consult our *Natural Organic Beauty Book*, published by Robert Speller and Sons.

Man, the only animal who has the ability to think and reason, has brought upon himself many worries. In his highly developed civilization he has acquired illnesses unknown in the animal kingdom. He runs the gamut from rheumatism to insomnia and accepts these as conditions of everyday life. How often we hear the expression "learn to live with it." But there are things to be done to improve both health and appearance, and, in the process, your outlook on life.

Many diseases and conditions are caused by improper eating habits, and though most meals are prepared with an eye toward a balanced diet, improper methods of cooking, including overcooking may remove vitamins and minerals important to the sustenance of cells and the maintenance of health. And our processed and denatured foods often offer us only a small percentage of their original nutrients.

A lack of vitality leaves the body vulnerable to germs and viruses, and lack of fresh air, which many people who work in cities or spend most of their time indoors may suffer from, tires the body because oxygen is so important to revitalization. To counteract the effects of stale air, breathe deeply from the diaphragm and exhale slowly through the nostrils when you do go outdoors. This is one of the easiest exercises but will help your health, your looks, and your disposition—if you remember to do it.

More specific exercises follow for particular areas of the body, but exercise alone will not bring about improvement. Proper eating habits must become as much a part of your beauty program as the physical care you give your body. Some beauty creams and treatments are mentioned here, and details on health are given elsewhere in this book.

WRINKLES

Wrinkles are a sign of physical or spiritual debility and learning to relax and relieve body tension is a primary factor in preventing them. The following exercises, in combination with the proper diet, will also help.

Before retiring, air your entire body for a few minutes and perform some of the facial exercises mentioned below. In the morning, before you dress, stretch, relax and contract all the muscles and tissues of the body. After a cool shower, massage the scalp and slap cold water on your face gently until the blood supply is increased and the face is rosy. Breakfast should consist of energy-giving fruits, which must prepare your body, after a foodless twelve hours or more, for an entire day's activity.

FACE

Exercises and action of tissues create a free circulation of blood which acts as an agent for rebuilding tissues and cells. Should the blood be toxic or full of poisons, the new tissues will be of an inferior quality and will appear worn and haggard and, above all, flabby. You can see, therefore, that taking facial exercises will not, by itself, remove wrinkles unless the blood carried to the face contains the necessary materials for rebuilding.

There are sixteen elements necessary for the rebuilding of tissues. When the intake of foods supplies only five or six elements, or does not exceed seven or eight, your body will shrivel and you will continue to become older, day by day. Your facial tissues and muscles will be left depleted, and as a result you will look older than you actually are.

The first exercise one must learn is smiling. It lifts your face immediately and relieves tension throughout the entire body. And it may even improve your mood—which may help prevent wrinkles because tension and frowning shut off the circulation and starve your tissues of nutrients flowing through the bloodstream.

Some other facial exercises follow.

Tense all your facial muscles and bring the eyes inward. Try to turn them to the bridge of the nose. When you do this, hold the tension long enough to cause pressure on the weaker tissue cells. When you release the tension, the fresh arterial blood carries in new material to rebuild the worn-out, lifeless cells which form wrinkles.

If you have a double chin or a flabby neck, try the following: Tense your facial muscles with the chin lowered, making pressure against the double chin. Eyes at this time should be tightly clenched. This destroys the weaker cells around the eyes, which are broken down during this exercise.

To remove forehead wrinkles and deep lines along the side of the nose, draw your mouth together as tightly as possible, open your eyes as wide as possible and, with the chin lowered, put pressure on it. This will also be beneficial in removing crowsfeet around the eyes.

To get rid of lines between the nose and upper lip, tighten your lips and distend your cheeks. Push your chin down. This exercise will also add color to your cheeks.

Stretching and pulling the muscles of the neck, as well as the facial muscles, can be done by tensing the muscles on one side of the face and turning your head in the opposite direction. These exercises repeated four or five times in the morning and evening will firm flabbiness and rejuvenate the texture of the skin by reviving or activating the cells.

EYES

Improper diet and poor elimination may cause the eyes to strain and lose their brilliancy. The muscles of the eyes react to exercise and proper food as does any other muscle of the body. To relieve wrinkles around the eyes, close them and open them several times before retiring and upon awakening. Also practice blinking and shifting your eyes to distant and close objects. These simple exercises stimulate the circulation and rebuild the shriveled tissues and strengthen weak eyes.

HAIR

Hair frames the face and can add luster to the face and the individual. Daily common-sense care includes diet, fresh air and plenty of exercise. Because hair is elastic it thrives on exercise, and brushing and massage circulate the blood and feed the scalp. Overexposure to sun and heat will cause hair to become brittle and lose its sheen and vitality. Healthy hair is beautiful hair, no matter what the shade. Soft, shiny and bouncy hair is the envy of women and a sight men don't forget.

Dry hair should be washed with a mild oil-based shampoo, and followed up with a cream rinse to restore lost oil and give it luster and manageability.

Oily hair should be shampooed at least twice a week with a soap that whips up the greatest amount of lather. Sudsing is a must to remove excess oil. Rinse the hair with warm water and massage the scalp gently.

The most important service you can do your hair is brushing. The improved circulation brought about tends to normalize both oily and dry scalps. Oily hair benefits from brushing by the equal distribution of the oil throughout all the hair, and the distribution of oil to the ends of the hair will help dry and splitting ends. If your hair is dry, wrap an old nylon stocking around your brush to catch any flakes from the scalp; if it is oily, cover the brush with a piece of cheesecloth to absorb the oil.

The best comb for hair is sturdy and flexible, with rounded teeth that won't scratch the scalp. A hard rubber comb with large teeth is excellent.

Never brush wet hair because that may stretch and break it. The scalp should be treated gently; use a soft towel to dry the hair; squeeze the water out. If possible, dry your hair outdoors, but not in direct sunlight. When this is impossible, fluff your hair dry with a towel.

Hairdryers tend to dry the scalp and should be shunned whenever possible. Conditioners will help avoid damage if they are used regularly.

NATURAL RINSES

The hair texture of blondes, brunettes, and redheads differs, and there are different natural rinses for each.

For blondes, the juice of two lemons strained through cheesecloth and mixed with an equal amount of lukewarm water is used. If possible, leave this solution on the hair and let it dry in the sun. If you do wish to rinse it out, use cool, clear water.

A tea rinse is often recommended for redheads to enhance highlights and give extra bounce to the hair. Camomile tea makes a wonderful rinse. Strain it through cheese cloth and mix with a pint of water. Pour it through your hair and use a cold water rinse.

Brunettes use a vinegar rinse. It adds extra highlights and tone. Add 4 tablespoons of vinegar to three glasses of water. (Cider vinegar is preferred.) Massage the mixture gently through the hair and rinse with cool, clear water to remove the vinegar odor. Blondes may also use vinegar, but only white vinegar.

For gray hair or loose, thinning hair see chapter on Vitamins.

A hundred brushstrokes a day will benefit any shade or texture hair.

HOT OIL TREATMENT

Dry hair is a result of the inactivity of the sebaceous oils in the scalp. The most important thing you can do for your hair is to keep it lubricated. A hot oil treatment is effective as a pre-shampoo conditioner. Warm olive oil or castor oil is placed in a receptacle and applied with cotton pads to your scalp. Wrap your head in a hot towel for at least twenty minutes. Then massage the oil into your scalp, wrap your head in a fresh hot towel and keep it on for an hour. Shampoo your hair at least three times to remove all the oil.

EGG SHAMPOO

This is a nourishing conditioner for dry or damaged hair and can be used for all types. Eggs are a natural way to condition the hair and make it shine. Separate the white of an egg from the yolk; whip the white to a peak. Add a tablespoon of water to the yolk and blend until the mixture is creamy; then mix the white and yolk together. Wet your hair with warm water, remove the excess moisture, and apply the mixture to your scalp with your fingertips. Massage gently until the froth is worked into your scalp, and then rinse the hair with cool water. Keep applying the mixture until it is used up and then rinse until all of the egg is washed away.

TENSION

Tension makes dry hair dryer and oily hair oilier. In other words, it activates the present condition of the hair. Normal hair becomes lifeless and lacks luster under this condition. Frequent short naps may reduce tension. Also try soaking cotton pads in witch hazel, then lie down over two pillows with your feet elevated, and place the pads on your eyes. Relax. Take time out from your household chores. Sit upright at a table, place both your elbows on it and put the palms of your hands on both your eyes. Or sit in a straight chair, close your eyes and black all thoughts out. Then concentrate on relaxing each part of your body individually.

EXERCISE YOUR HAIR

A massage of the hair and scalp just five minutes a day will do wonders for the hair and benefit the complexion at the same time. A scalp massage is a pre-shampoo must. A ritual should be: Massage, brush, and shampoo. Electric vibrators are often used, but a most satisfying massage may be given with the fingertips. Use your fingers in a circular motion. Push your hands together, so that the folds of the scalp are pushed up between your fingertips. This should be done over the entire head until the scalp has been covered and relaxed.

Pulling the hair gently is also an effective exercise which has been used for centuries to strengthen the hair and bring about good circulation. Start at the front of the hair and pull gently, then try another section and pull gently with interlocked fingers. You will feel exhilarated after this treatment, and the increased circulation in your face from this will also tone your complexion.

SOME TIPS

If your hair is oily, avoid fried foods, nuts and butter. These foods increase the production of sebaceous oils. If your hair is dry, try to avoid permanent wave lotions, bleaches and detergent shampoos which make the hair dryer and cause scaling of the scalp. Dry, indoor air and too much sun and wind have the same effect on your hair. Hairspray dries the scalp. Sleeping on rollers or wearing them for a long period may break the ends of the hair and cause splitting. Change your part from time to time. A sun-bath after shampooing is healthy for the hair and can be a beneficial tonic. It should never be done to excess, however.

SKIN

Each cell of the skin must receive food, and your circulation determines the kind of nourishment it gets. Face creams are also applied to cleanse, soften and improve the skin, but one should be aware that many popular lotions and creams which are deemed harmless contain lead, mercury, antimony and bismuth which are absorbed by the body tissue and may harm the health of the skin.

In this busy day and age, it is difficult to find time to make one's own creams and powders, but a few suggestions may help you eliminate some of these commercial products.

Pure baby oil not only removes makeup but lubricates the skin naturally. Olive oil can be heated and applied to the skin around the eyes, in a circular fashion, to smooth wrinkles and make eyelashes silky. To open the pores and cleanse away imbedded dirt and oil, a kettle of steaming water will serve as a facial sauna.

Cosmetics can, and should be, good enough to eat. Some commercial cosmetic products are now utilizing foods, plants and herbs. There are face creams on the market now which contain lemons, cucumbers, honey, strawberries, eggs and milk. Some bath oils contain shrubs, evergreens, bitter oranges, plants, and flowers. Many pharmacies are using herbal preparations for the hair and almond meal for complexions.

Some of the finest skin packs, often used in salons, can be made at home very inexpensively. One of them is a combination of honey and egg-white whipped together and applied to the face. This acts as an astringent and also feeds the skin with the different vitamins it contains. Oatmeal and cucumber facials were used by our grandmothers to soften their skin and prevent wrinkles. Vegetables are now recommended for everything involving skin care, and so are fruit juice extracts and creams made from the papaya fruit. This would not have surprised our female ancestors at all; old beauty books are crammed with these remedies. Wines, whiskeys and brandies were used as astringents years ago, and skins glowed. Beer, made from malt, which is made from grain and barley, was also used frequently.

The greatest "wonder mask" is pure egg white. Separate

the yolk from the white and smear the white over the face with two pieces of cotton. Allow this to dry. The lines of the face seem to disappear after one of the above applications. Egg white was formerly used in some of the more complicated facial masks: Ladies of the French court used the white of the egg together with camphor and alum to clear up blemishes and tighten the skin. You can still purchase these ingredients in your neighborhood drugstore. The same mixture can be used on the neck and arms.

Another egg mask used for thousands of years is made by combining three ounces of barley, one ounce of honey and sufficient egg white to make a thick paste. Plain egg white, however, does a good job and is the simplest to use.

Cucumber juice is an old favorite as a beauty recipe and can be used in the following manner: 3 ounces cucumber juice, 3 ounces of distilled water and 1½ ounces rose water. Rub this mixture into the skin with the finger tips. A refreshing hot weather beauty trick is to wash the face with cold water in which some cut-up cucumbers have been mashed.

BLEMISHES

The facial masks mentioned in the previous paragraphs can be used effectively in the treatment of pimples, blackheads and large pores. For serious conditions, a dermatologist should be consulted. The following home treatments are for the minor blemishes that affect most people at one time or another:

Mix equal parts of pure lanolin, glycerine and castor oil. Melt this concoction over low heat, let it cool and keep it in a glass jar. Apply to pimples until healed. *Never mix any of these beauty recipes in a metal utensil unless it is a glazed, heavily enameled ironware cooking pot. It is best to use enamel, china, glass or earthenware.*

Brown or yellow laundry soap applied to pimples will bring them to a head, or even dry them up. This treatment is also an excellent remedy for boils. Another is onions— cooked in lard until they are transparent, allowed to cool, and placed between pieces of cheesecloth as a poultice. Camphor is also a remedy for pimples. You can buy a bottle at the drugstore and carry it with you while traveling. Pat camphor on a pimple until it disappears. If it comes to a head, squeeze it gently and then apply camphor. It may sting a little, but it prevents infection and causes the blotch to heal rapidly.

BLACKHEADS

The best thing one can do for blackheads is to keep the face clean. Steaming daily and scrubbing gently with soap and water are good, as are most of the masks mentioned previously. An old-fashioned meal wash is excellent for blackheads too. Mix it as follows: 16 ounces powdered oatmeal, 8 ounces powdered almond meal, 4 ounces powdered orris root and 1 ounce powdered castile soap. Mix thoroughly and add one spoonful of hot water to make a paste. Apply to the blackhead area and rinse with cold water. An old remedy for blackheads around the nose is to rub them gently with lemon juice. Another is to rub them with a solution of bicarbonate of soda dissolved in 8 ounces of distilled water. Liquid green soap mixed with 3 ounces of witch hazel, a complexion brush and hot water have been used successfully. It is also good for large pores. Cooked oatmeal, mixed with white wine and lemon juice and left on the face overnight gently forces blackheads out and closes the pores.

BLOTCHES

Cod liver oil is one of the best remedies for blotches. In its natural state it contains a high content of vitamin A, which is a natural skin healer. It works like a charm on rashes, pimples, blotches, fever blisters, or cold sores. Boric acid dissolved in boiling water can be used on blotches, and calamine lotion is good, as it heals and stops itching of a rash. Borax dissolved in water may also be used as a solution for removing blotches.

LARGE PORES

Large pores are caused by incorrect cleansing, acne, blackheads and improper diet. There are many masks that can be used to shrink these pores. One is, of course, the egg white mask. It does wonders for this problem. Buttermilk has an astringent effect on pores and can be used as a daily treatment. Allow it to dry for about ten minutes and rinse it off with cool water.

Equal parts of vinegar and hot water can be used as a facial wash to refine the pores. There is also a camphor wash used as a substitute for water which refines the texture of skin. Cornmeal and oatmeal masks are highly praised by some women for reducing the pores, as is powdered alum, which is also used as an astringent.

Raw tomatoes have been used for centuries to tighten the skin. The pulp of the tomato contains certain vitamins, minerals and acids and has an astringent effect on the skin. Use old sheets or bath towels around your head and neck when applying the tomato pulp. (The amino acid in the tomato is the ingredient which clears the skin.) The juice of garden lettuce, the juice of cucumbers, and poultices of bread and milk are used for enlarged facial pores.

FRECKLES

In olden days freckles were considered an abomination. Today they are a sign of wholesomeness, and are not worried about as they used to be. A few freckles sprinkled on the nose can be quite youthful and piquant. But for those who wish to rid themselves of freckles, lemon juice or buttermilk helps. Buttermilk seems to work better and is a favorite old remedy. Lemon juice diluted with Jamaica rum has been used quite often and successfully.

For light freckles, an old-time, harmless remedy may be used. Dissolve borax in lemon juice and hot water. Put rose petals in the solution and leave them soaking for about an hour. Then strain the solution through cheese cloth. Let the clear liquid stand for 24 hours. Add glycerine and pat it on the freckles. Use 3 drams of lemon juice, 1 ounce hot water, 2 drams borax, 1 ounce red rose petals and 1 ounce glycerine.

Another old-fashioned remedy for persistent freckles is 30 grains of powdered borax and 2½ ounces of lemon juice mixed. Apply this at bedtime and leave it on all night. It should help if used continually.

SUNBURN

Sunburn can be extremely dangerous to the skin. An overdose of anything is not recommended, especially solar rays. Many different types of moles have been attributed to an overdose of sun. It also dries out the natural moisture of the skin, and at times causes pigmentation of an indelible sort. Should you overexpose your skin, the following home remedies may be tried:

1. Vinegar. Take any commercial vinegar and pat it on
   lavishly over the sunburned area, to remove the sting.
2. Calamine lotion. It may be purchased in any drugstore.
   Apply it over the sunburned area and let it dry.
3. Make a pack of baking soda and milk and apply it to
   the face or any other area.
4. Equal parts of lime water and linseed oil.
5. Cod-liver oil or desitin ointment is soothing and
   healing.

FLABBY SKIN

Exercise, of course, will help correct this and may prevent
the skin from becoming flabby. The proper nutrition and
vitamins will also alleviate this condition. The following
is an old-fashioned remedy which, if used persistently, will
result in a firmer skin. Mix equal parts of milk and whiskey.
Wash the face with a pure soap and, after drying, pat
the mixture all over the face with absorbent cotton pads.
Leave it on for several hours or overnight. It will take
about a year for obvious results.

GREASY SKIN

Wash your face with soap and water at least three times
a day and then pat on an astringent. Witch hazel is one
of the best astringents and has a mild, drying effect. White
Rhine wine for fair skins, and red wine for olive complexions are also used. The juice of fresh strawberries or
cucumbers has been prescribed too. This should be applied
about once a week. Always remove old makeup with soap
and water or use one of the commercial products sold in
any drugstore to refresh your face. They will remove
makeup and grease and leave your skin clean, dry and
ready for the next application of makeup. An excellent
refresher is the sauna, described below.

DRY SKIN

Dry skin should always be protected by a moisturizer,
and an extremely mild soap should be used for washing.

Soaps made with lanolin are best. Rubbing the face with olive oil or castor oil is highly recommended, and the juice of honeydew melon does wonders for the face by activating the natural moisture of the skin.

STRETCH MARKS

Pregnant women are often advised by their doctors to oil the skin of the abdomen nightly in order to prevent the stretch marks, or wrinkles, that follow childbirth. The best thing for this purpose is warm coconut oil. (Olive oil is used on occasion, but it is greasy and must be covered to prevent its rubbing off.) Massage gently into the stomach area and repeat every night, if possible. It helps the skin retain its resiliency.

WARTS

Though the electric needle, or scraping, is the modern approach used by doctors, there are home remedies for warts too. Castor oil or the juice from milkweeds, applied regularly, could cause a wart to disappear.

THE SAUNA

Finnish women, with their pink and white complexions, have the most fabulous skins in all of Scandinavia. The sauna is their beauty secret. Saunas are found in private homes and basements of new apartment houses. There are public saunas, executive saunas, prefabricated saunas for weekends at the shore. The Finns credit the stimulating action of the steam for keeping their skins soft, silky and dewy.

The sauna is not a Turkish bath or a steam bath. It is a thermal bath that produces a high, dry heat. A wood-walled room can be heated to the temperature of 200 degrees, yet be comfortable because the humidity never rises above 10 percent. The dry heat causes free perspiration in a matter of minutes, opens the pores and steps up the circulation. The result is a rosy, clean and petal-soft skin. The sauna works like a tranquilizer, too, for the atmosphere is one of dim lights, quiet, and steam.

FACIAL SAUNA

To reproduce the effect of a sauna for your face, boil sufficient water to fill your basin, or simply stand over a large kettle. Use a terrycloth towel to make a tent over your head, and remain under your tent, letting the steam envelop your face for at least five minutes. If your skin is dry or normal, apply rich cream or complexion oil to your face and throat before steaming. Afterwards splash your face with cold water and pat it dry. Apply a lotion or cream immediately.

If you have oily skin, lather your face and throat with an antiseptic soap before steaming. When you emerge from the tent, splash on cold water or ice and pat dry. Then apply an astringent.

BATH

Your bath should be a daily ritual. It gives you a luxuriant feeling and keeps your skin clean. A bubble bath will take care of oily skin, and bath oil can improve dry skin. If your skin is normal use them both. There are many stories about milk baths, dating back to the Romans. A packet of skimmed milk poured with running water into the tub will keep your skin soft.

FACIAL MASSAGE

The result of a facial massage can be quite dramatic if it is done correctly. The purpose of a facial is to tone the skin, not to stretch it, and a proper facial is the ideal exercise for facial muscles. Some areas of the face seem to grow lazy, and the right facial will increase the skin's resiliency.

The best way to massage your skin is to pat it gently with upward and outward movements. The fingertips should be used ever so lightly. The following rules illustrate the Swedish method of massage:

Start at the collarbone and run your fingers over your throat with a gentle upward and outward movement.

Place the backs of both your hands under your chin and flutter your fingertips against your chin, working from the center outward toward the earlobes.

Place your index finger at the corner of your mouth, and with a circular motion lift the skin upward and outward.

Start at the sides of your nose and with your index fingers curve your hands up and out along the cheekbones all the way to your hairline.

Stroke your fingers gently over the eye area. Work from

the inside tip of the eye, upward and outward to the eye bone.

Stimulate the forehead, nose and chin with a circular motion, but never stretch the skin.

Pat your fingers lightly over your entire face, press slightly and lift gently.

EYES

A cube of ice wrapped in a washcloth and pressed gently on closed eyes will help to reduce puffiness. If you have wrinkled eyelids and crowsfeet, try the following: A pound of pure lanolin and a small bottle of pure almond oil. Melt the lanolin in a double boiler and slowly add enough of the almond oil to make a cream which spreads easily. The mixture should have the consistency of cold cream. At night before retiring, place some of the cream on your index fingers and, with a circular motion, keep spreading it around the eyes. Start from the tip of the eye and continue all the way around. Do this about 25 times. You can also use this cream for the neck, for rough elbows, hands and feet.

Another remedy for wrinkles around the eyes is a raw potato, grated onto cheesecloth and placed on the eyelids for fifteen or twenty minutes. Freshly squeezed orange juice is sometimes recommended but it may be too acid for your particular type of skin.

FIGURE

There are many books on the market describing the exercise required for trimming the various parts of your body. Walking is one of the greatest exercises there is. Trains and buses are over-crowded these days, so if you can manage to walk a mile or two you will trim your figure, take in the oxygen you need for revitalization, and increase blood circulation. Jogging, too, is recommended if your heart is good. Stretching helps the entire body; any part of your body you stretch is also being trimmed.

A favorite exercise for a straighter, prettier back follows: Stand facing the wall with your feet together and your toes about three feet from the base of the wall. Lean forward so that the palms of your hands are flat up against the wall. Your hands should be level with your shoulders and a shoulder width apart. Keep both feet flat on the floor and allow yourself to sink toward the wall. Your elbows will protrude to the sides. Keep your back straight. Feel that stretch?

Now push away from the wall and let your back sway. Remember to keep both palms flat against the wall. Then drop your head down as far as you can without changing the position of your hands and feet. Lead with your chin and raise your head up. As you do the last position, your back will arch. Repeat this at least 5 times.

There is a tummy exercise which is really a toughener: lie perfectly flat on your back on the floor, feet together and arms at your sides. Relax. Then slowly raise both feet about 3 or 4 inches off the floor, at the same time raising your head just high enough to see your toes.

Holding that position, start to climb an imaginary rope, hand over hand to the count of 20. Feel your tummy tighten? Do this about five times and increase one count every week. If you keep this up you will never need a girdle.

If you want a shapelier bosom, try the following. Either stand or sit with this exercise. Hold your left elbow with your right hand and your right elbow with your left hand. Pull, as though you were trying to tug your two arms together, jerk them, and then relax. If you repeat this exercise 20 times a day or more you will see marvelous results.

Skipping rope a few times in the morning, after your breathing exercises, will increase the circulation of your blood and help you to enjoy your breakfast as well.

Swimming is another of the best exercises. It stretches, firms, balances and invigorates your entire body.

The things suggested here will put you on the road to a good figure. One more suggestion: when dieting, substitute, whenever possible, fish for meat. It supplies as much energy, more iron and less fat than meat, and is easier to digest. And use honey instead of sugar. It gives you the required energy as well as potassium and iron which plain sugar lacks.

HERBS

Mankind has been provided with remedies for every disease that might afflict him, and possibly no other source of medicinal properties is more beneficial for our good health than Herbs.

Herbs were recorded in use as early as 2500 b.c. The Assyrians knew the virtues of more than 250 herbs. It was recorded in early scrolls that the ancient Egyptians used elderberry, pomegranate bark, wild lettuce, wormwood, hemlock and other herbs. Similarly, the Greeks used herbs such as mustard, cinnamon, gentian, rhubarb and others. Many prominent scientists felt that the study of herbs was the mother of all scientific discipline.

Herbs were used as medicine extensively until about 1500 when Tohemhein started the practice of using chemicals to treat disease. He convinced most medical men that the human body could be purified chemically, and thus transformed the medical practice. After his death, people took up the practice of giving chemicals in place of herbs, roots and barks.

The study of herbology as a science is called by various names other than herbology, such as materia medica, botany, pharmacology, vegetable drugs, or pharmacognosy.

Herbs and *spices*   The dictionary defines an herb as a seed plant which does not develop woody persistent tissue, as that of a shrub or tree, but is more or less soft or succulent. A spice is any of the various vegetable productions which are fragrant or aromatic and pungent to the taste. Thus herbs may be spices as well as herbs.

The first medicines used by mankind were those derived from the vegetable kingdom. Any vegetables appearing on the table are considered as foods, while any bitter tasting vegetable is now considered as a medicine. It is almost forgotten that not too long ago, bitters were common to the table. They were made from herbs that had ample potash and were good tonics because they contained potassium, a mineral that is the building cement of muscle and nerve tissue.

Herbs act as astringents, alkalinizers, acidifiers, tonics, diuretics, diaphoretics, laxatives and serve several other purposes. Since the fundamental principle of natural healing calls for a return to organic remedies, the following pages of lists of herbs with their effects and reported usage should be an important guide and reference for your continued good health.

DEFINITION OF MEDICINAL PROPERTIES OF HERBS

Alterative: Producing a healthful change without perceptible evacuation

Anodyne: Relieves pain

Anthelmintic: An agent which expels worms

Antibilious: Acts on the bile, relieving biliousness

Antiemetic: Stops vomiting

Antiepileptic: Relieves fits

Antiperiodic: Arrests morbid periodical movements

Anthilitic: Prevents the formation of calculi in the urinary tract

Antirheumatic: Relieves rheumatism

Antiscorbutic: Helps prevent scurvy

Antiseptic: Opposed to putrefaction

Antispasmodic: Helps relieve spasms

Aperient: Gently laxative, without purging

Aromatic: Causes contraction and arrests discharges

Astringent: Causes contraction and arrests discharges

Carminative: Expels air from the bowel

Cathartic: Evacuating the bowels

Cephalic: Used in ailments of the head

Cholagogue: Increases the flow of bile

Condiment: Improves flavor of food

Demulcent: Soothing, relieves inflammation

Deobstruent: Removes obstructions

Depurative: Purifies the blood

Detergent: Cleansing to boils, ulcers, and wounds

Diaphoretic: Produces perspiration
Discutient: Dissolves and removes tumors
Diuretic: Increases the secretion and flow of urine
Emetic: Produces vomiting
Emmenagogue: Promotes menstruation
Emollient: Softening and soothing to inflamed parts
Esculent: Eatable as food
Exanthematous: Remedy for skin eruptions and diseases
Expectorant: Facilitates expectoration
Febrifuge: Abates and reduces fevers
Hepatic: Remedy for diseases of the liver
Herpatic: Remedy for skin eruptions, ringworm, etc.
Laxative: Promotes bowel action
Lithontryptic: Dissolves calculi in the urinary organs
Maturating: Ripens or brings boils, tumors, and ulcers to
a head
Mucilaginous: Soothing to inflamed parts
Nauseant: Produces vomiting
Nervine: Acts specifically on the nervous system
Ophthalmicum: A remedy for disease of the eye
Parturient: Induces and promotes labor at childbirth
Pectoral: Remedy to relieve chest or lung afflictions
Refrigerant: Cooling
Resolvent: Dissolves and removes tumors
Rubifacient: Increases circulation, produces red skin
Sedative: Tonic on nerves, also quieting
Sialagogue: Increases the secretion of saliva
Stomachic: Strengthens and gives tone to the stomach
Styptic: Arrests hemorrhage and bleeding
Sudorific: Produces profuse perspiration
Tonic: Remedy which is invigorating and strengthening
Vermifuge: Expels worms

TONICS

A tonic is an agent that is used to give strength to the system. It is always good to take tonic herbs when convalescing from any disease or ailment. The following are all tonic herbs.

White pond lily, boneset, ginger root, capsicum, bitter root, balmony, poplar bark, golden seal, white willow, black horehound, broom, centaury, comfrey, cudweed, ground ivy, elecampane, dandelion, valerian, meadow sweet, mistletoe, mugwort, wood betony, self heal, agrimony, sanicle, skullcap, red raspberry leaves, yarrow, sage, and vervain.

Specific Nerve Tonics Golden seal is a pure tonic to nervous systems and mucous membranes. It acts as a powerful cleanser to all the mucous membranes in the system.

White willow, Skullcap, Valerian, Mistletoe, Wood Betony, Agrimony and Self Heal are all excellent for nervous tremors.

Tonic for Lungs One teaspoonful equal parts of the following: comfrey, black horehound, cudweed, ground ivy, elecampane, ginger root, and one-half teaspoon of cayenne is reported to have had soothing effects to the lungs.

Tonics for general debility and loss of appetite Century, dandelion, ground ivy, meadow sweet, mugwort, wood betony, self heal, agrimony, capsicum, balmony, poplar bark, black horehound, broom, sanicle, yarrow, and sage.

Different herbologists recommend varying amounts and recipes to achieve the desired effect of different herbs. Often, one source does not agree with another source on the exact method or amounts to prepair the herbs for human use. Therefore, rather than giving the dosage for each herb, we suggest that you discuss this with the herbologist or chemists from whom you purchase your herbs. Any herbs which are purchased through the mails must state the exact method of preparing it for human use. There are probably thousands of general practitioners across this country who are knowledgeable in the use and preparation of herbs.

Most of the more popular and readily available herbs are sold with directions for their usage right on the label of the box or package. If, however, you are still in doubt as the the exact amounts for your own needs, consult your doctor, *never* try to prescribe for yourself.

Again let us state that *no* herb can be considered a *cure* for any given ailment, by itself. They have, however, been known to have varying degrees of benefit in helping arrest or improve various ailments.

Should you have a particular ailment which you are going to try and treat with herb therapy, you *must* consult your doctor, first. Never undertake such a program by yourself, HERBS: IF NOT USED IN THE PROPER MANNER CAN BE HARMFUL!

In researching the material for this comprehensive chapter on herbs, we found certain books and manuals of great use and would recommend them for the casual or inquisitive reader on the subject of herbs. They are:

Modern Encyclopedia of Herbs, J. M. Kadans, M.D., Ph.D. *Parker Pub.*

Eat the Weeds, B. C. Hasris, *Barre Publishers*

Herbal Manual, H. Ward, *L. N. Fowler & Co. Ltd.*

The Healing Power of Herbs, Mary Bathel, *Wilshire Books*

Back to Eden, J. Kloss, *Longview Publishing House*

Natural & Folk Remedies, C. Wade, *Parker Publisher*

Ginseng and Other Medicinal Plants, A. R. Harding, *A. R. Harding Pub.*

Materia Medica and Pharmacology, Culbreth, *Lea & Febiger Pub.*

God-Given Herbs for The Healing of Mankind, W. K. McGrath, *McGrath Pub.*

The Place of Herbs in Rational Therapy, E. Robinson, *E. Robinson Pub.*

HERBS

Abscess Root: Also known as American Greek Valerian, False Jacob's Ladder, Sweatroot. Botanical name: Polemonium retans. This herb has a stimulating effect upon glands so as to produce considerable perspiration. It has been recommended for various lung diseases, coughs, colds and bronchial disturbances.

Acacia: Also known as Gum Arabic, Egyptian Thorn, Gum Acacia, Tamarisk Catechu. Botanical names: Acacia Senegal, Acacia Arabica, vera, decurrens. Habitat: Northern Africa, Egypt and Middle-east. The gum has a soothing or softening effect upon the skin or mucous membrane to which it is applied. It also has an astringent effect, contracting and hardening tissues so as to limit secretion of glands. Acacia is also said to have nutritive qualities, nourishing tissues to which it is applied. Due to its high tannic acid content, widely known for use in treatment of burns, acacia may be applied to burned areas, preventing air from contacting the burn, and preventing blistering.

Aconite: Also known as Monkshood, Wolfsbane, Cuckoo's Cap, Blue Rocket, Friar's Cap, Jacob's Chariot. Botanical name: Aconitum Napellus. The effect of this herb is that of a sedative or depressant. It has also been used to reduce pain and fever and helps in combating inflammation of the stomach (gastritis), nerve pains of the face (facial neuralgia), inflammation of the mucous membrane (catarrh), ulcerated tonsils, croup and heart spasm.

Acorn: This is the fruit of the Oak tree. Botanical name: Quercus robur. The acorn tends to contract and harden tissues and to limit secretion action by the glands. This astringent action has made the mixture applicable for treatment of diarrhea.

Adder's Tongue: Also known as Serpent's Tongue, Dog's Tooth Violet, Yellow Snowdrop, Rattlesnake Violet, Yellow Snakeleaf. Botanical names: Erythronium Americanum and Ophioglossum vulgatum. Habitat: United States. When swallowed, it will cause vomiting and so is an emetic. When placed directly upon tissue, it has a soothing and softening effect and so it is also an emollient. Another reported use for this herb is for the relief of swelling due to accumulation of fluid in various body cavities known as dropsy.

Adrue: Also known as Guinea Rush. Botanical name: Cyperus articulatus. The aroma of this herb tends to reduce the desire for vomiting and is therefore recommended in conditions where it is desired that a person retain the food taken. This herb also acts as a sedative.

Agar: Also known as Agar-Agar, Japanese Isinglass, Vegetable Gelatin. Botanical names: Gelidium amansii, Gelidium corneum of the family Gelidaceae. Habitat: In Japan, Yellow and China Seas, along the eastern coast of Asia, and in the Pacific Ocean. This is an algae which has been used to soothe and relieve inflammation. It has also been used as a mild laxative when mixed in mineral oil.

Agaric: Also known as White Agaric, Larch, and Purging Agaric. Botanical names: Polyporus Officinalis, Boletus laricis. This herb will limit secretions of mucous membranes and glands, thus producing an astringent effect. When taken internally, the effect upon the bowels has produced a cleansing result and is therefore also a purgative.

Agrimony: Also known as Stickwort, Cocklebur. Botanical name: Agrimonia eupatoria. Habitat: Europe. This herb has an astringent effect, as it contracts and hardens tissue. When absorbed into the system, it also strengthens and tones the muscles and is therefore a tonic. This herb also affects the cells of the kidneys, allowing fluids to pass more readily through the kidneys, and is therefore also a diuretic. It can reduce and relieve diarrhea. It can also be used to improve the stomach, liver and bowels and assist in the treatment of stones and gravel in the kidneys. It has been used as a gargle for reducing soreness of the mouth and throat.

Alder, Black, American: Botanical name: Prinos verticillatus. The bark of this tree, when steeped in hot water, produces a solution that has a strong laxative effect.

Alder, English: Botanical name: Alnus glutinosa. The leaves are useful when applied to inflammed parts of the body. The bark also produces a mixture which has been used as a tonic and as a gargle for sore throats. It has also been recommended as an astringent, as it tends to contract tissue and reduce secretion of fluids.

Alkanet: Also known as Dyer's Bugloss, Spanish Bugloss, Anchusa, Orchanet. Botanical names: Alkanna tinctoria, Lithospermum, tinctorium, Anchusa tinctoria. This herb is an emollient. It also has the effect of contracting tissue and causing a cessation of the flow of body liquids. It can be used as an antiseptic for treatment of wounds and when taken internally, it has also destroyed body worms.

Alfalfa: Also known as Buffalo Herb, Sweet Lucerne. Alfalfa is one of the richest land-grown sources of sub-nutritional trace minerals. Most plants are shallow surface feeders. Alfalfa is very high in iron, magnesium, phosphorus, sulphur, sodium, potassium, chlorine and silicon. It is very potent in plant calcium. It is also high in vitamin K, which is so essential to the clotting of blood. It contains eight known enzymes, all of which are necessary to make foods assimilable by the body. It is a good blood builder, good for teeth and bones and inflamed bladder. It helps to produce milk for nursing mothers and aids in the elimination of various drug poisons from the body. In its total effect, it is one of the all-round best herbs in nature.

All-Heal: Also known as Wound-Wort. Botanical name: Brunella vulgaris. This European herb has antiseptic qualities and can also help to relieve muscular spasms. It has also been used to assist in starting menstrual flow when irregularities occur.

Allspice: Also known as Pimento, Jamaica Pepper. Botanical name: Pimenta Officinalis. This herb is an aromatic. It is also a stomachic in that it excites activity in the stomach. It is a carminative in that it tends to remove gases from the upper intestinal tract. Inasmuch as it imparts flavor to almost any food, it is also a condiment. It has been used in cases of diarrhea.

Aloes: Also known as Bombay Aloes; Turkey, Mocha, Zanzibar, Socotrine, Curacao, Bitter, and Cape Aloe. Botanical name: Liliacae Family; Aloe socotrina. It acts as a cathartic, stomachic, aromatic, emmenagogue, drastic. This is reportedly one of the best herbs to clean out the colon and promote menstruation when suppressed. It helps to clean morbid matter from the stomach, liver, kidneys, spleen and bladder. It has been used for burns, radiation burns, cuts and bruises. It is reportedly very soothing to the stomach and can be used in any case where a laxative is needed.

Alstonia Bark: Also known as Fever Bark, Australian Quinine, Australian Febrifuge. Botanical name: Alstonia constricta. This can act as an agent and tonic for reducing fever. It has also been effective in some forms of rheumatism.

Althea: Also known as Mallow family, Marshmallow. Botanical name: Althea Officinalis. This herb acts as demulcent, emollient and pain-soother. It has been used as a douche for irritation of the vagina, bathing inflamed eyes, in making poultices and for irritative diarrhea or dysentery.

Amaranth: Also known as Red Cockscomb, Love-lies-bleeding. Botanical names: Amaranthus hypochondriacus, Amaranthus melancholicus. This herb is an astringent, having the effect of contracting tissue and limiting secretion of glands. It is helpful for excessive bleeding during the menstrual period and is reportedly good for stopping diarrhea as well as bleeding from the bowels. The liquid is also useful as a wash for ulcers and sores and as a gargle for the throat and mouth.

Ammoniacum: Also known as Persian Gum Ammoniacum. Botanical name: Dorema ammoniacum. This is a gum resin that is a natural exudation from the plant and serves as a stimulant, causing removal of secretions of the bronchial passages. It has been used for use in asthmatic conditions involving spasms of the bronchial passages.

Angelica, European: Also known as Garden Angelica. Botanical name: Angelica archangelica. This herb acts as a stimulant, carminative, emmenagogue, tonic, aromatic, diaphoretic, diuretic, and expectorant. This has been used as a tonic for the stomach, heartburn, gas, colic, colds and fever. This herb has reportedly been found to be valuable in various lung diseases including coughs and shortness of breath. It also has the effect of opening passages in the liver and spleen. Due to this herb's unique ability to clear tiny passages, it has been used to relieve dimness of vision and hearing by placing drops of the fluid into the eyes and ears. It is reported that it heals ulcers and helps restore the normal tissues.

Angostura: Also known as Cusparia Bark. Botanical names: Cusparia febrifuga, Galipea officinalis, Bonplandia trifoliata, Galipea cusparia. This native plant of Venezuela is a tonic and an aromatic. It stimulates functional body activity and has been used for diarrhea, intermittent fevers and for conditions where there has been accumulation of water in the tissues and cavities.

Anise: Also known as Anise Seed, Sweet Cumin and Anisum. Botanical name: Pimpinella anisum Linne. This acts as a stimulant, aromatic, diaphoretic, relaxant, tonic, carminative and stomachic. This is one of the old herbs, and has many valuable properties. It has helped to prevent fermentation and gas in the stomach and bowels. It is reportedly a good stomach remedy for overcoming nausea and colic.

Arbutus, Trailing: Also known as Gravel Plant, Ground Laurel, Mountain Pink, Winter Pink, Mayflower. Botanical name: Epigae repens. This herb is an astringent in that it has the effect of contracting and hardening tissue and checking secretions of mucous membranes. It has reportedly helped persons who have weak bladders or bladders containing so-called gravel or crystalline dust, which are often called bladder stones. It has also been helpful when the urine contains blood or pus.

Areca Nut: Also known as Betel Nut. Botanical name: Areca catechu. This herb contracts and hardens tissue and checks secretions of mucous membranes, and is thus an astringent.

Arenaria Rubra: Also known as Sandwort. Botanical names: Lepigonum rubrum, Tissa rubra, Buda rubra. This herb acts as a diuretic, stimulating functioning of the bladder. It has been used for inflammation of the bladder, known as cystitis, as well as for bladder stones.

Arnica: Also known as Leopard's Bane. Botanical name: Arnica montana. This herb is used for bruises, strains, sprains, pain, muscular rheumatism, externally in liniments. When taken internally it is reportedly effective as a sedative for the nerves, lessening the irritability of nerves and increasing nerve energy. It has been used for cases of hysteria or high nerve tension. It can reportedly also be used effectively in connection with stimulation of the menstrual function due to obstructions in the flow.

Arrowroot: Also known as Bermuda Arrowroot. Botanical name: Maranta arundinacea. This herb is used as a nutritive drink for infants and convalescents. It also has had a soothing and softening effect upon mucous membranes, in addition to being nutritious.

Asafetida: Also known as Gum Asafetida, Devil's Dung, Food of the Gods. Botanical name: Umbelliferae, Ferula foetida Regel. This herb, which is found only in Iran, India and Afghanistan, is a stimulant due to its effect on the brain and nervous system. It is also an expectorant, tonic, laxative, diuretic (urine producing), diaphoretic (produces perspiration), emmenagogue (stimulates menstrual flow), anthelmintic (expels putrified matter from the intestinal tract) and has been reported to have a stimulating effect on the sexual glands. It has been found valuable in cases of excessive air in the stomach of infants, known as colic. It has been helpful to persons who suffer from stomach irritation, hysteria and spasmodic nervous conditions.

Asarabacca: Also known as Hazelwort, Wild Nard. Botanical name: Asarum Europaeum. This herb has been used as an emetic, inducing vomiting, and has also been used as a purgative in cleansing the intestinal tract.

Ash: Also known as Common Ash, Weeping Ash. Botanical name: Fraxinus excelsior. This herb has been used as a laxative as well as for general relief from arthritis and rheumatism.

Asparagus: Botanical name: Asparagus officinalis. This commonly used plant also contains special healing properties. It has been used as a diuretic for stimulation of action of the kidneys, and as a mild laxative and sedative for the nervous system. It has reportedly been recommended for persons who suffer from enlarged heart and for conditions involving accumulation to an excessive degree of fluids in tissues and in body cavities.

Avens: Also known as Colewort, Herb Bennet. Botanical names: Geum urbanum, Radix caryophyllata. This herb has an astringent effect, in that it checks secretions of the mucous membranes and contracts and hardens tissue.

It has been used for its effect in contracting blood vessels so as to stop hemorrhages, thus having a styptic effect. It is also a tonic as it has been reported to have restored power and strength in cases of weakness and debility. It has also been used in cases of diarrhea, as it tends to diminish constant watery discharges from the intestines.

Azadirachta: Also known as Nim, Margosa, Neem. Botanical name: Melia azadirachta. This herb is well known for its use in relieving intestinal worms (anthelmintic) as well as a purgative.

Bael: Also known as Bel, Indian Bael, Bengal Quince. Botanical name: Aegle marmelos. This herb has the effect of contracting tissue and reducing the flow of liquids or fluids from the glands. It is also used in cases of diarrhea and it is reported as non-constipating. It has been recommended for other ailments where there is inflammation of mucous membrane accompanied by ulcers or fever.

Balm: Also known as Sweet Balm, Lemon Balm. Botanical name: Melissa officinalis of the Family Labiatae. This herb acts as a diaphoretic, carminative, febrifuge, stimulant and tonic. It has been used in cases of feverish colds, and for relieving headaches. When taken cold, it reportedly relieves fever; when taken hot, it promotes perspiration. It has also been used for painful or suppressed menstruation. It is often used to aid digestion and for relief of nausea and vomiting.

Balm of Gilead: Botanical name: Populus Balsamifera or Candicans. This herb stimulates the body organs and also has nutritive value, therefore being both a stimulant and a tonic. It has been used for ailments of the chest, lungs, stomach and kidneys. The ointment has also been found useful for relieving the pains of rheumatism and the gout.

Balmony: Also known as Bitter Herb, Snake Head, Turtle Bloom. Botanical name: Chelone glabra. This herb has many uses. It is a tonic, giving strength to the tissues; it is an anthelmintic, helping to relieve the intestinal tract of morbid matter; it is a detergent, in that it cleanses harmful bacteria from the vital organs; and it is antibilious, being used for disordered conditions of the liver that cause constipation, headache, loss of appetite and vomiting. It also increases the gastric and salivary secretions, and stimulates the appetite. It has been used for sores and eczema.

Bamboo Brier: Also known as Wild Sarsaparilla. Botanical name: Aralia nudicaulis. This herb is used as an alterative, that is, it alters the processes of nutrition and excretion, restoring the normal functions of the system. It has a tonic effect, increasing the strength and tone of body tissue, and is used in cases of rheumatism and diseases of the skin. It is also used as a blood purifier.

Barberry: Also known as Berberis, Oregongrape Root, Trailing Mahonia, Rocky Mountain Grape. Botanical name: Berberis Linne; Berberis vulgaris; Berberis aquifolium. This herb acts as an astringent, a tonic and stomach aid. It also has alterative qualities, changing nutritive processes to a normal state. It has been used for relief of pain, soreness and burning sensations along the biliary ducts as well as the urinary tracts.

Barley: Also known as Pearl Barley, Perlatum. Botanical name: Hordeum distichon, of the Family Graminaceae. Barley is a nutritive food, containing protein, starch, enzymes and vitamins, and is therefore a valuable food for the sick and convalescent. In addition, this food is soothing to irritated surfaces and can be easily digested. It can also be used for diarrhea or inflammatory conditions of the bowels or other inflammatory conditions of mucous membranes of the body.

Basil: Also known as Common Basil, Sweet Basil. Botanical name: Ocium basilicum. This herb acts as a stimulant, condiment, nervine, aromatic. It is commonly used on areas of the skin that are swollen from insect bites or ivy poison. It also allays excessive vomiting and is effective in aiding digestion.

Bayberry: Also known as Bayberry Bush, Myrtle, Tallow Shrub, Vegetable Tallow. Botanical name: Myrica cerifera. This herb is used as an astringent, tonic and stimulant. This is one of the most useful herbs. The tea has been used as a gargle for sore throat and to aid in cleansing the throat of all putrid matter. It has restored the mucous secretions to normal activity and cleansed the stomach. It can be used as an emetic after narcotic poisoning of any kind, and it is good to follow with a lobelia emetic. It has been used for all varieties of hemorrhages, whether from the stomach, lungs, uterus, or bowels. It is reportedly used to check profuse menstruation and in cases of leucorrhea. It is one of the best herbs for the female organs, also has an excellent effect on the uterus in pregnancy, and makes a good douche.

In case of gangrenous sores, boils, carbuncles, it has been used as a wash and poultice. It also is beneficial to spongy and bleeding gums. Bayberry has been used in treatment of adenoids and catarrh.

Bay Leaves: Also known as Bay Tree, Indian Bay, Bay Laurel. Botanical name: Laurus nobilis. A pleasant tonic, which gives tone and strength to the digestive organs. It expels wind from the stomach and bowels and has been used for cramps.

Beech: Also known as Beech Tree, Beech Nut Tree. Botanical name: Fagus ferruginea. This herb has been used as a tonic, astringent, and antiseptic. It has been known to improve appetite and to aid the softening and healing of wounds and ulcers. Reportedly used in diabetes, internal ulcers, skin diseases, dyspepsia. It is also used for ailments of the liver, kidneys and bladder.

Bearsfoot, American: Also known as Uvedalia, Leaf Cup. Botanical name: Polymnia uvedalia. This herb acts to stimulate the glands of the body and produces a laxative effect as well as a pain relieving effect, serving as an anodyne. It has also been reported to have helped cases of liver and spleen congestive conditions. It also aids in digestive conditions known as dyspepsia, especially hepatic dyspepsia, resulting from liver disease.

Belladonna: Also known as Deadly Nightshade, Dwale, Black Cherry Root. Botanical name: Atropa belladonna. This herb serves as a diuretic, increasing the secretion of urine. It also serves as an anodyne relieving pain, and relaxes overcontracted smooth muscle and is therefore a sedative. It depresses sensory nerve endings. Its action also makes it effective in the condition involving loss of semen involuntarily, known as spermatorrhea. Despite its sedative action, it helps stimulate the circulation.

Benne: Also known as Sesam, Gingelly, Sesame. Botanical name: Sesamum indicum. The leaves and seeds of this herb are used as a demulcent and as a laxative. This herb, in its tea form, has been used in various ophthalmic complaints, such as inflammation or soreness.

Benzoin: Botanical name Styrax benzoin, Styrax benzoin dryander, Styrax tonkinensis. Also called Benjamin tree, benzoin laurel, gum Benjamin, gum benzoin, palembang benzoin, siam benzoin, sumatra benzoin. A dry powder is prepared from the sap of this herb, and a tincture made with alcohol. An expectorant, it is useful in treating coughs and bronchitis and often used in cough medicines. Used externally it helps relieve wounds and sores. It also acts as an antiseptic and a stimulant.

Berberis: Botanical name Berberis vulgaris. Also Barberry. The Egyptians used this bitter tonic for treating fevers, and the American Indians ate the berries in a jelly or jam and as a tonic for liver ailments. During the 19th century it was used in New England as a medicine for consumptives. Its action is similar to that of Golden Seal and it is used in the same way.

Bethroot: Botanical name Trillium pendulum and trillium rectum. Also Birth-root, Dough Root, Ground Lily, Indian Shamrock, Jew's Harp, Lamb's Quarters, Milk Ipecac, Three-Leaved Nightshade, Trillium, Wakerobin. Besides acting as a tonic and alterative, this herb helps as a pectoral in treatment of bronchial troubles, coughs, lung hemorrhages and pulmonary consumption. It reportedly is used to stem excessive menstruation and as a douche for leucorrhea and other vaginal problems. In an enema, bethroot soothes rectal irritations; the herb is also used for diarrhea and dysentery.

Bilberries: Botanical name: Vaccinum myrtillus. Also Huckleberries, Whortleberries, Hurtle berries. This herb has been valuable during typhoid epidemics both as a preventative and as a treatment. A tea from the dried berries relieves dropsy and kidney or bladder stones, and has been used for diarrhea and bowel derangements. It also may serve as an enema, a diuretic, a gargle for sore throats and as an astringent for wounds. The ripe fruit reportedly relieves fever and quenches thirst, and the leaves yield a substance known as Myrtillin, which helps reduce blood sugar as does insulin.

Birch: Botanical name: Betula alba. Also known as White Birch. A bitter, this herb increases the tone of the gastro-intestinal mucous membrane and produces an oil (from the bark), Oleum Rusci, which is used in the relief of gonorrhea and skin diseases such as eczema.

Birthwort: Aristolochia longa. Besides its aromatic properties, birthwort has been successful in relieving the symptoms of gout and rheumatism because it is a stimulant for both circulation and glandular functions.

Bistort: Botanical name: Polygonum bistorta. Also called Adderwort, Dragonwort, Easter Giant, Patience Dock, Red Legs, Snake Weed, Sweet Dock. This herb acts as a powerful astringent and has been used in cases of cholera, diarrhea, dysentery and leucorrhea and as a wash for sores on the mouth or gums, as well as external open or running sores (i.e. smallpox, measles, pimples, insect stings, snake bites). Powdered, it is a styptic and will stop bleeding when applied to a wound. It reportedly decreases or regulates menstrual flow when used in a douche. It is also a diuretic and alterative.

Bitterroot: Apocynum and rosaemifolium. Also called Catchfly, Dogsbane, Flytrap, Honey Bloom, Milk Ipecac, Milkweed, Wandering Milkweed, Western Wallflower. The root of this plant seems to have an excellent effect on the liver, kidneys and bowels and can aid in digestion and help to expel worms. It has also been used in treating diabetes and diseases of the joints and mucous membranes such as rheumatism and neuralgia. It has been known to rid the system of impurities (i.e. gallstones) and to remedy fevers of various kinds.

Bittersweet: Solanum dulcamara. Common names are Fever Twig, Felenwort, Garden Nightshade, Nightshade, Nightshade Vine, Scarlet Berry, Staff Vine, Violet Bloom, Wolf Grape. A soothing anodyne when used externally, this is also an hepatic used as a salve or ointment either by itself (in leprosy), with yellowdock (for skin diseases and sores), or with camomile (for bruises, sprains and corns). It will also purify the blood, make the kidneys and other glandular organs active and increase menstrual flow. Thus it is a deobstruent and aperient or laxative as well. It is also used as a resolvent.

Bittersweet, American: Celastrus scandens. Also False Bittersweet, Waxwort. This alterative acts, also, as a diuretic, thereby aiding in normal functioning of the liver. It has been found helpful in treating leucorrhea and in bringing about delayed menstruation. Perspiration may be induced by drinking the tea.

Blackberry: Rubus Villosus, of the Rose family, Rosaceae. Also known as Bramble, Rubus, Dewberry, Gout Berry, Cloud Berry, Rudi Fructus. Having both an astringent and a tonic effect, this plant has been highly esteemed in relieving diarrhea. An invigorating tonic and gargle.

Black Cohosh: Cimicifuga racemosa. Also called Black Snake Root, Bugbane, Bugwort, Rattleroot, Rattlesnake's Root, Rattleweed, Rich Weed, Squaw Root. This herb acts as a nervine and antispasmodic. As such is used in cases of hysteria, St. Vitus's Dance (chorea), epilepsy, and convulsions. It has been known to be an effective pain reliever in childbirth. It has been used for dropsy, rheumatism, meningitis, asthma (it is an astringent and expectorant), delirium tremens and snake and insect bites. As a syrup it quiets coughs and soothes liver and kidney troubles. It is also an emmenagogue, alterative and diaphoretic.

Black Currant: Ribes Nigrum. Besides the nutritive value of the fruit, this plant's leaves are a diuretic and have been used as a tonic and for hoarseness, cleansing wounds and ulcers, and to reduce fever. The juice is an antiseptic and blood purifier, thereby of value in anemia, malnutrition and general debility.

Black Haw: Viburnum rufidulum rafinesque. Also American Sloe, Stagbush, and Viburnum Prunifolium. Reportedly the principal use of this herb is during pregnancy for nervous disorders, pain relief, and to prevent miscarriages. It is also used as a uterine astringent to draw together the soft tissue and prevent painful menstruation. It has also been used to check uterine bleeding.

Black Willow Bark: Salix nigra, salix discolor. Commonly called Calkins Willow, Marsh, Pussy Willow. This astringent and antiseptic has been used as a douche to relieve inflamed and ulcerated surfaces of mucous membrane of the vagina and for relief of ovarian pain. It is a treatment for nocturnal involuntary emissions and a depressant for the sexual glands where irritation of the sexual organs results from genito-urinary problems. In powdered form the bark has been known to relieve inactive ulcers or gangrene. The herb is also effective for rheumatism and inflammation of the joints, muscles and nerves.

Bloodroot: Sanguinaria canadensis. Also Indiana Plant, Pauson, Red Paint Root, Red Root, Red Puccoon. In small doses bloodroot stimulates the heart and digestive organs; a large dose acts as a sedative. It is effective in speeding the process of healing of piles and nasal tumors (and American Thomasonians use it to treat adenoids), sores and diseases of the skin; and as a relief for chest diseases such as coughs, colds, bronchitis, pneumonia.

Blue Cohosh: Caulophyllum thalictroides. Also Blue Berry, Blue or Yellow Ginseng, Papoose Root, Squaw Root. A most valuable herb to women, it is used in chronic uterine problems, leucorrhea, vaginitis and cramps. American Indians use it to facilitate childbirth and induce labor. As an emmenagogue it is also used to regulate menstruation. It has been used for dropsy, colic, hysteria, heart palpitations, high blood pressure and diabetes. It has been reported to soothe hiccoughs and other spasms such as epilepsy and whooping cough. It contains the minerals potassium, magnesium, calcium, iron, silicon and phosphorus which help to alkalinize the blood and urine.

Blue Flag: Iris versicolor. Also Flag Iris, Flag Lily, Fleur-de-lis, Flower-de-luce, Iris, Liver Lily, Poison Flag, Snake

Lily, Water Flag, Water Lily. This herb was used before the discovery of penicillin in curing syphilis. For liver troubles, it increases the flow of urine (diuretic action), thereby eliminating poisons from the blood and relieving indigestion and its accompanying dizziness and headaches. It is also a laxative and vermifuge. The powdered herb will induce sneezing to clear nasal passages or, if applied to a wound, will speed healing. It is also a remedy for insect bites and stings. The juice reportedly relieves hemorrhoids and is relaxing and stimulating.

Blue Mallow: Malva sylvestris. Also called Cheese Flower, Common mallow, Mauls. A drink prepared by pouring boiling water over the herb has been found to be popular for coughs, colds and similar ailments. It will also soothe and soften the skin when it is applied directly to the body part in powder form.

Blue Violet: Viola cuculata. Also Common Blue Violet and Violet. Among those ailments said to have been remedied by the leaves of this plant are tumors, gout, coughs, colds, sore throat, sores, ulcers, cancer, scrofula, syphilis, bronchitis and difficult breathing due to gases and morbid matter in the stomach and bowels. It also relieves internal ulcers and as a mucilaginous herb soothes headache and head congestion and whooping cough. Combined with nerveroot, skullcap, or black cohosh it serves as a soothing nervine. It is also a laxative, an emetic and an alterative.

Boldo: Peumus boldus. Sometimes called Boldea, Boldu, or Fragrans. This herb is a native of Chile and its leaves are imported for use in the treatment of various disturbances. It stimulates the secretion and excretion of urine, serving as a diuretic, and is therefore used in chronic hepatic torpor. An antiseptic as well, it prevents the growth of microorganisms and has been reported to be effective in cases of inflammation of the bladder and ridding the urinary tract of gonorrhea germs.

Boneset: Eupatorium perfoliatum. Common names are Indian Sage, Thoroughwort. It is both a febrifuge and an expectorant and provides relief for coughing spells and catarrh. It may also be used as an ointment for some skin diseases.

Borage: Borago officinalis. Burrage or Common Bugloss. The tea is used to bathe sore, inflamed eyes. Taken internally, the tea cleanses the blood by diuretic action and is effective for fevers, yellow jaundice, to expel poisons of all kinds due to snake bites, insect bites. It has been known to strengthen the heart and is used for coughs; it soothes itch, ringworms, tetters, scabs, sores, ulcers and, as a gargle, ulcers in the mouth and throat.

Box Leaves: Buxus sempervirens. This herb, acting as a depurative, is helpful in curing yellow jaundice. It may be made into a tea or swallowed directly, and is used as a tonic for general weakness or debility.

Broom: Cytisus scoparius. Also Irish Broom. The leaves and stem are used with uva ursi, cleavers and dandelion as a diuretic to cleanse the kidneys and bladder. It may also be used internally to relieve toothache, dropsy, ague and gout. Externally it may be made into an ointment for lice or vermin. It contains potash.

Bryony: Tamus communis, Linn. Sometimes Black Bryony, Blackeye Root, Bryonia, English Mandrake, Mandragora. A pulp made from the root of this plant is rubbed into areas of the body affected by rheumatism, gout or paralysis. Bruises and discolorations as well as freckles also seem to be removed by this procedure (thus the name "blackeye" root). A tincture prepared from the herb will act as a diuretic; it has also been used for accumulation of fluid in body cavities or tissues and for coughs, influenza, bronchitis. It is also reported to heal sunburn and effectively cleanse ulcers on the skin and is used in malarial and zymotic diseases.

Buchu: Barosma betulina. Common names are Bookoo, Bucku, Buku, Thumb, Diosma. Used as a tincture or as a tea, buchu is reported to be one of the best aids for urinary problems. Taken warm it produces perspiration and soothes leucorrhea and enlargement of the prostate gland and irritation of the urethra. It has also been used successfully for rheumatism and dropsy and in the early stages of diabetes.

Buckbean: Menyanthes trifoliata. Also Bitter Trefoil, Bitter-worm, Bog Bean, Bog Myrtle, Brook Bean, Marsh Clover, Marsh Trefoil, Water Shamrock. Buckbean seems to be especially effective in cases of stomach complaints. It is used to treat dyspepsia and stomach catarrh, and to promote digestion. Taken in large doses it is emetic and anthelmintic. A tonic and bitter, it is also used to relieve rheumatism, scrofula, scurvy, jaundice and other liver troubles, and intermittent fevers.

Buckthorn Bark: Rhamnus frangula. Sometimes called Alder Buckthorn, Black Alder Dogwood, Black Alder Tree, Black Dogwood, European Black Alder, European Buckthorn, Persian Berries. Taken internally, the bark of the buckthorn seems to relieve constipation and keep the bowels regular. (The fruit is a purgative.) It has been used for gout, dropsy and skin disease and, taken hot, produces profuse perspiration. An ointment of the herb provides relief from itching and has been reported to be helpful in the removal of warts.

Bugle: Ajuga reptans: Sometimes known as bugula. This aromatic herb is a tonic which tones the gastrointestinal mucous membrane. It is also an astringent and widely used to stop hemorrhaging and for bile disorders.

Bugleweed: Lycopus virginicus. Also Sweet Bugle, or Water Bugle. This mild narcotic has been used for coughs and to relieve pulmonary bleeding. It has a sedative as well as an astringent effect, tending to contract tissues of the mucous membrane and reduce fluid discharges.

Bugloss: Echium vulgare. Sometimes called Blueweed, Viper's Bugloss. The action of this herb is expectorant, diaphoretic, and demulcent, used to reduce fever due to colds and inflammation of the respiratory tract.

Burdock: Arctium lappa. Bardana, Beggar's Buttons, Burrs, Burr Seed, Clot-bur, Grass Burdock, Hardock, Harebur, Hurrburr, Lappa, Turkey Burr Seed. It is the seed of this plant which has medicinal properties. The dried, first-year root is also used. A seed tincture has been found to be a stomachic tonic and has aided in the relief of the chronic skin condition known as psoriasis inveteratar, as well as boils and carbuncles. Applied externally a decoction made from the root is used for gout, rheumatism, scrofula, canker sores, syphilis, sciatica, and gonorrhea. It seems to be one of the best blood purifiers. In the form of a salve or tea it helps relieve swellings, burns and hemorrhoids. The plant produces *inulin* which is used in the production of fructose which has been used in the diet of diabetics.

Burnet: Pimpinella saxifraga. Also Burnet Saxifrage, European Burnet, Pimpernel. A stomachic used to cleanse the lungs and stomach. It helps heal cuts, wounds, sores, piles, and relieve tooth and earache. It also has a pleasant odor.

Burr Marigold: Bidens tripartita. Also Water Agrimony. This garden or wild plant is astringent, diuretic and diaphroetic and has been recommended for dropsy, gout and hemorrhages of urinary and respiratory organs.

Butter-Bur: Petasites vulgaris, Tussilago, Petasites. Also Common Butterbur. This valuable herb is a stimulant and diuretic and has been effective in strengthening the cardiac muscles.

Butternut Bark: Juglans cinerea. Also Kisky Thomas Nut, Lemon Walnut, Oilnut, Oilnut Bark, White Walnut. This plant has several medicinal qualities: it is an alterative, anthelmintic, astringent, cathartic and cholagogue. It will also expel intestinal worms and relieve fevers and colds.

Calamus: Acorus calamus. Also Grass Myrtle, Myrtle Flag, Sea Sedge, Sweet Cane, Sweet Flag, Sweet Grass, Sweet Myrtle, Sweet Root, Sweet Rush, Sweet Sedge. The root of this plant is especially effective for stomach complaints: it improves gastric juice and keeps the stomach sweet while preventing acids, gases and fermentation in the stomach. It is also good for dyspepsia and increases appetite. It is claimed to destroy the desire for tobacco. A tea of the herb may be applied to burns, sores and ulcers and is valuable in treating scrofula.

Calumba: Jateorhiza calumba. This root is used for stomach troubles and indigestion in general. It acts as a febrifuge and is a bitter tonic.

Calotropis: Calotropis procera, asclepias procera. Sometimes called Mudar Bark. It is reported that the powdered bark mixed with water, olive oil or antiseptic vaseline may be applied directly to the skin for relief of eczema. Taken internally, it has been found beneficial for diarrhea and dysentery.

Camomile: Anthemis nobilis. Common names are Chamomile, Ground Apple, Whig Plant. A well-known home remedy, a tea made from the blossoms is an excellent tonic and beneficial in the treatment of many ailments, among them dyspepsia, colds, bronchitis, bladder troubles, ague, dropsy and jaundice. The tea is a soothing wash for sore eyes, as well as other sores and wounds. As a poultice it is used on swellings and pains. It promotes menstrual flow, softens skin, is effective for colic in infants, intermittent fever, and the early stages of typhoid. It is good in hysteria and nervous diseases. It is also a popular table tea. In pulverized form the flowerheads may be made with soapwort into a shampoo, especially for fair hair.

Camphor: Cinnamomum Camphora, Laurus Camphora, Camphora officinarum. Sometimes referred to as Gum Camphor or Laurel Camphor. As an anodyne, it is especially beneficial in cases of gout, rheumatism and neuralgia, and is used to relieve irritation of the sexual organs. Externally it may be applied to inflamed or bruised areas. Taken internally it is a sedative and is valuable for colds and their accompanying symptoms. Perspiration may be induced by ingestion of the herb and fever reduced. Physicians will sometimes use oil of camphor as a heart stimulant.

Caraway: Carum carui. Sometimes called Kummel or Caraway Seed. The seeds may be taken in hot water or milk for colic and colds. It is a digestive aid, strengthening and toning the stomach and preventing catarrh on the alimentary tract. The powdered seeds may be made into a poultice to remove bruises. It is also used to flavor other herbs and prevent griping, as well as in baking. The root may be eaten as turnips are.

Cardamoms: Elettaria cardamomum. The seeds of this fruit, taken warm, are an aromatic helpful in flatulence. It is a carminative and a stomachic.

Carrot: Daucus carota. Bee's Nest Plant, Bird's Nest Root, arden Carrot, Queen Anne's Lace, Wild Carrot. Both the root and seeds are used. Grated, they make an effective poultice for ulcers, abscesses, carbuncles, scrofulas, cankerous sores and severe wounds. A carrot diet has sometimes relieved bladder, liver and kidney problems. They are used for dropsy, gravel, painful urination, to increase menstrual flow, and expel worms from the bowels. The powdered seeds make a tea which is reported to relieve colic and increase the flow of urine.

Cascara Sagrada: Rhamnus purschiana. Bear Wood, Bearberry, Bitter Bark, California Buckthorn, Chittam Bark, Coffee Berry Bark, Dogwood Bark, Persian Bark, Purschiana Bark, Sacred Bark. The fresh bark is a powerful gastro-intestinal irritant and emetic sometimes recommended as an intestinal tonic and as for relief of gallstones. It has been used for chronic constipation and digestive disorders, and is not habit forming. It increases the secretion of bile and has been used for liver complaints, especially enlarged liver. Other uses are in gout, dyspepsia, piles and to regulate the bowels.

Castor Oil Plant: Ricinus communis. Also Palma Christi. This is a well-known purgative and cathartic which is gentle enough for use by children and pregnant women. Besides being a treatment for constipation, it is effective in colic in infants and in cases of diarrhea resulting from slow digestion. Applied externally the oil tends to soothe itch, ringworm, and cuts on the skin.

Cayenne: Capiscum annuum. Also called Cayenne Pepper, Chili Pepper, African Red Pepper, Spanish Pepper, Bird Pepper, Pod Pepper, Cockspur Pepper, Red Pepper. Red pepper is reportedly one of the best and quickest stimulants among the herbal medicines and also has the advantage of causing no negative side effects: it stimulates the heart but does not increase the blood pressure. It is used as a tonic. It has been used as a healing application for bruises, sprains, wounds, burn and sunburns, and pyorrhea. A plaster of cayenne has been used to relieve internal inflammation most efficaciously and therefore has been used in connection with pleurisy and rheumatism. One author reports that, with an emetic, an enema, sudorifics, and cayenne he has cured cases of rheumatism overnight. The effect of this herb is to equalize circulation, as well as to stimulate the glands, and has been used for ague, spring fever, and in cases of excess mucus in the respiratory passages, as it facilitates expectoration. For its astringent quality, it has been administered for sore throat and diphtheria as a gargle. With bayberry it helps to stop uterine hemorrhages. It has reportedly been used as a remedy for hangover, and for cold feet a small amount may be sprinkled in the socks. To relieve toothache, cotton wool saturated with oil of capiscum has been packed into the tooth, where it acts as a stimulant and an antiseptic. It has none of the irritating effects of black pepper or mustard.

Catnip: Nepeta cataria. Commonly called Cat Mint, Catrup, Cat's Wort, Field Balm. One of the oldest household remedies, it is an antispasmodic and anodyne helpful in convulsions. Further, it reportedly restores menstruation and allays gas or acids in the stomach and bowels. It also prevents griping. Reportedly, an enema is soothing and relaxing and will induce urination when it has stopped. For the treatment of colds, it has reduced fever and produced perspiration. It is also a tonic.

Cedron: Simaba cedron. Sometimes called Rattlesnake's Bones. The tea of this plant has been recommended as a generally invigorating and strengthening drink. It reportedly prevents gas in the stomach and is effective for intermittent fevers. As an antispasmodic it has been used for fits and nervous disorders and any kind of spasm. Externally, a strong tea may be used for snake or insect bites.

Celandine: Chelidonum majus. Not to be mistaken for Small or Lesser Celandine (Pilewort), this herb has been found helpful for jaundice, eczema and other skin diseases. It may be applied directly to abrasions and bruises and the fresh juice to corns and warts. It is claimed that a decoction of the herb or roots boiled in white wine serves as a deobstruent for liver and bladder.

Celery: Apium graveolens. Also called Smallage. The seeds and the ripe fruit (dried) of this plant have reportedly had an excellent tonic and stimulant effect. They affect the kidneys, producing an increased flow of urine. It has been used in cases of nervousness, neuralgia, and rheumatism. It is also a diaphoretic. The stalks are a popular food and the seeds are a delicious flavoring.

Chickweed: Stelleria media. Commonly known as Adder's Mouth, Satin Flower, Starwort, Starweed, Stitchwort. This garden pest has multiple healing properties and may be used as a food (prepared like spinach) as well. Reportedly, any form of internal inflammation is soothed and healed by its application: colds and coughs, hoarseness, bronchitis, pleurisy, inflamed bowels. It has been used as a soothing poultice for boils, burns, skin diseases, sore eyes, and wounds. It is said to be one of the best remedies for tumors, piles, swollen testes, ulcerated throat and mouth, and deafness. It may be taken internally for blood poisoning and as a poultice applied externally. A salve of the powder may also be applied, in addition to bathing with the tea. A bath in the tea has been used for sores and skin problems. It is also given to pigs for a disease known as white scour.

Chaulmoogra: Taraktogegnos Kurzii. The powdered seed may be taken or an oil made from the seed may be administered as an ointment or taken internally. A laxative and febrifuge when taken internally, it helps relieve skin eruptions and stiffness of the joints.

Chicory: Cichorium endiva: Blue Sailors, Garden Endive or Garden Chicory, Endive, Succory. The root of this plant is best known for its use with coffee, but is also effective as a hepatic and for disorders of the urinary canal, stomach and spleen. It has been used to settle an upset stomach by expelling morbid matter, while also toning up the system.

Cherrylaurel: Prunus laurocerasus. When taken internally, its powered leaves have been used as a sedative and have often been used to relax the muscles involved in coughing. It has been used for asthma and whooping cough and other diseases involving severe coughing.

Chiretta: Swertia chirata. Sometimes called Chirayta, Griseb. A bitter tonic. With suitable hepatics and laxatives, it sometimes forms part of a soothing tonic for liver complaints, dyspepsia and constipation.

Cinquefoil: Potentilla reptans. Also Fivefinger, Five Leaf Grass. When an astringent skin lotion is called for this herb has been applied. It has also been taken as a gargle and internally for diarrhea.

Cleavers: Galium aparine. Also Bedstraw, Burweed, Catchweed, Cheese Rent Herb, Clabbergrass, Cleaverwort, Clivers, Eriffe, Goose's Hair, Goose Grass, Goose-share, Goosebill, Gravel Grass, Grip Grass, Hayriffe, Milk Sweet, Poor Robin, Savoyan, Scratch Weed. Reportedly, an infusion of this herb is very effective for kidney and bladder problems and may be combined with broom, buchu, gravelroot, marsh mallow, and uvu ursi to act as a diuretic. It seems to dissolve bladder stones. For fever, scarlet fever, and measles its refrigerant and diaphoretic properties are said to be excellent, and it has been used both as a skin cleanser and for skin diseases. As a blood purifier it has been used in connection with gonorrhea and jaundice. Applied to a bleeding wound it reportedly causes clotting and stops bleeding, as well as hastening healing. The oil of the herb may be applied for earache.

Clover, Red: Trifolium pratense. Also Cleaver Grass, Cow Grass, Marl Grass. This attractive and common flower may be made into a tea for both internal and external use. It may also be combined with blue violet, burdock, yellow dock, dandelion root, rock rose and golden seal to make a concoction for remedy of growths and leprosy. The warm tea has been said to be very soothing to the nerves and therefore has been helpful for spasms and severe coughing. It has been used as a mild stimulant. As a salve it may be applied to wounds.

Gather the blossoms when in full bloom. Dry in the shade and hang in paper bags in a dry place. A tea can then be made from them.

Clover, White: Trifolium repens. Common names are Melilot, Shamrock, Sweet Lucerne. A salve may be made of the clover blossoms and yellowdock in equal parts. A strong tea applied to external sores helps speed healing, and, taken internally, serves as a cleanser and blood purifier.

Cloves: Eugenia aromatica. Sometimes called Clavos. A powerful carminative, this reportedly relieves gas pain in the stomach and bowel. Because of its stimulant effect, it has improved digestion as well as promoted the flow of saliva and gastric juices. It is an excellent carminative to reduce griping of other herbs. Cloves have been used to relieve pain of toothache, lumbago, rheumatism, muscle cramps and neuralgia.

Coffee: Coffee arabica. In the popular drink, the ground coffee seeds are a diuretic, causing an increase in the activity of the kidneys. It is often used to aid in expelling the effects of alcohol and prevents vomiting by acting as an anti-emetic. The caffeine in coffee is a stimulant and increases the heartbeat. It has also been used to dispel stupor and drowsiness when they are caused by excessive use of narcotics, thus acting as an anti-narcotic. There are also claims that it is helpful for bladder stones, rheumatism and gout.

Colombo: Cocculus palmatus. A very fine but bitter tonic, this reportedly will strengthen and tone the entire system. It is an antiemetic that can be used in pregnancy and for chronic colon trouble, diarrhea and cholera. It has been used to improve the appetite.

Coltsfoot: Tussilago farfara. Sometimes called Coughwort, Horsefoot, British Tobacco, Flower Velure, Ginger Root. The leaves of this plant often constitute one ingredient in cough medicines for asthma and whooping cough as they are both pectoral and emollient. It has also been found in medicines for lung ailments such as tuberculosis and catarrh. It has been used in cases of sinusitis, ague,

piles, fever and swellings and has been applied externally
to scrofulous tumors (or taken internally) or to the lungs
and throat. The leaves have also been smoked to soothe
the mucous membranes of throat and lungs and relieve
congestion of asthma or bronchitis.

Comfrey: Symphytum officinale. Also Blackwort, Consolio-
dae, Gum Plant, Healing Herb, Knitback, Knitbone,
Nipbone, Slippery Root. This reportedly popular cough
remedy has also been taken for arthritis, coughs, catarrh,
consumption, excessive expectoration in asthma, sinusitis,
and ulceration of the stomach, kidney or bowels. It has
been used in cases of bloody urine. To relieve swellings,
bruises, sprains and fractures a compress of the hot tea
has been applied. It has also helped to relieve the pain.
This same treatment reportedly also works on breasts
sore from excess milk, headaches, eye injuries, tonsilitis,
anal or rectal itching, arthritis or gout, gangrene and
burns. As an infusion comfrey has been used to treat
female debility, anemia, leucorrhea and gall and liver
conditions, diarrhea and pulmonary diseases such as
pneumonia. It has been said to be a good general cleanser
when taken internally and is reportedly rich in calcium
and protein and may be added to fruit juice for a nutritious drink.

Coral: Corallorhiza odontorhiza. Sometimes called Crawley,
Chicken's Toes, Dragon's Claw, Fever Root, Turkey
Claw. This root has been used for skin diseases, boils,
tumors, scrofula, scurvy, menstrual cramps, pleurisy, and
is said to be effective for enlarged veins. It acts as a diaphoretic and febrifuge without exciting the system. It is
sometimes combined with blue cohosh to produce an
emmenagogue.

Coriander: Coriandrum satium. This pleasant flavoring
strengthens and tones the stomach and acts as a carminative as well. It has also been used to alleviate pain in
the bowels caused by laxatives.

Cornsilk: Zea mays, Stigmata maidis. Also known as Corn,
Maize Jagnog. This is the yellow silk of sweet corn;
reportedly used for irritation of the urinary organs and
for painful urination caused by stones in the bladder or
trouble with the prostate gland. It seems to be an excel-

lent remedy for kidney and bladder troubles, such as enuresis.

Cotton Root: Gossypium herbaceum. The powdered bark of the root of this herb has been used to bring on retarded menstruation.

Couchgrass: Agropyrum repens. Sometimes called Twitchgrass or Quickgrass. The powdered root of this herb has been used to stimulate activity of the kidneys and bladder and increase the flow of urine. It could therefore be helpful for bladder and urinary problems and a mild purgative. It may be taken for gout and rheumatism and to soothe the mucous membranes.

Cowslip: Primula veris. Also Herb Peter, Paigles, Palsywort. This antispasmodic seems also to be effective in soothing restlessness and insomnia. Cowslip has been used at times for rheumatism, gout and paralysis but its value for these diseases has been disproved.

Cramp Bark: Viburnum opulus. Guelder rose, High Cranberry, Snowball Tree. In a decoction, this has been used as a nervine and antispasmodic, soothing cramps and other muscular spasms.

Cranesbill: Geranium pratense. As a douche with bistort this has been used for leucorrhea. It reportedly will also stop bleeding, both internal and external, and has been used as an astringent and tonic for the kidneys.

Creeping Jenny: European Bindweed. The roots of this plant have been said to act very rapidly as a styptic for wounds.

Cubeb Berries: Piper cubeba. Also Java Pepper, Tailed Cubebs and Tailed Pepper. It has been said that this tasty seasoning can also serve as a tonic for the stomach and bowels, as an aid in bronchial troubles and for chronic bladder troubles. As an aromatic it has been used in gonorrhea and leucorrhea. It is also carminative, a purgative, and a diuretic.

Cudweed: Gnaphalium uliginosum. Also Cotton Weed, or Marsh Cudweed. This herb is an astringent and has been used as a gargle for inflammation of the salivary glands.

Culver's Root: Veronicastrum virginicum, Leptandra virginicum. Also Black Root, Bowman's Root, Culver's Physic, Tall Speedwell, Tall Veronica. The root and rhizome of this plant have been used to treat indigestion resulting from insufficient flow of bile from the liver. When fresh, the root is a strong and rather violent cathartic, and in mild doses it is a tonic.

Damiana: Turnera diffusa. Sometimes called Turnera. It will reportedly increase the flow of urine, has a mild laxative effect, and has been used as a nerve tonic in cases of physical or mental exhaustion.

Dandelion: Taraxacum officinale. Also Blow Ball, Cankerwort, Lion's Tooth, Priest's Crown, Puff Ball, Swine Snout, White Endive. Dandelion greens are used in salads and as a nutritious vegetable. The root may be ground, roasted and prepared as coffee, and it has none of the bad effects of that drink. Prepared this way and drunk regularly it reportedly acts as a mild laxative and diuretic. The sodium salts in the plant should act as blood purifiers. The herb is reportedly useful for dropsy, eczema, scurvy, scrofula, diabetes, inflammation of the bowels, and fevers.

Devil's Bit: Scabiosa succisa, or Ofbit. An infusion of this herb has helped to relieve coughs and fevers.

Digitalis: Digitalis pulverata and Digitalis purpurea. Also Cottagers, Dead Men's Bells, Fairy Bells, Fairy Cap, Fairy Fingers, Fairy's Glove, Fairy Thimbles, Flopdock, Foxglove, Folk's Glove, Figwort, Ladies' Glove, Throatwort. A heart toner and stimulant, this herb must be used with the greatest care as it can also cause overstimulation and paralysis. A doctor's direction is strongly recommended. For burns or scalds an ointment made by beating the blossoms into lard is reportedly soothing. The berries contain large amounts of vitamin C.

Dill: Anethum graveolens. Sometimes called Eneldo. This popular food seasoning is also used in digestive disorders. It reportedly expels wind from the stomach and bowels and prevents gas and fermentation. It has been used for colic in children. It has been used to soothe pains and swellings, quiet the nerves, and to stop hiccoughs.

Echinacea: Brauneria angustifolia. Common names are Black Sampson, Cornflower, Kansas Niggerhead, Purple Cove Flower, Red Sunflower, Sampson Root. This reportedly excellent blood purifier has been used in any disease resulting from impurities in the blood, including blood poisoning. It is also said to relieve dyspepsia and gastrointestinal pain, and to be an analgesic. It has also been used as a gargle.

Elder: Sambucus nigra. Elderberry. The flowers of this familiar tree have often been used, with peppermint and yarrow, to reduce fever in colds and as a bath to relieve inflamed eyes. Elderberry wine has been taken for colds and influenza.

Elecampane: Inula helenium. Also Aunée or Scabwort. Though a very popular medicine in the seventeenth century, the claims for elecampane have been greatly revised. In combination with other herbs it has been used in dough medicines and for asthma and bronchitis. It is an expectorant and a tonic for the lungs and mucous membranes. It is also an emmenagogue used to bring on menstruation, and reportedly acts to expel kidney and bladder stones and to relieve retention of urine.

Ergot: Claviceps purpurea, Secale cornulum. Also known as Spurred Rye or Smut of Rye. This is the fungus obtained from rye grains. It has been used for dysmenorrhea (painful menstruation) and amenorrhea (abnormal stoppage of menstruation) and leucorrhea (a whitish vaginal discharge). It is also said to be helpful in male disorders such as enlarged prostate and involuntary discharge of semen and in gonorrhea. Another use has been as a styptic for internal bleeding.

Eryngo: Eryngium maritimum. Also Sea Eryngo or Sea Holly. Eryngo root has been used in bladder disorders. It is usually used in combination with other herbs, such as barberry bark or wild carrot.

Eucalyptus: Eucalytus globulus. Also Blue Gum Tree. The leaves and oil from this tree are an extremely potent but safe antiseptic. It is also inhaled for sore throat or bacterial infections of the bronchial tubes and lungs. It is soothing to inflamed mucous membranes and therefore a relief for asthma and croup. It has been applied to ulcers and cancerous growths, sores or other wounds. The oil must not be used internally except in small doses.

Eyebright: Euphrasia officinalis. Also Birdseye, Bright eye. As the name indicates this herb has been used largely for eye disorders and weakness of the eyes. Combined with golden seal it may be prepared as a lotion to soothe inflammation of the eyes and general eye irritation. It has also been applied externally to arrest hemmorrhages. It is both a tonic and an astringent.

Fennel: Foeniculum officinale. Also Hinojo. The licorice flavor of this herb makes it a popular seasoning. It has also been used for gas, acid stomach, gout and colic in infants. Reportedly, a tea of the herb is a soothing eyewash, and is used for snake and insect bites. Boiled with barley it seems to increase milk in nursing mothers. It has been known to increase menstrual flow.

Fenugreek: Trigonella foenum graecum. For a sore throat the tea has been said to be an excellent gargle and reportedly, when applied externally to sores it prevents blood poisoning. It has been used to lubricate the intestines and has had a cooling effect on the bowels.

Feverfew: Chrysanthemum parthenium. Also Featherfew, Featherfoil. This unpleasant tasting herb has been given for hysteria, to promote menstruation and to expel worms.

Fig: Ficus carica. A tea has been used to relieve earache, to wash sores and remove soreness and discoloration of bruises and aid in circulation. The milk which escapes when an unripe fruit is broken from a branch has been said to remove warts. The fruit itself is a mild laxative. It has also been used to hasten the healing of boils when split and applied directly. Fig juice with lemon juice added is reputed as excellent for coughs and lung diseases.

Figwort: Scrophularia nodosa. Sometimes called Carpenter's Square, Rosenoble, Scrofula Plant, Throatwort. As a poultice applied directly to wounds, abscesses and skin eruptions, this herb reportedly is a pain reliever and has a cleansing effect. Taken internally as a tea it has been used as a diuretic.

Fireweed: Eretchthites hieracifolia. Common names are Pilewort, Various Leaved Fleabane. The oil of this herb is an astringent and a reported pain reliever, used for hemorrhoids. Being an antispasmodic, it has also been used for colic and hiccoughs. It has also been applied locally for gout and rheumatism.

Figroot: Monotropa uniflora. Bird's Nest, Convulsion or Fit Weed, Corpse Plant, Dutchman's Pipe, Ice Plant, Indian Pipe, Nest Root, Ova Ova. This sedative and nervine has been used as a replacement for opium and quinine. It has been taken for fevers and spasmodic afflictions, as well as restlessness and nervous irritability. As a tea with fennel seed it has been used as a douche for inflammation of the uterus and vagina and a wash for irritated eyes.

Flaxseed: Linum usitatissium. Commonly called Linseed or Winterlien. Mixed with other herbs and boiling water, the ground flax seed has been made into a poultice for sores, carbuncles, boils, tumors and inflamed areas. The oil has been helpful for coughs, asthma and pleurisy.

Fleabane: Erigeron canadense. Also Blood Staunch, Butterweed, Colt's, Cow's or Mare's Tail, Fire Weed, and Scabious. Reportedly used as an enema for cholera, dysentery and colon trouble in combination with other herbs. Taken internally it has been used to aid in bladder troubles, scalding urine and hemorrhages from the bowels and uterus.

Fluellin: Linaria elatine. This is an astringent which has been used both internally and externally. It reportedly stops nosebleed and excessive menstrual bleeding.

Fo-Ti Tieng: Also known as Hydrocotyle Asiatic. This herb is said to promote clear thinking and rejuvenating effects on brain cells, endocrine and ductless glands. It has been used also for treatment of fevers and piles.

Fringe Tree: Chionanthus virginica. Sometimes known as Old Man's Beard, Snowdrop Tree. Applied both as a lotion and an injection, it has been used for digestive complaints as an alterative, diuretic, hepatic and tonic. With other herbs it has been used for gallstones and female disorders.

Fumitory: Fumaria officinalis. Also called Earth Smoke. This is a mild tonic which has been used as a gentle laxative (aperient) and a diuretic. It has also been applied for skin blemishes.

Garlic: Allium sativum. Mixed with honey, a teaspoon of garlic juice has been helpful in cough, colds and asthma. It also increases perspiration, serves as a diuretic and has helped remove mucus from the throat and lungs.

Giant Solomon Seal: Convallaria multiflora. Commonly called Dropberry, Seal Root, Sealwort. Taken internally or applied as a poultice it has been known to be useful for inflammation of the skin or mucous membrane (erysipelas), female disorders, neuralgia, to ease pain and disperse congealed blood from blows and bruises. It has also alleviated vomiting.

Gelsemium: Gelsemium nitidum, Gelsemium sempervirens. Also Wild Woodbine, Yellow Jasmine. This herb is a sedative, nervine and has been used in cases of insomnia. It reportedly relaxes the nervous system, particularly nerves in the arterial blood vessels, relieves neuralgia, toothache, and diarrhea or dysentery resulting from inflamed bowels. It is also a febrifuge and diaphoretic.

Gentian: Gentiana lutea. Also Baldmoney, Bitter Root, Bitterwort, Felwort. The root of this plant is the most popular of all herbal tonics and stomachics. It has been used to tone the stomach nerves and as a blood purifier. Acting on the liver and spleen, it reportedly is effective for jaundice, improves the appetite, allays dysentery and dyspepsia, and improves digestion. It has been used to improve the appetite, increase circulation and generally invigorate the system. It acts as an emmenagogue and diuretic and is said to act as a counter-poison for insect, snake and animal bites.

Ginger: Zingiber officinale. Also African Ginger, Black Ginger, Race Ginger. This popular condiment stimulates the salivary glands and has been used for paralysis of the tongue and sore throat. Taken hot it assists to bring on suppressed menstruation and causes increased perspiration. It is a carminative when combined with other laxative herbs and therefore, also used for bronchitis, cholera, gout and nausea. The tea has been used for colds, grippe, and nausea.

Ginger, Wild: Asarum canadense. Sometimes called Canadian Snakeroot. Reportedly, taken hot, this herb is a stimulant for use in colds and amenorrhea and acts on the uterus to bring about labor and childbirth and when taken warm it acts as a carminative for digestive and intestinal pains.

Ginseng: Panax quinquefolia. Also Five Finger Root, Garantogen, Ninsin, Red Berry. The Chinese have used ginseng for centuries as a preventive and treatment of diseases of all kinds. It also is a diaphoretic when taken hot. It has been used for lung afflictions and for relief of inflammation in the urinary tract. Because it is said to give comfort for headache and backache, it has been used in cases of lumbago, sciatica and rheumatism. It has also been said to increase appetite, allay hiccoughs, and alleviate some problems of eyesight such as double-vision.

Goa: Andira araoba. Common names are Araoba, Bahia Powder, Brazil Powder, Chrysarobine, Ringworm Powder. An ointment of the powder has been helpful when applied locally for eczema, acne, psoriasis and other skin diseases. Taken internally, it is said to destroy tapeworm.

Goat's Rue: Galega officinalis. This herb has been used as a diuretic, to increase the flow and secretion of urine, and a vermifuge to expel worms. It also seems to help promote the flow of milk in nursing mothers.

Golden Rod, Sweet: Solidago odora. The fresh or dried leaves make a tea (with peppermint). The American Indians used this common herb for sore throat and general pain. It has been used also as a diaphoretic for coughs, colds, and for relief of rheumatism.

Golden Seal: Hydrastis canadensis. Also Eye Balm, Eye Root, Ground Raspberry, Indian Plant, Jaundice Root, Ohio Curcuma, Orange Root, Turmeric Root, Yellow Eye, Yellow Indian Paint, Yellow Paint Root, Yellow Puccoon. This herb is one of the best and most generally effective remedies of all. It is used widely in conjunction with other herbs and is useful alone. It reportedly has a good effect on all mucous membranes and body tissues; it is excellent for all catarrhal conditions, whether of the throat, nose, bronchial passages, intestines, stomach or bladder, is a tonic for spinal nerves and helpful in spinal meningitis. It has also been combined with hops and skullcap for this purpose. It has been said to alleviate pyorrhea or sore gums by brushing the teeth and gums with the tea. The tea has also been used as an eyewash and for sores and skin diseases such as eczema, ringworm and smallpox. For throat troubles, such as tonsilitis, it has been combined with a little myrrh and cayenne. This same combination reportedly improves the appetite and aids digestion. It has been used to equalize the circulation and, combined with skullcap and red pepper, strengthen the heart. For ulcers of the stomach and duodenum, for dyspepsia and enlarged tonsils or mouth sores, it has been used with myrrh. Taken frequently in small doses it is said to alleviate nausea during pregnancy. As a snuff it reportedly helps nose problems. It has also been used to treat bowel and bladder disorders (with alum) and as a laxative. This has also been used for treating hemorrhoids and prostate problems. The herb in tincture form or taken internally has been used for leucorrhea and ulcers of the vagina and uterus.

Gooseberry: Ribes oxyacanthoides. Also Feverberry, Groser. Besides its popular use as a fruit in cooking and preserves, a warm tea has been taken to reduce fever and colds. The wine has been taken as a tonic.

Grape, Wild: Vitis. The wine made from grapes has been taken as a tonic appetizer to increase and improve digestion. It reportedly will reduce acid conditions of the urine and is slightly laxative and diuretic.

Gotu-Kola: This is said to be a longevity herb and is known for its revitalizing effects on the brain and body. It also acts as a diuretic which stimulates kidney and bladder.

Gravel Root: Eupatorium purpureum. The root of this plant is used as a diuretic and stimulant.

Grindella: Grindelia camporum. Sometimes referred to as Gum Plant. This is often combined with euphorbia and Yerba Santa for asthma and bronchitis. It has also been used as a tonic and diuretic.

Ground Ivy: Glechoma hederacea. Synonyms are Alehoof, Gill-go-over-the-ground, Haymaids, and Runaway Jack. As an astringent it reportedly works well as a poultice, in combination with camomile or yarrow, applied to abscesses. As a diuretic it has been used for kidney ailments and dyspepsia. It has been used as an anti-scorbutic.

Groundsel: Senecio vulgaris. This garden weed has been used as a hepatic and a diuretic, and, in stronger doses, as a purgative and emetic.

Hartstongue: Scolopendrium vulgare. Has been used as a mild laxative and to relieve coughs. It has also been used as a deobstruent for the liver, spleen and bladder.

Hawthorn: Crataegus oxycantha. Also Haw, May, Whitethorn. This herb should be used under a doctor's direction as a tonic for the heart. It has been found helpful in arteriosclerosis and dyspnea.

Heartsease: Viola tricolor. Wild Pansy. This is a diaphoretic and diuretic and has been used as a very mild treatment for skin eruptions.

Hedge Mustard: Sisymbrium officale. The dried and powdered herb has been used in connection with hoarseness and weak lungs.

Hellebore, False: Adonis vernalis. This heart tonic should be used with a doctor's supervision. It has also been helpful in kidney ailments.

Hemp (See Indian hemp)

Henna Leaves: Lawsonia inermis. Also Alcanna, Egyptian Privet, Jamaican Mignonette. The bark of this plant is known for its use as a dye, while the leaves have been used for jaundice and skin infections (including leprosy), and the root as an astringent.

Hollyhock: Althaea rosea. Part of the mallow family, its demulcent and emollient properties are similar to those of the ground and marsh mallow.

Holy Thistle: Carbenia benedicta. Blessed Thistle, Cardus, Spotted Thistle. Though used mainly for digestive problems, this tonic and diaphoretic has reportedly proven helpful in curing colds and to promote the secretion of milk. There are also claims for its reducing headaches and migraines and purifying the blood. It may be combined with the roots of red dock, yellow dock and burdock.

Honeysuckle: Lonicera caprifolium. It facilitates expulsion of mucus from the mucous membrane and it has therefore been used in asthma and disorders of the respiratory organs. It is also a mild laxative and aids in ailments of the liver and spleen.

Hops: Humulus lupulus. A nervine, it is an old-fashioned remedy for insomnia. A pillow stuffed with hops is also said to be effective in bringing on sleep. Hop poultices are reportedly soothing for inflammations, swellings, boils, tumors, and old ulcers. It is an anodyne and has been used for earache, toothache, neuralgia, and used for gonorrhea, as a diuretic and a cholagogue. It also has a sedative effect.

Horehound: Marrubium vulgare. Hoarhound, Marrubium. Its usefulness as an expectorant has been declaimed for hundreds of years and it is probably one of the best known herbal remedies for coughs, croup, colds, hoarseness, and pulmonary ailments. When taken hot it acts as a diaphoretic, producing profuse perspiration. The syrup has also been taken for asthma and difficult breathing. Taken warm, the tea is reportedly a mild laxative and brings on retarded menstruation. It has also been used to eliminate poisons and expel afterbirth. It has been used externally for skin diseases and to cleanse sores and ulcers. It is this herb from which the popular candy is made.

Horehound, Black: Ballota nigra. Also Crantz, Marrubium Nigrum. This is similar to white horehound (Marrubium vulgare, above) in its diaphoretic, expectorant, and stimulant qualities, and is used similarly.

Horsemint: Monarda punctata. This has been used in skin diseases such as athlete's foot, impetigo, psoriasis and ringworm. It is also an antiseptic, and a stimulant and nervine. It has been known to expel wind from the bowels and increase the flow of urine. It also acts as a diaphoretic, causing perspiration.

Horseradish: Cochlearia armoracia. This is now mainly used as a digestive. Modern herbalists rarely prescribe it for dropsy, though its stimulant and diuretic properties are said to be helpful.

Houseleek: Sempervivum tectorum. A poultice of the fresh leaves, bruised and applied locally, is said to relieve burns, stings, warts and corns, and reduce discharge, while acting as an astringent.

Hydrangea: Hydrangea aborescens. Also Sevenbarks. Reportedly used for bladder and kidney troubles, rheumatism, paralysis, scurvy and dropsy. It also acts as a sialagogue.

Hyssop: Hyssopus officinalis. This is a customary ingredient in cough and cold prescriptions and for other pulmonary conditions and asthma. It is a cleanser and, taken with honey, it reportedly destroys intestinal worms. With figs it is said to cleanse the intestines and reduce secretion of lymphatic fluid from body cavities or tissues. It has also helped restore the spleen to normal when taken with figs. Boiled with wine and applied directly to a bruise, it has been known to remove the discoloration. The green herb may be sprinkled on a cut or wound to speed healing.

Iceland Moss: Cetraria islandica. Also called Iceland Lichen. Besides its considerable nutritive value, the demulcent quality of this lichen affects the lungs, reportedly relieving obstinate coughs, bronchial catarrh and other pulmonary complaints.

Indian Hemp: Pilocorpus selloanus. Sometimes called Brazilian Jaborandi Root. The tea has been used to stimulate growth of the hair by massaging it into the scalp. It has been taken internally for mumps, or applied as a poultice to reduce the swelling. Its action as an expectorant makes it helpful in breaking up colds and influenza. It has been said to be effective in various fevers, in diabetes, dropsy, jaundice, pleurisy. It is a diaphoretic and causes profuse perspiration.

Ipecac: Psychotria Ipecacuanha Cephaelis. A mouthwash and gargle for pyorrhea has been reported to be soothing. It has been used for coughs and colds, since it is an expectorant and diaphoretic. Taken internally in small doses it has been known to relieve dysentery. Larger doses may cause vomiting.

Jambul: Eugenia jambolana. Common names are Java Plum, Jamun. It is claimed that the seeds of this plant are able to reduce blood sugar to an extent great enough to be a treatment for diabetes mellitus.

Jewel Weed: Impatiens aurea. Also called Balsam Weed, Pale or Spotted Touch-me-not Speckled Jewels. It has been said that the juice of the plant may be applied directly to remove corns, warts, and other skin growths and that it also relieves ringworm.

Juniper Berry: Juniperus communis. Also Horse Savin Berries. As a diuretic, the berries and bark are helpful in bladder, kidney and urinary problems. It has been combined with other herbs as a douche for leucorrhea, and to treat gonorrhea, dropsy and scorbutic diseases. Other herbs used in combination with juniper are broom, buchu, cleavers, and uvu ursi. As a spray the berries are excellent for fumigation and they have been chewed or gargled as a disinfectant. Bathing the skin with a juniper solution is said to be beneficial for itches, scabs and even leprosy. Drinking the infusion is reported to help hemorrhoids and prostate troubles, aid in digestion and rid the bowels of worms. Too large a dose may cause irritation of the urinary passages.

Jurubeba: Solanum insidiosum. An emmenagogue, it has been used for liver and spleen disorders.

Kelp: Fucus vesiculosis. Common names are Black Tany, Bladderwrack, Bladder Fucus, Sea Oak, Seawrack, and Seaweed. Because of its high content of iodine, kelp is especially beneficial to the thyroid and therefore valuable for obesity. Other minerals in this plant are manganese, silicon, calcium, sulphur, copper and iron. These are reported to be effective in toning the skin, to prevent falling hair, strengthen fingernails, prevent indigestion, relieve anemia, and strengthen tissues in the brain and heart. It has also been used to cleanse toxic substances from the colon and thereby relieve nervous disorders, headaches and kidney troubles caused by the presence of these poisons.

Knapweed: Centaurea nigra. Also Black Ray Thistle, Hardhead, Ironweed, Star Thistle. This herb has been used like gentian as a general tonic and is said to be equally effective.

Ladies' Mantle: Alchemilla vulgaris, or Lion's Foot. As an astringent and nervine it has been used for excessive menstruation, and also used for spasmodic nervous problems.

Ladies' Slipper: Cyprepedium pubescens. Sometimes called American Valerian, Moccasin Flower, Nerveroot, Noah's Ark. The rhizome of this flowering plant is an antispasmodic, nervine and tonic, and therefore helpful in nervous diseases and hysteria. It is said to relieve pain and has no narcotic effect.

Larkspur: Delphinium consolida. Sometimes called Lark's Claw or Heel, Knight's Spur. A tincture of this herb has been used for external parasites and insects, such as hair lice. Taken in small doses it has also been used in the relief of asthma and dropsy.

Lavender: Lavandula vera. A tea made by steeping the flowers is said to be a good general tonic and has been used to allay nausea and prevent fainting. It is also an aromatic. The flowers and leaves are most commonly used for their fragrant scent.

Lemon: Citrus limonum. A refreshing drink, lemon juice has been used as a tonic and cold remedy. It has been helpful in fevers, headache, and other cold symptoms, especially coughs.

Licorice: Glycirrhiza glabra. This popular ingredient in candy has been used as an expectorant, to soothe irritation, and promote bowel action.

Lily of the Valley: Convallaria majalis. Also May lily. The root has been used for calming the heart. Reportedly helpful in convulsions of all types, and is said to generally clear and strengthen the brain and alleviate dizziness.

Linden (or Lime Flowers): Tilia europoea, Tilia americana. The flowers of this tree are both nervine and stimulant. They are a popularly used remedy to help clear up excess flow of mucus from inflamed mucous membranes of the nose and throat. They reportedly have an excellent effect on the digestive and nervous system. The tea has long been substituted for the more widely used English and Chinese teas.

Lobelia: Lobelia inflata. Also called Asthma Weed, Emetic Herb, Eyebright, Gag Root, Indian Tobacco, Puke Weed, Vomit Wort. There is a great deal of controversy over this herb. While many herbalists contend that it is the most valuable botanic remedy, it is classified in some countries as a poison. It is used chiefly as an emetic and an expectorant, for fevers, pneumonia, meningitis, pleurisy, etc. It has been applied as an enema with catnip; with pleurisy root for pleurisy; with slippery elm bark for poultices to treat abscesses, boils and carbuncles. It is also reported to be a powerful relaxant and helpful in asthma and spasmodic vomiting.

Low Mallow: Malva rotundifolia. Also Cheese Plant, Dwarf Mallow. This has both a demulcent and emollient action and has been used to soothe inflammation and irritation of alimentary, respiratory, and urinary organs.

Lucerne: Medicago sativa. Commonly called Alfalfa. Used as a tea or powdered and mixed with cider vinegar and honey, it is reportedly used for arthritis and to aid in weight gain. It seems to be a strength-giving tonic as well.

Lungwort: Pulmonaria officinalis. Also called Jerusalem cowslip, Jerusalem sage, spotted comfrey. Because of its action as a demulcent, an expectorant, a pectoral and a mucilaginous, lungwort is used for colds, coughs, influenza, and for diseases of the chest and lungs. It decreases excessive menstruation and has been used as a bath for genital ulcers.

Lycopodium: Lycopodium clavatum. Sometimes called Common Club Moss, Foxtail, Lamb's Tail, Vegetable Sulphur, Wolf's Claws. The spores of this plant have been used as a medicinal dusting powder. Taken internally it is reported helpful for indigestion and diseases of the lungs and kidneys. Because of its reported healing effects on mucous membrane, it has been used for swellings of arteries and to relieve itching of the anus.

Magnolia: Magnolia glauca. Common names are Bay Beaver Tree, Holly Bay, Indian Bark, Red Bay, Red Laurel, Swamp Laurel, Swamp Sassafras, Sweet Magnolia. There are claims that the bark of the magnolia tree reduces craving for tobacco. It has been used as a tonic and is reportedly helpful in intermittent fever, dysentery, dyspepsia, and erysipelas. For leucorrhea it has been used in a douche. Externally it has been applied directly for skin diseases.

Mandrake: Podophyllum peltatum. Also called American Mandrake, Duck's Foot, Ground Lemon, Hog Apple, Indian Apple, May Apple, Raccoon Berry, Wild Lemon, Yellow Berry. The rhizome of this plant is a hepatic and purgative, but it is so powerful that it should only be taken under the direction of a physician. It has often been combined with other herbs to regulate liver and bowels, for uterine disorders and intermittent fever.

Maple, Red: Acer rubrum, or Swamp Maple. This is a popular salve, used originally by the American Indians, for sore eyes. It is also an astringent and reportedly helps eliminate fluid discharges.

Marigold: Calendula officinalis. The flowers and leaves have been made into a salve for direct application to skin eruptions, as in measles, and to varicose veins and chronic ulcers. A hot fermentation is said to relieve sore muscles. It has also been taken for amenorrhea.

Marjoram: Origanum marjorana. Also Sweet Marjoram, Knotted Marjoram. This herb is often used with gentian and camomile and is reportedly an excellent general tonic. It has been helpful for indigestion, sour stomach, nausea, colic, loss of appetite, and suppressed menstruation. For toothache a few drops of oil on the aching tooth is said to stop the pain. It is also a diaphoretic when taken hot and is therefore able to cleanse the system and expel poisons from the body.

Marsh Mallow: Althaea officinalis. Sometimes called Althaea, Guimauve, Mallards, Mortification Root, Schloss Tea, Sweet Weed, Wymote. This herb is said to be very soothing and healing and taken both internally and externally. It has been used as a poultice for sore or inflamed parts, as a tea to bathe sore eyes, and as a douche for irritation of the vagina. It is also a mucilaginous and has been taken for lung troubles, hoarseness, catarrh and pneumonia. As a diuretic it has been helpful in kidney diseases.

Masterwort: Heracleum lanatum. Sometimes known as Cow Parsnip, Madnep, Madness, Youthwort. This plant is reportedly a good antispasmodic for asthma and epilepsy. As a carminative it has caused gases to be expelled from the gastrointestinal tract. It has been taken for colds, kidney stones, suppressed or painful menstruation, cramps, dropsy, palsy and apoplexy. Externally it is said to be a good wash for sores and ulcers.

Meadowsweet: Spiraea ulmaria. Common names are Bridewort, Dolloft, Queen of the Meadow. This herb is mild and therefore reported safely used for infantile diarrhea. It also has aromatic, tonic and diuretic qualities which make it popular for use in herb beers.

Melilot: Melilotus officinalis. Also King's Clover. An infusion can be made for flatulence. It is also an emollient used in poultices. See also White Clover.

Mescal Buttons: Lopophora lewinii, Anhalonium lewinii. Also called Pellote. Very small amounts of the tea have been taken to relieve angina pectoris, but an excessive amount may cause vomiting. It is also a narcotic and can bring on a stupor or complete unconsciousness.

Milkweed: Asclepias syriaca. Sometimes called Silkweed, Silky Swallow Wort. This is reportedly an excellent remedy for gallstones when used with marsh mallow. It is a diuretic and therefore has been used in dropsy and kidney and bowel troubles. It has also been taken for asthma, stomach complaints, female disorders and scrofulous conditions of the blood.

Mint: Monarda punctata. Also Horsemint, Origanum. A carminative, the tea has reportedly caused expulsion of gas from the stomach and intestines. It is also an emmenagogue and has been known to bring on suppressed menstruation. It is very quieting and reportedly eases pain. It is also a stimulant and diuretic, has been used to increase the flow of urine and for nausea and vomiting.

Mistletoe: Viscum flavescens. Also Bird Lime, Golden Bough. As an antispasmodic and nervine the leaves of this plant have been used for epilepsy, convulsions, and hysteria. It reportedly acts as a tonic and is recommended for suppressed and painful menstruation, uterine hemorrhages, and has been suggested for high blood pressure. It is also a narcotic, producing sleep, stupor, or unconsciousness.

Motherwort: Leonurus cardiaca. Also Lion's Ear, Lion's Tail, Throwwort. This plant is an emmenagogue, reportedly increasing menstrual flow; a nervine and an antispasmodic, said to relieve menstrual cramps. It has also been helpful in nervous complaints, convulsions, hysteria, and liver affections. Reportedly it will kill worms and is a good remedy for chest colds.

Mountain Flax: Linum cartharticum. Also known as Purging Flax. This herb is a laxative and cathartic and rarely causes griping. It has been used with diuretics for bladder and gall stones and dropsy. Sometimes it is taken with gentian and calumba root.

Mousear: Hieracium pilosella. Common names are Hawkweed, and Pilosella. As an astringent and expectorant this reportedly makes a useful medicine for whooping cough and other coughs.

Mugwort: Artemisia vulgaris. Sometimes called Felon Herb. This is an emmenagogue. It is said to have been helpful for fevers, gout, kidney and bladder stones and swellings. A drink of the warm infusion has often relieved bowel or stomach pain.

Mullein: Verbascum thapsus. Also called Bullock, Candle Flower, Cow's Lungwort, Flannel Flower, Hare's Beard, Lungwort, Pig Taper, Shepherd's Club, Velvet Plant, Verbascum Flower, Woolen Blanket Herb. The leaves and root of this plant are used internally and externally in many ways. As a poultice the herb has been known to relieve swelling of all types. A fermentation has been used for piles, tumors, mumps, tonsilitis, and sore throats. It has been taken internally for dysentery, diarrhea, bleeding bowels, dropsy, catarrh, swollen joints. A tea from the leaves has been taken for asthma, all lung afflictions, and hay fever. It is also reportedly good as a gargle, for toothache and for cleansing open sores. A tea made from the flowers is said to induce sleep, relieve pain, and in large doses act as a physic. Inhalations of fumes from the burning root have been used for treating asthma.

Muira-Puama: Liriosma ovata. The powered root of this herb has been used as a nerve stimulant.

Mustard: Sinapis alba. Also known as kedlock. A laxative, stimulant, condiment and emetic. A mustard plaster made with this herb has been used to relieve irritation of the kidney. Reportedly used to induce vomiting.

Myrrh: Balsamodendron myrrh. Also known as Gum Myrrh Tree. An antiseptic, this reportedly is an effective treatment for pyorrhea and also removes halitosis. As an ointment combined with golden seal it is said to be an excellent treatment for piles. With charcoal it has been used to hasten healing of sores and ulcers. As an expectorant it has been taken for cough, asthma, tuberculosis and all other chest afflictions. It is both a tonic and stimulant and has been used for bronchial and lung diseases. As a stimulant, it has been used in cases of shock and prostration.

Nettle: Urtica dioica. Also known as Stinging Nettle. The tea made from the root and leaves of the nettle is said to be an excellent hair tonic, bringing back natural-color and removing dandruff. It has also been given for dropsy, kidney troubles and bladder stones, when a diuretic is needed. The boiled leaves are a styptic but must be used carefully as they may cause blistering if left in contact with the skin too long. It has also been taken internally for hemorrhaging, and as an expectorant and emmenagogue. For chronic rheumatism the bruised leaves have been rubbed on the skin. With Seawrack it has been used as a reducing aid. The green leaves, cooked like spinach, are said to be a good blood purifier.

Night-Blooming Cereus: Cereus grandiflorus. Also Sweet-scented Cactus. As a heart stimulant this herb is reportedly able to bring relief in angina pectoris, palpitations, cardiac neuralgia and irritations of the prostate gland, bladder and kidneys. It has also been used for headaches during menstruation and acts as a diuretic.

Nutmeg: Nigella sativa. Common names are Bishop's Wort, Black Caraway, Black Cumin, Flower Seed, Nigella Seed, Small Fennel Flower. This popular seasoning is a sialagogue, increasing the flow of saliva, and stimulating the appetite. It has been known to prevent gas from forming in the bowels, intestines or stomach, and reportedly brings on or increases menstruation. It is a deobstruent and diaphoretic.

Nux Vomica: Strychnos nux vomica. Also Poison Nut, Quaker Buttons. The seeds of this herb have been used as a general tonic and stimulant and are reportedly valuable for impotence, general debility and neuralgia. It stimulates peristalsis and has thus been used as an aid for constipation. An excessive dose could be poisonous.

Oats: Avena sativa. Sometimes called Groats, Panicle Oats, White Oats. A drink of oatmeal has been taken for indigestion and constipation and as a general tonic. A poultice of oatmeal has been applied to relieve itching. It has also been used as a nerve tonic and seems to strengthen cardiac muscles. Because of its reported relaxing effect on the nerves, oatmeal may facilitate sleep in cases of insomnia. It is also reported to remove spots on the skin and freckles when applied as a mash.

Olive: Olea europae. Also Lucca Oil, Provence Oil, Salad Oil, Sweet Oil, Virgin Oil. This has been used for constipation, often being substituted for castor oil. It is also reportedly used for intestinal worms and to remove stony deposits from the bile. Externally it has been applied directly to burns, scalds, bruises and other skin conditions. It is also reported helpful for rheumatism.

Onion: Allium cepa. Boiled onion has been eaten to relieve colds and to stimulate the kidneys. Roasted and made into a poultice it has been applied to tumors or ulcers and reportedly will help draw out pus. The same poultice has been said to be helpful for earaches.

Origanum: Origanum vulgare. Also Mountain Mint, Wild Marjoram, Winter Marjoram, Winter Sweet. This plant reportedly helps toothache, swellings, sprains, boils and sore throat. It has been said that it is strengthening to the stomach and promotes appetite, relieves sour stomach, expels gas, relieves dyspepsia, colic and nausea. It seems to be soothing for bad coughs and consumption. It is also a diuretic and an emmenagogue.

Ox-Eye Daisy: Chrysanthemum leucanthemum. Also Field Daisy, Horsegowan, Marguerite, Moon Daisy. This herb has a tonic effect similar to camomile. It has been used in whooping cough and asthma for its antispasmodic properties, and it is reportedly used externally for wounds and ulcers and as a douche for leucorrhea. Large doses taken internally have been said to produce vomiting.

Paraguay Tea: Ilex paraguayensis. Also Brazil Tea, Jesuit's Tea, Mate, Yerba Mate. The leaves of this herb have a diuretic effect and, because of the presence of caffeine, are also a stimulant. It has been used for rheumatism and gout and reportedly, in large doses, acts as a purgative.

Parsley: Petroselinum sativum. Also called March. The root and leaves of this well known garden plant have been used for liver and kidney problems, including stones or obstructions, dropsy, difficult urination, jaundice and various fevers. It is also reported to have been used for syphilis and gonorrhea. It has also been classed as a preventive herb. It has been used with buchu, black haw and cramp bark for female troubles. Externally a hot fermentation has helped to relieve insect bites and stings. A poultice of the bruised leaves has been applied to swollen glands and swollen breasts, or to dry up milk. The tea will reportedly kill vermin in the hair.

Parsley Piert: Alchemilla arvensis, or Breakstone Parsley. An infusion of this herb has been given to regulate bladder and kidney functions.

Passion Flower: Passiflora incranata. Sometimes called Maypops, Passion Vine, Wild Passion Flower. As a nervine this herb is reportedly helpful in nervous conditions, such as insomnia, hysteria, high blood pressure, headache, and asthma. In some cases it has relieved neuralgia pains.

Peach: Amygdalus persica. The leaves of this common tree have been used as a sedative, a laxative, or a demulcent. They are said to relieve morning sickness in pregnancy and dyspepsia. They have also been taken for abdominal inflammation and to expel worms. It has been said that for bladder and uterine disorders a tea may be imbibed, and in small doses the hot tea helps reduce vomiting. For sores or wounds, a powder of the bark or leaves has been applied to hasten healing. The buds are said to restore hair growth in baldness.

Pellitory-of-the-Wall: Parietaria officinalis. As a diuretic this herb has been used for bladder and kidney disorders, such as gravel or suppressed urine. It is often used with wild carrot and parsley piert.

Pennyroyal: Hedeoma pulegioides. Also Mock Pennyroyal, Squaw Mint, Stinking Balm, Thickweed, Tickweed. As a sudorific this herb has been taken to reduce fevers. It is also an emmenagogue and has been said to bring on suppressed menstruation, and should not be used by a pregnant woman. It is also reportedly used for toothache, gout, leprosy, colds, consumption, congested chest and lungs, jaundice, dropsy, itch, ulcers, to ward off and heal insect bites, and stings; the oil has been used in liniments. As a carminative it has been used to relieve intestinal pain, colic, and griping. Its sedative effect reportedly soothes nervous headache, hysteria and convulsions. Used as a poultice and wash it has been used to relieve bruises and skin diseases.

Peony: Paeonia officinalis. This is reportedly used as a tonic and antispasmodic for chorea and epilepsy.

Peppermint: Mentha piperita. Balm Mint, Brandy Mint, Mint. This is an old and popular household herb. It is a general stimulant, stronger than liquor, and will reportedly bring back warmth and equilibrium to the body in case of fainting and dizziness. It has been said to strengthen the heart, aid in digestion and soothe indigestion. It has also been used to relieve headaches and is better for the body than drugs taken for the same purpose. The leaves, chewed until they are easily swallowed, are said to have the same effect as the tea. The oil has been applied locally for rheumatism and neuralgia. Peppermint enemas are reported to be excellent in cholera and colon troubles.

Peruvian Bark: Cinchona calisaya. Also Calisaya Bark, Jacket Bark, Jesuit's Bark, Yellow Bark, Yellow Cinchona. This bark has been taken as quinine but is itself harmless. It is a good febrifuge, and has been used in abating and reducing fevers. It has also been taken for dyspepsia, neuralgia, epilepsy, and female debility. It is said to strengthen the lungs, and has therefore been used for pneumonia.

Periwinkle: Vinca major. This has been taken as a drink for internal hemorrhages and diarrhea, as a gargle for sore throat, and as a douche for leucorrhea and excessive menstruation. There is some evidence that this herb is beneficial in diabetes.

Pilewort: Ranunculus ficaria. Also Lesser Celandine, Small Celandine. As the name indicates, this has been used for hemorrhoids because of its astringent and detergent properties.

Pinkroot: Spigelia marilandica. Sometimes American Wormwort, Carolina Pink, Demerara Pinkroot, Indian Pink, Maryland Pink, Wormgrass. This is one of the best vermifuges and has been taken with a laxative such as senna.

Pitcher Plant: Serracenia purpurea. Also Flytrap, Saddleplant, Watercup. The powdered root of this plant has been used to treat smallpox. It is a laxative and diuretic and is reportedly helpful for derangements of the stomach, liver and kidneys.

Plantain: Plantago major. Also Cuckoo's Bread, Englishman's Foot, Ribwort, Ripplegrass, Waybread. To check bleeding, the fresh leaves pounded into a paste have been applied and reportedly have a soothing, cooling and healing effect. It has also been applied for skin irritations and diseases as a tea. It has been injected for hemorrhoids or applied externally on a piece of gauze. Reportedly used as a douche for leucorrhea and syphilis and as a tea for diarrhea, kidney and bladder trouble and their accompanying symptoms. The mashed green leaves have also been applied as a poultice for insect and snake bites, boils, carbuncles or tumors. As an astringent, plantain contracts tissues and has been used for excessive flow in menstruation. It has also been used for dropsy, toothache, inflamed eyes, as a vermifuge, and, with yellow dock, as a wash for itching skin, ringworm, or running sores.

Pleurisy Root: Asclepias tuberosa. Also Butterfly Weed, Canada Root, Flux Root, Orange Swallow Wort, Tuber Root, White Root, Wind Root. As the name suggests it has been used in bronchial and pulmonary diseases, including colds, grippe and pleurisy. It is reportedly good for the kidneys and to treat suppressed menstruation, dysentery, scarlet and rheumatic fevers, typhus, measles and other fevers.

Poke Root: Phytolacca decandra. Sometimes called American Nightshade, Cuncer Jalap, Garget, Pigeon Berry, Pocan Bush, Red Ink Plant, Scoke Coakum, Virginia Poke. The leaves of this plant have often been eaten as a vegetable, which acts as a general tonic. It is reportedly good for treating enlarged glands, particularly the thyroid, and therefore used as a treatment for goiter. Taken internally or used as a poultice, it has been applied to growths and chronic enlargement of bones caused by injury. A tea has been used for treating the skin.

Prickly Ash: Xanthoxylum americanum. Also Suterberry, Toothache Bush. This has been used widely as a stimulant and for general debility as a tonic. It has been effective, reportedly, for paralysis of the tongue and mouth and for rheumatism and hepatitis. The berries are said to be helpful for poor circulation.

Psylla: Plantago psyllium, Plantago ispaghula. Also Branching Plantain, Flea Seed, Flea Wort. This herb is said to have the effect of removing toxins from the intestines and colon, toning and ridding them of sluggishness. It has been used therefore for colitis, hemorrhoids, and ulcers.

Pulsatilla: Anemone pulsatilla. Sometimes called Easter Flower, Meadow Anemone, Passe Flower, Wind Flower. Because of its nervine and antispasmodic qualities this has been taken by women for nervousness and fatigue, especially when it results from menstruation. It is also reported good for all of the mucous membranes.

Purslane: Portulaca oleracea. Sometimes called Pussley, Portulaca. This is an especially nutritious plant and the leaves may be served uncooked and included in salads. It may also be steamed or cooked and served like spinach. Its effect is to cool, and it has been taken for fevers and to stimulate the appetite.

Purple Loose-Strife: Lythrum salicaria. Sometimes known as Purple Grass or Willow Strife. This is most often used with other herbs. It is an astringent which has been said to be especially helpful in diarrhea. It has also been used to reduce fevers and as an alternative.

Quassia: Picrasma excelsa. Also Bitter Wood or Bitter Ash. Cups known as "bitter cups" are made of the wood from quassia trees; water allowed to steep in the cup acquires the medicinal properties of the wood. Otherwise chips of the wood may be soaked in water, which has been taken in small doses for expelling worms and as a bitter tonic. It is also said to dispel the desire for alcohol.

Queen of the Meadow: Eupatorium purpureum. Also Gravel Root, Joe Pye, Kidney Root, Purple Boneset, Trumpet Weed. This herb is reportedly used with blue cohosh, lily root, marsh mallow, and uva ursi for female disorders, diabetes and Bright's disease. It has also been taken alone or with other herbs for urinary and bladder disorders (e.g. stones), dropsy, rheumatism and neuralgia. It is a mild nervine.

Queen's Delight: Stillingia sylvatica Linne; Euphorbiacae. Also Silver Leaf, Queen's Root, Yaw Root. Reportedly used for purifying the blood and for conditions such as scrofula or infectious diseases. It has been said to stimulate action of the kidneys. Combined with sundew it has been taken for laryngitis or as a cough remedy; with bittersweet for eczema and as a relaxant; and with milkweed and Indian tobacco for bronchitis.

Quince: Cydonia oblonga, Pyrus cydonia. Sometimes known as Cydonium, Cydonia Vulgaris, Semen Cydoniae. The seeds of the quince fruit are sometimes used in a skin and hair lotion; their effect is to contract tissues and skin. For conjunctivitis it is reportedly a soothing eyewash, and it has been taken for diarrhea and dysentery. A lotion of the crushed seeds and water is said to make a healing cream for skin abrasions or cracks in the mucous membrane.

Ragwort: Senecio jacobaea. Also Dog Standard, Fireweed, Ragweed, St. James' Wort, Staggerwort, Stinking Nanny.

As a decoction this reportedly makes a good gargle and has been applied externally to ulcers, wounds and inflamed eyes. It is a diaphoretic as well and has been used for coughs, colds, influenza, catarrh, sciatica or rheumatic pains.

Ragwort: Senecio aureus. Cocash Weed, Cough Weed, False Valerian, Golden Senecio, Liferoot, Squaw Weed, Uncum, Waw Weed. Because of its effect on the female organs, it has been used for leucorrhea and amenorrhea. It is said to relieve urinary diseases and gravel.

Raspberry: Rubus stringosus. A tea of the leaves has been a popular drink during pregnancy, as it is believed to aid in parturition. It is an astringent and has been used as a mouthwash and gargle and for cleansing wounds and ulcers. It has been taken with ginger and pennyroyal for stomach and bowel disorders in children, and with slippery elm as a poultice. It also has been claimed that it decreases menstrual flow.

Red Pepper: See "Cayenne."

Red Root: Ceanothus Americanus. Synonyms are Bobea, Jersey Tea, Mountain Sweet, New York Tea, Walpole Tea, Wild Snowball. Because of its astringent and expectorant properties, the root of this plant has been used for dysentery, asthma, bronchitis, whooping cough, consumption, tonsillitis, and piles or hemorrhoids. It is said to be especially effective in any spleen trouble and diabetes.

Rhatany, Peruvian: Krameria triandra. Also Rhatanhia. As an astringent this herb is reportedly used to stop bleeding or hemorrhaging, in menstrual disorders where fluid discharges occur, and has been used in bowel malfunctions. As a tonic it is said to restore strength and muscle tone and has been taken to regain control of sphincter muscles to control incontinence of urine. For pyorrhea a small amount of the powder has been applied to the gums.

Rhubarb: Rheum palmatum. Also Rhizoma Rei or Chinese or Turkish Rhubarb. This is not the ordinary garden variety of rhubarb but a larger member of the same family. An effective cathartic value for its very mild action, it is also an astringent, contracting tissues and tending to alleviate diarrhea and stomach troubles. It is reportedly a stomach tonic taken to improve digestion and increase appetitie.

Rock Rose: Helianthemum canadense. Also Frost Plant, Frost Weed, Frostwort, Scrofula Plant, Sun Rose. A poultice of the leaves reportedly helps ulcers and tumors and it is said to make an excellent gargle for sore throats and scarletina. Taken internally it has aided in diarrhea, syphilis and gonorrhea.

Rosemary: Rosmarinus officinalis. Also Garden Rosemary, Romero. This herbal tonic has reportedly been used for many years for colds, colic and nerves—including nervous headaches. It has been used as a mouthwash for sore mouth, gums or throat. It has been used too for female disorders and is said to strengthen the eyes and prevent premature baldness.

Rue: Ruta graveolens. Also Country Man's Treacle, Garden Rue, Herb of Grace. This is one of the oldest and most internationally-known medicinal herbs. As a tea it is said to relieve uterine congestion, and has been used in amenorrhea, painful menstruation and has a tonic effect on the uterus. It reportedly helps in stomach troubles, including colic, cramps in the bowels, and is an anti-spasmodic taken for convulsions and hysteria. It is also a vermifuge. Some herbalists recommend a tea of this plant to clear the mind and relieve headache pain. A poultice of rue is said to relieve sciatica, gout and pain in the joints.

Rose, Wild: Rose canina. Also Dog Rose, Brier Rose. A tea of the leaves and dried petals of the wild rose bush are used as a tea substitute and it is said to be soothing to persons with arthritis or dyspepsia. It has none of the tannic acid of coffee and tea, nor does it have the effect of stimulating the heart. The petals contain acids which reportedly help to dissolve gallstones and gravel. The hips, or fruit, contain sixty times the vitamin C of lemons, as well as natural sugar, and the puree, powder, and extract have been used to prevent colds.

Saffron: Carthamus tinctorius. The flowers and seed of this plant, besides being a popular condiment, have been used for measles, scarlet fever, and other eruptive skin maladies. Because it is a sudorific it has been taken for colds and influenza to produce perspiration. It is also an emmenagogue, reportedly stimulating and increasing menstrual flow. It is also a carminative and diuretic.

Sage: Salvia officinalis. Also Garden Sage. This favorite among kitchen herbs is a digestive as well. It has been used for sores and ulcers in the mouth, laryngitis and inflamed throat. The healthful tea is reputedly helpful in cases of dyspepsia and gas in the stomach or bowels. As a vermifuge both adults and children may use it. It is a nervine and said to be soothing to the nerves and delirium from fever. As an astringent, it has been used to halt bleeding as well as to cleanse wounds. Reportedly, for liver and kidney trouble the tea is taken internally, as it is for spermatorrhea; to stop the flow of milk in the breasts, the tea is drunk cold; taken hot it reduces fever by producing free perspiration and strengthening circulation. There are also claims for it as a hair restorer and a dandruff remedy.

Sage, Red: Salvia colorata. Sometimes called Purple-Topped Sage. This has been taken for its healing effect in lung trouble, including bronchitis, asthma, coughs, colds, grippe, sore throat and tonsillitis. For diphtheria a gargle with a strong tea of red sage has been said to have a soothing effect. It is also an emmenagogue, having been used to promote menstruation; as a diuretic, detergent, tonic and astringent it is reportedly beneficial in preventing gas or fermentation in the stomach. It is slightly laxative and has been used as a liver cleanser. Taken in cases of nervousness or nervous headache it is said to act as a nervine and a stimulant. As a healing poultice for inflammations, it has been applied for smallpox and measles and has been taken internally for typhoid and scarlet fever.

St. John's Wort: Hypericum perforatum. An oil of this plant has been applied to wounds, swellings and ulcers to soothe and heal. It is also an expectorant and has been taken for coughs and colds, and its effect as a diuretic has made it useful in disorders of the urinary system.

Sanicle: Sanicula europaea. Also Pool Root. Though there have been claims for this as a remedy for consumption, they are unproven. It is, however, a powerful alterative and an astringent which has been taken in diarrhea and leucorrhea and has been used externally for erysipelas and rashes.

Sarsaparilla: Smilax. Though it was first introduced in the 16th century for syphilis, this claim has long since been disproven. It is, though, an excellent alterative and has been used when a blood purifier is indicated. Reportedly an excellent demulcent it has been applied to skin diseases, rheumatism, scrofula and gout. It has been used as an anti-toxin, an eyewash, a diuretic, and a carminative.

Sassafras: Sassafras officinale. Sometimes referred to as Ague Tree, Cinnamon Wood, Kuntze Saloip, Saxifrax. This is a favorite spring tonic reportedly taken to purify the blood and cleanse the entire system. It has been said to relieve colic and gas in the stomach and bowels; that for sore and inflamed eyes it is a soothing bath; and that the oil will relieve a toothache. It has also been applied to skin sores and diseases; claims are made for it as a cure for varicose veins too. Because of its agreeable flavor it may be used to flavor other medicines, and rubbed over the skin it reportedly repels flies.

Saw Palmetto: Seronoa serrulata, Sabal serrulata. Sometimes called Dwarf Palmetto Pan Palm. This is reportedly a valuable treatment for any disease in which there is excessive discharge of mucus from the head or nose, such as asthma, colds, bronchitis, grippe, whooping cough and sore throat caused by the mucus. It has been said to be an excellent herb for toning and strengthening glandular tissues and muscles, and has been used, therefore, for debility caused by tuberculosis, or other enfeebling diseases. It has also been used for diseases of the reproductive organs, nephritis, and diabetes.

Scopolis: Scopola carniolica or Scopolia atropoides. Reportedly, a small amount of this herb acts as a sedative and brings relief from pain and coughs.

Skullcap: Scutellaria lateriflora. In some areas this is known as Blue Pimpernel, Helmet Flower, Hoodwort, Hooded Willow Herb, Mad Dogweed or Madweed. Combined with other herbs or by itself this has been used as a tonic for the nerves. It acts as an antispasmodic, as well as a pain reliever, and has been taken for neuralgia, delirium tremens, rheumatism, poisonous insect or snake bite, St. Vitus' dance, rabies, fits or convulsions, and epilepsy. With golden seal and cayenne it is reportedly a good heart tonic. The herb deteriorates rapidly from age and heat and should be stored in an airtight container.

Scurvygrass: Cochlearia officinalis. Also known as Spoonwort. This herb is rarely used now, but before dietetic remedies for scurvy were known, it was recognized as a powerful antiscorbutic.

Sea Lavender: Statice limonium. Sometimes referred to as Marsh Rosemary. This herb which, in spite of its name, has no scent, is an astringent and has been used as a mouthwash and gargle for inflammation. It has been taken too for some cases in which there are urinary, uterine and vaginal discharges.

Seawrack: Fucus versiculosus. Also Black Tany, Kelpware, Sea Oak, Bladder Fucus, Bladderwrack. This is an herb reportedly taken for glandular problems, such as goiter, and for obesity. It has been said to have a favorable effect on the kidneys.

Self-Heal: Prunella vulgaris. Also called All-Heal. As an astringent this has been taken in small doses for internal bleeding, as a douche for leucorrhea, and as a gargle for sore throats.

Senna: Cassia acutifolia. Also known as Locust Plant. Reportedly taken for minor ailments such as dsypepsia and constipation, this is a mild laxative. It should be combined with an aromatic herb (such as ginger) to prevent griping. It has been said to be effective for expelling worms in combinations with other herbs.

Shepherd's Purse: Capsella bursa pastoris. Common names are Cocowort, Mother's Heart, Pepper Grass, Pickpocket, Poor Man's Pharmacetty, St. Anthony's Fire, St. James' Weed. This reportedly is used for halting internal hemorrhages of all kinds and to check menstruation; is taken for bleeding piles and hemorrhoids; in intermittent fever; and as a remedy for diarrhea. An infusion has been used for kidney complaints and dropsy. It is sometimes used with pellitory-of-the-wall and juniper berries: Added to coleslaw, it has a delicious peppery flavor.

Simaruba: Simaruba officinalis. Also Mountain Damson. This herb has been used for aiding digestion and has been taken for loss of appetite, especially during convalescence. It reportedly serves to strengthen the muscles and tone the tissues.

Skunk Cabbage: Ictodes foetidus. Sometimes called Collard, Fedit Hellebore, Meadow Cabbage, Polecat Weed, Skunk Weed, Swamp Cabbage. This is an old-fashioned remedy for bronchial and lung problems, including tuberculosis, catarrh, asthma, whooping cough, pulmonary consumption, and pleurisy. Externally it has been applied to tumors and sores for relief of pain. It has also been taken for rheumatism, dysentery, nervousness, spasms, convulsions, hysteria, dropsy and epilepsy. It has been used during pregnancy as a general tonic.

Slippery Elm: Ulmus fulva. Also Moose Elm, Red Elm. The powdered bark of this tree reportedly makes one of the best poultices for skin eruptions such as boils; it has been said to be healing and soothing and to draw out impurities. Its emollient effect has been used for inflammation of the mucous membranes of the bowels, kidneys and stomach. The tea has been used as an enema and as a douche for inflammation of the vagina. As a nutritious gruel it has been used for general debility and both bronchitis and gastritis reportedly are helped by its soothing and healing properties.

Snake Root: Aristolochia serpentaria, Aristolochia reticulata. A febrifuge that has been taken for typhoid, this herb is also a diaphoretic inducing perspiration, and a stimulant which promotes the activity of the glands. As a tonic it reportedly strengthens the muscles and the tissues. It has also been said to be a pain reliever and antispasmodic.

Soap Tree: Quillaja saponaria. Common names are Panama Bark, Quillaia, Soap bark. Reportedly for coughs or bronchial and lung ailments, this herb has also been applied externally to cleanse skin eruptions. It is also a diuretic.

Solomon's Seal: Convallaria polygonatum. Reportedly, solomon's seal is prepared as a poultice for inflammations and wounds and a wash to soothe erysipelas, poison ivy, and other sores. As a tea it has been taken internally for female disorders and neuralgia.

Sorrel: Rumex acetosa. Also Garden Sorrel, Sourgrass. Sorrel has been taken as a blood cleanser and for its warming effect on the heart. It is a vermifuge too. It has been said to reduce excessive menstruation and stomach hemorrhage. Reportedly, a tea from the flowers has been used for gravel in the kidneys, black jaundice, internal ulcers, scrofula, and for skin diseases. The leaves, eaten like spinach, are very nutritious.

Southern Wood: Artemisia abrotanum. Common names are Lad's Love, Old Man. A garden plant cultivated for its pleasant aroma, reportedly taken to remove menstrual obstruction, combined with mugwort and pennyroyal. The fragrance is claimed to be a repellent of various insects, especially moths.

Spearmint: Mentha viridis. Also called Mint. As a diuretic and carminative, spearmint has been used for gas in the stomach and bowels, colic, dyspepsia, nausea and vomiting, gravel in the bladder, dropsy and suppressed urine. For piles it has been injected into the rectum. It has been said to soothe inflammation of the kidneys and bladder and that it is quieting to the stomach and nerves and has been used after an emetic to soothe the stomach.

Speedwell: Veronica officinalis. Also Bird's Eye, Cat's Eye, Fluellin. As a tea this has been used on minor skin blemishes and for coughs and catarrh. It is similar in taste to Chinese teas but has none of the negative effects.

Spikenard: Aralia racemosa. Petty Morrel, Spignet. Because of its strength as an alterative, it has been used in rheumatic and uric acid disorders, as well as in some skin diseases.

Squaw Vine: Mitchella repens. Sometimes called Checkerberry, Deerberry, Hive Vine, One-berry Leaves, Partridge Berry, Winterberry, White Clover. Alone, or in combination with red raspberry leaves, squaw vine has been used during pregnancy and is said to ease childbirth. With olive oil or cream it is reportedly a good bath for sore nipples. It is claimed to be a good and mild wash for sore eyes and has been given to children for this purpose. It is usually combined with equal parts of witch hazel leaves and raspberry leaves. As an injection for mild leucorrhea, dysentery and gonorrhea this has been given, and it has also been used for gravel, uterine and urinary troubles, female disorders, and to increase the menstrual flow.

Squill: Urginea scilla. Commonly known as Scilla. As an expectorant and to relieve irritated mucous membranes, squill has been taken for coughs and bronchial afflictions. A large dose of the herb is reported to be an emetic.

Strawberry: Fragaria vesca. This is the common garden strawberry, and it is claimed that both the berries and leaves have medicinal properties. A tea of the leaves is a tasty, caffein-free substitute for the usual table tea and has been said to be a tonic for the entire system. It has also been said to be a stomach cleanser and useful for bowel troubles. Taken internally it reportedly helps eczema, diarrhea, and dysentery, and weakness of the intestines. It has also been used externally as a wash and as an enema. A gargle has been used for sore mouth and throat.

Sumach: Rhus glabrum. Equal parts of sumach berries and bark, white pine bark, and slippery elm have been said to be effective for syphilis and gonorrhea. This tea is reportedly an excellent cleanser for the system and an aid for leucorrhea, scrofula and internal sores or wounds. A tea of sumach berries alone has been reported helpful in bowel complaints, fever and diabetes. They are also an emmenagogue, stimulating menstrual flow.

Summer Savory: Satureja hortensis. The carminative effects of this herb have reportedly made it valuable in wind colic. As a warm tea it is said to increase menstrual flow and to bring on suppressed menstruation. It has also been taken for colds and toothache, and is a popular condiment.

Sundew: Drosera rotundifolia. Sometimes called Dewplant, Flytrap. Because of its reported effect on dry, tickling coughs, this has been taken for whooping cough.

Sunflower: Helianthus annuus. Also Marigold of Peru. The seeds of this plant contain 53 percent protein, making them an excellent meat substitute. They have been used for centuries as a medicine and a preventive, as well as a staple food. Reportedly pulmonary afflictions, snake bite, and dry hair have all been aided through application of the plant. And no part of the plant need go to waste: the leaves have been added to cattle and poultry feed, and the seeds themselves have been fed to chickens to increase laying; the stem fibers have been used by the Chinese in the manufacture of paper and silk; the pith of the stalk is so light that it is employed in the manufacture of life-saving equipment; the flowers make a color-fast dye; and any left-over part of the plant may be applied as a mulch or composted for an organic fertilizer rich in potash.

Tansy: Tanacetum vulgare. Commonly called Arbor Vitae, Hineheel, Yellow Cedar. Often grown by gardeners as an insect repellent, this has been used as a tonic for the stomach and bowels. It has reportedly been used for indigestion and to expel worms. Although this has been used for suppressed menstruation and female nervousness or hysteria, it should never be taken during pregnancy as it may cause a miscarriage. It is said to strengthen weak veins, and that an application of the herb, hot, soothes bruises, swellings, inflammations, and sore eyes. This remedy must be used with caution, as it is a narcotic and an overdose may be fatal.

Thyme: Thymus vulgaris. This is the common garden plant and popular seasoning. Taken hot, it causes profuse perspiration and has been used for treating colds. As an antispasmodic, taken cold, it reportedly checks coughs, whooping cough, cramps, and other stomach ailments, including diarrhea. It is a nervine and emmenagogue.

Toad Flax: Linaria vulgaris. Common names are Butter and Eggs, Flaxweed, Pennywort. This has been used most often with other herbs in an ointment to treat skin diseases or piles. It is reportedly used in cases of jaundice and as a hepatic.

Tormentil: Potentilla tormentilla. Sometimes called Septfoil. This herbal tonic is an astringent, and has been used in diarrhea and as a gargle.

Turkey Corn: Corydalis formosa. Also Choise Dieyltra, Squirrel Corn, Staggerweed, Wild Turkey Pea. This is reportedly an antisyphilitic and used for all skin diseases. Taken as a tea it is a tonic and an herbal astringent.

Turpentine: Pinus palustris or Pinus Maritima. This is a product formed naturally in the wood of various conifers. Though it is dangerous to take the oil internally, it is used in some pharmaceutical prescriptions and reportedly has been applied externally for rheumatism and pulmonary complaints, and sprains. With castor oil, it is said to expel tapeworm. The vapor is an irritant and provokes coughing, causing the expulsion of phlegm which has been said to be helpful in cases of bronchitis and pneumonia.

Twin Leaf: Jeffersonia diphylla. Also Ground Squirrel Pea, Helmet Pod, Rheumatism Root, Yellow Root. Because of its effects as an antispasmodic and antirheumatic, this has been claimed to be useful for neuralgia, cramps and rheumatism. As a poultice it has been said that it relieves pain and, in severe pain, should be taken internally. It also has been used in cases of syphilis and as a gargle for throat afflictions.

Uva Ursi: Arctostaphylos uva ursi. Also Bearberry, Bear's Grape, Kinpikinn Ick, Mealberry, Mountain Box, Mountain Cranberry, Sagckhomi, Universe Vine, Wild Cranberry. This is used a great deal in combination with other herbs. Taken internally or as a douche it has been said to be effective for female disorders and gonorrhea. An infusion has been used in diabetes, Bright's disease, dysentery, hemorrhoids, and discharges from the bladder. It has astringent, nephreticum, and tonic properties as well.

Valerian: Valeriana officinalis. Sometimes referred to as All Heal, Set Wall, Vandal Root. As a nervine and antispasmodic, this has been taken for hysterics and colic and to induce sleep. Taken hot, it is an emmenagogue. It has been said that it is mild enough to give to children for measles and scarlet fever, but in excessive doses may cause headache. It also is claimed to soothe ulcers in the stomach and to prevent fermentation and gas. Taken internally and applied externally at the same time it reportedly promotes the healing of pimples and sores. With licorice, raisins and anise seed it has been used for cough, shortness of breath, and to expectorate phlgm. It has also been used for bladder stones. Often it has been used with skullcap, mistletoe and vervain.

Vervain: Verbena officinalis, Verbena hastata. Also Simpler's Joy, Traveler's Joy, Wild Hyssop. As a powerful diaphoretic, this has been claimed to be effective against fevers, colds, whooping cough, pneumonia, and has been taken also for its expectorant property in asthma and ague. As an emmenagogue, it reportedly increases menstrual flow and will help other female troubles as well. It is also a vermifuge, and it is said to cause the expulsion of worms; a tonic for the entire system; and a vulnerary.

Violet: See Blue violet.

Wahoo: Euonymus atropurpureus. Also Arrow Wood, Bitter Ash, Burning Bush, Indian Root, Pegwood, Spindle Tree, and Strawberry Tree. This is a laxative and has been used for dyspepsia, dropsy, and fevers. It is claimed to be a better remedy than quinine for the same ailments.

Watercress: Nasturtium officinale. This herb grows wild or cultivated in gently moving streams and may be eaten in salads and as a vegetable. It is an excellent source of the B-Vitamin complex, as well as Vitamin C and several others, and also supplies many health-fortifying minerals. It is therefore an antiscorbutic and has been used to strengthen the bloodstream and serves as a stomachic.

Waterdock: Rumex aquaticus. Sometimes called Bloodwort or Red Dock. This herb is both an alterative and detergent and has been taken for skin diseases, sluggish liver, and, as a mouthwash, for ulcers. The powdered root is claimed to be a medicinal tooth cleaner.

Water Pepper: Polygonum punctatum. Sometimes called Smart Weed. Its astringent properties make water pepper reportedly valuable in any cases where tissues must be drawn together, such as coughs or colds. For scanty menstruation, it has been given hot as an emmenagogue; it is said to be helpful in uterine troubles, gravel in the bladder, bowel complaints, and kidney disorders. It has been used as an enema or a hot fermentation externally applied, or for erysipelas, as a cold water wash.

White Bryony: Bryonia alba, Bryonia dioica. Sometimes known as Bryonia, Bryonin, English Mandrake, European White Bryony, Mandragora, Wild Bryony. For a diuretic, it is said to have a soothing and cleansing action and to clear the lungs and bronchial tubes and remove excess fluids from the glands. It has therefore been used in cases of pleurisy, dropsy, bronchitis, coughs and influenza and pneumonia. It reportedly tends to reduce the swelling fo glands (in tonsillitis) and inflammation, especially of the heart, caused by rheumatism or gout.

White Clovers See clover, white.

White Oak: Quercus alba. Also referred to as Tanner's Bark. Both the leaves and the bark of the white oak tree are used, the inner bark being the most potent part. It is said that a strong tea may be used internally and externally to remove varicose veins. This tea is also good as a douche for leucorrhea and other uterine troubles. It has been used as an enema for piles, hemorrhoids, or any rectal problem. It has also been taken to stop internal hemorrhages.

White Pond Lily: Nymphaea odorata. Also Cow Cabbage, Toad Lily, Water Cabbage, Water Lily. As a strong astringent the root of the water lily has been given for leucorrhea (both as a douche and internally), diarrhea, scrofula, bowel ailments; its reported effect on the mucous membranes and inflamed tissues makes it a popular home remedy for sore throat and gums, swellings, boils, ulcers and dropsy. It is said to be mild enough to be given to children for bowel troubles, and has also been used in kidney troubles, catarrh of the bladder, and irritation of the prostate. Applied to wounds and cuts, the leaves reportedly hasten healing.

White Willow: Salix alba. Sometimes known as Withe, Withy. This bark has been used to reduce fever and chills. It is reported to have a good effect on stomach troubles and heartburn. A tea of the leaves and buds has been used in gangrene, and eczema, used both as a tea and applied directly. It is said to stop bleeding of wounds, nosebleed, and to serve as an eyewash, diuretic and for rheumatism and ague. It is reportedly more effective than quinine when used for the same purposes.

Wild Alum Root: Geranium maculatum. Sometimes American Kino Root, American Tormentil, Cranesbill, Crowfoot, Geranium, Storksbill, Wild Dovefoot. The powerful astringency of this root makes it helpful, both internally and externally. It has been taken for cholera, dysentery, diarrhea, piles, chronic ulcers, or mucous discharges from any part of the body (also used for this with golden seal). It reportedly also stops hemorrhaging, bleeding wounds, nosebleed and excess menstruation. As a douche it has been used for uterine troubles and leucorrhea.

Wild Carrot: Daucus carota. See Carrot.

Wild Cherry: Prunus virginiana. Sometimes called Black Cherry, Black Choke, Cabinet Cherry, Rub Cherry. As a tonic, the inner bark has been used to tone the system. It is said to loosen phlegm in the throat and chest, acting as a pectoral, and to be effective in relieving colds, grippe, tuberculosis and asthma. It also has been used in dyspepsia, fevers and high blood pressure.

Wild Oregon Grape: Berberis aquifolium. Also California Barberry, Holly-leaved Barberry, Mahonia. This has been said to be a blood purifier, helpful for skin diseases, uterine problems and liver and kidney troubles. It has also been used as a tonic and alterative, and is said to relieve rheumatism, leucorrhea and constipation.

Wild Plum: The bark is claimed to be the "best remedy for asthma."

Wild Yam: Dioscorea villosa. Also China Root, Colic Root, Devil's Bones, Yuma. Because of its soothing, nervine effects, this has been used for any type of nervous excitement and for neuralgia. Taken during pregnancy (it may be combined with squaw vine) it reportedly relieves pain, allays nausea, and, with ginger, helps prevent miscarriage. It is said to be helpful in expelling gas from the bowels, for cholera, rheumatic pains, and afflictions of the liver. It is also an antispasmodic.

Wintercress: Barbarea vulgaris. Also known as Yellow Rocket. This herb makes an excellent addition to any salad or the leaves and stems may be steamed and eaten as a vegetable. It has been used primarily as an anti-scorbutic.

Wintergreen: Gaultheria procumbens. Common names are Beerberry, Boxberry, Caudad tea, Checkerberry, Chink, Ed Pollom, Ground Berry, Grouse Berry, Hillberry, Ivory Plum, Mountain Tea, Partridge Berry, Redberry Tea, Spiceberry, Wax Cluster. This is a well-known, old-fashioned herb that has been used for colic and gas in the bowels. The oil is reportedly useful in liniments for swellings, boils, ulcers and inflammations. In small doses it is said to stimulate the heart, respiration and stomach. The tea has been used as a wash for sore eyes, a douche for leucorrhea, and a gargle for sore throat and mouth. It reportedly is sometimes taken for rheumatism, rheumatic fever, scrofula, skin diseases and any bladder problems.

Witch Hazel: Hamamelis virginiana. Common names are Hazel Nut, Pistachio, Snapping Hazel, Spotted Alder or Elder, Striped Elder, Tobacco Wood, Winter Bloom. Because of its astringent property, the bark or leaves of this plant are claimed to arrest excessive menstruation and hemorrhages. For piles, especially when they are bleeding, it is reportedly used in an enema; this, it is said, will allay dysentery or diarrhea. The same tea has been used as a douche, for leucorrhea and gonorrhea. As a poultice or wash, the same tea reportedly soothes sore eyes, inflammations, bed sores and piles.

Wood Betony: Betonica officinalis. Betony, Bishopswort, Louse Wort. This herb, taken with skullcap and Calamus Root, has been known for a hundred years for its excellent effect as a stomachic and its effectiveness for digestive disorders in general. It is said also to stimulate, mildly, the heart. It reportedly will relieve the pain of headaches, gout, neuralgia, colic, and other pains in the head and face. More effective than quinine, it has also been taken in jaundice, palsy, convulsions, dropsy, grippe, colds, consumption and nervous ailments. It is a vermifuge and has been used to cause worms to be expelled from the system.

Wood Sage: Teucrium scorodonia. Also Garlic Sage, Wood Germander. This is a tonic and has been used to promote the appetite. Externally has been applied, with chickweed, to sores, ulcers, swellings and boils to soothe and heal. In combination with ragwort and comfrey, wood sage has been used as a poultice for tumors. It reportedly will increase the flow of urine and menstrual flow, and has been taken for colds, fever, kidney and bladder problems, and palsy.

Wood Sanicle: See Sanicle.

Wood Sorrel: Oxalis acetosella. Sometimes known as Cuckoo Sorrel, Allelujah. This has been given as a cooling medicine (it is a refrigerant) to reduce fevers. It has also been used with other diuretics in some urinary conditions.

Wormwood: Artemisia absinthium. Also Ajenjo, Old Woman. Applied as a fermentation, this has been used for rheumatism, swellings and sprains. The oil has been used in liniments that are used for sprains, bruises, lumbago, and so on. It reportedly may be taken internally for liver troubles, including jaundice, and intermittent fevers, diarrhea, and leucorrhea. It is claimed to be an excellent appetizer, and will act as a vermifuge.

Yarrow: Achillea millefolium. Sometimes called Ladies' Mantle, Milifoil, Millefolium, Noble Yarrow, Nosebleed, Thousand Leaf. This has been used for lung hemorrhages, and, if taken early in a cold, reportedly will break it up. It is also a powerful febrifuge when taken hot and has been used for dyspepsia, scanty or suppressed urine, and mucous discharges from the bladder. It is said to have been used successfully for typhoid fever too, and in diabetes, and Bright's disease. For piles and hemorrhoids an enema has brought relief, as it seems to have an excellent effect on the mucous membranes. A douche of yarrow has been used for leucorrhea and other vaginal problems. It is claimed that an ointment will help to heal wounds, ulcers, and fistulas, and is helpful in measles, smallpox, and chickenpox.

With elder flowers and peppermint in equal quantities it has been taken for influenza.

Yellow Dock: Rumex crispus. Also called Curled Dock, Garden Patience, Narrow Dock, Sour Dock. The root of this plant is depurative. As a detergent, it has been applied to leprosy, running ears, impetigo, itch and sores. It is used both in the form of a tea and an ointment. Its astringent quality makes it useful for such diseases as scrofula, glandular tumors, swellings, and syphilis. For glandular tumors and swellings it has been applied as a fermentation wrung from the hot tea.

Yerba Santa: Eriodictyon glutinosum. Also Consumptive Weed, Gum Plant, Bear's Weed, Mountain Balm, Tar Weed. Because it is a tonic and an expectorant, invigorating the system and facilitating expectoration, this has been used in chronic bronchitis, laryngitis, and other lung troubles. It reportedly brings relief of rheumatism and reduces discharge from the nose. It is often an ingredient in asthma prescriptions.

Yerba Mate: See Paraguay tea.

POISONS IN YOUR FOOD

Chances are if you live in the United States you eat a lot *more* and a lot *less* than you really intended. Suppose you had orange juice, or rather benzoic acid (a chemical preservative), dimethyl polysiloxane (antifoaming agent) DDT and related compounds, parathion or one of the other potent phosphorus nerve-gas pesticides and saccharin. If the company producing the juice was complying with the standards of juice content suggested by the Food and Drug Administration in May, 1968, then there would also be at least 50 percent pure orange juice in the drink. As of April, 1970, however, these standards had not yet been adopted so that it is also conceivable that the container you hold labeled "orange juice" contains as little as 10 to 20 percent pure orange juice, the remainder being water and chemicals.

Two slices of white bread go into your stomach. Perhaps you didn't understand some of the things the label did and didn't say: the product of bleach interaction in flour, ammonium chloride (dough conditioner), mono and digylcerides and polyoxythylene (softeners) ditertiary-Butyl-para-Cresol (antioxidant), nitrated flour or coaltar dye (to give it the yellow color suggestive of egg yolks and butter), vitamin fortifiers (to replace nutrients lost in milling), DDT and related compounds, and parathion and related compounds.

Certainly nothing was added to that egg you ate. An egg is an egg. But what about the hen that laid it? Do you know what chemicals went into her feed and sex hormones and antibiotics into her system?

That tossed salad with dressing you had for lunch—were you aware of the sodium alginate (stabilizer), mono-isopsopyl citrate (antioxidant to prevent fat deterioration),

DDT and related compounds, phosphorus insecticides and weed killers it contained?

The juicy piece of roast beef you had for supper contained DDT and related compounds, methoxychlor, chlordane, heptachlor, toxaphene, lindane, benzene hexachloride, aldrin, dieldrin and other pesticides, particularly in the fatty parts, stilbestrol (artificial female sex hormone), aureomycin (antibiotic), mineral oil residue from wrapping paper; and the gravy contained DDT and other pesticides that were in the meat, antibiotics, products formed from the interaction between the chlorine-dioxide bleach used on the flour and the flour nutrients.

What about that all-*American* apple pie—a fitting dessert of butylated hydroxyanisole (antioxidant in lard), chemical agents in flour and butter or margarine, sodium o-phenylphenate (preservative), and several if not all of the following pesticides used on apples: DDT, dinitro-orthocresol, benzene hexachloride, malathion, parathion, demeton, lindane, lead arsenate, nicotine, methoxychlordane and others.

Are you feeling sick? Is nothing safe or sacred?

Large corporations are dehumanizing and in particular encourage conformity and intellectual mediocrity at the expense of individuality, enterprise and variety (Graham Bannock, *The Juggernauts*, p. 25). Technological development combined with the growth of the population are leading to an increasing disparity between the private and social costs of economic activity. Pollution, noise and the destruction of the countryside are already recognized as major problems. (Ibid, p. 322)

When one examines our national food supply and the activities of the Food and Drug Administration to regulate its quality, it becomes apparent that the chief difficulties with food available to the consumer stem from large and powerful economic and political forces which are more interested in their own profit than in the welfare of the entire population . . . and more tragically . . . the population of succeeding generations.

These vague and distant charges become real and horrifyingly close when a loved one dies of botulism poisoning because he was unlucky enough to eat from the wrong can; or when you look in the mirror and see aged, pale, flabby skin and remember your grandmothers with rosy cheeks; or when you see the "elderly" cheerfully riding their bicycles through Swiss Alpine cities—and you huff and puff up one flight of stairs.

What is wrong with our food? Pollution and processing . . . the natural vitamins and minerals are taken out and replaced by non-nutritive . . . and often far from harmless chemicals. In addition, known harmful chemicals are constantly coming into contact with our food supply through the use of insecticides and water pollution.

What does this mean in terms of you and me and what we eat everyday? Bon Vivant Soup can be avoided—but what about bread, and milk, and meat, and fruit, and vegetables? What's being done (which isn't included in advertisements) to the very things which determine whether we will be able to open our eyes tomorrow morning?

Americans are slowly beginning to realize that they are not the healthy, well-fed nation they once assumed they were. Dr. Stanley N. Gershoff, Associate Professor of Nutrition, Harvard School of Public Health, who has worked long and hard to alert the public to the problems of hunger in America, stated in 1969 that a survey of nutritional studies conducted between 1950 and 1968 showed a deterioration in the American diet, especially since 1960. He found a significant portion of the population examined were taking in less than half the recommended daily requirements of vitamins and that many had biochemical indices in the deficient range. Since the people he studied were primarily from the middle class, these findings are particularly striking.

Our statistics on disease verify Dr. Gershoff's findings. According to the Metropolitan Life Insurance Company, in 1968 the United States had an infant mortality rate higher than that of twelve other countries. Deaths of children occurred at the rate of 22.1 per 1,000 live births. Chronic illness is suffered by more than half the population—babies included. More than 225,000 die each year of cancer and an estimated one out of every three Americans will develop cancer sometime during his life. Heart disease claims more than 817,000 lives annually and accounts for more than half the nation's deaths. More than 7,000,000 Americans suffer from arthritis and other rheumatic ailments, and mental institutions become the habitations of one out of every ten Americans at some time during their life.

While antibiotics and sulfa drugs alone saved 1,500,000 lives during the first fifteen years of their use according to the United States Public Health Service; and the number of deaths from infectious disease dropped from 676 to 66 per 100,000 between 1900 and 1948 (and the number of maternal and infant deaths also dropped considerably) —the unpleasant truth is that a man of forty today can anticipate living only about two years longer than a man of forty in 1900.

What is most disturbing about these figures is that while we rank first in man-hour productivity in agriculture and industry, and in per capita income—the factors which should make excellent health readily attainable by all—we stand twelfth in the ranks of physical health. This disparity clearly stems from our national diet.

Not only are we not getting enough nutrients and consuming too many chemicals in our food, but also there are too many reported cases of food poisoning in the United States—with the number on the increase rather than the decline. According to Kenneth R. Lennington, the FDA salmonella project officer, in 1967 "on a nationwide basis, the total number of reported salmonella food-borne outbreaks are running staphylococcus [staph] a close second." By conservative estimates between 10,000,000 and 20,-000,000 cases of food poisoning occur in this country annually. Poliomyelitis and infectious hepatitis, caused by viruses contained in fluid milk, raw shellfish, cooked and cold-cuts meats, salads, frozen strawberries and reconstituted orange juice have also occurred all too often. In addition cases of Clostridium perfirgens food poisoning associated with eating meat, fish and poultry and causing profuse diarrhea and frequently accompanied by abdominal pain are not as rare as they should be.

Kenneth Lennington has explained why he feels this problem of food poisoning is more likely to get worse rather than better: "Our mode of living and technology probably renders us more susceptible to food-borne infection today. The convenience foods, ready-to-eat items, and frozen prepared dinners requiring only minimum heating prior to serving open avenues for mass infection. Our production and distribution system is such today the output of a plant may be distributed nationwide, or even worldwide. This means that an infected employee or a breakdown or deterioration of some phase of plant sanitation can infect thousands of consumers instead of a limited surrounding community. Our population concentration, human and food animal, with the resultant waste disposal and pollution problems, is likewise conducive to spread of infection . . . Effective control of the foodborne infections, whether they be bacterial or viral in nature, entails a much higher and more rigid level of sanitation than generally has been practiced, or required, by industry, or by health and regulatory officials."

In 1940, our draft boards had been confronted with the alarming fact that over half of the first two million men drafted had diseases or physical defects which warranted note, and nearly one third of them were unfit for active service. The National Nutrition Conference for Defense met six months after Pearl Harbor as a result of these startling revelations, assembling our nutritionists and food technologists to assess what was wrong with our diet.

The Conference had little trouble in agreeing that our nutritional woe was caused by a diet in which two thirds of our food calories were derived from devitalized polished rice, white flour, white sugar, and hydrogenated fats.

Where then did the first part of our dietary horror story begin? It was with the crushing, separation and devitalization of what nature intended to be whole and complete. The later and more tragic part of the story . . . the tale of the chemicals in our foods and the poisons in our bodies . . . has hardly started to unravel yet.

The first major nutritional disaster occurred in this country when our coarsely ground whole wheat grains were turned white and refined. Just after the turn of the twentieth century, Minneapolis became the major center for milling flour because of its superior productivity due to its use of the new steel roller mill. The former stone mills which for centuries had ground grain coarsely were now replaced with steel rollers which crushed the grain and destroyed the cell structure. The part of the grain which most readily passed through the reel-separators was the starch cells. By the turn of the century most of the flour consumed in the United States came from these roller mills which extracted 60 to 70 percent of the original content from the wheat berry. In nutritional terms this meant that much of its protein value was lost since it was now low in lysine and tryptophane—amino acids essential to cell growth.

The mineral content of refined white bread produced from roller mills was also greatly inferior to its whole wheat ancestors, with an average of one quarter less iron, calcium, phosphorus, potassium, copper and manganese than whole wheat flour.

But it was in terms of vitamins that the roller mill dealt its most devastating blow to the American diet. The "straight run" product of the roller mill contains 16 percent of the thiamin present in the wheat berry and white "patent" flour as little as 6 percent. Riboflavin, nicotinic acid, pyridoxine, biotin and perhaps other undetected members of the vitamin B complex present in the outer coatings of wheat undergo similar though varying losses. Since wheat germ is one of only four known sources of the complete B vitamin, this is a very significant loss.

Besides the outright loss, once the flour is milled, the nutritive value deteriorates quickly especially in the finely ground grains of white bread where the exposed surface to the oxidative processes are at a maximum. The longer the "shelf-life" in "modern" supermarkets, the less the nutritive value.

We see what was taken out of bread for commercial reasons (certainly not for nutritional ones)—what then was done to replace the nutritional value of one of the basic foods in the American diet?

In 1939, the convention of the American Institute of Nutrition (when war was imminent and food an essential weapon for every country involved), produced a formula for allowing industry to continue selling its white bread and at the same time give the consumer something to eat that some nutritionists would accept as a substitute for whole wheat bread.

Not all those present at the meeting were in accordance with saving "white bread" at whatever the cost. Dr. Sebrell of the United States Public Health Service, a participant in the meeting, condemned the restoration-fortification proposals in these terms:

> I think we can safely say that there are so many unknown factors involved in both the question of what to add and how much of each to use in fortifying a food that it would be prudent not to undertake it at this time as a public health measure . . . Finally, to me it does seem a little ridiculous to take a natural foodstuff in which the vitamins and minerals have been placed by nature, submit this foodstuff to a refining process which removes them and then add them back to the refined product at an increased cost. If this is the object, why not follow the cheaper, more sensible and nutritionally more desirable procedure of simply using the unrefined, or at most, slightly refined natural food?

The enrichment program did eventually go through however. At first thought of as a temporary wartime measure leading to the eventual return to whole wheat or high extraction flour—by January, 1943, the originally voluntary enrichment program became mandatory and developed the markings of permanence. Six states passed permanent enrichment laws a year later, and the Board of Governors of the American Baker's Association's Planning Committee had urged retention of enrichment after the war.

The result of these enrichment laws was that at first *three* and later *four* out of a known *twenty-two* nutrients, largely removed from the wheat berry in the milling process, were restored. Compared to whole wheat bread, however, the product was still impoverished and yet ironically whole wheat bread could not be legally labeled "enriched" and therefore suffered a sales disadvantage.

Among the nutrients in the original wheat berry, important in their role in human physiology, which are not restored are: biotin, pyridoxine, pantothetic acid, calcium, phosphorus, potassium, manganese, copper and the protein amino-acids lysine and tryptophane. Since it is believed that many of these nutrients depend on each other for their own effectiveness, the removal of any one of these essential factors might well destroy the effectiveness of the others.

While there is perhaps some improvement furnished by the enrichment program, at least twice as much might have been done had the nutritionists been tougher and the government less afraid of the baker's lobby. More importantly, this marked the beginning of the new, unprecedented philosophy of taking natural foods, expensively devitalizing them and then at an additional expense partially restoring them by use of synthetic supplements.

The story of the former "staff of life" doesn't end with nutrition however. There is the non-nutritional side as well ... chemicals. The current FDA food standards for bakery products allows 93 different ingredients (few of them nutrients) to be added to bread products at the discretion of the processors *without requiring that they be mentioned on the label*.

In the beginning there is the seed—and the organic mercurials or similar agents used to treat them for protection against plant diseases. Then there is the soil fertilized with chemical fertilizers. Selenium (an extremely poisonous mineral substance) may be extracted from the soil and be synthesized into the growing plant.

Improvers, oxidizing agents such as nitrogen trichloride, persulfate and bromate which affect protease (anienzyme which digest proteins) activity and gluten properties are used in the milling of the flour.

Nitrogen, chlorine or benzoyl peroxide is then used as a bleaching agent to convert the yellow carotenoid pigment to colorless compounds because the consumers "desire" white bread. For compulsory "enrichment" vitamins and minerals are added. To stabilize the gas-retaining properties of flour, gluten and mineral salts may be added. Cyanide or chlorinated organic compounds may be used in fumigating the resulting flour while it is stored.

Alum, soda ash, copper sulfate, and chlorine might be used to purify the water. Lime, sulfur dioxide phosphates and charcoal are used to refine the sugar. Iodide may be in the salt, and calcium and magnesium carbonates may be used to promote "free running" and prevent caking.

Yeast nutrients may actually be ammonium salts and other chemicals. Sodium bicarbonate, alum, tartrates, phosphates, starch and cream of tartar which are probably the leaveners. The shortening is a refined, bleached, deodorized product possibly hydrogenated to change liquid oil to plastic fat which in turn contains traces of nickel, or the shortening may be glycerinated and contain antioxidants.

The list of chemicals doesn't end here. The margarine, eggs, milk and flavor will also be chemically tampered with. What is left of the whole wheat berry continues to be molested practically until the time it reaches your table. The part of the wheat grain which does survive is the starchy anemic material which does an exceptional job of holding the chemicals and water which make up its bulk.

Even insects shy away from this product—showing marked preference for the whole grain breads and cereals. As Samuel Lipkovsky of the College of Agriculture at the University of California in Berkeley and author of *The Bread Problem in War and in Peace* observed: "instead of being alarmed at the decreased nutritive value of white flour as shown by the inability of insect pests to thrive on it, the production of white flour was hailed as a great forward step."

In that next package of white bread you open . . . there's more food for thought than for your body.

The invention of centrifugal machines able to separate sugar from syrup, also occurring in the beginning of the twentieth century, was a second major technological disaster which befell our food supply. Now the "purest and best refined sugar in the world" could sell for only a penny more than the nutritionally superior brown sugar. The result was that brown sugar almost disappeared from the market while the use of white sugar, devoid of vitamins and minerals, steadily increased.

Because sugar has played an increasingly large part in the American diet as we have become more and more affluent and able to purchase more non-essential "treat" foods, this change in sugar's nutritive value is especially important. It is possible that excessive sugar intake of Americans is a factor in our widespread vitamin deficiencies. Research has shown sugar to be an indisputable factor in dental decay. It is at least a contributing cause in many ailments, including diabetes, many medical researchers are convinced.

Adelle Davis, a well-known nutritionist observed:

our American diet has become largely one of sugar
. . . it seems that the survival of every person unaware
of nutrition is at stake: caught in this tide, the inno-
cent victim is flooded by waves of sugar every time he
entertains or is entertained, every time he eats at a
restaurant, and often at every home meal and mid-
meal . . . This situation is not usually realized because
many sugars are hidden. Persons may consume one
or even two cups of sugar daily and still believe they
have eaten 'no sugar at all'.

Besides the obvious sugar added to such foods as
cereals, coffee, and fruits, or consumed in candy, jam
or jellies, as much as one or two table spoons or more
of granulated sugar is obtained in each small glass of
fruit-ade, ginger ale, cola drinks, cider, Manhattans,
and highballs; every serving of cake, pie, gelatin dessert, ice cream, pudding, custard, or canned fruit with
juice; or even a single cookie.

One should note that the body can easily fulfill its starch
and sugar needs through whole grains, fresh fruits and
vegetables and that these foods at the same time are also
supplying valuable vitamins and minerals. Concentrated
sweets and processed foods are almost wholly starches
with little positive food value . . . and much to be said
against them.

Milk, one of our most potentially valuable nutritional
sources in the United States, has also been consistently
adulterated so that Americans receive the minimum rather
than the maximum food value from it. The waste and loss
in quality and quantity at every stage of production, processing, distribution and consumption is another amazing
part of our food industry.

The quality of feed and forage determines to a large
extent the quantity and to some extent the quality (especially with respect to vitamins A and D) of milk our cows
yield. It is, therefore, entirely possible to raise the vitamin A value of winter milk (which tends to be thin),
50 percent by feeding legume forage to the cows at no
great additional cost. The vitamin A content of butter
would also be raised considerably by doing this.

In the handling of our milk, over 200 million pounds

of colostrum (the milk secreted by the cow immediately after calving) is thrown away annually. This milk contains about ten times as much vitamin A, three times as much vitamin D and riboflavin and twice as much ascorbic acid as normal cow's milk. But we have traditionally considered this unfit for human consumption—though the Swedes and Scots use it to make a pudding they consider a delicacy.

Our present pasteurization processes do much to further the destruction of our milk's vitamins and minerals. Unpasturized milk contains a third of the adult daily requirement of vitamin C. Every year we lose as much of this vitamin through pasteurization as is contained in our entire citrus crop. Why? Unpasteurized, certified milk with sufficient standards of dairy sanitation and inspection would be just as safe—especially since milk need no longer be a potential carrier of such diseases as bovine tuberculosis, septic sore throat, scarlet fever, typhoid, diphtheria and undulant fever.

We do in fact have the technological principles for conserving ascorbic acid during pasteurization if it was decided that the sanitary or economic considerations weigh in favor of continuing this process. De-aerating milk before it is shipped to the pasteurizing plant would save 25 to 40 percent of the ascorbic acid now lost enroute. Using brown, nonactinic bottles to contain milk would save additional vitamin C content as well as at least one third of the riboflavin now lost.

In a fifteen year study of 20,000 dairy products obtained from all over the world, Dr. Weston A. Price discovered that the vitamin content was lowest in samples from the eastern and far western states—soil which had been tilled the longest. The highest vitamin content was found in Deaf Smith County where the soil and pasture land was highly mineralized. He also discovered that high-vitamin butter containing both vitamin A and "Activator X" helped arrest tooth decay.

A high nutrient value in milk, therefore, could do much to raise the nation's daily vitamin intake and health. These nutritional losses are not inevitable and could be readily prevented if people were aware of the abuses and put enough pressure on our political leaders, our scientists and food suppliers so that it became important enough for them to find a *total* solution in the near future. It certainly seems hard to excuse our not producing an excellent quality milk far superior to the product we now consume.

What cannot be as easily corrected as keeping the vitamins and minerals *in* milk—is keeping the chemicals *out*. Because the FDA, in 1968, found it hopeless to try to maintain a zero pesticide tolerance for milk it has now set a tolerance for the known poisons, DDT, DDE and DDD of 0.05 parts per million for whole milk and 1.25 ppm for milk fat. This is certainly a strangely simple way of having companies keep within the law—change the law which was enacted for significant reasons (DDT, DDE and DDD are all known harmful poisons)—because the companies find it easier not to comply. Traces of radioactive fallout can also be found in too many milk samples.

The fact is, DDT is endemic. No matter how organically fed and non-pasteurized, your cow will produce milk which has some DDT in it. It will be concentrated however, in the fatty part. So one can reduce one's DDT intake by avoiding cream and butter . . .

Conceivably we could correct all of the devitalizing processes our food undergoes tomorrow if, as a nation, we were fully determined to do so. It is not as conceivable that we could alter the harm already done by the poisons which have become increasingly prevalent in all we eat. The most sinister of these are the carcinogens—cancer-causing substances that appear regularly in the American diet.

The great terror of carcinogens is their cumulative, irreversable effects. Yet, since the law doesn't require testing food chemicals for carcinogenicity, we really don't know how many chemicals on the "safe" list, (which are regularly poured into our foods and don't even have to be acknowledged on the label), may be capable of producing cancer. It is possible that up to 25 percent of the chemicals now labeled "safe" may prove to be carcinogenic when investigated further if we are to judge by the statistical results of previous tests of chemicals on this list, a frightening thought.

What happened with the chemical Aramite is typical of what happens with too many of the chemicals which you and I and our children—present and yet to come—continue to consume on a regular basis.

Aramite, a pesticide and acknowledged carcinogen was permitted to appear in our food for thirty months before it was banned by the FDA; that is, banned at least in foods crossing state lines.

Aramite was originally introduced into the market in 1951 after a five-year development program by Naugatuck Chemical Division, U.S. Rubber Company for the purpose of killing mites and at a cost of about $5,000,000. Mites, never a problem before the widespread use of DDT, became a significant threat to crops after DDT had killed off natural insect and bird predators. The 1952 Yearbook of Agriculture put out by the Department of Agriculture noted: "Never before have so many pests with such a wide range of habits and characteristics increased to injurious levels following application of any one material as had occurred following the use of DDT in apple spray programs."

At first Aramite was introduced on a limited test basis in 1951. Then in 1953 it was licensed for sale by the United States Department of Agriculture (USDA). In 1954, the Miller Act was passed by Congress requiring the FDA to set a tolerance for each pesticide chemical used on raw agriculture crops. As a result of this new law, in 1955 Naugatuck Chemical Company petitioned for a 2 parts per million parts (ppm) residue to tolerance of Aramite in or on certain fruits and vegetables, and a tolerance of 5 ppm on certain other raw agricultural commodities.

FDA tests of the substance showed that rats fed Aramite developed liver tumors and therefore, because of its carcinogenic qualities, the FDA ruled that it would grant a zero tolerance to Aramite. Naugatuck Chemical Company, which had made a substantial investment in time and money and knew that it had a ready market for its product, submitted a new petition requesting a tolerance of 1 ppm and also requesting that the new petition be referred to an advisory committee of experts for study and recommendations. The committee, after its one-day session, recommended approval of the known carcinogen into the lives of hundreds of thousands of Americans. The petition had made no mention of the cancer hazard and the casual reader would assume that a tolerance had just been set to permit sale of another new chemical—nothing out of the ordinary.

The FDA accepted the recommendation of the advisory committee although it was under no legal obligation to do so. This was a significant move because as Congressman James J. Delaney later pointed out: "It is . . . strange when we consider that the committee had before it reports of tests which showed that Aramite, when fed in certain concentrations, produced liver injury and malignant tumors in test animals."

Dr. William E. Smith, a cancer-researcher and now director of the Nutrition Research Laboratory at Fairleigh Dickinson University in Madison, New Jersey, called Congressman Delaney's attention to another striking feature in the Aramite decision. It established a precedent for granting "tolerances" to chemicals found to induce cancer. It was a precedent that benefitted the chemical manufacturers, but left consumers at the mercy of a lethal chemical.

What is also surprising about the FDA's advisory committees recommending a "tolerance" level for Aramite is that it had in its possession an interoffice memorandum which stated: "An experiment with any lower dosage level will not remove the onus that Aramite is a known carcinogen. The Division of Pharmacology cannot recommend that such a substance be used on human food." Still the FDA order permitted residue of Aramite on grapefruit, apples, grapes, blueberries, lemons, cantaloupes, celery, raspberries, tomatoes, strawberries, watermelons, sweet corn, green beans, cucumbers, oranges and peaches. Interestingly enough, it did not permit any tolerance level in forage—which makes one wonder why humans were allowed to consume Aramite in their food supply if cows were not.

Dr. Smith, among other noted cancer-researchers, in discussing the time bomb effect of carcinogens explained that young individuals eating such substances might not show any immediate adverse effects but could develop cancer later in life as a result of them. A man of fifty might not normally live long enough to develop cancer after being exposed to certain cancer-inducing substances—but a youth of twenty would probably die of cancer before he reached 50. Infants exposed to carcinogens from the very beginning of their lives might well die of cancer before they reached 30.

Irreversible and cumulative . . . once in your system there is no way of knowing when and how much carcinogenic material will begin to change your cell structure . . . no way of knowing what promoting factor will push the dormant cancer cells into active cancer production. For 30 months this known carcinogen was poured into our food supply until in 1958 additional testing showed that Aramite would not only cause tumors in rat's livers at lower dosages than originally thought, but also would produce liver damage and malignant tumors in the bile ducts and liver of dogs. It was at this point that the FDA rescinded its original order, changing the tolerance from 1 ppm to zero for Aramite.

If cancer is expected to afflict one out of every three Americans alive today at some time in their lives—one wonders what the statistics will read like 20 years from now. And for how many of us will the statistics no longer be numbers . . . but our own flesh and blood?

The real irony of pesticide stories like Aramite is that the bugs are doing a much better job of surviving them than the human beings that the spray is supposed to protect. Dr. Harvey Wiley, one of the most ardent crusaders for the Pure Food and Drug Act of 1906, had repeatedly pointed out that the nature of a chemical doesn't change just because a small dosage is used. Poison is still poison no matter how small the amount. While it is true a smaller amount may mitigate the immediate effect and make the harm go undetected, it does not mean that no harm is done. It is important to note that *none* of the chemicals introduced by man into food is necessary or even useful to life—and with only rare exceptions these chemicals have proven to be, upon extensive testing, antagonistic to living tissues. It is also important to realize that the food we eat becomes our blood, brain, bone and flesh, and the daily bombardment by nerve poisons and other toxic substances makes it difficult for a person to maintain a strong nervous system and good mental health.

One of the most interesting and least excusable uses (though no use is excusable) of carcinogenic chemicals is dyes—used exclusively to fool and confuse the consumer. It is hard to understand how these substances have been allowed to be poured into our foods. The majority of these dyes approved for use have been shown to cause cancer in animals. Some of them are chemical cousins to highly potent substances that have actually caused cancer in man. Some of them which are not carcinogenic have been found to be harmful to animals even in tiny doses.

The United States has the dubious distinction of leading the world in use of these synthetic food colorings. Their use between 1955 and 1965 shot up from 1.69 million pounds per year to 2.6 million pounds. This sky-rocketing use of dyes can be attributed mainly to more and more foods becoming ready-made, canned, bottled, packaged, shipped great distances, stored and stocked. Less fresh, less appetizing food is given a face lift with these chemical cosmetics so that few consumers know what the real substance looks like.

Originally these dyes were put on the market without any testing of their effects on living tissues. Their use was extensive for many years before it was decided to test a limited number of them. In 1938, under the Food, Drug and Cosmetic Act, nineteen dyes were certified—of which eight (almost half) have since been decertified.

Certification of a dye means that it is "pure and nonharmful" no matter how much is used. Wallace F. Janssen, former assistant to the FDA commissioner, has pointed out that "under the law, the colors are supposed to be certified as completely safe—so that no matter how much color is used it would not be harmful. No legal action is possible against anyone for using an excessive amount of certified color." Yet in 1957, Dr. Arthur A. Nelson of the FDA reported that ten out of the thirteen certified dyes tested (and in wide use) when injected under rat's skin had produced cancer. Earl Ubell, a science writer, said that from Dr. Nelson's figures "it was estimated that some [consumers] must get twice as much by mouth as some of the rats got under the skin."

The list of nine U.S. certified dyes and the foods they appear in are:

ORANGE No. 1—Fish pastes, carbonated beverages, jellies, confectionery, custards, blanc-mange powder, biscuits, cakes, ice cream, cordials, ice cream toppings, milk bar syrups, sausage casings, puddings, frozen desserts, soft drinks. (Now decertified)

ORANGE No. 2—Cheese, margarine, candies, edible fats, external coloring of oranges. (Now decertified)

YELLOW No. 1—Confectionery, macaroni, spaghetti, other pastas, baked goods, beverages. (Now decertified)

YELLOW No. 3 (Yellow AB)—Edible fats, margarine, butter, cakes, biscuits, candy. (Now decertified)

YELLOW No. 4 (Yellow OB)—Same as Yellow No. 3.

GREEN No. 1—Cordials, jellies, soft drinks, candy, bakery goods, frozen desserts. (Now decertified)

GREEN No. 2—Candies, essences, cordials, biscuits, cake, jellies, maraschino cherries, frozen desserts.

GREEN No. 3—Candies, jellies, desserts, bakery products.

BLUE No. 1—Icings, cordials, jellies, ice cream, ice cream toppings, milk bar syrups, candies, cake decorations, frozen desserts, soft drinks, puddings, bakery goods.

Orange No. 1, Orange No. 2, Yellow No. 1, Yellow No. 3, Yellow No. 4, and Green No. 1 have been withdrawn from government approval. Many years from now, long after we have forgotten these dyes were used in foods, the carcinogenic natures of these substances may prove fatal to the systems of those who once consumed them regularly.

The cancer hazard of Yellow AB and Yellow OB, widely used in the coloring of butter and margarine, has been repeatedly emphasized. They are both made from a chemical called beta-napt-thylamine. This chemical has a "remarkably low toxicity" according to Dr. Hueper, formerly of the National Cancer Institute, "while being one of the most carcinogenic substances known." Most large chemical manufacturers have, in fact, stopped its production due to its causing cancer in 50 to 100 percent of the workers exposed to it. The treachery of the FDA listing anything as safe is that its tests are primarily designed to uncover toxicity not carcinogenicity—which is often discovered accidentally.

The role of industry in perpetuating these "harmless" substances on the unsuspecting public is hard to reconcile. It is also hard to reconcile the government's complicity and the protection of industries' profits. In 1955, for example, when 200 children were made ill from eating dyed popcorn at a Christmas party and the FDA announced it would decertify the three dyes involved: Red No. 32,

Orange No. 1, and Orange No. 2, it allowed manufacturers to use up previously certified stocks of the color with the precaution that food containing excessive quantities of these colors could "cause illness to consumers." The manufacturers profits were protected—but what about the consumers' health?

Dyes used to mask the true state of our foods are numerous. As Consumers Research stated: "If the consumer buys dyed store cake on the assumption that the yellow means the cake contains egg yolks he is being cheated, for very often bright, attractive color indicates nothing except the presence of a coal-tar dye of uncertain safety that makes nutritionally skimped food resemble a food of better quality."

In another report on this matter, the Delaney Committee stated that: "there are indications that the use of artificial coloring matter is increased when quantities of whole eggs or egg yolks are reduced in commercial cake formulas. The addition of color to make pale winter butter look like summer butter which is more nutritious is another instance of using dye to deceive the consumer. There is also a tremendous amount of food coloring poured over oranges which are in fact green because they are picked before they have been allowed to ripen."

Who wants these artificial, potent, often proved harmful substances added to our food? Do we, the consumer, want it? Is it beneficial for us to be deceived as to the true nutritive value, taste and color of much of the food we eat? Should we be asked to foot the financial—and physical bill—for a small minority of people who care nothing about the health and safety of the public at large? Many who work in plants which handle these poisons are caused even more harm than the consumer. Is that the price they should be asked to pay to have a steady job? Is this how our economy is bolstered? Would the country collapse without such blatant deceit?

Chemicals used in growing foods are one of the major sources of poison in our daily diet. According to the Public Health Service, it is virtually impossible to find a meal in the United States that isn't laced with these poisons. DDT and other fantastic new poisons still in use cannot be washed off foods. They not only adhere to the outer surface of these foods, but penetrate the inner pulp of our fruits, vegetables and grains, and concentrate in the fats of the animals we eat. In fact it would be difficult to find a person alive in the U.S. today who doesn't have some DDT in his body cells. Even babies are born with this poison in their bodies.

DDT, discovered in Germany in 1874, didn't become popular as an insecticide until World War II. It was several years later that it became suspect as a hazard to man. By then, however, a tremendous vested interest had already been built up. It is easy to understand how economic and political expediency—especially since the government was embarrassed at having released DDT and endorsed its safety without adequate testing—dictated the policy of dismissing all warnings about its potential harm. As Dr. Morton S. Biskind, formerly a member of the headquarters staff of the Council on Pharmacy and Chemistry in the American Medical Association and in charge of the endocrine laboratory and clinic at Beth Israel Hospital in New York, commented to the Delaney Committee: "Some fantastic myth of human invulnerability has grown up with reference to the use of these substances. Because their effects are cumulative and may be insidious and because they resemble those of so many other conditions, physicians for the most part have been unaware of the danger." Dr. Biskind also noted that although there was much information available on the toxicity of DDT "the evidence has been treated with disbelief, ignored, misinterpreted, distorted, suppressed or subjected to some of the fanciest double talk ever perpetrated."

In 1958, Dr. Malcolm M. Hargraves, internationally known blood specialist at the Mayo Clinic, testified in Brooklyn Federal Court that he was *certain* that DDT and the solutions that carry it in sprays cause leukemia, aplastic anemia, Hodgkin's disease, jaundice and other fatal blood disorders.

Acute poisoning can be easily recognized—there may be nausea, vomiting, gastroenteritis, abdominal pains, coughing and sore throat—similar to the symptoms of the common cold or certain virus infections. Pains in the joints, general muscular weakness and fatigue, congestion of the lungs and pneumonia are also common findings. However, it is the long term effects which are more deceptive. When a person dies suddenly of a heart attack or cancer we know why he dies, but we don't necessarily know what caused the cellular malfunctions. These "bug killers" are becoming more and more suspect as "people killers" as well.

In chronic poisoning, a person may develop hypersensitive skin areas and numbness, tingling sensations, itching, headaches, twitching muscles and nerve involvement which interferes with walking. The brain may show signs of cell damage—loss of memory, inability to concentrate and dizziness. Apprehension and anxiety are also among the common complaints along with the hopeless feeling "I am going to die." It is possible that many of the new viruslike sicknesses since World War Two may be traced to such DDT poisoning according to Dr. Biskind.

Many studies have been made on the effects of DDT on all kinds of animals—from rats to horses to fish—and the results have shown that DDT causes functional disturbances and degenerative changes in the skin, liver, gall bladder, lungs, kidneys, spleen, heart muscle, blood vessels, brain, perihiperal nerves, gastrointestinal tract, blood and in fact in just about every cell in the body. The Yearbook of the American Journal of Public Health has reported that "contrary to previous beliefs, it now seems likely that a substance which is poisonous to one form of life is very apt to be found to some degree toxic for other animals, including men." Statistics on what DDT did to all forms of wildlife in sprayed areas seem to verify this statement.

It has also been shown that DDT destroys vitamins and inhibits the body's delicate enzyme systems. As Dr. John J. Miller, Chicago biologist has stated: "the very fact that a very small amount of a biological poison is ultimately able to effect a relatively enormous weight of animal tissue shows that the poison interferes with an essential line in a chain of vital processes."

Dr. Otto Warburg, a famous German medical researcher and Nobel Prize winner, has warned that any poison which interferes with the respiration of cells causes irreparable damage and inevitably leads to deterioration in the form of degenerative diseases, including cancer. Cumulative DDT certainly classifies as one such poison. The new poisons, however, which do not necessarily accumulate in the body are also potentially extremely harmful. A toxic substance does not necessarily have to accumulate in the body to have a cumulative effect of harm—each small dose adds to the effects of previous ones.

These new poisons which have replaced DDT have enjoyed tremendous success, if only because their menace has been skillfully underplayed. In 1939, the nationwide sale of pesticides was $40 million, by 1956 it had increased more than five times—the sales prediction for 1975 according to the chemical industry is one billion dollars.

Chlordane, rated by the FDA as at least four times as toxic as DDT, is still on the market even though the FDA found that pigeons could not survive in a small room treated with chlordane even after it was thoroughly scrubbed with alkali and subsequently aired for several weeks.

Ecologists will tell you . . . along with the priests and medicine men of all ancient cultures . . . that the balance of nature is very tenuous. One wonders what disastrous chain reactions will continue to be set in motion as we continue to act on the assumption that we must eradicate everything not sympathetic to us. What many fail to realize is how universally our food is already contaminated—and how long it would take to uncontaminate it even if *every* poison were taken off the market today.

The tale of what is done to our meat is a hundred times more harrowing than anything Upton Sinclair revealed in *The Jungle* if only because few animals in our meat supply, and therefore few meat eating consumers, escape the present continuing barrage of chemicals which rather than sudden death are more likely to lead to chronic illness and slow degeneration in our bodies. There is probably no article in the American diet as thoroughly tampered with. The average steer begins life by being artificially conceived, is raised on an artificial sex-hormone planted in its ear, is fed synthetic hormones, antibiotics and insecticides, is shot with tranquilizers and grazes on pastureland contaminated by radioactive fallout. Animals which survive this chemical feast are then slaughtered by generally inhumane methods and reach our tables as the primary source of protein in our diet.

A good part of the chemical adulteration takes place on the farm. Farmers seem to have forsaken their faith in nature, the seasons and the land. Today almost nothing that grows remains intact without some chemical alteration. The *Farm Journal* (June, 1968) informed farmers of still another chemical alteration which might be in store. Researchers are now working on forcing activated charcoal down the throats of cows to trap some pesticide residues, similar to the way filters trap tars in cigarettes. These cows would also be fortified by treatment with the enzyme-stimulating drug phenobarbital for which any veterinarian will be able to give a farmer a prescription. Then too, there are drugs used to slow down the metabolism of cattle so that with less food they will put on more weight.

While 90 percent of all cattle that go to market each year are estimated to be getting artificial hormones they are not alone in their chemical torture . . . 100 million chickens are receiving these hormones as well. Antibiotics and tranquilizers are fed almost universally to meat animals in this country. An antibiotic dip increases the shelf life of chickens and turkeys and the FDA has recently given milk farmers permission to feed their cattle antibiotics.

There is a continual arsenal of researchers looking for new and more powerful medications which would bring bigger profits for the chemical manufacturer, the packer and sometimes even the farmer. What about you and me, the consumers? We are still too unheard from in the rooms behind closed doors where the important decisions which affect our daily lives and health are made. Our role is to pay good money to reap the consequences of bad food . . . which destroys our bodies . . . more than it builds or maintains them.

By examining the story of stilbestrol, we will get some conception of what is permitted to be done to our meat, with no benefit to the consumer and of tremendous potential harm.

Farmers use stilbestrol, an artificial female sex hormone, for simple economic reasons—sixteen cents' worth of stilbestrol in a cow's ear brings an extra twelve dollars' worth of beef. Cattle gain weight fifteen percent faster on twelve percent less feed when this chemical is mixed with their feed. Annually, the use of stilbestrol is said to be worth 675,000,000 pounds of beef.

It is not exactly known why stilbestrol causes cattle to

increase their weight on less feed. The FDA has stated however: "Hypertrophy (excessive development) of the liver, of the adrenal glands, and of the pituitary without specific cellular changes has been reported. These observations seem to indicate that there is a change in the endocrine gland metabolism . . ."

Dr. Robert K. Enders, chairman of the department of zoology at Swarthmore College and an unsalaried advisor to the U.S. Department of Agriculture and the Department of the Interior, an outspoken critic of the use of stilbestrol in food, has said that it causes chicken skin to become very nice and smooth because of the water and fat under it. "It increases the attractiveness very, very much . . . I agree with those endocrinologists who say that the use of the drug to fatten poultry is an economic fraud. Chicken feed is not saved; it is merely turned into fat instead of protein. Fat is abundant in the American diet, so more is undesirable. Protein is what one wants from poultry. By their own admission it is the improvement in appearance and increase in fat that makes it more profitable to the poultryman to use the drug. This fat is of very doubtful value and is in no way the dietary equal to the protein that the consumer thinks he is paying for."

But the use of stilbestrol is more than an economic fraud and health hazard for what it doesn't do nutritionally—it is a health hazard and dangerous poison for what it can do chemically in our bodies. It is known to be capable of arresting the growth of children, bringing on excessive menstrual bleeding, fibroids of the uterus, premenstrual tension and painful breasts in women and causing impotence and sterility in men. It has also been shown to cause cysts and cancers of the uterus, cervix and breast, tumors of the testicles and leukemia in animals.

While it was assumed for a long time that by the time chickens with stilbestrol implants were killed the pellets would be dissolved, it was later discovered that this wasn't true. Male birds given this chemical rapidly lose many of their male characteristics: combs, wattles and reproductive organs shrivel and their propensity for crowing and fighting disappear. If the total pellet had been dissolved by the time the birds were killed then they would have reverted back to their male characteristics. They don't revert back.

The main justification for stilbestrol has always been that little estrogen activity remains in the meat after the animal is slaughtered. *Time Magazine* in September 1958 carried a story out of Rio de Janeiro where a newspaper had printed "TERROR IN BRAZIL—MEN FEMINIZED." According to *Time* "readers were shaken to their gonads" by this blaring headline. The panic was caused by a charge that a hen had been feminized by eating beef from a steer fattened with the aid of stilbestrol. There was nothing really serious to worry about, *Time* assured its readers, because Rio's state government had proclaimed: "The necessary measures will be taken to end this evil." *Time* also noted that hormone-fattening of meat is a common practice in the United States as well and again assured its readers that there was "probably" nothing to the claim since "nearly all the hormone is metabolized" and "virtually none can ever be found in meat if the hormone feeding is stopped (as required under U.S. regulations) 48 hours before slaughter." The scientific evidence does not back up this claim of stilbestrol being completely dissolved before humans eat it, as we have previously noted. "If the hormone feeding is stopped 48 hours before slaughter" is another point to be wary of. Farmers, untrained as scientists, biologists, chemists or nutritionists are known in many instances to take the warnings on labels of the hundreds of thousands of pounds of chemicals which go into our food each year—with a grain of salt. "If one pellet of stilbestrol is good to increase the market value of my chicken, Lord have mercy on what FOUR could do" must have been the reasoning of the farmer whose chickens were found to have remnants of as many as four pellets. Who knows how many such cases go undiscovered each year.

Farmers have also been known to kill their animals before the 48 hour "safety" period is up. If the price of his meat is good today it is not necessarily in his better interest to wait the two days before he kills his animals. Why should he suffer the economic loss just because some scientist from the big city who doesn't own any animals advised it? The money is coming out of his pocket—not the scientist's . . . and the poison is going into all of our systems. The poisons are too easily available—the checks not nearly sufficient.

The harrowing exposure of meat to chemicals does not end on the farm however. The list of chemicals used in curing and preserving cold meats is formidable—and all of them are poisons.

Sodium nitrate and sodium nitrite, widely used in luncheon meats (especially frankfurters) to accentuate the natural color, have on many occasions poisoned individuals who ate such meats containing larger quantities than legally permitted. In one instance, several years ago in New Orleans, several cases of severe illness were reported when wieners supposed to contain no more than 200 ppm nitrites were found to have up to 6,750 ppm.

Dr. Lehman of the FDA has reported cases of boric acid "dusted on hams during the curing process to keep off what they call skippers, a fly infestation. It has been used also as a preservative in waxy covering for certain fruits and vegetables." Boric acid is considered "poisonous per se" by the FDA and should not be used in any food products.

Prevention, a health food magazine, has reported that it discovered from the U.S. Department of Agriculture that one brand of synthetic sausage casings was made of synthetic resins, "modified by the addition of a small amount of harmless chemicals." Another brand was made of "regenerated cellulose" consisting of "wood pulp and cotton linters, and plasticized by treatment with alkali." A third brand's casings were made of "synthetic rubber modified by the addition of a small amount of harmless chemicals." *Prevention*, horrified by their findings asked: "But the meat has been packed in them for weeks (or perhaps months) before we buy it. How much of the synthetic rubber, resin, cellulose and 'harmless chemicals' have been absorbed by that meat before we make it into a sandwich?"

Sodium sulphite, one of the most infamous of the surreptitious chemicals—and illegal—can often be found in certain foodstuffs. This is also true of sodium benzoate. John Cullen, former Canadian food-inspection official, has warned that: "If the meat is of an unusually bright red color, it is reasonable to assume that it has been doped and doctored with sulphurous acid or sodium sulphite. This is especially true in the case of hamburger that has been made from stale meat trimmings, pork kidneys, pigs' hearts, sheep hearts and other meat by-products including large quantities of fat." It is a "great favorite with butchers and manufacturers of meat products generally . . . This preservative is very dangerous to health, especially when used in meat, because it will not only restore the color of putrid and almost black meat, but also because it will destroy the strong odor of putrefaction.

"Many butchers will contend that they use this preparation only because it arrests the spread of bacteria. Nothing, however, is further from the truth. Changes of the most dangerous character are continuously taking place in the meat, but the sodium sulphite obscures them and makes the meat appear to be fresh and of better value than it really is, and enables the seller to perpetrate an unscrupulous and deliberate fraud."

In supermarkets, poisonous bug killers, not uncommonly containing DDT, will also be illegally sprayed on the shelves. And so it goes with one poison after another being added up until the time you take your first bite—when the meat poisoning story ends . . . and your poisoning story begins.

A recent horror story that most of you remember and perhaps will never be able to forget if your body was involved—is the story of cyclamates in our food supply. This is an excellent example of how Americans are consistently permitted to be used as human guinea pigs of the food, drug, and chemical industries.

On October 18, 1969, then Secretary of Health, Education and Welfare Robert H. Finch released the following statement to the public: "I am today ordering that the artificial sweetener, cyclamate, be removed from the list of substances generally recognized as safe for use in foods." This was nineteen years (cyclamates originally went onto the market in 1950) and hundreds of thousands of pounds of cyclamated and consumed beverages, candies, desserts and baked goods later.

According to the Abbot Laboratories (the first company to officially file a drug application for a cyclamate product), it was "intended for use in foods and beverages by diabetics and by others who must restrict their intake of sugar."

It is worth noting that the FDA reviewed Abbot Laboratories' test data and found it useless due to the small test groups, the insufficient amount of autopsies and the vagueness of the report itself. The FDA would have rejected the application except for the fact that it had conducted experiments in its own laboratories for two years under the supervision of Dr. Lehman—who recommended the drug as safe. Almost twenty years later when cyclamates were finally removed from the market a review of the FDA data relied on by Dr. Lehman showed "a highly suspicious frequency of lung tumors . . . [which] assumed significant back-up importance." Other important factors ignored at the time when the drug was originally declared safe were six rare ovarian, kidney, skin and uterine tumors appearing in a test group of under a hundred rats. The normal occurrence of this disease would be in one out of every ten thousand rats—making the occurrence in these rats fed cyclamates 600 times what would normally be expected. Certainly these facts alone should have indicated the need for more testing before cyclamates were allowed to be marketed."

In 1954 came another significant warning about cyclamates. The Food Nutrition Board said "the priority of public welfare over all other considerations precludes the uncontrolled distribution of foodstuffs containing cyclamates" because it was "impressed with the fact that cyclamate has physiologic activity in addition to its sweetening effect, that there is no prolonged experience with its use, and that little is known of the results of its continued ingestion in large amounts in a variety of situations in individuals of all ages and states of health."

By 1962 there had been a steadily growing use of cyclamates in all kinds of food, especially in those which were supposed to be for people who wished to control their weight. At this time the Food Nutrition Board advised that when the rest of the diet was not controlled cyclamates "have no direct influence on body weight" though advertisers of cyclamate products used this as a main selling point.

The potential potency and destructive effects of cyclamates was again brought to the forefront when two Japanese scientists reported in 1966 that cyclamates passing through the body of man could create a different chemical called cyclorhexylamine (CHA). Later tests showed, in fact, that this change occurred in about one third of the population. The FDA in 1958 recognized CHA as clearly a dangerous chemical.[1]

The potential biological dynamite contained in cyclamates was strikingly pointed out in 1968, this time by two American scientists. Dr. Jacqueline Berrett, an FDA biochemist, reported to a high level FDA science seminar that she had discovered a firm relationship between cyclamates injected into chicken eggs and deformities of embryos taken from the eggs. She found that cyclamates caused "monstrous" deformities—a leg rotated in the socket, wings growing out of the wrong part of the body. Her findings were ignored by the FDA, however.[2]

Dr. Marvin Legator, a cell biology research chief of the FDA, several months later gave a report to *Medical World News* that he had discovered that cyclohexylamine could "break a significant proportion of chromosomes in both *in vitro* and *in vivo* animal studies."

James Turner, in Ralph Nader's Study Group Report on the Food and Drug Administration *The Chemical Feast*, reports that:[3]

> At least ten other danger signals, all of which FDA researchers had brought to the Commissioner's attention by December 12, 1968, brought no action. It seems likely that regular use of cyclamates might disrupt the effects of anticoagulants in humans, perhaps through inhibiting vitamin K effectiveness, an effect that could cause bleeding problems. Tests show unexplained effects on the liver. Cyclamates affect the intestinal tract, causing softening of the stool. Cyclamate use causes a change in the way the body absorbs certain drugs, by, for example, affecting the way substances bind themselves to plasma, probably altering the effectiveness of the drug. Cyclamate absorption into the body is increased by the consumption of caffeine, fats, and citric acid, and cyclamates are dis-

1. James S. Turner, Ralph Nader's Study Group Report on the Food and Drug Administration: *The Chemical Feast*, p. 11, Grossman Publishers, Inc., New York, 1970.
2. *Ibid.*, pp. 12, 13.
3. *Ibid.*, p. 14.

tributed through breast milk and across the placenta
. . . It appears that a significant portion of food-grade
cyclamates contains the dangerous and untested chemical cyclohexylamine (CHA) so that even that portion
of the population that does not convert cyclamates to
CHA is likely to be exposed to CHA if they consume
foods containing cyclamates.

HEW Secretary Robert H. Finch did not mention the
doubts expressed in fifteen years of reports on the chemical
when he announced that he would remove cyclamates from
the GRAS (Generally Recognized As Safe) list and the
market. He also minimized rather than highlighted the
potential danger of the chemical. There was no mention of
the severe limitations of scientific knowledge on chemical
hazards. Nor was there any discussion of the fact that the
law requires a food additive to be established as safe *before*
it is used.

It is hard to estimate the damage that cyclamates have
already done which cannot be eradicated by an order from
Secretary Finch or the people who originally allowed cyclamates to be put on the market. How many hundreds of
thousands of children, teenagers and college students (besides housewives and businessmen) lived on a cyclamate
diet beverage to keep their weight down or because it was
a readily available "in" drink? Besides the destruction these
Americans caused to their own bodies—how much genetic
damage will they pass on to their children? The answer will
come—perhaps too soon for many who had blind faith in
the food industry and our protective laws and didn't realize
the choice they had made or the possibilities of alternatives.

Cyclamates, if not in themselves cancer-producing (it is
not yet proven that they are not carcinogenic), are far more
dangerous in the genetic damage they produce.

What is most noteworthy about this recent case of a
disastrous chemical being allowed to adulterate our food
on a widespread basis is that such chemical abuse is the
rule and not the *exception* in the American food supply.

Until recently, when the Huckleby family hit national
headlines, the problem of mercury poisoning in our food
supply was given little attention. Few people knew about its
existence. Most are now aware that if you eat too much

tuna fish "it's not too good for you." And it's harder these days to find swordfish at your local market than it was two years ago. Why? The answer begins with the highly toxic organic mercury compounds used in slimicides, fungicides, mildew-killers, germ-proofing sprays, and crab-grass eradicators—it ends in our food—especially our fish.

The people in the quiet town of Minamata on the southwest coast of Kyushu, the most southerly of the main Japanese islands, discovered the dramatic effects on living organisms and human anatomy when indiscriminate "harmless" water pollution by mercury compounds takes place. The town was visited by a strange plague in April 1953. First it was noticed that some cats and crows which inhabited the town began doing peculiar things—the cats running into the waves to drown—the crows falling from the sky. Then the people began to fall down, become numb, lose all control of their bodies and become raving mad and die.

It took until 1957 to discover this horrible disease was brought about by eating fish from the mercury-polluted bay. The pollutor was a fertilizer factory which used mercury as one of its catalysts in processing. The treachery of such pollution is that the original effluent, mercuric chloride, an inorganic salt which is not extremely potent (certainly not potent enough to cause the cases of extreme mercury poisoning reported in Minamata) was changed into methyl mercury (highly toxic and capable of producing the Minamata disease) by bacteria which methylated the mercuric chloride in their bodies and excreted the deadly poison. "Modern" man often disrupts the natural biological chain before he can even begin to comprehend the ramifications —by then it is very, very late.

Mercury compounds first came into widespread use in 1940 as fungicides to protect seeds before planting from bunt, root rot, covered smut, net blotch, dry rot and blast. They were used on wheat, barley, oats, rye, corn, rice, sorghum, linseed, millet, cotton, flax, apples, pears, apricots, cherries, peaches, almonds, walnuts, strawberries, cucumbers, watermelons, pumpkins, squash and potatoes. Seven years later, in 1947, mercury compounds were placed on the zero tolerance list. Supposedly *no* mercury residues could be found on food shipped interstate—yet organo-mercurials are still used today by some farmers in the United States.

In Sweden in 1950, conservationists began to notice a decrease in the seed-eating bird population: pheasants, partridges, pigeons, finches. They also began to discover an increase in the number of bird carcasses strewn along the countryside. Two young radiobiologists, Dr. Goren Löfroth and Dr. Carl Rosén decided to investigate the cause of these deaths. In their experiments they found repeatedly high levels of mercury in the livers of these birds. By 1960 the predatory birds which feed on the seed eaters—buzzards, goshawks, sparrow hawks, owls and eagles were also showing high levels of mercury. In 1964 the Swedish Plant Protection Institute recommended the level of mercury concentrations in seeds be cut by 50 percent—no great victory for Swedish Conservationists—but a beginning. The Swedes became so concerned with the mercury problem by 1966 that they called an international symposium to discuss the hazards of mercury pollution. The U.S. attended—but apparently no one heard the alarm.

Not only have we polluted our lands but we have succeeded in polluting our seas as well. This is part of the unintentional biological chain we have set in motion. It's not as if we poured mercury into our oceans, lakes and streams to protect them from disease, or fatten them, or make them keep longer. We poured and are pouring these poisons into our bodies of water so they will magically disappear. It's not even as if we pour deadly methyl mercury into our waters. For the most part we are "careful" to pour the "much less harmful" inorganic mercuries. However, man does not control all of nature—though he might like to . . . and tends to forget that he doesn't. It wasn't his —that is our (for you and I have gone along) intention to have the microorganisms in the mud of our sea floors metabolize the metallic and inorganic mercury and excrete the highly poisonous methyl mercury. It just happens that way in nature. No matter what form the mercury takes when it is originally dumped into lake, stream or storm sewer, the biological systems slowly convert some unknown portion of it into deadly poison. The rest of the process which spreads the soluble mercury systematically throughout the aquatic environment has been understood for a long time and is called organic complexing. Mercury collects and concentrates in various biological pockets and eventually spreads to other plants, then fish and finally into birds and people.

Phytoplankton (microscopic plants) take the mercury directly into their bodies from the surrounding water and then pass it on to the zooplankton (microscopic animals) which eat them. Small fish eat the zooplankton, large fish eat the small fish and then other predators—including man eat the large fish. In each successive stage of the food chain the mercury becomes increasingly concentrated. The mercury concentration in the water is practically negligible —in a pike, however, it is 3,000 to one.

The 200 day half-life of mercury in fresh-water fish allows for these high concentrations to accumulate in the fishes' bodies. If a fresh-water fish takes in a certain amount of mercury today, half of it will still be left at the end of 200 days. 200 days later half of that will still be left and so on. As new mercury is added it simply increases the fishes' total body burden. It is a cumulative poison, therefore, which circulates in the blood unchanged for a long time.

Methyl mercury is lethal because of its ability to dissolve brain cells and attack the central nervous system. As yet we don't know how much of this poison it takes to harm the brain. We also don't know how much damage can be done before it becomes observable. It may be that "only one brain cell at a time may be killed," according to Dr. Alan Hinman at the Federal Center for Disease Control at Atlanta, "but eventually they add up."

As in the carcinogens (and it is not known yet if mercury is one of these) mercury is not only capable of doing tremendous genetic damage (as has already been shown by human guinea pigs) but may also have the cumulative time bomb effect as do the cancer-producing carcinogens. According to Dr. Neville Grant, professor of medicine at Washington University (St. Louis) Medical School:

From the nature of the injury in nerve tissue caused by mercury poisoning, it is clear that the absence of symptoms does not mean the absence of damage. The damage may go on out of sight for some years and may be of great significance as the poisoned person ages. The malfunction of the nerve cells damaged by mercury may at first be compensated for by viable neighbors, but as these normal neighbor cells are removed by the aging process, neurological abnormalities could become markedly enhanced.

The half-life for mercury in human beings is 70 days—plenty of time for it to circulate throughout the body in the bloodstream, doing its work, concentrating in particular spots: the cortex of the brain, the gonads, and the fetuses of pregnant women.

By March 1969, Dr. Löfroth of Sweden had completed an extensive study of methyl mercury. Seven months later, the U.S. Embassy in Stockholm alerted Washington to the doctor's frightening message. A State Department airogram sent from Stockholm on October 29, 1969 attached a copy of Löfroth's study. His findings were:

a) Crops grown from mercury-treated seeds can cause accumulation of this poison in the food chain leading to man, both when the crop is consumed directly and when it is consumed via the animal products he eats.

b) Biological systems can methylate mercury. In certain Swedish waters, commercial fishing was banned because of the dangerous levels of methyl mercury in the fish.

c) Mercury in pregnant women concentrates in the fetus. Mercury poisoning which would be hardly noticeable in the mother, therefore, can cause tremendous harm to the unborn child.

d) Even at very low levels, mercury is known to cause serious genetic damage.

Though the Department of Health, Education and Welfare received several copies of this aerogram, it stirred little action.

The most potent danger of mercury poisoning is the genetic damage it causes. According to the Mrak Commission Report in 1969 (Report of the HEW Secretary's Commission on Pesticides and Their Relationship to Environmental Health, named after the commission's chairman Dr. Emil M. Mrak) some mercurials are known mutagens, presumably owing to their content of HG [metallic mercury]. The report states that mercury pesticides (chiefly methyl mercury) are "compounds which by their structure may possibly affect DNA either directly or after enzymatic activation into reactive compounds."

The Mrak Commission report forcefully states its warnings of possible genetic damage caused by mercury poisoning:

> a particularly subtle danger from wide-scale use of pesticides lies in the possibility that some of them may be damaging to the hereditary material. If this is so, we may be unwittingly harming our descendants. Whether this is happening, and if so, what is the magnitude of the effect, is regrettably unknown. Surely one of the greatest responsibilities of our generation is our temporary custody of the genetic heritage received from our ancestors. We must make every reasonable effort to insure that this heritage is passed on to future generations undamaged. To do less, we believe is grossly irresponsible . . . The risk to future generations though difficult to assess in precise terms, is nevertheless very real. The prevention of any unnecessary mutational damage is one of our most important and immediate responsibilities.

Mercury is known to be one of the chemical mutagens having strange effects upon normal mitosis and meiosis (the cell dividing process which produces sex cells), causing the chemical structure of cells and their chromosomes to go haywire.

The effects of even minute doses of mercury on test animals have been shown to be significant in causing genetic damage. Geneticist Theodosius Dobzhansky and author-scientist Isaac Asimov have written:

> An important assumption (in genetic experiments on fruit flies) is that the machinery of inheritance and mutation is essentially the same in all creatures and that therefore knowledge gained from very simple

POISONS IN YOUR FOOD 377

species (even from bacteria) is applicable to man. There is overwhelming evidence to indicate that this is true in general, although there are specific instances where it is not completely true and scientists must tread softly while drawing conclusions.

Fruit flies are known to suffer chromosome abnormalities from mercury when given such small amounts as 50 parts per *billion*. But what does this mean in human terms? Certainly nothing terribly encouraging when we consider the revelations of Claes Ramel and Jan Magnusson after two years research in Sweden. (Since the U.S. is even more highly industrialized than Sweden all of the Swedish figures for mercury pollution have been found low in comparison with ours.)

The observations are of interest from a practical point of view in relation to the mercury pollution of the environment . . . This pollution includes some important human food stuff, like eggs, and fresh water fishes and therefore it obviously is of interest to establish what kind of human health risks may be involved. With reference to the experimental data, the genetic effects of such a health problem primarily concern the risk of an induction of cells with aberrant chromosome numbers. This might cause an increase for instance of trisomic defects like mongolism or Klinefelter's syndrome.

(Mongolism involves certain physical deformities and moderate to severe mental retardation. Klinefelter's syndrome is characterized by atrophied testes, the absence of living spermatozoa in the semen and sometimes excessive development of the male mammery glands.)

The horror of mercury pollution became dramatically apparent to Americans when the Huckleby family was stricken with a strange disease after eating a hog which had been fed seed treated with a mercurial fungicide. Amos Huckleby, 14, became deaf and blind, Dorothy Jean, 20, became raving mad, Ernistine, 8, also blinded, lapsed into a coma which lasted eight months, and Michael, only a fetus when his mother ate the poisoned hog, was born blind.

It was only after NBC News spread the story of the Huckleby family across the country on February 18, 1970, that Dr. Harry Hays, then director of the Pesticide Regulation Division of the U.S. Department of Agriculture announced the conclusion of a "ten year" study on the dangers of mercurial pesticides. "Mercury," he said, is an "'imminent hazard," therefore he would cancel registration of 17 alkylmercury fungicides, chiefly the group known as "panogen." He also ordered the major panogen supplier, Nor-Am (a subsidiary of Morton Norwich and a chemical conglomerate) to recall its fungicide from dealers' shelves.

In March of 1970, Norvald Fimreite, a graduate student researcher at Western Ontario University, released to the press his discovery of very high mercury levels—7.09 ppm —in fish from Lake St. Clair, a major commercial fishing area. Four days later the Ontario government closed its side of the lake to commercial fishing and on April 7 the state of Michigan closed the American side. Within a short period of time 1,500 miles of fishing water in five Canadian provinces were closed. Ohio closed its portion of Lake Erie to commercial fishing and also requested a federal investigation of mercury pollution in Ohio waters. Victor Cohn of the *Washington Post* learned from sources within the FDA that its officials weren't sure about the so-called "safe" level of mercury it had established for food fish.[4] By June 18, Secretary of the Interior Walter J. Hickel announced a ban on use of 16 pesticides including mercury compounds on 534 million acres of federally controlled lands. Other agencies were also encountering the mercury problem. The Bureau of Water Hygiene (a unit under the Department of Health, Education, and Welfare) discovered that it had no idea how much mercury might be safe in drinking water. It then adopted a standard set by the Soviet Union 10 years before. Under judicial scrutiny, however, the U.S. Department of Agriculture's attempt to ban mercury compounds from agricultural use almost fell apart. Nor-Am was upset that the USDA demanded that existing stocks of panogen be recalled from dealers' shelves. It claimed that recall would create an insurmountable and

4. *Ibid.*, p. 73.

hazardous hardship for the company.[5] The USDA's decision was ultimately upheld however, although the product continued to be sold during the months while the case was fought.

The new U.S. Environmental Protection Agency which took over the USDA's pesticide regulation authority in December 1970 says it plans to enforce this ban on mercurials. Nor-Am, on the other hand, says it will go to the U.S. Supreme Court for the right to sell methyl mercury to farmers and seed dealers. The alkyl mercurials are still doing a good business in the U.S. today. Ralph Nader has been able to get the Interior Department to announce the names of the nation's 50 major mercury pollutors. At the same time Secretary Hickel reported a nationwide reduction in industrial mercury discharges from 287 pounds per day to 40. However, these figures seem questionable since the U.S. Bureau of Mines and the U.S. Geological Survey both estimate that since 1930 mercury losses into the American environment have averaged one million pounds per year of 2,729 pounds per day—40 times higher than Hickel's figures. To date, not one of the companies accused of violations has paid a cent in fines nor has any corporate executive risked jail for polluting.

The question again in the poisoning of our food is 'how safe is safe?" While the FDA has continued to allow mercury in four out of eighteen cosmetic classifications— creams, lotions, hair preparations, and facial make-up— which millions of Americans pour on their bodies on a regular basis—it was quick to pounce on 25,000 vitamin pills made from seal livers and marketed through an obscure health food store.[6]

In 1970, the FDA hurriedly set a "safe" standard of 0.5 ppm under which quotient fresh-water fish in 33 states had been discovered "unsafe." The standard in itself is also very vague since a fisherman eating two safe fish of 0.4 ppm will actually be consuming considerably more than the 0.5 safety level. The World Health Organization had recommended a standard of 0.05 ppm in 1963. One won-

5. *Ibid.*, p. 75.
6. *Ibid.*, p. 89.

ders for what health reason ours could be allowed to be 10 times higher . . . perhaps there is no healthy reason.

Richard Ronk, mercury project officer in the FDA's office of compliance reported on October 30, 1970 that several states in the West had warned pregnant women to avoid eating fish from contaminated areas. Although Ronk's office has since reaffirmed this opinion, the FDA has apparently made no effort to publicize this important piece of information to the public.[7] Around the same time, Professor Bruce McDuffie of the State University of New York at Binghamton, disclosed that he had found tuna fish mercury levels up to 0.86 ppm. After sampling only 138 cans which averaged .37 ppm mercury the FDA calculated that 23 percent of the 900 million cans of tuna processed in 1970 contained levels above the officially allowed 0.5 ppm. By mid-March 1971, tuna testing revealed only 3.6 percent of the cans contaminated, while the remainder were judged "safe." The treacherous part about such statistics is that "unsafe" cans were found to contain as much as 1.12 ppm, over twice as much as our already high standard allows. By December of 1970 it was found that 89 percent of all swordfish on sale in the United States was also contaminated above the permissible 0.5 ppm. These contamination levels reached as high as 2.4 ppm— an extremely serious level for anyone eating such fish.

Even the small list of chemicals added to our food daily which we have reported here is discouraging . . . and very frightening when we contemplate the proven and potential harm that the vast majority of these substances can cause in our bodies. What is more disheartening and perhaps frightening are the reasons that our food is allowed to be so thoroughly contaminated.

The Food and Drug Administration is the government agency which is supposed to protect the consumer from such gross aberrations of faith, safety and health. Obviously it has failed on many accounts. It has permitted our food to become devitalized and poisoned by failing in its monitoring of the food industry. Why?

The FDA has become an entrenched bureaucracy which has developed a distinct propensity for intrigue and play-

7. *Ibid.*, p. 93.

ing cops and robbers with the "little guys" who are only marginal health threats, if even that, rather than taking on the "big guys." It has consistently gone after the small purveyors of vitamins and health foods and Scientology—a fuzzy area of its jurisdiction Since the Food and Drug Law was not designed to deal with problems raised by sharp and strongly held differences of opinion about how to live and what to eat, such crusades are misguided. The area where it should have been pulling most of its talent and resources—i.e., protecting the consumer from the large corporate producers of most of the food consumed by Americans—it has shied away from.[8]

In the hearings conducted by Senator Edward Long of Missouri which took place in Missouri, Senator Long testified that there has been "instance after instance of FDA raids on small vitamin and food supplement manufacturers. These small, defenseless businesses were guilty of producing products which FDA officials claimed were unnecessary for the average human diet. Here again, we have the same Federal agency setting itself up as the judge of what should and should not be eaten by the general public." It was also revealed in these hearings on invasion of privacy by government agencies that the FDA has one of the largest and most sophisticated collections of snooping devices in the Federal government.

In hearings a year later, it was admitted to a special subcommittee of the House Committee on Interstate and Foreign Commerce by Dr. James Goddard, then Commissioner of the FDA that "We do have equipment that is used . . . to record oral promotional claims made by health food lecturers at public meetings and by door-to-door salesmen who offer such things as vitamins as cures for disease." As this book has attempted to demonstrate, we believe that claims of "health food lecturers" and purveyors of vitamins as "cures for disease" are far more accurate and less fraudulent than the claims of the food industry at large. They would have the consumer believe that proven poisons are harmless and "enriched" food is that which has been devitalized and had synthetic substi-

8. Turner, p. 33.

tutes added which hardly have the healthful qualities of the natural nutrients originally destroyed.

The FDA has developed a "safe" attitude towards the large, powerful food industry to avoid the industry's putting excessive pressure on it and also because many who leave the FDA do so to take on jobs in the very industry that they were once supposed to regulate. Many FDA officials, therefore, tread cautiously on the toes of their potential future bosses.

It is a convenient attitude that the FDA has developed when it assumes that all but a tiny number of food and drug manufacturers can be trusted to place the public interest ahead of their own profits.[9] The FDA's own statements do not even substantiate the assumption that there are only a "tiny" number of purposeful violators. According to FDA reports "In the food area over 80 percent of the establishments subject to the provisions of the Food, Drug and Cosmetic Act are in substantial compliance with its provisions." More clearly put, this means that close to a full 20 percent of the establishments are not in compliance. Also: "The FDA's major food objective is to achieve compliance with good manufacturing practices in at least 90 percent of the industry or industry segments where the potential of microbiological contamination producing disease states in the consumer is the highest. Present compliance levels in this area are estimated to be approximately 65 percent." This means that approximately 35 percent of the food industry does not comply with good manufacturing practices designed to eliminate microbiological diseases —a figure well below the FDA's own recommendation for compliance.

It is easy to understand why the tremendous health hazard stemming from the food we eat continues to exist since the FDA bases its policies on the assumption that there is little need for vigorous action to assure major manufacturers' compliance with its policies. The FDA, by its own admissions, has seen that this method of self-regulation by the industry does not work, yet they continue to formulate their policies and activities on the assumption that it does.

9. *Ibid.*, p. 37.

Former FDA Commissioner Herbert L. Ley's desire to have more extensive two-way communication with food manufacturers is a typical example of what happens when the FDA deals with major producers. *Food Engineering*, a trade publication, highly praised the Commissioner for his work along these lines in its October 1968 issue:

> Some of the Commissioner's enthusiasm comes from a recent achievement. FDA officials sat down at the conference table with executives of member companies of Grocery Manufacturers of America. The purpose was to solve common problems and iron out differences. Resolution of one worrisome question is cited. Agreement was reached on a definition of "withdrawal." When a food product is still under the control of the manufacturer, taking it off the market does not constitute an FDA "withdrawal." In the absence of legal action, such a move is merely a voluntary removal. This is to the benefit of the industry in a public relations way.

The problem with such commendable resolutions is that they keep accurate consumer information from the public —the Commissioner's constituency—to protect the "public relations" image of the food industry he is supposed to regulate—not collaborate with. If the FDA has discovered food requiring recall because it is putrid, dangerous or adulterated, why should the responsible company be allowed to obliterate this from the public record and therefore the consumer's attention as was achieved by Commissioner Ley's method of "public relations."

Substantial doubts about the inherent willingness of industry to comply with the law have been raised on many occasions (though the FDA continues to disregard this). One such instance of substantial non-compliance was reported by the Department Task Force on Environmental Health and Related Problems, headed by Ron M. Litton. In a statement to the Secretary of Health, Education, and Welfare, Litton said:

> In 1965 a total of 711 firms suspected of producing harmful or contaminated consumer products refused

to let Food and Drug Administration conduct inspections. Some 515 refused to furnish quality or quantity formulas to the Administration; 26 denied the Administration the opportunity to observe manufacturing procedure. And 153 refused Food and Drug Administration personnel permission to review control records. Also, 111 would not permit the Food and Drug Administration to review complaint files and 216 refused permission to review shipping records.

None of these statistics speak in favor of the food industry's inherent good will or its wish to comply in good faith to the existing laws which tend to be minimal rather than maximal.

Time and time again the FDA has shirked its responsibility to prosecute the food industry because, in the words of James S. Turner, author of the Nader Study Group on the Food and Drug Administration *The Chemical Feast*: "The FDA moves cautiously against major components of the food industry because it is much smaller and weaker than they are."[10]

Why has the FDA failed the consumer so badly? Why has it allowed dissemination of the pesticides, the cyclamates, the dyes, the mercury compounds and an endless parade of other chemicals not nutritional and healthful and suspected to be deadly poisonous into our systems over a long enough period of time?

According to the Kinslow Report aimed at stemming the tide of criticism the FDA anticipated after a Ralph Nader Study Group investigated it in the summer of 1969, the FDA's difficulties were:

Our responsibility is simply stated. The consumer has virtually no control over the quality of vital products which he uses every day. When industry fails to exercise adequate control, he must rely on regulatory agencies such as the FDA.

The problem is simply stated. Increasing volume and sophistication in types, production and marketing of consumer goods under our jurisdiction has outstripped

10. *Ibid.*, p. 12.

our ability to assure the public that all is well with respect to these products.

The result is simply stated. We are forced into reacting to meet individual problems rather than acting to head off impending crises.

Beyond this very little else is simple.

Ralph Nader's Study Group, however, did not agree with what they felt to be a misleading apology. They felt Commissioner Ley's assessment, once he had left the FDA, was much more accurate and to the point:

A majority of the medical staff people are retreads, persons who have suffered coronaries or who have personality problems; at the moment they're the only people that the FDA can get.

Merely putting more money into the agency will not change it. A more highly motivated staff and better administration is also needed.

If the Administration really wants to get better scientific people into FDA, the time is now because the squeeze on university research funds has made talent available.

We also need to sit down and find out what the gaps are in the consumer protection and that the FDA is responsible for, then what the needs are, then what can be done.

The FDA also has to be raised to the status of a policeman-type activity.

It is not that Congress has failed the FDA in not providing enough "legislation, manpower and money" as the Kinslow report would have us believe. The problem is more fundamental. It has failed to develop sophisticated methods to go after meaningful violators. Rather than building a thorough knowledge of the food industry's technology and economics so that its expertise would match that of industry, the FDA has spent its time and money developing spy techniques. This has meant that between 1950 and 1965, when the food industry went through its fastest period of growth, it was practically unmonitored. During this time chemical food additives became major threats to our health—especially since modern mass-distribution systems made these chemically tampered with food available to everyone. Pesticide residues in food also became prevalent during this period as well as brand new synthetic foods made up entirely of chemicals. All of this happened without the FDA taking serious or effective action.

James S. Turner in *The Chemical Feast* aptly describes the FDA's impotence in the face of much needed consumer protection: "Whenever supporters of more vigorous regulation of the food industry, both on the inside and outside of government, seek broader FDA authority from Congress, they are faced with convincing arguments from strong food lobbies that the FDA is not responsibly handling the authority it already has. The very people who most benefit from FDA weakness use that weakness as an argument against strengthening the agency. They point to inspectors who leave the FDA to go into industry jobs, harrassment of small and relatively defenseless businesses, and foolish wastes of energy such as the vitamin hearings, and convince Congress that the FDA cannot handle more authority."[11]

When the consumer naively believes, therefore, that the healthfulness and safety of the food he consumes daily are guaranteed by the FDA—he is tragically mistaken.

The weakness of the FDA is only part of our nutritional problem. The tremendous strength of the food industry is the other essential in the catastrophe which has befallen a large part of our food supply.

Looking at the food industry, it becomes clear that the consumer's health and nutrition are the least important factors in the marketing of their products.

The food industry is the largest retail industry in America with a total sales of approximately $125 billion in 1969.[12] It is also a high money-maker which has attracted large corporations to buy into it. Greyhound, for instance, known for its buses, has taken over Armour, the nation's second largest meat packer. Continental Bakery has been taken over by International Telephone and Telegraph. The industry is, in fact, moving towards monopoly. In 1966, the National Commission on Food Marketing reported a

11. *Ibid.*, p. 46.
12. *Ibid.*, p. 82.

sharp rise in conglomerate acquisitions in the past two decades.

What does this monopolization mean to the consumer in terms of quality, service and cost? According to the Marketing Commission: "High concentration in the food industry is undesirable because it weakens competition as a self-regulating device by which the activities of business firms are directed toward the welfare of the public at large. When large firms dominate a field, they frequently forbear from competing actively by price; competition by advertising, sales promotion and other selling efforts almost always increases; and the market power inescapably at the disposal of such firms may be used to impose onerous terms upon suppliers or customers."

American breakfast foods, 85 percent of which are produced by four large companies (Kellogg, General Foods, General Mills, Quaker Oats) is an excellent example of what happens when too much power is put in too few hands with no one really overseeing that the power is constructively used for all involved.

Between 1954 and 1964 the retail price for breakfast food per pound increased 45 percent—nearly twice the average of price increases for any other food. Unfortunately these higher prices did not mean better food—or even maintaining the same quality. Much of the increased revenue was poured into advertising. Cereal manufacturers spend 19 percent of their budget on advertising and sales promotion (compared to less than 3 percent spent by automobile companies). As long as a food can look good and sell well, its content is secondary.[13]

Other food producers have similar records. As early as 1958, 80 percent of all food companies in the United States had been classified as oligopolies. The twenty-two largest of these also spend about 18 percent of their sales on advertising. The result has been continued inflation for the consumer, who has paid more and more for less and less nutrients and more chemicals which are consistently being proved harmful to him. While food consumption per person has remained stable since 1939—cost has increased 37 percent.

Among the many examples of the callousness of the food

13. *Ibid.*, p. 83.

industry and its irresponsible attitude towards the consumer is the story of the purposeful and economically motivated pollution of baby food by baby food manufacturers.

Baby food manufacturers began to replace the amounts of fruits, vegetables and meat in each container as the price of these items rose. The cheaper ingredients, starch and sugar, were used as substitutes. Since the resulting product was blander or sweeter, salt and monosodium glutamate were added in an effort to restore the taste. (It must be remembered that baby food manufacturers are selling their food to mothers who must approve the taste.) The added starches, however, would break down quickly and become watery when the opened containers were allowed to sit for any length of time. Also, the baby's saliva which got into the food while he was eating it would begin to "digest" it. The food manufacturers' simple cure?—Add modified starch which does not break down as readily—neither on the baby's plate nor, some researchers believe, in his digestive system.[14]

Industry's justification for these additives was that it wanted to make the baby food tastier to the infant. In reality, most infants when they begin eating baby food have not yet developed a discriminatory taste. *Teaching* infants to eat sweet and salty food is also believed to be a contributing factor in the excessive candy eating habits which many American children develop as they grow older. If the industry really had the baby's interest in mind, it seems logical that they would have left the original more nutritious ingredients in.

Some researchers believe that developing a taste for highly salted food is related to the development of hypertension which is now appearing in patients in their teens and twenties. Previously it had appeared mainly in people in the thirty and forty age group. Dr. Lewis Dahl, chief of the Brookhaven National Laboratory, who conducted a series of studies on the relationship between high salt consumption and hypertension has stated: "A child gets a salt appetite [from eating salted foods as an infant] which then must be satisfied the rest of his life. If there is a family

14. *Ibid.*, p. 86.

history of hypertension, and he takes a lot of salt in his food, he may get it early in life."

Industry's response to Dr. Dahl's report is typical. Dr. Robert A. Steward, director of research for Gerber Products Company replied: "Before the boon to mothers of preserved baby food is jeopardized, several questions must be answered. Does excess dietary sodium chloride cause human hypertension? Several mechanisms affect hypertension. Salt may be involved in one of them. . . . If salt does cause hypertension in the adult, will it produce changes in the infant leading to hypertension later in life? There is no evidence one way or another. . . . Is there a strain of salt-sensitive people (and, therefore, infants) resembling rats? No one knows. . . . Until these questions are answered definitely, too few data are available to invoke some hypertension later in life." This reasoning is certainly not in the consumer's interest. Why not put the burden of proof on the industry. Let the manufacturer prove that salt is absolutely safe rather than allow our infants to be used as guinea pigs.

The monosodium glutamate (MSG) added to baby food has caused the biggest vocal controversy however. Dan Gerber states the manufacturers' position well in a letter to Gerber share-owners on November 14, 1969:

On May 9, 1969, John Olney, an associate professor of Psychiatry at Washington University in St. Louis, reported that MSG injected under the skin of 2 to 10 day old mice caused a specific type of brain damage and speculated that similar damage might result in human infants fed foods containing MSG . . .

Although a committee of experts was appointed as an ad hoc committee to the Food Protection Committee to study the scientific data on MSG and make recommendations for its use in foods, public pronouncements by Dr. Olney and by Dr. Jean Mayer, nutrition adviser to the President of the United States, denounced the use of MSG in baby foods. These statements were publicized on TV and the newspapers and the U.S. public became very concerned. An attempt was made to counteract the adverse publicity by presentation of the accumulated data demonstrating the safety of MSG when used in normal feeding procedures, but this information, although its validity was recognized by the scientific community, received little coverage in the news media and came too late to head off the public's reaction. Qualified scientists who have reviewed the written work of Dr. Olney as well as unpublished data in his laboratory are not convinced that his work is relevant to human feeding. It is the generally accepted consensus that further work must be done with different species of animals in order to validate the conclusions drawn by Dr. Olney.

Here again is the basic industry stance that until a product is *proven* harmful it should be allowed to remain on the market. This hardly substantiates the FDA's faith in industry that it will self-regulate itself. Industry's own spokesmen will in fact admit that in a profitable area no industry will do anything to possibly jeopardize that profit unless it is forced to. As *Chemical Engineering News* quoted one industry man in a 1966 special Supplement on Food Additives: "If an established product is grinding out millions of dollars a year for a company, you know darn well the company is not going to mess around with it." Where does this leave the hundreds of thousands of American babies who were fed Gerber baby food with salt and MSG in the first essential months of their growth?

It was only tremendous public pressure which finally forced MSG to be taken out of baby food—five months after the original reporting of Dr. Olney's significant findings. The FDA, which should have taken the legal action to force its removal, had again failed in its job.

If food manufacturers can violate the health and well being of babies through empty rationales of profit and safety, it is hard to imagine whose health they can be trusted with.

The story of our food supply—how it is adulterated, and why—doesn't end here. It begins again each day as new and different chemicals are invented and become part of our diet . . . and as we progressively harvest the results of all that we have eaten.

BIBLIOGRAPHY

In addition to the selected list of reference books and manuals listed at the beginning and end of several chapters, we have compiled a list of the books on health and nutrition which you may find useful.

Title	Author	Publisher
Add Years To Your Heart	Max Warmbrand, M.D.	Pyramid Books
About Allergy	Albert E. Hughes	Thorsons Pub.
About Bread	Harvey Day	Thorsons Pub.
About Biochemistry	Esther Chapman	Thorsons Pub.
About Bronchitis	Publisher	Thorsons Pub.
About Drugs	C. V. H. Cleary	Thorsons Pub.
About Food Values	Barbara Davis	Thorsons Pub.
About Fruit, Vegetables and Salad	P. E. Norris	Thorsons Pub.
About Herbs	Dr. Benedict Lust	Thorsons Pub.
About Molasses	P. E. Norris	Thorsons Pub.
About Mothers, Children & Nutrition	T. K. Basu	Thorsons Pub.
About Nuts & Dried Fruit	P. E. Norris	Thorsons Pub.
About Preservation of Food	John B. Lust	Thorsons Pub.
About Raw Juices	John B. Lust	Thorsons Pub.
About Salt Free Recipes	Nancy Lloyd	Thorsons Pub.
About Scientific Fasting	Linda B. Hazzard	B. Lust Pub.

Title	Author	Publisher
About Yeast	P. E. Norris	Thorsons Pub.
About the Water Cure	Russell Sneddon	Thorsons Pub.
About Wheat Germ	P. E. Norris	Thorsons Pub.
About Vitamins	P. E. Norris	Thorsons Pub.
Acid-Alkaline Balance	Mira Louise	Author
A New Look at Vitamin A	R. Adams & F. Murray	Larchmont Press
Arthritis	Dr. Philip M. Lovell	Natural Health
Arthritis & Rheumatism	George S. Weger, M.D.	Health Research
Arthritis & Rheumatism	Publisher	Ball Clinic
Back To Eden	Jethro Kloss	Longview Pub.
Basic Nutrition & Cell Nutrition	R. F. Milton, Ph.D.	Provoker Press
Be Happier, Be Healthier	Gaylord Hauser	Fawcett Book
Be Your Own Doctor	William Utrecht	Author
Bio-Organics	James Rorty & N. P. Norman, M.D.	Lancer Books
The Bloodstream	Isaac Asimov	Collier Books
The Blood Poisoners	Lionel Dole	Gateway Books
Blood Washing Method	Dr. Benedict Lust	Author
Body & How It Works	Natural Health Assn.	N.H. Assn.
Body Chemistry Health & Diseases	Melvin E. Page, D.D.S.	Page Foundation
Body Mind & Sugar	E. M. Abrahamson, M.D.	Pyramid
Bragg System; Building Nerves	Paul Bragg	Author
Bragg System; Cider Vinegar	Paul Bragg	Author
Breathe Deeply	Emanuel M. Josephson, M.D.	Chedney Press
Building Skin Beauty	Mary MacFadyen, M.D.	Emerson Books
Cancer; Disease of Civilization	Ebba Waerland	Provoker Press
Cancer Prevention	Cyril Scott	Athene Books
Case for Unorthodox Medicine	Brian Inglis	Berkley Books
Catarrh	W. R. C. Latson	Health-Culture

Title	Author	Publisher
Cells: Structure & Function	E. H. Mercer	Doubleday
Changing Years: Menopause	Madeline Gray	Signet
Chemical Feast	Ralph Nader's Study Group	Grossman Pub.
Chest Complaints	Milton Powell	Vegetarian Soc.
Children's Diet	M. Bircher-Benner, M.D.	C. W. Daniel Co.
Chinese Folk Medicine	Heinrich Wallnofer	Bell Pub.
Chlorophyll	Theodore M. Rudolph, Ph.D.	Nutritional Pub.
Comfrey & Chlorophyll	Vincent Licata	Health Research
Common & Uncommon uses of Herbs	Richard Lucas	A. R. C. Books
Complete Book of Food & Nutrition	J. I. Rodale	Rodale Press
Control for Cancer	Glenn D. Kittler	Paperback Lib.
Crown of Grapes	Josiah Oldfield	Living Lib.
Crude Black Molasses	Cyril Scott	Athene
Diabetes: Its Causes & Treatment	Dr. Andrew Gold	Vegetarian Soc.
Dictionary of Foods	Hauser & Berg	Beneficial Book
Dictocrats'	Omar V. Garrison	A. R. C. Books
Diet Does It	Gayelord Hauser	Cap. Giant Book
Diet For A Small Planet	Frances Moore Lappe	Ballantine Book
Diet & High Blood Pressure	Bertrand P. Allinson	Vegetarian Soc.
Dr. Carlton Fredericks' Diet	Carlton Fredericks	Award Books
Dr. Silvers' Remedies	Lewis J. Silvers, M.D.	Paperback Lib.
Drink Your Troubles Away	John Lust	Beneficial Book
Eat Right-Live Longer	Lelord Kordel	Health Today B.
Eat the Weeds	Ben Charles Harris	Barre Books
Eat Without Fear	Marvin Small	Larchmont Press
Eat Your Troubles Away	Lelord Kordel	Belmont Books
Ecological Eating	Lesley Vine	Tower Books
Edgar Cayce on Diet & Health	Anne, Read, Hugh L. Cayce	Paperback Lib.

Title	Author	Publisher
Enzymes: the Agents of Life	David M. Locke	Crown Pub.
Enzymes! The Spark of Life	John H. Tobe	Modern Pub.
Enzymes	Carlson Wade	A. R. C. Books
Everybody's Guide to Nature Cure	Harry Benjamin, N.D.	Health for All
Faith, Love, and Seaweed	Ian F. Rose	Award Books
The Fasting Cure	Upton Sinclair	Health Research
Feel Like A Million	Catharyn Elwood	Pocket Books
Folly of Meat-Eating	Otto Carque	Author
Folk Medicine	D. C. Jarvis, M.D.	Fawcett Crest
Food Combining Made Easy	Herbert M. Shelton	Shelton's Health
Food Facts & Fallacies	Carlton Fredericks, Ph.D.	A. R. C. Books
Foods That Alkalinize & Heal	Mary C. Hogle	Health Research
For Good Nutrition	Carlton Fredericks, Ph.D.	A. R. C. Books
Fruit: Medicine For Man	Morris Krok	Essence-Health
Fundamentals of Normal Nutrition	Corinne H. Robinson	MacMillan
Get Well Naturally	Linda Clark	Author
Ginseng & Other Medicinal Plants	A. R. Harding	Author
God-Given Herbs for Healing	William K. McGrath	Benedict Lust
Grape Cure	Johanna Brandt	London Press
Has Dr. M. Gerson a Cancer Cure?	S. J. Haught	A. R. C. Books
Healing Crisis	C. Leslie Thomson	Kingston Clinic
Healing Power of Herbs	May Bethel	Wilshire Books
Healing With Water	Jeanne Keller	Parker
Health & Happiness are Twins	Ethel Foresman	R. Speller & Sons
Health From the Kitchen	Eric F. W. Powell	Health Masters
Health Foods & Herbs	Kathleen Hunter	A. R. C. Books
Heart Disease & High Blood Pressure	Kenneth C. Hutchin	A. R. C. Books
Helping Your Health With Enzymes	Carlson Wade	A. R. C. Books

Title	Author	Publisher
Herbs; How To Use Them	Shirley A. Boie	Author
Herbal Manual	Harold Ward	Fowler Pub.
Herbs, Health & Healing	J. Hewlett-Parsons	Health-Harmony
Honey for Health	Cecil Tonsley	Award Books
Honey for Your Health	Bodog F. Beck, M.D.	Bantam Books
How Good Is American Diet	Bob Hoffman	York Barbell
How Nature Heals	H. A. McGowan	Author
How to be Healthy-Natural Food	Edward E. Marsh	A. R. C. Books
How to live with Diabetes	Henry Dolger, M.D.	Pyramid
How to live with Hypoglycemia	Charles Weller, M.D.	Award Books
Hunza Health Secrets	Renee Taylor	Award Books
Key to Good Health Vitamin C	Fred R. Klenner, M.D.	Graphic Art Fnd.
Let's Cook It Right	Adelle Davis	World Pub.
Let's Eat Right To Keep Fit	Adelle Davis	World Pub.
Let's Get Well	Adelle Davis	World Pub.
Let's Have Healthy Children	Adelle Davis	World Pub.
Live At Peace with your Nerves	Walter C. Alvarez, M.D.	Award Books
Live Food Juices	H. E. Kirschner, M.D.	Author
Look Younger, Live Longer	Gayelord Hauser	Fawcett Crest
Low Blood Sugar	Clement G. Martin, M.D.	A. R. C. Books
Lower Your Pulse, Live Longer	J. I. Rodale	Rodale Press
Magic Minerals	Carlson Wade	A. R. C. Books
Magnesium	J. I. Rodale	Pyramid Books
Materia Medica & Pharmacology	Culbreth	Lea & Febiger
Medicinal Value of Natural Food	Dr. W. H. Graves	Author
Minnesota Dr.'s Home Treasury	John E. Eichen-laub, M.D.	Award Books
Miracle of Fasting	Paul C. Bragg	Health Science

Title	Author	Publisher
Modern Encyclopedia of Herbs	Joseph M. Kadans, Ph.D.	Parker Books
More About Biochemistry	Mira Louise	Author
Mirror, Mirror On The Wall	Gaylelord Hauser	Fawcett Crest
Mucusless-Diet Healing System	Arnold Ehret	Author
Muscle Building	Michael Fallon	A. R. C. Books
Muscles	Therese C. Saw- cher Pfrimmer	Vantage Books
My Experiences with Living Food	Dr. Kristine Nolfi, M.D.	Author
Natural & Drugless Better Health	M. O. Garten, D.C.	A. R. C. Books
Natural & Folk Remedies	Carlson Wade	Tower Books
Natural Foods	Wendy Pritzker, R.N.	Dafran House
Natural Health & Pregnancy	J. I. Rodale	Pyramid Books
Natural Way to Beauty & Health	Carlson Wade	Bantam Books
Natural Health through Fasting	Carlson Wade	A. R. C. Books
Nature's Healing Grasses	H. E. Kirschner, M.D.	H. C. White Pub.
Nature's Healing Law	M. L. Scott, M.D.	Author
Nature's Medicines	Richard Lucus	Award Books
Nerves & Muscles	Robert Galambos	Doubleday
Medical Dictionary	Robert E. Rothenberg	Signet Books
Nursing	Natural Health Assn.	N. H. Assn.
Nutrition in a Nutshell	Roger J. Williams	Dolphin
On the Causation of Varicose Veins	T. L. Cleave	Author
Overfed But Undernourished	Dr. Curtis Wood, Jr.	Tower Books
Poisons In Your Food	William Longgood	Pyramid Books
Pollen & Royal Jelly	G. J. Binding	Thorsons Pub.
Practical Methods in Preparing Health Food	Royal Lee	Author

Title	Author	Publisher
Protein	Bob Hoffman	York Barbell
Protein Problem	Mira Louise	Author
Raw Food Treatment of Cancer	Dr. Kristine Nolfi	Vegetarian Soc.
Rebuilding Health	Ebba Waerland	A. R. C. Books
Rejuvenation	Eric J. Trimmer	Award Books
Rejuvenation Vitamin: Vitamin E	Carlson Wade	Award Books
Rodale's System for Mental Power	J. I. Rodale	Pyramid Books
Roots of Health	Leon Petulengro	Signet Books
Royal Jelly	Dr. Reynaud Allen	Benedict Lust
Secrets of Health & Beauty	Linda Clark	Pyramid Books
Skin Troubles	Harry Clements	Health for All
Stay Young Longer	Linda Clark	Pyramid Books
Therapeutic Fasting	Arnold De Vries	Chandler Book
Truth About Arthritis	Horace Markley	Author
Truth About Colds	Ian Leslie Doran	Author
Tumors	J. H. Tilden, M.D.	Author
Victory Over Cancer	Cyril Scott	Health Science
Vitamins & Minerals	Arthur W. Snyder, Ph.D.	Hansen's
Vitamins	Henry Borsook, Ph.D.	Pyramid Books
Vitamin E	Dr. Evan V. Shute	Larchmont Press
Vitamin C	Linus Pauling	Freeman
Water	Kenneth S. Davis	Science Lib.
Weight Control through Yoga	Richard L. Hittleman	Bantam Books
You Are All Sanpaku	Sakurazawa Nyoiti	Award Books
Your Allergic Child	Herman Hirschfield	A. R. C. Books
Your Overweight Child	Milton I. Levine, M.D.	Signet Books

You can obtain copies of most of the above books at your local book store. However, if you have difficulty locating a book, author or publisher, write to NUTRI-BOOKS Denver, Colorado 80205. They have the largest collection of Health & Nutrition books in the country.

GARY NULL is a playwright, poet, and author of many books, and articles. His books include:

BLACK HOLLYWOOD
ITALIAN-AMERICANS
SITTING ON THE OHIO
WINDSOR: AN EARLY PORTRAIT
THE CONSPIRATOR WHO SAVED THE
  ROMANOVS
THE SPERM TREE
NOWHERE BUT TOMORROW
THE COMPLETE HANDBOOK OF NUTRITION
HERBS FOR THE SEVENTIES
GROW YOUR OWN FOOD ORGANICALLY
THE NATURAL ORGANIC BEAUTY BOOK
THE COMPLETE QUESTION & ANSWER BOOK
  OF NATURAL THERAPY
THE COMPLETE QUESTION & ANSWER BOOK
  OF GENERAL NUTRITION
SURVIVING AND SETTLING IN NEW YORK
  ON A SHOESTRING
BODY POLLUTION
HEALTHY EARTH, HEALTHY SOIL, HEALTHY
  MAN
SECRET CIRCLE SERIES
WHITE PAPER ON THE RED MAN
PROTEIN FOR VEGETARIANS
COMPLETE HANDBOOK OF FOOD COMBINING
THE FORGOTTEN WAR
THE ART OF NATURAL WINE MAKING
SEX & NUTRITION: FACT & FALLACY
A six-volume set of 'HOW TO' self-help books
A twelve-volume set of 'Hobby' books

Gary owns several health food stores and has his own nationally syndicated radio series on nutrition called "Natural Living." He is on the faculty and teaches Mental Health & Nutrition at G.R.O.W. college. He is also the editor-in-chief of his own health magazine and writes articles for other magazines each month. He is a popular lecturer on college campuses and in major cities across the nation, in addition to conducting a weekly lecture on Nutrition at the Creative Institute. Gary lives in New York, is 26 years old, and quickly becoming the youngest and most knowledgeable spokesman for the health food industry.

STEVE NULL acts as his brother's right hand and does the research for Gary's many books. Steve is the originator of many significant innovations in the Health Food field including: Health Food Push Carts, Health Food in Cafeterias, Door-to-Door Health Food Salesmen, etc. He writes articles each month for their own magazine, as well as other publications. He shares lecturing duties with Gary and is an essential part of the Creative Institute, their organization which helps minority groups and creative individuals develop and market their ideas, inventions, and programs.

INDEX

Dell BESTSELLERS

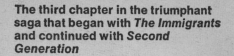

The third chapter in the triumphant saga that began with *The Immigrants* and continued with *Second Generation*

The Establishment

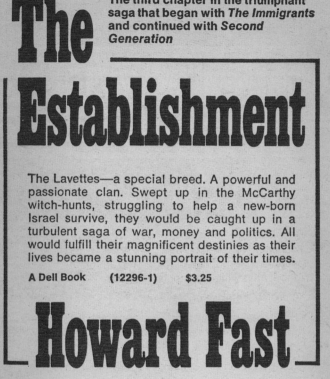

The Lavettes—a special breed. A powerful and passionate clan. Swept up in the McCarthy witch-hunts, struggling to help a new-born Israel survive, they would be caught up in a turbulent saga of war, money and politics. All would fulfill their magnificent destinies as their lives became a stunning portrait of their times.

A Dell Book   **(12296-1)**   **$3.25**

Howard Fast